Bitter Roses

An Inside Look At
The Washington Huskies'
Turbulent Year

Sam Farmer

Forewords by
Dan Raley and Edward Cunningham

Sagamore Publishing
Champaign, IL 61820

©1993 Sam Farmer

All rights reserved.

Production supervision
    and book design: Brian J. Moore
Cover and photo insert design: Michelle R. Dressen
Editor: David Hamburg, Russ Lake
Proofreader: Phyllis L. Bannon

Publisher's Cataloging in Publication

(Prepared by Quality Books Inc.)

Farmer, Samuel W.
    Bitter roses: an inside look at the Washington Huskies'
turbulent year / Sam Farmer.
    p. cm.
    Preassigned LCCN: 93-84960.
    ISBN 0-915611-80-5

    1. Washington Huskies (Football team) 2. University of
Washington--Football.   I. Title.

GV958.W3F37 1993   796.33'263'0979777
                                                         QBI93-1128

To my parents, Jerry and Susan.
Better than pals.

Contents

Forewords

The first play I saw went for a touchdown. Ninety yards.

Staring at a fuzzy, black-and-white television picture, I watched Steve Bramwell tuck a season-opening kickoff under his arm and dart upfield for an instant score against Air Force.

That was my introduction to University of Washington football. That was exactly 30 years ago.

My grandfather encouraged me to watch the game with him. The afternoon was meant to be a diversion. My father had died in a car accident the month before.

Little did I know that Husky football would shadow everything I did from then on, influencing my own athletic pursuits, my schooling and even my job.

When I was 12, my basketball coach at the neighborhood parks and recreation department was a Husky football player. A starting offensive tackle and the biggest player on the team, he was an intimidating figure, always dressed in a dark purple blazer with a yellow "W" emblazoned across it. My teammates and I wanted to ask him for his autograph. He asked us to run laps.

When I was 18, the chief drug supplier to players on my high school football team was a Husky football player. His Saturday exploits were widely known. His off-field transactions were highly secretive. We were all more than a little amused when he later became a teacher, coach, and school administrator.

Growing up, Washington football was everywhere. I lived within walking distance of Husky Stadium. The three daughters of Jim Owens, the Husky coach in 1957-74, were classmates of mine from grade school to high school. Players from my high school became Huskies. Friends from opposing high schools became Huskies.

Even my grandfather had a deep-rooted connection. For the better part of two decades, he was in charge of all student-section ticket takers at Husky Stadium on game day. Close friends of his were Ivan Travis, Husky ticket manager, and Clyde Robinson, Husky program manager. Another friend and pallbearer at his funeral was Wendell Broyles, Washington's longtime football public-address announcer.

For nine years, I didn't miss a game. I ran errands for my grandfather. Just before kickoff, I turned in attendance totals encompassing half the stadium to an obscure office hidden beneath the south deck. When my grandfather retired from his duties, I sold programs for Robinson.

Most of all, I had free reign to wander Husky Stadium. I remember having 50-yard line seats (OK, so they were located in the aisleway, and I got stepped on a lot). I remember being in the locker room. I remember being the envy of my friends, who showed up every Saturday looking for ways to sneak into this fall fantasy world and never found them.

Today I have a worse seat and no locker room access, but some of my friends still profess envy. For the past six years, I have been the Husky beat writer for the *Seattle Post-Intelligencer*.

My exposure to this sporting enterprise, now a 103-year tradition, is one that leans to the extreme, but a heavy dose of this activity is not an isolated experience in Seattle.

Husky Stadium attracts more college football fans on an average Saturday afternoon than all but a handful of places nationwide, none west of Lincoln, Nebraska, Walk down any street in Seattle and you will pass someone wearing a Husky hat, T-shirt, or sweatshirt, demonstrating an intense level of devotion not enjoyed by the three local professional sports franchises.

For that matter, Husky football came before there were SuperSonics, Mariners, or Seahawks, holding at least a 75-year head start.

My view of Husky football initially was awe but has grown cynical over the years, which in some ways is an unspoken requirement of my journalistic profession. The program's warts are as visible as its flowery accomplishments. But that was the case well in advance of quarterback Billy Joe Hobert's improper personal loans, which set off the recent maelstrom of allegations, investigations, and general controversy.

In three decades, Husky football has undergone great change, not all of it welcome. The role before was similar to Robin Hood's—Washington was a poor second cousin to Southern Cal and UCLA, an occasional Rose Bowl entry, ignored by the polls and national exposure, and mostly interested in stealing from the rich.

Now the Huskies have become the wealthy. Innocent expectations have been replaced by a certain degree of arrogance, both in the stands and on the field. Upsets involve only Washington defeats, not victories. It is far more noteworthy when the Huskies fail than succeed. Southern Cal and UCLA have taken back seats.

A 90-yard touchdown run would be hard to remember 30 years from now.

—Dan Raley

*   *   *

When Sam called with his idea on this book, I was both excited and concerned. Being an alumnus of the University of Washington, I have nothing but fond memories of my senior year there. I captained the greatest team in Husky history to the school's only national championship. The reason I was concerned was, like most of you reading this book, I was simply a fan when all of 1992's troubles hit the program. I was not there to see how truly hard these allegations of cheating and crime hit my former teammates. I could only sit back and hope the team and coaches were able to weather the storm.

The key to reading this book, for me, was realizing that the "storm" I refer to was merely a stiff breeze when broken down to its essential elements. As I began to read about Billy's loan and Danianke's drug deals, I realized for the first time that these guys made poor life decisions. It had nothing to do with Don James, Barbara Hedges, or anyone else involved in Husky athletics. Billy and Danianke simply screwed up. They knew what they were doing was wrong, were told somewhere along in their Husky careers it was wrong, but as *individuals* they chose to continue. For that, no one but Billy and Danianke should be held accountable.

Then I read what hurt me the most: Former Huskies, most of whom I played with, accused the program of cash payments, no-work jobs, and boosters giving cars to players. Ask any current or former Husky player who does not have a reason to tarnish the program, and you will get the real answer to this puzzle. Husky football is one of the hardest, most competitive things anyone can go through, and some simply do not make it. Grades, behavior, poor play—any one of these will land you on the bench or off the team. Some cannot handle that. I have never heard a player who has had a successful career bad-mouth Don James or his program. Find a player who did not reach his goals at Washington, and you may hear a different story.

I am not saying every successful player likes Don James, but that player probably respects him and the program he has built. Perhaps the best argument against these allegations is very simple: If you were a rich alumnus, who would you give your money to? Ask Mario Bailey if he got a car from a booster. Ask Steve Emtman if he received cash payments. Ask Greg Lewis if he had a job he did not have to work at to earn his paycheck. These are the best players in recent Husky history, and wouldn't they have benefited had cheating occurred?

After reading this book, it also became very clear how the press can alter a situation. As I read the section on Billy's bogus loan, I was appalled not only at Billy's stupidity but how the story broke. A student-athlete receiving improper money is a big story, but it's not the *Exxon Valdez* or the spotted owl controversy. It's a kid making a mistake. Yet two of Seattle's best investigative reporters, one a Pulitzer Prize winner, were put to work for *months* after an anonymous tip. Great story, guys, but you aren't winning any prizes for this one.

Even though Washington football went through some troubled times last year, it is still an outstanding system, and this book gives great examples why . The biggest reason is the guys who play. Sam's portrayal of Dave Hoffmann was one of the most accurate I have ever read. Shivers ran down my spine when I read about his hunger on the playing field. But to really know Dave, you must know him off the field. Dave is a true gentleman.

Kind, intelligent, funny, hardworking. Dave Hoffmann's the definition of what Husky football is all about. I would say there are more Dave Hoffmanns than Kevin Conards or Vince Fudzies in the program, and that's what you need to remember when reading this book. A few bad apples spoiled it for everyone last season, but do not forget the standouts the program has produced.

Finally, I would like to share a letter I wrote to Stanford head coach Bill Walsh. Coach Walsh made some very strong, false allegations against the Husky football program. I was offended and decided someone needed to speak out. Because even though he apologized, he never retracted his statement.

June 8, 1993
Dear Coach Walsh:

Before you read any further, I want you to know that this is not another hate letter from a University of Washington alumnus. I am a current NFL player and graduated from Washington in 1991. Although this will be only my second season in the league, I truly respect your accomplishments as a coach at this level. To keep a team at that level as long as you did is astonishing. But I ask you to bear with me while I tell you a little bit about my experience at the University of Washington that makes me feel the way I do about my alma mater.

When I arrived in the fall of 1987, the program was on a serious downslide. After nearly winning a national title in 1985, Don James was being challenged for his job. After a very disappointing 1988 season when we missed a bowl game for the first time in over a decade, Coach James made some serious changes. These changes, however, were made on and off the field. The academic side of our program became as competitive as our play on the field, and Coach James was right in the middle of both. He has extremely strict rules about class and study table attendance, grades, and most importantly, graduation progress. But the best thing he did was have former players we thought would play pro ball and did not, come back and tell us the importance of graduating. I will not argue that Washington's athletic program is devoid of academic problems, but major progress has been, and is being made.

The easy part to tell you about is the on the field changes he made, so I will not bore you with what you already know. However, I would like to share my success story with you. I was born and raised in Washington, D.C., thousands of miles away from my eventual choice of college. The most asked question I heard was why I traveled so far to go to school. There is a simple answer. There are very few schools in this country that combine the academic and athletic superiority that the University of Washington has to offer. What occurred during my career at Washington was a dream come true. After struggling through a few tough seasons, we began to play incredible football.

It all came to an apex when we won the national title my senior year. Shared or not, we earned that championship, and if you have seen that team on film, you know what I'm talking about. That was one tenacious football team, and no one would or could have beaten us that season.

On the personal side of this story, I will argue with anyone who believes we cheated to win or broke rules to get players. I was Captain of the team that won the title, and feel I have a great knowledge of what it took to build that team. But my knowledge does not end in 1991. I also know painfully well about the problems of the 1992 Huskies. I found it extremely hard to believe that a small handful of my former teammates would break rules and laws so easily, and tarnish the program's accomplishments. The nation now sees Washington as just another "football factory" and I believe that is what you meant with your comments. Coach Walsh, I spent five great years in Seattle, and seriously hope that you reconsider your opinion. Coach James has built a program of honesty and integrity. Most importantly, he has built a program that builds hardworking, good men.

I wish you the best of luck at Stanford (except when playing the Huskies!), and hope your players have the same positive experience that I had while at Washington.

Sincerely,
Edward P. Cunningham
Phoenix Cardinals

Introduction

Any half-baked notions I entertained of surviving a series of downs in Division I football were dashed in Boulder, Colorado. I was standing on the Folsom Field sidelines in 1990 watching the last two minutes of a nail-biter that pitted the Golden Buffaloes vs. the University of Washington. Husky receiver Mario Bailey ran a crossing pattern and left his feet to make a catch at the Colorado 10-yard line. CU safety Tim James jammed his helmet between Bailey's shoulder blades as if shot out of a circus cannon. The collision sounded like a car accident. Bailey not only hung onto the ball, but he bounded to his feet and jogged to the Husky bench. I was close enough to see wooziness in his eyes, but otherwise he seemed all right.

I was amazed at how a guy five inches shorter and 30 pounds lighter than me could withstand a knock so punishing. I played football in high school; a pop that ferocious would have sent me off to see the Wizard. When Bailey reentered the game, I glanced at my fellow reporters to check if I was the only one agape. I was; they had seen it before.

So this was big-time college football.

But I would learn that Washington Huskies football is about more than high pain thresholds and crowds louder than a jet engine, about more than superheroes and Saturday afternoons. Washington Huskies football is about college students living four to five years of their private lives in the public eye, about the triumphant and the troubled, the aboveboard and the under-handed. A snapshot of society.

Bitter Roses is a story that needed to be told. Maybe because of space constraints or conflicts of interest or bias, the full account of Washington's turbulent year was never given. Before now.

When I first met Don James, coach of the Huskies, I realized he had no burning desire to chat with me. That's not his way. James lives a life that is meticulously scheduled. He takes time to answer questions but avoids idle conversation. He gives the same access to reporters from the school paper that he does to those from *Sports Illustrated*. Once, he was busy when I called him at his home. "Can I call you back in five minutes?" he asked. I could have set my watch by that return phone call.

James always has treated me fairly. In this book, I extend him the same courtesy. Since the torrent of allegations ravaged the Husky football program, the longtime coach has felt anywhere from slighted to betrayed by the media. He keeps a list of reporters he will never speak to again.

"First of all, coaches would like to see media guys report on the games instead of digging into lives," he told me. "But I think we recognize with the profession that we're in and the visibility that we're in that there will be stories if any of us cross over the line or stumble in life. The thing that we always hope is that there would be some balance. I think in my case it appears as though some people in the media are out to do whatever they can to damage my career and my reputation.

"I would have hoped that they investigate any possible thing that they get their hands on. If, for instance, they did go through my phone calls and they couldn't find excessive calls or business calls or whatever, that they would come out and say, 'We've analyzed a year of phone calls and they looked OK,' or they go through a year of my travel and say, 'Looks like he's not trying to make money off the university.'

"(Reporters) are not really interested in the fact that I made 72 speeches in 1992 that were free for service clubs, auctions, youth groups, churches. It just seemed like there was never any balance to show the good side of anything, Billy Joe Hobert or Don James. I think that was probably the discouraging point. The fact that on Easter Sunday you wake up and read a story about graduation rates. So it hasn't been a lot of fun."

This book aims for balance. Whenever possible, I have taken pains to seek many sides of the reports that rocked the program, sides that have never before appeared in print. Some sources requested anonymity and provided information so valuable it overrode my reluctance to use their comments. Whenever possible, I have used uncensored quotes and unedited excerpts from court documents. My aim is not to be an apologist for the UW program or the media, but to present the story each has given. Let the reader judge.

Acknowledgments

To help pull together the many disparate strains into a single narrative, I have relied on maps—previous reporting that covers the territory over which I travel. Journalists who will find their work reflected in this account are Bud Withers, Art Thiel, Sheldon Spencer, John Owen, Paul Shukovsky, and, in particular, Dan Raley of the Seattle *Post-Intelligencer*; Dick Rockne, Duff Wilson, Tom Farrey, Eric Nalder, Steve Kelley, Blaine Newnham, and Hugo Kugiya of the *Seattle Times*; John McGrath, Bart Wright, Robert Kuwada, Ron Newberry, and, in particular, Don Borst of the Tacoma *Morning News Tribune*; Gary Nelson, Rich Myhre, and Larry Henry of the *Everett Herald*; Rick Alvord of the Bellevue *Journal-American*; Terry Mosher of the *Bremerton Sun*; Jeff Hood of the *Stockton Record*; Gail Wood and Jeff Redd of the *Olympian*; Ed Sherman of the *Chicago Tribune*; Mitch Albom and Steve Kornacki of the *Detroit Free Press*; John Niyo of the *Michigan Daily*; Jim Cour and Rick Warner of the Associated Press; Gary Klein, Elliot Almond, Danny Robbins, Steve Elling, Jerry Crowe, Mal Florence, Vince Kowalick, John Lynch, Mike Hiserman, John Cherwa, and Bill Dwyre of the *Los Angeles Times*; and, of course, Austin Murphy of *Sports Illustrated*.

I want to express sincere thanks to *Valley Daily News* managing editor Bob Jones and my co-workers, particularly Mark Moschetti, Matt Massey, and Calvin Karbowski, who picked up the slack in my absence.

Thanks to Ed Cunningham for his candor, sense of humor, and willingness to go out on a limb for the project. You are a good friend.

Several people graciously gave up their time and resources to help me with this book, and without them, this project would have never happened. First on this list is Jim Vanderslice, who, with his crew at Microsoft—including David Ward, Jim Walsh, and Umesh Madan—devoted an amazing amount of time and energy to this endeavor.

Heartfelt thanks also go to Scott Eklund, who photographed the front and back covers of the book and, having followed the Washington program for years, gave invaluable input for the text. Lui Kit Wong's photographs for the middle of the book were fantastic. Steve Elders provided editing that was thorough beyond belief but never affected the integrity of the copy. Brian Murphy lent his literary expertise and inspiration, as did Austin Murphy, Tim Cahill, and H. G. Bissinger.

Others who provided crucial information and resources include Keith Shipman, Bob Rondeau, Jeff Riley, Brendan Healey, Kevin Pike, and Dr. Gary Connor. I would also like to thank Washington coaches, players, Emily Hill, and several people in the athletic department, including Chip Lydum, Jim Daves, Dan Lepse, Paul Kirk, Jeff Bechthold, Jina Solis, and Joan Burton, who provided thousands of pages of information and were extremely professional in their dealings with me. Some people who have helped me prefer anonymity. I thank them without making eye contact.

I give special thanks to the family and friends of Travis Spring, who bared their grief—and happy memories— for this account. This project never would have gotten off the ground were it not for Joe Bannon, Jr., Brian Moore, Michelle Dressen, David Hamburg, Russ Lake, Phyllis Bannon, and the rest of the good people at Sagamore Publishing, and Dan Raley, who showed enough faith in me to encourage me in this direction.

My lower back thanks Dr. John E. Dunn of the Seattle Orthopaedic Fracture Clinic for his precision with a microscope and scalpel.

Several people served as true inspiration for me, including Bob Stewart, Elizabeth Perry, Jerry and Sue Farmer, Pete and Helen Farmer, Tom and Jill Farmer, and, most of all, Cresey Stewart, who patiently listened to hours and hours of passages and always reminded me that fairness is the most important thing.

1

The Rose And Fall

The greeting on Billy Joe Hobert's answering machine sounded anxious, curt: "Hi, I'm kind of busy. Looking for something." *Beeeep.*

Life can be hell when you're in a freefall from grace. Hobert was learning all about that.

The life of the beleaguered University of Washington quarterback was a carnival ride spinning wildly out of control. The latest problem: his car was stolen. Not just any car, mind you, but a bad-assed machine. A 1992 Chevrolet Camaro packed with a 3.1-liter, V-6 engine, and a custom $4,000 stereo that could rupture the eardrums of any grunge rocker in town. A bone-white trophy on wheels.

On the morning of Sunday, December 13, 1992, Hobert stepped outside his apartment to find his pristine cruiser missing. Frantic, he called the police, who hours later found the Camaro vandalized and stripped along a rural dirt road in Maple Valley, Washington, a few miles from his apartment.

The crime scene wasn't pretty. The car's windshield had been bashed by a boulder. Its sleek body, in showroom condition a few hours earlier, was dented and battered. "You can't afford this B. J." was spray-painted on one side and dollar signs on the other. The thief or thieves were never caught, but their artwork put a sinister spin on an otherwise common crime.

Could it have been a vendetta?

Was karma catching up to Billy Joe?

Hobert certainly had his detractors. An improper loan that he took out in spring 1992 cost him his NCAA eligibility, not to mention his peace of mind. Hobert and his expectant wife, Heather, natives of Washington, ultimately moved to Arizona to escape the bad vibes they were getting in their home state.

Hobert's story had the makings of a Greek tragedy. His triumphs were well documented. During the course of his short-lived college career, he went 17-0 as a starting quarterback and led Washington to a share of the 1991 national championship, the first national title—in any sport—in the school's history.

Then cash seduced him. He sought and received a $50,000 loan from Charles Rice, an Idaho scientist and father-in-law of Hobert's golfing pal. The money was easy to accept, easier to spend. He wasn't shy about indulging in the spoils of his success. For three months, until his lender cut him off, he enjoyed the hedonistic life of a playboy. He paid cash for cars, guns, and golf clubs and bankrolled wild weekends with his buddies. "I'd buy new golf clubs," he boasted once, "and if I didn't like them, I'd give them away." Put simply, he lived large.

What made these revelations more painful for the Huskies and their fans was that they surfaced during a dream season. When the Hobert story broke, Washington was 8-0, ranked No. 1 in the nation, and riding a 22-game winning streak. A third consecutive Rose Bowl berth was all but guaranteed and a second national title was in reach. Nebraska left Seattle a loser. So did USC. So did Stanford. This was a time to paint the town purple, celebrate the dominance of the Dawgs, soak in the glory of a team that packed Husky Stadium with more than 70,000 people week after week.

The Huskies had risen from the ashes of a 6-5 season in 1988, a year in which they were denied a bowl berth, to go undefeated in 1991 and gnaw through foes like a buzz saw through balsa.

Washington football became more than a source of pride for fans in the Pacific Northwest, it was a *raison d'etre,* a grand tradition as reliable as rain and majestic as Mount Rainier. The program had been recharged by a new generation of Huskies. These were flower children, in that they were consumed by one goal: to inhale the sweet fragrance of those Pasadena roses for a third time. Leading this monomaniacal mission were guys like Mark Brunell and Dave Hoffmann and Shane Pahukoa and Joe Kralik and Walter Bailey and Andy Mason.

And yes, Billy Joe Hobert.

Hobert, who grew up in Orting, Washington, reached hero status in these parts. He clung to vestiges of his blue-collar roots. His skills on the field were unquestioned. He had some mobility but was best when given time to throw darts from the pocket. "I'm no slug butt," he claimed once, yet he had the build of one. Bulky. Jutting jaw. Thick like a linebacker. He swaggered with his arms out to the side like a guy carrying a couple of invisible suitcases, forever searching for a place to set them down. His unflappable confidence gave him a special charisma. He was likeable, glib, and shot from the hip. Good ol' boy talkin', crafty eyes watchin'.

Then came the blunder, the largest improper loan to an NCAA athlete ever discovered, putting not only his future but the reputation of his team in jeopardy. Many disillusioned fans who cheered the golden-armed junior from the stands now viewed him as a self-centered opportunist who, because of his lust for money, sullied a football program whose reputation was once as spotless as that beautiful Camaro. Many teammates supported Hobert, but others were less than sympathetic when it came to his woes.

"When I heard about what happened to his car, I laughed my butt off," said center Ed Cunningham, who snapped the ball to Hobert throughout the championship season. "I thought, 'Damn straight. I hope someone on the team did it.'" Cunningham was one of the Huskies who felt Hobert used shoddy judgment in accepting money based on his earning potential as a professional football player. "Ninety-nine percent of the guys on that team are good, upstanding citizens," he added. "Billy made us all look like crooks."

Steve Emtman, an All-America defensive tackle and the No. 1 selection in the 1992 NFL draft, was another former Washington player disappointed by the choices Hobert made. "Billy's an idiot," Emtman confided. "He thinks about stupid things. He thinks of himself before anyone else. He's not all bad, he's just a little self-centered. I don't know if he was trying to take the whole team down with him or not."

Whatever Hobert's motives were, the article that chronicled his spending spree was the first ground to give way in an avalanche of allegations and innuendo, rattling the once-stalwart Washington program. Problems existed long before Hobert took out the improper loan, yet reports of his violation changed the perception of the Huskies.

"It seemed like every reporter suddenly became an investigative reporter," Brunell noted.

Story after story popped, CRACK-CRACK-CRACK, like the angry report of an assault rifle strafing the proud Husky mystique. The improbably bright spotlight of adulation bathing the co-national champions now looked closer to a police floodlight. Cast in that harsh glare of scrutiny, impurities in the Washington program began to show:

•The Pac-10 Conference considered forcing Washington to forfeit all the 1992 games in which Hobert played, then decided to conduct a comprehensive investigation with a price tag of $150,000 (billable to the UW) and possible penalties to the Husky football program.

•Reserve defensive end Danianke Smith was arrested on charges he sold narcotics to undercover investigators, dealing cocaine out of the Conibear Shellhouse, a university dormitory filled mainly with athletes. Smith allegedly also attempted to arrange the sale of automatic weapons.

•Several Huskies were interviewed by the Secret Service as part of an investigation into cellular telephone fraud in the Seattle area. Electronically altered phones were apparently sold to a handful of Washington players, who used the phones to make "free" calls for two or three months during summer 1991.

•Reports surfaced of many UW football players routinely ignoring traffic tickets and court dates. According to court records, the players owed thousands of dollars in unpaid fines.

•Washington boosters allegedly provided cash, jobs, and other benefits to Husky football players in a violation of NCAA rules. Hobert apparently was one of those recipients. Five former Washington players told the Los Angeles Times they made as much as $10 an hour doing little or no work in summer jobs arranged by boosters. Three players making the allegations were parties in failed lawsuits against the university.

•Former Husky tailback Vince Weathersby said he felt pressure to change his story about the boosters by Jim Heckman, president of Sports Washington magazine and then the son-in-law of UW coach Don James. In a message left on Weathersby's answering machine, Heckman suggested that the former tailback recant his allegations. "Whether it's, hey, you're pissed off and you said those things because you're mad and you didn't mean it," Heckman said in the message, "it would make everyone in the community feel great if you could say it." Heckman later was accused of trying to coerce Notre Dame linebacker Demetrius DuBose and Washington State safety Signor Mobley to transfer to Washington. Under NCAA rules, representatives of a university's athletic interests cannot contact athletes for recruiting purposes at any time. When asked whether the Pac-10 was looking into his dealings with DuBose, Heckman said: "That's untrue. Those rumors are untrue."

Coaches and players insisted they would not let the transgressions of Hobert and the other accusations become distractions. But their efforts to block out the off-field revelations fell short. After winning 22 consecutive games, the Huskies lost three of their last four and missed an opportunity to become the first team to win a third straight Rose Bowl by losing to Michigan.

James likened his situation to that of Queen Elizabeth, who deemed 1992 an *Annus Horribilus* because of the insufferable bouts between the Royal Family and Fleet Street tabloids. "Yes," he agreed, "1992 has not been a very good year."

Yet it began with such promise.

2

Pandemonium, Thy Name Is Pasadena

A red line of taillights snaked, inch by inch, up Rosemont Street to Orange Grove Boulevard. Leaving the Rose Bowl meant battling an ugly snarl of traffic. There were few reasons to dash out and, particularly for Husky fans, plenty of reasons to stay. Scores of them did.

On the field, benign chaos. Long after Michigan retreated to its locker room, Washington players and coaches danced, embraced, rolled in the grass. Reporters followed, shouting questions, furiously scribbling in their note pads. In the stands, fans stood in their seats and cheered, ran down the aisles, leaned over railings to collect autographs or simply touch their heroes. The Husky band played "Tequila" over and over. The ditty was intoxicating.

On this, the first evening of 1992, Pasadena was the axis of college football's universe.

At last, the Rose Bowl figured in the national championship equation. Miami was playing Nebraska three thousand miles away, yet the Orange Bowl was scarcely under way. This game had been decided: Washington 34, Michigan 14.

Cornerback Walter Bailey could have slept right there, pitched a tent on the floor of the bowl. Ripped off his Washington helmet and used it to drive the stakes into the soft turf. "I couldn't cry, I couldn't speak, I couldn't do anything but look around," he recalled. "I didn't care if we were voted national champions or not. Everything I'd ever wanted was right there, and it all happened that night. If I had a blanket and pillow, I wouldn't have left."

These hulking football players were reduced to children. Billy Joe Hobert's transformation was one of the strangest. He wept openly after the game and looked up into the stands, searching for his wife. He wanted to share the moment with her.

He wrapped his powerful arms around Don James and squeezed. Like the first time Magic hugged Kareem, this awkward embrace was an emotional mismatch. Hobert, the team's wild hair, putting a bear hug on James, as stoic a coach as imaginable. Hobert couldn't contain his emotions and blurted to his coach, "I love you, man."

Reporters gathered around the Huskies' mountain of a defensive tackle, Steve Emtman. Moths to a lantern. Bathed in the television kleig lights, Emtman moved slowly, talking as he walked.

What about Miami? Should the Hurricanes be national champs?

"I don't care about Miami," Emtman said, vaguely backhanding the air. "We're No. 1. I'm sick of hearing about Miami. We're too legit."

He was wearing a red baseball cap with NEBRASKA stitched in white. The reason for his new found loyalty to the Cornhuskers: If Nebraska, which Washington defeated early in the season, could beat Miami, or even give the Hurricanes a good game, Washington almost certainly would win the national championship outright. "Tonight," he said, "I'm the biggest Nebraska fan there is."

On the star scale, Emtman was already a supernova in Seattle. And this 21-year-old kid was the dancing bear in this media circus. When word got out that he had the flu a couple of nights before the game and spent a night in the hospital to receive fluids intravenously, it was big news. Would the greatest defensive player in UW history miss the Rose Bowl? The nature in which that story was covered indicated just how dearly people held this team.

Wrote Art Thiel, columnist for the *Seattle Post-Intelligencer*: "The Seattle-area media contingent (in Pasadena) is only slightly smaller than the one that covered the eruption of Mount St.

Helens. What is remarkable is that the only news for an entire week has been Steve Emtman's sore throat. Perspective, thy name is not UW football."

Maybe not. But pandemonium, thy name is Pasadena. A pack swarmed around a temporary platform erected on the field for the presentation of the Rose Bowl trophy. Receiver Curtis Gaspard made his personal pitch to national pollsters via a TV camera. "We're No. 1!" he yelled into the lens. "Are you convinced? Are you convinced?"

Handed out in the locker room later were white cotton shirts with "1991 National Champions" embroidered on the pocket and a tiny Washington helmet on the right chest. Ordering the mementos wasn't James's idea. He was far too superstitious to be so bold. "If I heard about this beforehand, I would have killed whoever brought these," James admitted. "But I like the way it fits now."

Washington players felt ignored by the national media all year. Lost in the upper-left corner of the country. A poor sister to Notre Dame, Miami, Colorado, even USC. Bitter fans deemed sports writers who they thought didn't give the Huskies due respect "East Coast Mafia."

Michael Martinez of the *New York Times* lent credence to the notion when he wrote, "Notre Dame has the Four Horsemen, Penn State has Joe Paterno, even Southern Cal has Tommy Trojan standing tall in the center of its Los Angeles campus. Washington has, well, a lot of rain."

James downplayed the East Coast Mafia theory, saying: "I never thought it was an Eastern bias as much as I thought it was a lack of national visibility. I've had a number of Eastern writers tell me that they go to bed Saturday night not knowing if we won or lost."

All that was changing. After the best season in the school's history, recognition was beginning to trickle in. Winning the Pac-10 race was no longer enough to satiate Washington. Winning the Rose Bowl wasn't enough—the Huskies did that the year before, whipping Iowa. But a national championship, now THAT was enough. A year before, the team's secret mantra for the 1990 season was "Nothing But Roses." Washington had a brush with greatness that year and a shot at that national title but was stunned at home by UCLA, a 22-point underdog. As it happened, winning that game would have clinched a championship.

The Dawgs came back in 1991 with a new motto, "Hungrier Than Ever." They then proceeded to feast. Michigan turned out to be little more than a light dessert.

"We were just starving for this win," Hoffmann said after the Rose Bowl game. "And I'll tell you, we were going to get it."

The Huskies came into the Rose Bowl at No. 2 in the Associated Press writers poll, a few points behind No. 1 Miami, and deadlocked with the Hurricanes in the *USA Today*/CNN coaches' poll. Both teams were 11-0. Beating fourth-ranked Michigan, the Dawgs reasoned, was proof positive of where at least a share of the No. 1 mantle should lie.

"Hey," Emtman crowed, "if we don't win it, I don't want it."

The numbers made a pretty strong case for the Huskies. They went undefeated for the first time in their history and chewed through opponents like a saber saw through sapling. Stanford was the first to fall. The Cardinal lost, 42-7, followed by 10 more regular-season victims: Nebraska (36-21), Kansas State (56-3), Arizona (54-0), Toledo (48-0), California (24-17), Oregon (29-7), Arizona State (44-16), USC (14-3), Oregon State (58-6), and Washington State (56-21).

Eleven Washington players would be selected in the 1992 NFL draft—the largest representation of any school—and a 12th, defensive tackle Tyrone Rodgers, made the Seattle Seahawks as a free agent. That means every UW senior who started in the Rose Bowl was drafted and/or made an NFL roster. Emtman, a junior who entered the draft a year early, was chosen by the Indianapolis Colts as the No. 1 selection overall. Cornerback Dana Hall went in the first round to San Francisco.

In his first year as a starter, Hobert completed 60 percent of his passes for 2,271 yards and 22 touchdowns. He was a better drop-back passer than Mark Brunell, who lost the starting job after sustaining a major knee injury during spring 1991. That injury came three months after Brunell won Rose Bowl MVP honors by leading the Dawgs over Iowa, 46-34. Brunell made a spectacular recovery and passed for 333 yards as a backup but could never unseat Hobert in 1992. Brunell was blazing fast, even after knee surgery, and was deadly on options. In his first start, against San Jose State, he took his second snap and scrambled 47 yards on a broken play. By his admission, his left-handed throwing style was a tad ungainly. "When I look at a left-hander throwing, it looks different to me," he conceded. "I'm used to guys like Montana and Elway. When I see Boomer (Esiason), it looks kind of weird."

Carrying the ball out of the one-back set were Jay Barry and Beno Bryant. Barry was a churning runner, built like a pit bull, and good on short-yardage situations. Occasionally, he would bust a big run between the tackles. He broke away at Nebraska and at Cal. At season's end, he had accumulated 718 yards on the ground.

Bryant, who finished with 943 yards, was more of a slippery back. More susceptible to getting hurt but more explosive. He rocketed upfield when he got to a corner. He was one of the team's most popular players. A natural comedian, he'd slip in and out of a falsetto voice during interviews, playfully mocking teammates. Reporters loved him for his quotes. After the Cal game, he sat down with about 20 scribes and filled their note-books with quips. His impersonation of crooner Terence Trent D'Arby at a team talent show brought down the house.

After the Rose Bowl, he and his mother made an excursion to Las Vegas, about a five-hour drive from her home in Los Angeles. A lucky streak on the one-armed bandits lined Beno's pockets with $600 of a casino's money. Then he began to lose. And lose. And lose some more. He left Nevada with five bucks, a sprained ankle from the game, and a smile wide as the Vegas Strip.

Star wideout Mario Bailey was named an All-America for good reason: He caught 62 balls for 1,037 yards and 17 touch-downs. He made some pretty spectacular grabs, but was best *after* catching the ball. More twists and turns in that 5-foot-10 frame than a dime-store mystery novel.

Orlando McKay was the primary deep threat, who stretched out the secondary and created seams for Bailey. A 47.09-second quarter miler, McKay had pretty good hands, too, catching 47 passes for 627 yards.

Assessed Oregon coach Rich Brooks, "(The 1991) Washing-ton team was the most dominant I've seen in this league since the 1972 USC team. And Washington's defense was the best college team I've seen anywhere."

The heart of this Husky team was its defense, ranked No. 1 in the nation, and spearheaded by Emtman. He didn't bother much with "swim" moves. He bull rushed over guys, plain overpowering just about everyone he lined up against. That made for chaos in the middle. Just two teams gained more than 100 yards on the ground against the Dawgs—Nebraska, which relied primarily on the option, gained 135 yards, and Cal, which featured Heisman hopeful Russell White and burner Lindsey Chapman, totaled 114.

History favored the Huskies on New Year's Day: The Pac-10 had won 18 of the previous 22 Rose Bowls, and on 14 of those 18 occasions, the Pac-10 team was ranked lower than its opponent. Also, Washington was riding a nine-game winning streak against Big Ten foes.

So Michigan, a seven-point underdog, had its hands full. But those were pretty talented hands. The 1991 Wolverines, in fact, were among the school's best teams. Michigan's defense yielded 15.4 points a game during the regular season, fewer than any other Washington opponent, and had not given up a rushing touchdown in the past 22 quarters. The team was No. 1 in the Big Ten against the run. Leading the defensive charge was senior starter Erick Anderson, who led the team in tackles for four consecutive years and won the Butkus Award, given to the nation's best linebacker. He and wideout Desmond Howard, winner of the Heisman Trophy, were the first two Michigan players to receive individual awards in the past 40 years.

Elvis Grbac and Howard were the marquee names in the Michigan offense, but running backs Ricky Powers and Tyrone Wheatley could do damage. James called Michigan the Huskies' most complete opponent in five years. Said All-America offensive lineman Greg Skrepenak, "If we beat Washington, I think we deserve to be called No. 1."

Gary Moeller, Michigan's coach, seemed pretty loose at the final press conference held at the Wrigley Mansion, headquarters for the Pasadena Tournament of Roses Association.

Moeller said he sought advice from Bo Schembechler, the former Wolverines coach who was 2-8 in Rose Bowls. "I let him put in five plays," Moeller quipped. "Three of them involve the fullback."

That brought hearty laughter from the press corps. Moeller smiled. James, sitting next to him, seemed more tense. He was asked how he celebrated his 59th birthday, which was the day before. "I didn't even remember it was yesterday," he said, forcing a smile. "Somebody just reminded me of it a minute ago."

Don James had better things to worry about than his birthday. He was, after all, eyeball to eyeball with destiny. Earlier in the week, in a meeting scheduled to last 30 minutes, James talked for about 45. That might not be unusual for some coaches, but it was for James. First, he could hardly be classified as long-winded, and second, he was meticulous about time. Recalled Dana Hall of the meeting: "Guys were asking me, 'Do you think he's scared or just excited?'"

Things started well for the state of Michigan on January 1. The General Motors entry was named the best float in the Rose Parade. Meanwhile, the Honda Motors float failed to start and had to be towed along the parade route.

The flint-gray clouds that blotted out the sun since Christmas gave way to streaks of sunshine. A monsoon-type storm that drenched the Southland for much of the week was over. By noon, it was 70 degrees. Perfect football weather. The Rose Bowl turf was especially soft from all the rain, but the grass was fairly dry. A day before, a helicopter was lowered a few feet from the floor of the bowl, blowing huge curls of mist toward the sidelines.

Outside the bowl, almost a palpable sense of expectation. Not since 1979, when third-ranked USC defeated No. 5 Michigan, had the Rose Bowl game determined the national champion. A crescendo had been building in Seattle all fall, and fans who made the trip south were banking on a scrapbook of memories. Some Washington fans went to extremes to show their loyalty to the team. Laurie Hobert, aunt of the starting quarterback, met a couple from Omak, Washington, who were about to get married in the parking lot of the Rose Bowl. They asked her to be their maid of honor. Their wedding song? "Bow Down to Washington," of course.

The atmosphere was electric, and when kickoff arrived at 2 p.m., the Rose Bowl brimmed with 103,566 people.

An attacking defense, one that regularly sent seven or eight pass rushers, punished Grbac. Got in his face. Planted him. The Huskies sacked him six times, equaling the number of sacks Michigan surrendered all season. "I can't remember being sacked that many times," he said. "Not even in high school. They're 10 times better than Notre Dame or Florida State."

Emtman, named co-MVP of the game, wrought havoc from the start. On the Wolverines' third play from scrimmage, he powered up the middle and shouldered his man into Grbac, who dropped the ball and pounced on his own fumble for a 7-yard loss. After big defensive plays like those, Emtman would lean back in a limbo stance, yank imaginary six-shooters out of an invisible holster, and fire them into the sky. The move always whipped the Washington crowd into a frenzy. Other Huskies would celebrate by shaking uncontrollably, convulsing their bodies in a dance called the "Compton Quake," named after a city near South-Central Los Angeles.

Hobert, who shared MVP recognition with Emtman, struggled to find a groove in the first half, but came back strong after the intermission, throwing touchdown passes to tight ends Aaron Pierce and Mark Bruener. He also scored the game's first touchdown, on a 2-yard sneak in the opening period, halting the streak of the Wolverine rush defense at 22 quarters.

Always the maverick, Hobert wore white shoes in the game. Every other Husky wore black. "I just wanted to be different," he explained. "No, not really. The cleats on those shoes were just right for this field, even though I did slip a couple of times."

Hobert sauntered into the postgame press conference wearing an oversized T-shirt with JUST BE ME written on the front in huge letters. When a reporter suggested he lean closer to the microphone, he shrugged, "I will, but I don't need it."

Less effusive was Brunell, who entered for series in the second and fourth quarters. He was razor sharp, completing his first six passes and putting the Dawgs in position for a second-quarter field goal that snapped a 7-7 tie. On the first play of a fourth-quarter series, he lofted a 35-yard touchdown pass into the hands of Mario Bailey. "All I did was drop back and throw it up there," Brunell said. "Mario did the rest." The two used the same play for similar results, a 31-yard score, against Iowa in the 1990 Rose Bowl.

His 7-for-8 outing left Brunell itching for more playing time. "I just wanted one more quarter. Just one more," he recalled. "I felt really good that game. Some games you go out and you're unstoppable. Things were clicking that game."

Not for everyone. Desmond Howard left Pasadena having made one catch in the most important game of his life. "Magic," as his teammates called him, had disappeared. Shutting him down required a defensive feat. When it came to speed, Howard was world class. He notched 23 touchdowns, at least one against every team he faced in 1991. He caught 61 balls and struck paydirt just about every possible way—scoring by reception, punt return, kickoff return, and reverse. No one was able to stop him. Even Florida State, which humbled the Wolverines in Ann Arbor, 51-31, was burned for two scores by Howard. And torched on both of those was Terrell Buckley, the Seminoles' All-American defensive back. Grbac had a face full of purple, and the Husky secondary was well prepared to bottle the Heisman winner.

Despite separating his shoulder on the game's first play, Washington free safety Shane Pahukoa twice knocked the ball out of Howard's hands on fly patterns up the middle. On one, Walter Bailey was nearby and picked off the tipped ball.

During the two weeks before the game, Travis Spring and Shermonte Brooks, redshirt freshmen, were assigned to mimic Howard. Both wore No. 21, just like the All-America wideout. Both were fast and ran crisp patterns, yet neither was quite the real deal. "It's not the same thing," Dana Hall said. "But it makes you very aware of the guy when you see No. 21 all over the field." The simulation might have been more realistic if, instead of rotating downs, Spring and Brooks ran routes at the same time. Covering Howard could be as tough as covering two guys at once.

Bailey's numbers for the regular season were strikingly similar to, and sometimes better than, Howard's. Bailey caught 62 balls for 1,037 yards and 17 touchdowns. Howard caught 61 for 950 and scored 19 touchdowns. Similar in stature to Howard, Bailey had to put up with some episodes of mistaken identity on game week. Twice, he was approached by writers during a meet-the-teams press conference who wanted a Howard quote. Irritating gaffes, to be sure. "The only difference between me and Desmond Howard," Bailey said, "is he's at Michigan and returns punts and kickoffs."

Some reporters snickered at that assessment, dismissing it as a bad case of sour grapes. Bailey, fast but not blazing, wasn't even mentioned in the same breath as the Heisman. His pass patterns hardly left NFL scouts drooling. Before the season, Bailey worked out with former Washington receiver Lonzell "Mo" Hill, who played for the New Orleans Saints, and Chris Chandler, the former UW quarterback who now plays for the Phoenix Cardinals. Bailey played receiver, Hill a defensive back. The matchup was a mismatch, and Bailey was on the ugly end. Hill knocked him to the turf, stepped in front of him to bat down balls, disrupted his routes.

"He was just killing me," Bailey said of Hill. "Sometimes I couldn't even get past him. That kind of stuff really gets to you and makes you work harder and harder because he's really talking in your ear and telling you: 'You gotta keep going. You gotta keep going.'

"He's a receiver, so I thought he wasn't going to be able to cover me. I was amazed. He would just jam me up. I wouldn't be able to get off the ball."

That humbling experience paid dividends. Six months later, in the most important game of his life, Bailey caught six passes for a game-high 126 yards and a touchdown, showcasing his talents to a sold-out stadium and a television audience of millions. The most memorable move he made wasn't a juke but a jab. With 13 minutes to play, after making a diving catch of a 35-yard touchdown pass from Mark Brunell that put the Huskies up, 34-7, Bailey popped to his feet in the end zone and struck the Heisman Trophy pose, something Howard had done against Ohio State while campaigning for the trophy.

Bailey planned the move long before kickoff. Fans had written him letters suggesting it. "Everybody told me to do it, so I did," he said. "I told my mom and stepfather that I wouldn't do it in the first quarter. It might come back to haunt me. I'd do it in the fourth quarter when I knew we'd have the game wrapped up." So with Michigan on ice, Mario did the freeze-frame.

"I wanted to prove that there is another receiver whose name is not Desmond Howard," Bailey said. "It's no longer Mario who? It's Mario Bailey. It's No. 5, not 21."

Showered and smiling, Howard loped into the interview room wearing an Armani/Beach Boys outfit. Offsetting his blue blazer and tie were blue jeans and sandals. He took a seat behind a microphone at a long table and answered question after question about his futile afternoon. Fatigued, he began to look like a man late for a plane. He shifted in his seat. What of Bailey's pose? "If he's into the Heisman Trophy," Howard snapped, "he can come over to my house and see the real thing."

Word of the remark traveled fast. Bailey, mobbed by reporters outside the interview room, was asked if he'd be needing a
map to the Howard abode. "That's OK," he said, chuckling. "I'm
going to have a national championship. He can have the Heisman
Trophy."

II

It was odd to see Don James smile, bizarre to see him cry.

But there he was, on January 2, 1992, standing on a dais in the
ballroom of the Anaheim Marriott, with a bouquet of microphones under his chin, fighting back tears. Unsuccessfully. He
planned to answer questions about the Huskies winning the *USA
Today*/CNN coaches' poll. The words were hard to come by. His
chin quivered. His voice cracked and sounded as if it were
filtering through an electric fan.

"Tears," he said haltingly. "It's so difficult to express the
feeling I have for these kids . . . I don't know what more our kids
could have done."

Washington edged Miami for first place in the CNN poll,
receiving 33 1/2 first-place votes and 1,449 1/2 points to Miami's
25 1/2 first-place votes and 1,440 1/2 points. The AP poll was
even closer: The Hurricanes got 32 first-place votes and 1,472
points, and the Huskies got 28 No. 1 votes and 1,468 points. The
four-point spread was the narrowest margin of victory in the 57-
year history of the AP poll.

Sitting among the reporters at the Marriott was Carol James,
who cried along with her husband. They seldom cried together,
maybe twice in their 40-year marriage, and only on sad occasions. This was one of their happiest moments. Both were a little
punchy after a sleepless night. So many well-wishers. The Jameses
had gotten a call in the middle of the night, informing them the
Associated Press vote went to Miami. That wasn't a shock. The
Hurricanes blanked Nebraska, 22-0, in the Orange Bowl, a showing that allowed Miami to maintain its narrow advantage in the
AP poll. There were a few defectors for Washington: Gary Long,
a *Miami Herald* writer and AP voter, made a change during the
final week and cast his No. 1 vote for the Huskies.

"Splitting the atom must have been simpler," Long wrote of
his inflammatory stance. He argued that Washington's wins over

No. 8 California, No. 15 Nebraska, and No. 20 Stanford—all of which came on neutral or hostile turf—were more impressive than Miami's victories over No. 3 Florida State, No. 5 Penn State, No. 15 Nebraska, and No. 22 Tulsa. Besides, he wrote, "Had Miami beaten Florida in the Sugar Bowl instead of a made-to-order Nebraska that also arrived intimidated, my final vote would have been Miami No. 1 and Washington No. 2."

All that was moot to the Jameses. The AP vote was history. All Don and Carol could do was wait for the coaches' vote. They decided to ignore all phone calls and knocks on the door until around the time the CNN votes were tabulated. They were basically hiding out in their 19th-floor suite. The polls closed at 8:30 a.m. Eastern Standard Time. Counting votes would take an hour, so if Washington won, James figured, he'd be getting a call around 6:30 a.m. his time.

When the sun rose, hopes began to sink in a certain 19th-floor suite. Don James, a guy who had won 114 games, more than any other coach in Husky history, was losing this mind game. Would a national title be snatched from him again? He remembered 1984. Always will. That's when his team finished 11-1 and beat No. 2 Oklahoma in the Orange Bowl, 28-17, only to be edged out of a title by undefeated Brigham Young. That couldn't happen again, could it?

The phone calls to the suite died off, and James wondered if they would ever start up again. Six-thirty had come and gone. Wracked with disappointment, Don turned to his wife.

"It's 9:30 on the East Coast," he said. "We haven't won it. Nobody's got the nerve to call us and give us the news."

Eleven painful minutes passed. For a man who had spent his whole life breaking hours into minutes, minutes into seconds, those 11 minutes felt like an eternity. "We just felt every kind of bitter disappointment," Carol recalled. "It was unbelievable, the feeling—everything went through our hearts and our minds. It was almost like somebody in the family had died. I know that's not fair to compare—we've been through that. But that's the feeling we had, more for the team than for ourselves."

Finally, the phone rang.

"Should I get it?" Carol asked.

"Might as well," Don said.

It was Bob Roller, a representative for the ad agency that handles the coaches'-poll trophy, sponsored by McDonald's.

Washington, Roller gleefully informed her, was the coaches' No. 1 team. "I didn't want to keep them in any suspense," Roller explained. "So I told her who I was and that they had won it . . . She sort of gasped and dropped the phone and said, 'Don, you've won!'"

The call was a short one. Carol hung up and frantically began dialing close friends. It was early, but so what? This was the best news in 101 years of Washington football. Sharing a national title didn't seem so bad after all. Washington and Miami were on top of the mountain, and James would take that any day.

Word of the coaches' vote trickled to the Husky players, some of whom got calls in their rooms from reporters. Around 8 a.m.— just in case there were any late risers—Mario Bailey ran up and down a 15th-floor hallway pounding on doors and screaming, "We're No. 1!"

ESPN had called Brunell in his room at 3 a.m. and asked him if he would come down to the lobby for an interview. The network wanted his reaction on losing the AP vote. He hung up and went back to sleep.

Hobert got a similar call. "I was too tired to care," he confessed. "But when (Jeff) Woodruff called to tell me about the CNN poll, that woke me up pretty good."

It was the second consecutive year the polls disagreed on who to call the national champion. The writers chose Colorado after the 1990 season, and the coaches picked Georgia Tech. This was the first national championship, in any sport, that Washington had won. In fact, every other school in the Pac-10 had some type of national title in its trophy case. The UW, sandwiched by Lake Washington and Lake Union, has a powerhouse rowing program, but that is not recognized as an NCAA-sanctioned sport.

Something about winning praise from the coaches, Washington players would say, made the CNN poll more credible than its AP counterpart. Coaches knew football. Writers were more likely to vote with their heart. Not everyone agreed. Mike Price, head coach at Washington State, made the mistake of telling reporters he voted Miami No. 1 because he went to high school with Hurricane coach Dennis Erickson in Everett, Washington. The two are buddies. It was a bad move, especially because, unlike writers, coaches do not have to disclose their votes. What's worse, Price admitted to this during the week preceding the Apple Cup, the annual game between Washington and Washington State.

No, the CNN poll wasn't perfect. After the bowl games, one coach ranked Miami third. Erickson was rankled and shed any facade of disinterest when he heard that. "I'd like to know what he was drinking last night," the Miami coach fumed. "I'd like to think we're all accountable for something like this."

Erickson has a lot of ties to the Pacific Northwest. A native of Snohomish County, just north of Seattle, he coached Washington State in 1987 and '88. Keith Gilbertson, the Huskies' former offensive coordinator who's now the head coach at California, is one of his best friends. In fact, Erickson is the godfather of Gilbertson's daughter. That isn't Erickson's only connection to the UW, either.

"My cousin used to be the crew coach at Washington," he said of Dick Erickson, who now handles all the docking of boats in the open end of the Husky stadium. "How do you think he's leaning? All my family up there changed the 'o' to an 'e' at the end of their last name for the last month."

When asked a few days before the first of the year if his players were planning to watch part of the Rose Bowl before they squared off against Nebraska, Erickson said: "We'll probably have about 10 TVs going in the locker room. Look, they wouldn't be human if they weren't interested."

But the coach pulled a reversal the day before the Orange Bowl. When he walked into the Hurricanes' locker room and found two TVs, he ordered them removed from the premises. His boys didn't need Pasadena on their minds.

The Hurricanes had a reputation for flash. It seemed a new dance craze was born out of every Miami touchdown. Washington players danced, too, and were frequently flagged by officials for excessive celebrations. Yet for some reason, the Huskies did not bear the hot dog label.

Wrote the *PI*'s Thiel, "Washington is the virtuous Dudley Do-Right, square of jaw and stout of heart, while Miami is the Snidely Whiplash, tying sorority girls to railroad tracks."

Bad reputation or not, folks know something about winning national titles in Miami, where they have three in six years and four in 10. But this was uncharted territory for the Huskies. The community of Seattle made a pretty stiff pitch for the crown. A columnist for the *Seattle Times* drew up a form for readers to fax to AP voters, begging them to lean Washington's way. Many voters, whose machines were clogged with the forms, said if anything, that ploy pushed them closer to Miami.

A Seattle radio station bought billboard space on Miami's Northwest 12th Avenue, in the shadow of the Orange Bowl. On the sign was a huge dog eating bite-sized Hurricane helmets out of a dish labeled "Husky Chow." Above him, bannered across the purple background, was "No. 1 is going to the Dawgs." It wasn't going to win any advertising awards and didn't draw high praise from locals. If a similar Miami sign were erected in Seattle, it would have been promptly torched.

Don James set five passing records as a quarterback for the Hurricanes during the early 1950s and didn't mind sharing the national title with his alma mater. Plenty of other folks called for a playoff between the teams. Maybe, as *Seattle Times* columnist Steve Kelley suggested, a showdown should have been held at a neutral site on the idle Sunday before the Super Bowl. "It's dreaming," Husky co-captain Ed Cunningham said of the suggestion. "That's all it is, dreaming. The NCAA has their heads so far up their butts, they're not going to let it happen."

Cunningham had a way with words. As the team's elder statesman and an academic All-America, the offensive lineman was always good with a quip. He was quoted on absolutely every subject. If a writer was doing a defensive back story, he'd talk to Cunningham. Need to gauge a quarterback? Cunningham's your man. Want a weird angle on a linebacker? Well, you get the idea. Gilbertson, himself a quotable rube, once moaned that Cunningham wound up in the newspaper more often than the coaching staff. Any more ink, he playfully warned the senior center, and there would be some extra running to do after practice.

When asked about the battle for national respect, Cunningham said Miami players "don't have the testosterone to be No. 1," adding, "And you know where testosterone comes from, don't you?"

Of Miami All-America defensive end Rusty Medearis, also recruited by Washington, Cunningham spouted, "He didn't come here because he knows he wouldn't start. He'd be a permanent scout-teamer."

Talk about drenching a campfire with gasoline. Bad blood already flowed between these teams. They might have been at opposite corners of the U.S. map, but they were nose to nose in the newspapers. Playoff talk was rampant, but James and Erickson would have none of it, even if the NCAA had sanctioned a showdown. Twelve games are enough, they argued, especially when the players aren't being paid.

"I think everyone wanted to see that game," says Cunningham, now a second-year pro with the Phoenix Cardinals. "It still goes on today. Guys are always asking me, 'Do you think Washington would have won that game?' Everyone wants to know who was better, the '91 Huskies or '91 Hurricanes?"

Miami defensive back Charles Pharms suggested the school settle the score in March, when they were scheduled to meet the president. "Let's play a little sandlot game in the Rose Garden," Pharms said. "It would have to be a pretty clean game at the White House, in front of the president. Maybe a little seven-on-seven."

Just because there wasn't an actual playoff didn't mean *Sports Illustrated* couldn't pretend. In the tradition of Sidd Finch—the mythical New York Mets pitcher with the supersonic fastball—the magazine conjured an imaginary football game, complete with doctored photos showing Washington and Miami sharing a field. The article, "The Dream Game," was written by Austin Murphy. Played in a temporary stadium built behind the aptly dubbed Mirage Hotel in Las Vegas, the Fracas in the Cactus ended with Washington winning, 18-17. Emtman and his defense rounded up quarterback Gino Torretta and his "Ruthless Posse" of receivers. Hobert iced the win, settling the score that could never really be settled, by sneaking in for a two-point conversion.

Plenty of readers responded. "Half the Miami fans who called were furious Washington won," Murphy said. "The others were furious it wasn't televised."

Save the *SI* scenario, there was no barometer of how the teams would fare head-to-head. Both whipped Nebraska—which, interestingly, lost to co-champs Colorado and Georgia Tech a year earlier. Who was better, Miami or Washington, was fodder for a heated debate. Bob Devaney, the former Cornhuskers coach who now serves as Nebraska's athletic director, was one of the few college football authorities to make a distinction between the teams. After losing the Orange Bowl, Devaney remarked, "We've played them both. And Washington is not in the same ballpark as Miami." Don James posted that clip on a locker room bulletin board. Devaney would pay for his comments when Nebraska came to Seattle nine months later.

But James wasn't thinking of vindication January 2, the most triumphant day of his coaching career. He was more concerned about keeping his overflowing emotions in check.

"This," he told the reporters in the Marriott, "is a great day in the life of a football coach."

And in the life of an athletic department. "I think it re-emphasizes Washington's great football tradition," Athletic Director Barbara Hedges said. "It will have a positive effect on the entire athletic program."

Reaching the top of the mountain means one thing, UW faculty athletic representative Dick Dunn gushed, "A clean program *can* win. That's what it means."

Dunn's assertion that this program was squeaky clean would be tested less than a year later but, as it stood, the only controversy surrounding the football team was no parade was scheduled. The Hurricanes were thrown a block party in Miami, yet there was no ticker-tape reception down University Avenue for the Huskies. Insiders at the UW Athletic Department said James was too superstitious to allow a parade to be planned before the Michigan game and was too busy with recruiting after the Rose Bowl. Wrote *Tacoma Morning News Tribune* columnist John McGrath, "Without (James's) approval, it's difficult to get within the same telephone prefix as the players, let alone arrange for them to holler and whoop before tens of thousands of towns-people."

A somewhat anticlimactic ceremony to honor the co-national champions was held in front of a relatively small crowd at halftime of a Husky basketball game. Championship rings were distributed at the spring football game.

Four University of British Columbia engineering students held their own private parade, heisting the $3,000 Rose Bowl trophy and toting it across the border. Sometime on the night of February 3, 1992, or early morning hours of the next day, the four broke into the UW Tubby Graves building, which houses the athletic department. They smashed the glass in the trophy case and heisted the Rose Bowl booty as part of UBC's "prank week."

The crime led local newscasts. The search party for D. B. Cooper was smaller.

No doubt those students took first place for zaniest prank. And the reddest faces. They turned the trophy over to Canadian authorities on the night of February 4. The mounties met UW police at the border and returned the stolen goods along with a note from the students.

> Dear Sirs:
>
> We would like to express our sincere regret for the damage we have caused you.
>
> We understand now the ramifications and the negative impact of our actions. We intended to cause no injury to the University of Washington, the Husky football team, or their fans.
>
> We wish to compensate you for any damages you have incurred as a result of our actions. Please send us a bill.
>
> Sincerely,
> Phil, Brent, Mike, and Jesse

Washington asked for $450 to replace the glass in the trophy case. Coaches breathed a collective sigh of relief and immediately went to work on a third league title.

3

Parting With The Past

The champagne uncorked to toast the co-national champions had scarcely gone flat and already the winds of change had whipped through the Montlake Cut. The Husky program proved to be a catapult for the careers of assistants Keith Gilbertson, Matt Simon, and Larry Slade.

Simon, who coached Husky running backs, took the offensive coordinator post at New Mexico, and Slade, Washington's secondary coach, accepted the position of defensive coordinator at Maryland. Chris Tormey, who coached outside linebackers, was wooed by Navy to take the defensive coordinator position there but decided to stay at Washington, where he was moved to defensive secondary coach.

Most significant was the loss of Gilbertson, UW's offensive coordinator and a guru of the one-back set, hired to replace Bruce Snyder as head coach at California. Snyder accepted the top job at Arizona State, a position for which Gilbertson also was considered.

Gilbertson, 43, edged Steve Mariucci, Cal's popular offensive coordinator, and accepted the Golden Bears' job Jan. 14. He got the nod because of his head coaching experience; he ran the show at Idaho in 1986-88. "That may have been the deciding factor," Cal athletic director Bob Bockrath said. "But it was real close." The pact Gilbertson signed paid him $200,000 per year and included a clause that barred him from taking a job at any Pac-10 school for five years.

Gilbertson, a native of Snohomish, Washington, and a close friend of Miami coach Dennis Erickson, built a reputation of a freewheeling players' coach with an eagle eye for finding a soft spot in a defense. His relaxed approach complemented Don James's rigid, scheduled-to-the-second coaching style. He was UW offensive coordinator for just one season, replacing Gary Pinkel, who moved on to take the top job at Toledo. Under Gilby, as his players called him, the Huskies averaged a league-leading 471.9 yards a game. It had been bandied that Gilbertson would take over the Huskies when James retired, but Gilbertson downplayed that notion. "I don't want to touch that," he said four games into his Cal career. "He (James) never asked me and I never answered . . . I don't think that's fair for me to do that. It's not fair to the people who think they have a chance, and it's not fair to put that on my players."

Jeff Woodruff, a nine-year veteran of the Husky staff and a son-in-law of James, was appointed offensive coordinator, and Steve Morton was hired to assume Gilbertson's responsibilities as offensive line coach. Hired to coach UW cornerbacks was former Husky Ron Milus, a cornerback and punt returner for the school in 1982-85. Al Lavan, who coached running backs for the Dallas Cowboys (1980-88) and San Francisco 49ers (1989-90), took over for Simon.

The defection that likely hurt the Huskies most wasn't that of a coach, but a player—someone considered in these parts as much a natural wonder as Mount Rainier.

II

By the time Steve Emtman took his place behind the podium on January 31, 1992, every reporter in the Husky Hall of Fame room knew what he was going to say. The mystery about his future no longer concerned whether he would stay for his senior season. That notion was reserved for ardent fans, blinded by optimism.

Emtman was holding a press conference to declare his eligibility for the NFL draft. Talking to media was becoming a chore. Reporters were getting under his skin. They badgered him, his friends, his parents, trying to get notice of whether the Dawgs would have a new man in the middle come spring. Emtman changed his phone number and, to escape it all, went on a fishing trip after the Rose Bowl.

Meanwhile, the subject—Will he or won't he?—was dissected on radio call-in shows, in newspapers, and in barrooms all over town.

Reasons to leave were compelling. Why should he stay? The Outland Trophy and Lombardi Award were already on his mantel. Twice, he was named Pac-10 defensive MVP, sharing the honor in 1990 with Arizona cornerback Darryl Lewis. Washington had an undefeated season, won two Rose Bowls and a national championship. The only conquest left was the Heisman Trophy, and Emtman finished fourth in the voting two months earlier. No defensive player has ever won it, and only two linemen have taken home the Heisman since its inception in 1935: Larry Kelley of Yale (1936) and Notre Dame's Leon Hart (1949).

Sticking around for the Heisman would have been dumb. Much as he wanted No. 90 to stay, Don James didn't question the decision. If he were Steve's dad, James said, he would have "gathered up all the information that he got and probably would have thought along two lines. No. 1, make sure you get your education. You've got to get your degree because, as Steve knows, he's only one play away from being done with football. I would have insisted that, No. 1, he had a plan to get his degree, and No. 2, probably go the way he did."

The NFL beckoned. If he stayed, the specter of a rookie salary cap and the possibility of an injury loomed. Both, as it happens, came true. A rookie salary cap *was* instituted, and Emtman—selected by the Indianapolis Colts as the first pick in the draft—underwent knee surgery in November 1992, two weeks after tearing a ligament in a loss to the Miami Dolphins.

Emtman probably chose to go pro long before he made the announcement. Still, he wanted to wait until the day before the deadline to tell the press. Maybe he didn't want to disappoint his coaches. Maybe he thought his decision to leave would affect recruiting. Maybe he was truly undecided.

Dan Raley didn't believe the latter. Eleven days before the press conference, the *Post-Intelligencer* reporter wrote a story headlined, "Sources say Emtman's bound for NFL." One of these sources warned Raley: "Don't you dare tell him I told you. I don't want his jeep pulling up out front."

Emtman felt betrayed.

He wanted to delay the decision, or at least the announcing of it, until the eleventh hour. If he was anything, he was loyal to UW, one of the few schools confident that he could pass a college class or play a lick of Division I football. Besides, he and Raley had established a good relationship. In summer 1991, Raley drove five hours from Seattle and spent time on the Emtman family farm, a 2,700-acre spread in Cheney, Washington, to do an in-depth feature on the most prominent Husky.

Raley told of the former fat kid who overcame his insecurities in the weight room. Emtman's is quite a tale. He grew up bailing, branding, and working 16-hour days on the family farm, where they raised cattle and grew wheat, barley, lentils, and alfalfa. Cheney is 90 miles north of Washington State University, one of the few schools besides UW to recruit Emtman. He was largely overlooked by most Pac-10 coaches and certainly coaches in the Midwest, South, and East. When his coach at Cheney, Tom Oswald, called coaches at the Arizona schools, they told him they had a full slate of defensive line recruits.

Some teachers at Cheney High tried to discourage Emtman, a marginal student, from accepting the Huskies' scholarship offer, insisting the school would be too challenging. Emtman, who took a developmental reading program at nearby Eastern Washington University, balked at the suggestion. He chose to attend Washington, where he carried a respectable 2.8 grade-point average.

Seattle Times writer Blaine Newnham followed Raley's story with a column admonishing reporters not to guess the lineman's plans. Emtman told him: "That a reporter can write a story like that really bothers me. I told him it was B.S. to print a story that I had made up my mind when I hadn't. He was just so hot for the story. It's been, 'Tell me first, tell me first. Don't hold a press conference.'"

Given his druthers, Emtman *wouldn't* have held a press conference. He told people in the Washington sports information department he didn't want to hold one. He suggested issuing a written release. No way, they said, reporters will want their questions answered.

Could the conference be held on a Saturday? That would leave the *P-I*, which doesn't publish Sunday, out in the cold. No, Emtman was told, he'd have to go by the book.

Emtman wanted revenge for Raley's story, and was delighted when the P-I reported he had all but hired Leigh Steinberg, perhaps the best-known agent in the business, when in reality he had inked a deal with Los Angeles power broker Marvin Demhoff.

Emtman showed little emotion as he read a prepared statement to the media:

> *I am here to announce that I have made the decision to forgo my final year of college eligibility and declare myself available for the 1992 NFL draft. This has been a very difficult decision. The main deciding factor was that of personal challenge. I feel I am at the top of my game at the collegiate level and want to challenge myself at a higher level. I have an intensity about myself when it comes to football and anyone who knows me understands that. I know that to maintain that intensity, I must move on to the pro level. I want it understood that this is not an issue of money, but rather to fulfill a life-long dream of playing pro football. I would like to thank my coaches and teammates for all the great memories such as the two Rose Bowl victories, a national championship, and a perfect 12-0 season, and, most of all, the friendships that have been built over the past four years. I am hopeful that they, along with all the great Husky fans will understand and support my decision. I plan on keeping close ties with this community and the university during my pro career. No matter where I play pro ball, this will always be home for me. I hope I can make you all proud.*

The speculation officially over, this country boy—a boy the size of a small country—had Washington in his rear-view mirror. Projected to be among the top three picks in the draft, he won the Outland Trophy, the Lombardi Award, and finished fourth in the Heisman race. When he announced his intentions, you could almost hear the sigh of relief from the coaching staffs of every other school on Washington's schedule. The mammoth defensive tackle was considered the most unblockable Pac-10 player in a decade.

Emtman finished his college career with 134 tackles, 71 of which were unassisted, and 14 sacks. He was named to the first unit of virtually every All-America team, including AP, UPI, Walter Camp, Football Writers of America, Kodak, *Football News*, *Playboy*, and *College and Pro Football Newsweekly*.

"You know all those X's and O's that we put up on the chalkboard?" Arizona coach Dick Tomey once moaned. "The problem is, that little line we draw to the guy in the middle of their defense . . . it was supposed to be a block . . . But nobody could ever block that guy, so nothing worked. And after a while, you get so far behind that you're trying to do what you don't do very well, and everything you do is wrong. That's what happened to people when they played Washington."

Tomey had cause for complaint. In Washington's 54-0 thumping of Arizona, Emtman sacked Wildcats quarterback George Malauulu on the first two plays from scrimmage. Husky Stadium was a crucible of anguish for Arizona, which ran the ball 39 times, losing yardage on 19 of those attempts while gaining more than 10 yards only once.

An overmatched Toledo offensive lineman, beaten down after down by Emtman, tried to slow him with a block, but "all I would see was a flash of purple, and he was gone."

Just as intense on the practice field, Emtman would mete out a pretty stiff penalty—a bell-ringing club to the head—if teammates didn't come at him full speed. One Washington defensive lineman complained of a sore knee and sat out of drills. Emtman and Tyrone Rodgers, a defensive tackle, gave him a sore ego, suggesting at full volume that he didn't have the balls to be a Husky, and he was damn lucky they didn't kick his ass on the spot.

"Steve wasn't this animal who was out to hurt people," lineman David Ilsley said of his All-America roommate. "He was just *really* competitive. . . . Not only was he 290 pounds and strong, but he was quick as hell. Lining up against him was almost impossible. Great explosion. You'd try to get in a good stance and he was already in your face."

During the 1990 season, the entire team wore white shoes, sort of a symbol of unity. Black shoes were painted white to conform with the rest. Before the 1991 Rose Bowl, Emtman walked onto the practice field wearing a pair of spanking new black Nike cleats. It wasn't a form of protest; he planned to paint them. But just in case, defensive line coach Randy Hart reminded him of the policy.

"Gotta get 'em painted!" said Hart, who had a way of sounding like a carnival barker when he conducted a drill. Sharp, rapid bursts of speech. So quick the words were hard to decipher.

"I'll do it after practice," Emtman promised.

"Gotta get 'em painted!"

"After practice."

"Gotta get 'em painted!"

"After practice."

"Gotta get 'em painted!"

No answer. Again, Hart prodded, "Gotta get 'em . . . "

"WHAT THE HELL DOES IT MATTER?"

The bellow was as loud as an air-raid siren. Recalled one Husky: "The whole team just moved back. It was like a meteor hit the Earth."

If he wasn't trying to dismember you, Emtman could downright disarm you. Folksy off the field, he had a way of making you feel like a friend. "He's really cool," teammate Joe Kralik said. "Whenever he has a party or anything, he's just one of the guys."

Music was at the center of Emtman's life, and like his playing style, he cranked it up to maximum volume. Everything from country to grunge rock to rap. He even had a classical compact disc to study to. He was fixated on his car and home stereo systems and always tinkering, trying to pump the tunes up one more decibel count. Wake the neighbors. "You'd get in his car and it sounded great," Ilsley recalled. "Then he'd go out and work on it some more. You'd listen to it again and it would sound like hell. I'd say, 'Steve, what did you do to this thing?'"

Emtman had a portable CD player that he tried to mount in the midsized Audi he owned before he bought a Jeep. Problem was, every time the car hit a stretch of bad road, the disc would skip. He slaved over the problem for months. "He tried everything," Ilsley said, laughing. "He put foam on the dashboard. He built some crazy thing out of drinking straws. He'd try to use suction cups on the windows. He even had the thing hanging with fishing line from the rear-view mirror. It was swinging back and forth."

Ilsley, an offensive lineman who lived with Emtman for two years, got a kick out of his buddy's resourcefulness. "He was into building his own speakers," he said. "Never did a great job. He'd crank it loud, as loud as you can get."

Emtman was accused of running a red light and causing a chain-reaction accident involving three cars in the University District in October 1990. He also was charged with leaving the scene of the accident. During the ensuing trial, an air of bemusement filled the courtroom when Emtman explained he had his music cranked and had no idea he had left an accident in his wake.

Riding in Emtman's Audi was an experience. There wasn't much passenger room with him behind the wheel. "You didn't want to ride in back behind him," said Ilsley, who was in that unfortunate position as a freshman on a drive to Cheney. With every gear shift, Emtman lurched back a little, rearranging the kneecaps of Ilsley, no small cargo at 6-foot-5, 280 pounds.

Speaking of leg crushing, Emtman did that on the field, too. He and Ilsley faced each other in a 1990 offense-on-defense drill. Emtman jumped to bat down a pass and was knocked down by offensive lineman Todd Bridge. Emtman fell on Ilsley's lower right leg. The force snapped Ilsley's tibia and fibula. "Obviously (Emtman), was sorry for it," Ilsley said. "But it's football. There's nothing you can do." Mark Brunell's knee injury was caused in part by an Emtman tackle, as was a broken leg sustained by Nebraska fullback Omar Soto.

Emtman had seen enough injuries to convince him to take out a million-dollar insurance policy with Lloyds of London for his junior season. He knew what his talents were worth. Scouts knew, too. Although one of the 451 college standouts invited to the NFL combine in Indianapolis, Emtman was the only no-show. A few NFL teams were miffed, but Emtman said his busy schedule, flying from one awards presentation to another, burned him out. "Being here could only have helped him," said Ken Herock, director of player personnel for the Atlanta Falcons. "This combine is a very important screening process for all 28 NFL teams. Anyone hoping to go in the draft should be here."

The decision didn't seem to bother those coaches and scouts who flew to Seattle to push, prod, time, and measure Emtman on March 25 in a personal tryout held in the UW weight room and on the football field. Colts coach Ted Marchibroda was there. So was Chuck Knox, coach of the Los Angeles Rams. So were reporters, TV cameras, and some students. The crowd swelled to about 70, following Emtman from station to station. They watched in awe as he got down in a crouch, exploded up, and recorded a vertical leap of 36 1/2 inches. He bench-pressed 225 pounds 29 times, four fewer than the record at the combine. He was disappointed with his 40-yard dash time, 4.85 seconds, but consistently had run a 4.75 the week before.

The Colts, who held the top two picks in the draft, were one of the few teams with high first-round selections that had yet to interview the bull-rushing lineman. "How can I draw a conclusion on Indianapolis?" Emtman asked. "I haven't met them. I haven't seen their facilities yet." But Colts vice president Jim Irsay didn't mask his intent to draft Emtman. "Defensive linemen are at a premium," he said. "When you have a chance to get a great one, you don't want to pass that up."

And Indianapolis didn't, inking Emtman to a four-year, $8.6 million contract, including a $3.8 million signing bonus. "I guess what it means is I'm set for life," said Emtman, recipient of the richest contract ever for a rookie defensive player. Enough cash to buy a car stereo or two. His first acquisition in Indy? He bought the house owned by besieged L.A. Raiders-bound running back Eric Dickerson, furniture and all.

Indianapolis, which chose Texas A & M linebacker Quentin Coryatt with its No. 2 pick, made Emtman the highest selection in Husky history. Other Washington players coached by Don James had gone in the first round —Blair Bush, Doug Martin, Curt Marsh, Ron Holmes, Joe Kelly, Reggie Rogers and Bern Brostek—but the highest selection before Emtman was Rogers, picked seventh by Detroit.

Before he sustained the knee injury, Emtman was having an all-rookie-type year. At Joe Robbie Stadium on October 25, he picked off Dan Marino on the game's final play and returned the interception 90 yards to give the 6-0 Dolphins their first loss of the season, 31-20. He made a two-handed snare of a bullet pass intended for Bobby Humphrey from point-blank range. The return was the longest for a defensive lineman in the history of the game. Emtman's coaches in Seattle were watching.

Recalled UW defensive coordinator Jim Lambright: " It was great seeing Steve do that. We all enjoyed it. We're so proud of him. It reminded us of how much we miss Steve and how much we'd love to have him back. . . . Coach James came running into our offensive and defensive meeting rooms when he'd picked up that Emtman had just done it. So we came running out to the television sets to watch the replays."

The departure of Emtman left some pretty big cleats to fill in the middle of the Dawgs' defensive line. D'Marco Farr, used sparingly in 1991, was heir apparent. No small burden. "No matter how well I'm playing or how many tackles I make," Farr said, "the first time I miss one, and probably every time I do something wrong, people are going to whisper to each other, 'Steve Emtman would have made that play.' I kind of feel like Steve made a parking place for a Cadillac and I'm pulling up in a Hyundai.

"Steve worked his butt off and made some plays that made people look at the film and decide they were either going to have to adjust their game plan to stop him, or they were going to lose a quarterback or a running back. It was that simple."

Farr, a 270-pound cousin of former UCLA and Detroit Lions receiver Mel Farr, found that just filling gaps wasn't sufficient to satisfy Washington coaches.

"I used to think that making a tackle was pretty good—get a guy at the line of scrimmage and it's no gain," he said. "But around here, that's not good enough. In the Cal game last year, I tackled Russell White, who's one of the best tailbacks in the country, for no gain. But at film review, I got yelled at because it should have been for a loss."

III

There were other holes to fill on both sides of the ball. Not far behind Emtman on draft day was Husky cornerback Dana Hall, picked 18th by San Francisco. With designs on converting him into a free safety who could fill the sizable void left by Ronnie Lott, the 49ers signed Hall to a three-year, $2.7 million deal. Interestingly, Hall gave up just three touchdown receptions during three seasons as a starter; two of those scores came at nearby Cal. "The Bay area isn't a jinx," he insisted. "I'll get used to it."

Four other Huskies went on the first day of the draft, broken into the first five rounds on Day 1, and the last seven on Day 2. In the third, Phoenix chose center Ed Cunningham, the New York Giants picked tight end Aaron Pierce, and offensive lineman Siupeli Malamala went to the New York Jets. Green Bay made receiver Orlando McKay a fifth-round selection. Two Washington State players were also chosen on Day 1: All-America kicker Jason Hanson, a second-round pick by Detroit, and cornerback Michael Wright, a fifth-round selection by the Giants.

The phone didn't ring at Mario Bailey's house. The under-sized receiver was not chosen until the morning of the second day, a sixth-round pick of Houston's. "Sunday (Day 1 of the draft) was the worst day of my life," Bailey moaned. "I'd never wish this upon anybody." Many felt the Oilers, of any NFL team, could use Bailey's pass-catching skills. He'd fit well in their "Red Gun" spread offense.

That Bailey wasn't drafted until the second day provided plenty of fodder for sports call-in shows on local radio stations. How, people wondered, could the NFL ignore a receiver so prominent in the Husky history books? Bailey held the record for most career yards (2,093), most receptions in a season (62), most career touchdown catches (26), touchdown catches in a season (17), and twice tied the record for touchdown catches in a game with three. NFL scouts, it seemed, were far more impressed by a receiver's size and speed. Although far from slow, Bailey wasn't going to leave anyone doing a double take at the stopwatch.

The snub of Mario Bailey further reinforced the notion that Washington football operated largely in the shadows of larger programs. Had Bailey played at Miami, Notre Dame, Penn State, or Michigan, his backers argued, he certainly would have been a high-round pick. Instead, the first day of the draft left him with a churning stomach, a lump in his throat, and bitter memories.

Another Husky player ignored until a late round was Donald Jones, who finished the 1991-92 season with 14 1/2 tackles for losses, and a team-high 8 1/2 sacks. He didn't get a call from an NFL team until New Orleans drafted him in the ninth round. Listed as an outside linebacker, Jones moved up to the line of scrimmage for the Huskies and was used primarily as a desig-nated pass rusher in a position deemed "studbacker." Too small for a pro defensive line at 6-feet-1, 225 pounds, Jones's NFL market value was hardly through the roof. The Saints released him, but later in the season he was picked up by the Jets.

Offensive lineman Kris Rongen and linebacker Chico Fraley were selected in the 11th and 12th rounds by Seattle, which ultimately cut them. Linebacker Brett Collins, not invited to the combine and one of the last picks in the draft, beat considerable odds and made Green Bay's roster. Tyrone Rodgers, who trans-ferred to Washington from Oklahoma and overcame a serious knee injury to start on the defensive line, impressed the Seahawks enough that they signed him as a free agent and kept him.

In all, 11 Huskies were drafted, the largest representation of any school. Florida, Oklahoma, Penn State, and Tennessee each had nine players selected, Notre Dame and Texas A & M eight.

The draft was a pleasant reminder to Pac-10 coaches that, in the case of Washington, all good things must end. "It isn't just Emtman," Arizona State's Snyder said. "There were, what, 11 guys drafted off that Washington team? Well, there are nine guys here (the Pac-10 coaches) who are hoping that makes a big difference this year."

4

All The President's Men

Miami and Washington finally met face to face . . . in Washington, D.C.

A party, consisting of a tour of the congressional buildings and White House and a customary congratulatory speech from President Bush, was thrown in honor of the co-national champions.

The trip to the nation's capital was, in a word, nuts. Plenty went on between the time the Huskies arrived Thursday, March 19, and when they returned to Seattle the next evening. In all, the excursion set the UW athletic department back $50,000. Why so expensive? Ninety-five people were on board the chartered flight, including Athletic Director Barbara Hedges, James, the assistant coaches, 58 players, support personnel, and school administrators. Also traveling with the team was James Kenyon, a wealthy and powerful Husky booster who, nine months later, would take a much less enjoyable sojourn through the eye of a hurricane of strife.

The flight to D.C. was a fiasco and tested the patience of everyone on board. The plane, a 727, didn't carry enough fuel to make a nonstop flight from Seattle to D.C., so the Huskies landed in Minneapolis for refueling. The stopover was supposed to last about 15 minutes. That delay ballooned to 3 hours, 45 minutes after problems with a fuel tank and the landing gear were discovered and corrected. It was a lengthy layover for such a short excursion.

A reception, given by the Washington State congressional delegation, was held for the team Thursday evening. Because of the delay, the Huskies arrived to find their buffet half eaten. The banquet room was packed with Husky fans. Speaker of the House Tom Foley was one. Fresh from dealing with the House bank and post office scandals, Foley posed with some players and quipped, "It's delightful to have my photo taken in public with people who are really popular." A native of Spokane, Foley attended Washington for his undergraduate studies and law school.

When the formalities ended Thursday night, the *real* partying began. Ed Cunningham, who was raised in nearby Alexandria, Virginia, had been waiting for this trip for some time. Toward the end of the 1990 season, when Washington had a chance to be No. 1, he started planning this party. UCLA proved a party pooper, however, and Cunningham had to postpone the bash.

Now, he and his teammates wanted to paint the town. A roommate of Cunningham's sister managed a D.C. bar, Lulu's New Orleans Cafe. That was designated Party Central. A group of 25 players crammed into a rented yellow school bus—dubbed "The Magic Bus"—and made a stop at the home of Cunningham's sister. After a round of beers there, they headed for Lulu's.

It being a Thursday night, the hangout was pretty dead when the players arrived. Not for long. Soon the place was hopping, the beer was flowing, and rock music was pumping. Walter Bailey, the outspoken defensive back who doubled as team comedian, danced with a broomstick out front. The bar gave out cups printed with its logo, and offensive lineman Frank Garcia walked off with his huge arms full of them. It was a wild scene.

The party raged until the wee hours. The Husky contingent consisted mostly of players, although Cunningham did give directions to Lulu's to some assistant coaches. "Of course," Cunningham said, "they couldn't hang with us so they turned in early."

Receiver Joe Kralik went back to his hotel room, and his roommate, Billy Joe Hobert, was passed out and sitting stark naked on the toilet. Kralik, not ready to turn in for the night, woke him up and left the room. When he came back a few hours later, Hobert was in the same position. Kralik woke him up again and went to bed. Hobert spent the entire night on the commode.

Two buses were reserved for the trip to the White House. The first left early, about 8 a.m., and was for those players who wanted to tour the Capitol. The second left later and was a straight shot to the White House.

Walter Bailey was on neither.

An unwritten code among Husky players dictates that, if there is a reason to get up early, the first guy awake shakes his roommate out of the sack. That way, no one misses a meeting or special event. Eric Bjornson, a sophomore quarterback, and Bailey shared a hotel room in D.C. An early-morning wake-up call from the front desk did the trick for Bjornson. Bailey didn't budge.

"Wake up, Walter," Bjornson said.

"I'm up," Bailey gurgled, none too convincingly.

Bjornson planned to take the early bus. He showered and dressed.

"Walter, get up!" he pleaded.

"I'm up," Bailey answered, face planted squarely in his pillow.

Bjornson gave it one more try as he closed the door. "WALTER! GET UP!" No use. Bailey was dead to the world.

Cunningham got on the early bus and received a standing ovation from his teammates. The party was a smashing success. "I saw a lot of pale faces on that bus," he recalled. "A lot of fixed stares. You know the one where you're looking at something real intently right in front of your face so you won't vomit."

This type of debauchery doesn't happen on regular road trips, Cunningham said, but the sojourn to D.C. wasn't a regular road trip. "The coaches really looked at it as a treat for the players," he said. "We could pretty much do what we wanted that night."

A congressman from Seattle gave the players a first-class tour of the Capitol, after which the group met the second bus at 1600 Pennsylvania Ave. It was a chilly morning, so the plans to have the reception in the Rose Garden were scrapped, and the event was moved to the East Room. The ceremony was brief. Washington and Miami players and coaches stood behind President Bush as he spoke. Always the diplomat, Bush recognized the teams in alphabetical order to not show favoritism.

"Some thought I should take the ball and go outside and try to settle this thing right now," Bush said. "I don't need this. I've got enough problems without getting in the middle of you guys.

"Lincoln Kennedy," the President continued, "you're nicknamed 'The Oval Office,' and at 6-7 and 325 pounds, 'The Pentagon' would be more like it. Incidentally, I want to salute your dad, a career navy man who served in the gulf." He added the Huskies "made 1991 an Ode to Billy Joe."

Bush received team jerseys and signed footballs from Mario Bailey and Miami kicker Carlos Huerta. "That was the most nervous I've ever been in my life," the Husky receiver confessed. "Shaking his hand and giving him the ball was more scary than going over the middle in the Rose Bowl."

Walter Bailey couldn't have been too calm at that point, either. While the team was getting its collective ego stroked by the commander in chief, Bailey was walking around the hotel lobby, trying to figure how he was going to make the plane home. The team had checked out of the hotel. As he was weighing his limited options, Bailey recognized some crew members from the flight to D.C. He told them of his quandary, and they promised him a lift to the airport.

Meanwhile, back in the East Room, Bush was winding down. Cunningham sensed this and positioned himself to shake the president's hand, something he had hoped to do ever since he learned the team would be going to D.C. Apparently, the 285-pound lineman was unfamiliar with the way Secret Service operates. When Bush finished speaking, the agents immediately surrounded their boss and whisked him out of the room. "Those guys don't mess around," Cunningham marveled. "They're throwing shoulders into guys like Lincoln Kennedy. They don't care. When it's time to go, it's time to go."

No handshake, but some valuable memories.

James first met Bush in 1984 and was burned by the fallout from that brief encounter. He introduced the then vice president to a forum in West Seattle and later rode in Bush's limousine. A few weeks later, President Reagan was in town, and James presented him with a Husky cap and an autographed football. It being an election year, some in Seattle saw James's actions as inappropriate. The coach received a slew of angry letters from fans, boosters, and faculty and a directive not to mix politics and football from UW president William Gerberding. In his autobiography, James called the episode "traumatic." No one could criticize this trip to the White House. The team earned this.

As the players boarded the return flight, they were greeted by a chipper flight attendant who bore a striking resemblance to their right cornerback. Instead of hunkering in the back of the plane, trying to avoid eye contact with his coaches, Bailey wore an apron and served them peanuts in first class. Brazen behavior? Perhaps, but typical of a guy as fearless as he was cocky.

To this day, Bailey insists that Bjornson made no attempt to wake him. "If he says he tried to get me up," Bailey says, "I'll kick his butt."

5

To An Athlete Dying Young

Today the road all runners come,
Shoulder high we bring you home,
And set you at your threshold down,
Townsmen of a stiller town.

—A. E. Housman
"To an Athlete Dying Young"

On April 28, 1992, Travis Spring lost his battle with cancer. The 19-year-old Washington wide receiver died at his mother's home in Seattle, just 63 days after he was diagnosed with the disease.

"In my entire coaching career, I have never had anything quite this tragic to deal with," a press release quoted Don James, out of town when the redshirt freshman died. "Travis was much more than a great athlete. He was a good kid and a good student."

Although he never played a down as a Husky, Spring was one of two players to mimic Desmond Howard on scout offense before the 1992 Rose Bowl. He was an all-state defensive back at Franklin High in Seattle, intercepting 25 passes during his career. He also caught 29 passes during his senior season, guiding the Quakers to a 10-1 record and a berth in the state semifinals.

He was memorialized during the 1992 season with a moment of silence before the home opener and stickers that bore 15, his jersey number, on the back of every Husky player's helmet. His locker stall remained empty during the season, and his picture hung in it. Tommie Smith, who also wore 15, changed his jersey number to 20 so he and his teammates could wear the helmet stickers.

The player who knew Spring best was his roommate, Demetrius Devers, a freshman linebacker. The 1992 season had special significance for him. Said Devers before the moment of silence at the Wisconsin game, "He was such a happy guy. What I'm trying to do—and we're all trying to look at it this way—is that (the moment of silence) is a celebration for Travis. I cried a lot and was so sad when he died, but since the funeral, all my thoughts have been positive."

Spring was survived by his father and stepmother, Terry and Joyce Spring, and mother and stepfather, Cheryl and Mike Lamb, three brothers and four stepbrothers, one sister and one stepsister, and his fiancee, Tanita Terry.

II

Theirs was a love story just like millions of others, but unlike any of them. Travis and Tanita. Tanita and Travis. They were inseparable. When they couldn't be together, they talked for hours on the telephone. Never hang up mad, that was their motto. "Don't you two ever get tired of each other?" their parents would tease. Never, they said, both lovesick for the first time.

They met as juniors in high school at a Seattle Prep dance. Travis went to Franklin High and Tanita went to Seattle Prep. They danced once that night. Tanita was hooked. She wanted to get to know this guy better. Travis was handsome, with heavy eyebrows and a warm smile that twisted into a devious smirk. His body was lean and muscular. "You," Tanita would tell him later, "could model underwear." Tanita had homecoming queen good looks, with high cheekbones under penetrating dark eyes and a wide smile that flashed two rows of impossibly white teeth.

Through mutual friends they met again. By spring, they were an item. Tanita liked to say she had a Type-A personality. She loved school, loved to read, and wrote everything down in a journal. She remembered tiny anniversaries—the first time she saw Travis, the first time they kissed, the last time she ever saw that smirking smile. They started going out April 17, 1990. Travis could never figure quite how Tanita came up with that date. That was just her way, always celebrating little anniversaries. He was sentimental, too, always writing her notes and sending cards. He called her "T." She has a scrapbook of mementos thick as five Bibles and filled with pictures and funny captions.

Tanita's room was neat as a pin. Had to be. She couldn't stand things being out of place. Spill juice on her carpet? Better try to wipe it up before she sees it. You could bounce a dime on her bedspread. Her checkbook balanced to the penny.

Travis was the opposite. He never seemed to get too upset about anything and worried more if someone else was upset. He couldn't stand that. He was the one who always ended arguments with "I'm sorry," whether he started them or not. He hated to fight. He'd tell a little fib, if he had to, to keep from hurting someone or making them mad. Like that time he bought Tanita those sneakers for Valentine's Day, wrote a check from their joint account, and found out later they had insufficient funds. He kept quiet about it and dreaded Tanita finding out. She did, of course.

Travis shared a dorm room in Terry Hall with Demetrius Devers, a freshman linebacker. Their room was typically messy, as if a giant hand lifted it, turned it upside down, and gave it a good shake. It was no wonder Travis spent most of his time in Tanita's room, where it was spotless and always smelled nice. He would put off getting a haircut until it was painfully obvious he could no longer hide it under his baseball cap. He had to be reminded to cut his fingernails. Tanita needled him about that occasionally. He usually dressed casually. Cutoff sweatpants, baggy sweatshirt, sneakers. They would share clothes. Travis always had some of Tanita's T-shirts in his dresser and vice versa. He didn't like getting too dressed up. When he started college, he sometimes wore a button-down shirt, jeans, and even a belt. "Hey," Tanita would tease him, "who are you trying to look so cute for? Is there someone I should be worried about?" But she didn't really get jealous. Travis did. He didn't like her spending too much time with other boys. That made him sad. He went a long time before introducing Tanita to any of his Washington teammates because he heard they had a reputation for stealing girlfriends. Tanita was the love of his life.

He didn't need to worry. Tanita loved him as much as she could love anything. Without question, this was the man she would marry. If she could pick a Hall of Fame made up of the world's greatest people, Travis would top the list. She loved the little things about him. The way he would try to carry every grocery bag, every suitcase. He didn't want her carrying anything, but he would playfully roll his eyes and give a sarcastic "Gee, thanks" when she would hold the door open for him. He would do all the laundry when they went to her parents' house for supper each Sunday night. She loved the way he was with little kids like her cousins, who would crawl all over him, smothering him like a thousand puppies. Travis would just laugh. He was the king of piggyback rides. He'd never say no to those requests.

Tanita loved the way he wouldn't act like a football star and didn't change the way he treated her just because his buddies were around. She came first, and Travis always remembered that. She loved the way he could charm people. Her mother collected dolls related to black history, and when she put a new one on the shelf, Travis would always notice. "Oh, wow," he'd remark, "you got a new doll." He always knew the right thing to say to her parents.

When Tanita took a night job at a campus store during her freshman year at the UW, she worked about a half block from her dorm. Travis would walk her there every evening and pick her up at 10:45 every night. Depending on the weather, he might drive her. He didn't want her walking by herself. He was pretty reliable, but occasionally he'd call about five minutes before he was supposed to pick her up and say he would be late. "Why'd you wait until 10:40 to call?" Tanita would ask. She knew the answer; that was just Travis.

There was one argument Travis would usually win—he could choose what show he wanted when the two would watch TV. Tanita liked soap operas and mushy movies, but if she ever left the room, Travis would change to a sporting event. When she would try to turn back, he would use the same ploy again and again: "Come on, T. We *always* watch what you want to watch. But I've been waiting to see this game." More often than not, it worked. ESPN was the bane of Tanita Terry's existence. They would rent videos, too, and saw one called "Dying Young," about a young man stricken with cancer. Overacted and corny, they agreed, two thumbs down. "You always pick out dumb movies," Travis teased.

Travis would always hog the blankets when they would watch TV. He was constantly cold. Tanita had a tendency to get too hot and frequently would turn on a fan and push open windows to get air circulating. They had their thermostat wars every so often.

Travis was of African-American and Vietnamese descent and was adopted as an infant by Terry and Cheryl Spring, a white couple who later divorced. He lived during high school with his mother, whose surname is now Lamb. His middle name was Trang, but he seldom talked about his Asian heritage and, Tanita figured, didn't seem too curious about it. He was a black man and proud of it. He and Tanita did name their hamster Trang, though.

Thinking about going to college scared Travis. He wasn't a very good student, and the only schools showing interest in him were those drawn by what he could do on the football field. Oregon and Oregon State sent him letters frequently, as did Washington State. But Tanita was going to Washington, and that had been decided. Once, Travis stayed up the whole night crying, wondering why he had to go to school on a football scholarship. Why couldn't he have studied like Tanita? Why was his whole future in the hands of a football coach? How could fate be so cruel? But when Washington began to pay closer attention to him as a football player, he started to relax. The Huskies offered Travis a full ride and he accepted right away. His heart was full again. All was right in the world. He could stay in Seattle, stay near Tanita. Maybe college wouldn't be so bad, after all.

Knowing he and Tanita would be together at Washington lifted a huge load off Travis's mind. He could enjoy the rest of his senior year at Franklin. Except for those darned allergies, or what he thought were allergies. He couldn't breathe well with his nose. He was constantly stuffed up and had to use an inhaler when he played basketball. It looked so strange to see Travis Spring—the guy with the underwear-model body—bent over, gasping, with his hands on his knees in the first quarter of a hoops game. He was drowsy a lot, too. Sometimes, he'd almost doze off at dinner and had to rest his elbow on the table and prop his head up with his hand. He blamed it on his summer job at the construction site, on lifting weights, and later on Husky football practice. His father, Terry, has a home movie of Travis as a toddler at the beach, standing in a tide pool, flinging handful after handful of sand into the waves. Travis stood in that tide pool forever, it seemed, fascinated by the way the sand hit the water. His energy was boundless and always was as he grew up. That made the new Travis, the one that was frequently running a fever, so hard to figure.

Maybe it was his stuffed-up nose, but he seemed to be losing his sense of taste. Food sounded good to him—especially his favorite things like sweet-and-sour prawns, strawberries and watermelon—but it never tasted quite so good as it did before. He picked at things and pushed them around his plate. That was a bad sign. He needed to keep weight on his 5-foot-10, 185-pound frame if he had designs on starting after his redshirt football season. His muscles ached after practice, but that wasn't unusual. Everyone creaks around after taking a pounding day after day.

Travis excelled on the field. He had a languid, loping running style that almost made him look as if he wasn't hustling, except that the defensive backs who tried to cover him would struggle to keep pace. His thighs were so muscular that he would have to buy oversized blue jeans that looked pleated after he cinched them with a belt. His powerful legs carried him along with beautiful fluidity. As with everything in his life, Travis didn't seem to be exerting too much energy along the way, yet he seemed to reach his destination awfully quick. Tanita marveled at how he could hang onto the football with his tiny hands, which were almost exactly the size of hers and perfect for holding. Some of those catches he made were simply spectacular and made him look as if he were a cartoon character moving at hyper-speed. People drew comparisons between Spring and Mario Bailey, also a Franklin graduate. "Someday," Spring told Joe Kralik while waiting in line during drills, "I'm going to break all of Mario's records." Kralik didn't laugh. It just might have happened.

Expectations from the coaching staff were sky high for Travis. He made the trip to the 1992 Rose Bowl and impersonated Desmond Howard in practice. Judging by the way Washington shut down the Heisman Trophy winner in the game, the acting performance should have won Travis an Oscar. It being his redshirt season, Travis didn't play in the Rose Bowl, but an ABC camera focused on him for about two seconds when he was standing behind Don James. Tanita was watching the game at home, and a few moments after the glimpse of Travis, her telephone rang. It was her grandparents calling. "Did you see him?" they asked, doing a poor job of containing their excitement. "Yes, I saw him," she said blandly, as if seeing her boyfriend on TV was an everyday event. But she was bursting with pride on the inside.

Things were tough when Travis returned from Pasadena. He still got sleepy quite often, and his appetite was shot. When offered a juicy strawberry, he'd give one of his trademark "Oooooweeee, look at that strawberry!" endorsements, then barely nibble at it. His nose was plugged all the time. Something was wrong. Something was very, very wrong.

Before the Rose Bowl, Travis had seen a general practitioner about the nasal problems. He went back when football season ended. Tanita came with him. Travis wasn't one to push doctors into action, but his girlfriend was. She told the doctor things weren't improving and she wanted something done. The doctor referred them to a specialist who discovered a growth in Travis's nose and scheduled him for surgery. The situation didn't seem too serious, and the doctor predicted the procedure would take about 30 minutes. But the operation, performed February 19, lasted close to three hours. Tanita sat in the lobby. Waited and worried. Finally, Travis came out of surgery. The growth was not a polyp, as the specialist had diagnosed, but a larger lump that needed to be tested to see if it was benign or malignant.

Time crawled for Travis and Tanita. The doctor tried to encourage them. It didn't help much. Emotions swirled inside. Fear, anger, hope, depression, disbelief. How could this be happening? Was this a dream? The procedure even changed the way Travis looked. The bridge of his nose was wide before. When the surgical packing was removed Sunday, his nose looked narrow, frail.

Five agonizing days passed. Finally, the news: the growth was malignant and Travis had cancer. *Cancer.* The word echoed through Tanita's head. Her whole body felt cold and numb. She saw Travis shed one tear in the office, just one. She made an entry in her journal at 4 p.m. that day:

Monday, February 24, 1992: Today, Travis was diagnosed with cancer. The first obstacle on our journey to forever. Although the days are seemingly longer and more filled with pain, we never lose the strength to thank God for each day he has offered us. Now it is clear that yesterday, today, and the many tomorrows are clearly a gift.

Neither was the type to give up. Never. Courage would carry them through. Tanita attacked cancer harder than she ever attacked math, or English, or Spanish, or any of those other subjects that she studied so diligently. If you had cancer, you'd want Tanita Terry on your team. She listened to every word that Dr. Ed Webber, Travis's oncologist, had to say, as if understanding cancer was the key to beating it. Her desk drawer was filled with pamphlets on lymphomas, carcinomas, all things "oma." She crammed her brain with anything and everything about the disease. She met things head-on. "Don't sugar-coat bad news," she told Webber, "Come to us first with information." To the corners of her soul, she hated this beast consuming the love of her life.

Just as he wouldn't confess about the bounced check, Travis would fib and say he felt fine when he clearly didn't. If he said his stomach hurt, people would worry, and he wouldn't want that, so his stomach felt fine. Just fine. Tanita would beg him in fits of frustration, "Travis, you *have* to tell the doctor *everything* that hurts. *Everything.*" But it was too late to teach him to complain, to feel sorry for himself. He simply wasn't wired that way. He stubbornly refused to read those pamphlets in her drawer.

Time was critical. The doctors worked fast. Two days after the lump was diagnosed as malignant, Travis was back in the hospital to begin chemotherapy. They were going to come at this thing with all guns blazing. The chemotherapy would make him sick, doctors warned, sicker than he had ever felt. He would vomit until his head throbbed and his stomach muscles ached. But Travis was strong. He would bounce back. If the cancer was confined to the nasal passages, there was an 80 percent chance he'd be alive in five years. But that 80 percent chance meant two people out of 10 die from this thing. *Die?* A week ago, he had a stuffed-up nose, and now people were talking about the remote possibility of his *dying*. This wasn't supposed to happen. He was supposed to break all of Mario Bailey's records. He was supposed to grow old with Tanita. He had a million more piggyback rides to give. This couldn't be happening.

But it was, and happening fast. He went back to the hospital two days later. His kidneys had failed. It was a dire situation, one that doctors did not expect. Webber said there had never been a reported case of that reaction to those drugs. The pain was severe, but as was his way, Travis didn't complain. He stayed in the hospital for nine days. Tanita had to keep up with her studies, making life doubly difficult. Travis was on her mind every minute, and when he came home to his father's house, she was with him.

The doctors weren't lying; Travis was sicker than hell. He couldn't hold down a sip of water, much less food, and his vomiting was violent. He was cold, and Tanita piled blankets on him. That movie they watched wasn't overacted. Cancer was a horrible thing. Just the sound of the sickness, the loudness of it, the way it reduced Travis to a shaking little boy. Suddenly, cancer wasn't just a word that bounced around in Tanita's head, it was real and it was absolutely ravaging Travis. No, that movie wasn't overacted. Not at all.

The pain overwhelmed him. He couldn't sleep and just got sicker and sicker. Life was being ripped from him, and he had no control over the situation. No one will ever know exactly how severe the pain was that caused him to go back to the hospital Sunday morning, but this was a kid who could pop to his feet and stroll back to the huddle after a bone-crushing hit on the football field. Football trained him to hide agony. But there was no hiding this pain. At about 5 a.m. Sunday, he couldn't take any more. His father and Tanita rushed him back to the hospital.

Travis's once-rippled abdomen was full of fluid, making it swell like a puppy's. Because his body could no longer filter out toxins, he had to be put on a kidney-dialysis machine. The procedure required that tubes be inserted at the base of his groin. The pain was excruciating.

Only a few days had passed since Travis was a lovestruck college freshman with a stuffed-up nose and on a collision course with the Husky record books. To Travis and Tanita those few days could have been a year, a lifetime. It was during that week-long stay in the hospital that doctors developed an unconfirmed suspicion that the cancer had spread to Travis's bone marrow. If that was indeed the case, his chances for survival plummeted to 30 percent. Somehow, that information never got to Travis or Tanita. They still had high hopes of his making it through this ordeal, maybe even playing football in the fall. His buddies were in the middle of Husky spring workouts then, vying for spots on the first team. Soon after Travis was released from the hospital, he and Tanita walked down a trail near their dorm. He told her about how he had taken football for granted. He missed being healthy. She wrapped her arm around him and helped him walk.

Travis was released from the hospital around the beginning of Tanita's spring break. The two took a trip to Port Townsend together and got a room at a romantic inn there. They had been to the beach the previous two years and spent their days shopping, running on the sand, wrestling, sometimes bickering. They had energy to burn. This time, Travis was drained. His back hurt. He wanted to stay around the inn and watch TV. Not understanding how ill he really was, Tanita tried to boost his spirits.

"Travis, you have to *want* to feel better," she told him. "You're only as sick as you think you are."

The two returned to Seattle the next day. Travis was running a high fever, and Tanita took him back to the hospital, where a chest catheter was reinserted for another chemotherapy treatment. Doctors were never able to administer the treatment, however, because Travis's damaged kidneys had begun to leak protein. The protein deficiency was killing him. Medicine piled up on his bed tray; he refused to take his pills after a while. Nurses wheeled in a cot so Tanita could sleep in the room. She stayed for a week and played cards, talked, and watched TV with him. He hated being in the hospital. His hair, which he wore in a flat-top style, began to fall out. He would tug it out in clumps, something that seemed to amuse him. Tanita winced when she saw that. His arms and legs atrophied. His voice became faint, more air than words. His body was tired. He loved having lotion rubbed on his swollen belly. He could never get enough of that.

Travis was released from the hospital, but at times, his blood pressure was too low for him to walk in on his own. He had to use a wheelchair. He objected strongly to going back to the hospital. He hated needles and was seeing plenty of them these days. Constantly being poked, cut into, and X rayed, he stopped eating for the most part. Maybe two bites of yogurt a day.

These two people so in love shared a private celebration in Tanita's dorm room April 17, their second anniversary. Because it was a special occasion, Travis didn't hook himself up to the intravenous unit usually attached to him 12 hours a day. He gave

Tanita an engagement ring she had picked out when the two were shopping. His father paid for it, and Travis worked out a repayment plan. He proposed and Tanita accepted, tears running down her face. The ring was a formality; as far as she was concerned, they were already engaged. They were already going to spend the rest of their lives together.

He also said something that will live in her memory forever: "Until death do us part." It shook her. "Don't say that, Travis," she pleaded, sobbing. It was the first time she really thought about living without him. She was convinced things would get better, and Travis would recover. Everyone seemed convinced of that, even the Huskies, who issued a statement saying they looked forward to his return to the squad in the fall. But those words—"until death do us part"—rattled down to her foundation. How could he die? He wouldn't even allow her to walk that half block to work; how could he ever leave her?

The two had their engagement party the next afternoon at Terry Spring's home. Travis wore a baseball cap and an ear-to-ear grin. He didn't look emaciated, yet his magnificent body was gone. His arms, shoulders, and chest were thin; his stomach and thighs were bloated. Too weak to budge, he sat on one end of the couch throughout the party. Everyone invited showed up, including one of his best boyhood friends, Vance Adams, who drove from school in Eastern Washington. Travis couldn't stop talking about that. He couldn't believe Vance drove all that way to see him. Seeing Vance was the highlight of the party.

The following day was Easter, and the two spent the day with Tanita's family at her grandparents.' There were lots of kids around, and Travis got his share of piggyback requests. Too weak to give any, he sat by himself and didn't eat much dinner. Spring break ended the next day, and Tanita went back to class. Concentrating on her studies was almost impossible. Travis stayed at his father's house until Wednesday, when he stayed the night in Tanita's dorm room. He didn't get much sleep because he spent most of the night coughing and vomiting.

His mother came and got him in the morning and took him directly to the doctor. A battery of tests was performed. His kidneys were not responding to treatment. That was bad news, and something Travis didn't want Tanita to worry about. According to Dr. Webber, Travis had a stage-four lymphoma.

"That's as bad as you can get," his surgeon, Dr. James Rockwell explained, adding, "This was a sick young guy." The cancer had spread around his body, yet it was in small amounts. The kidney failure was the most pressing concern.

Rockwell will never forget Travis Spring. At the height of his illness, Travis showed the doctor his Rose Bowl ring and said, "I would give this away if I could wake up tomorrow and be well." But Travis seemed to know his fate. He never banked on a last-second recovery.

When Tanita asked about the cause of the coughing and vomiting, Travis told her they weren't further complications from cancer but the flu. He just needed rest. Her reaction was part frustration, part relief. "The *flu*?" she thought. "How could he have the flu on top of all this other stuff?"

Travis spent the weekend at his mother's, where Tanita visited him. On Saturday, April 25, he and his mother went to the Washington Spring Game and arrived at Husky Stadium late in the second half. It was a chilly afternoon, and Travis watched from a team chair-stretcher. The disease had ravaged him, and when he shook hands with a few teammates, a handful of others didn't even recognize him. He and his mother left before the game ended.

Travis called Tanita around 11 p.m. Monday to say goodnight. His voice, reduced to a breathy whisper, was tinged with a hint of relief, almost happiness. He told her that the doctors had asked him to come back to the hospital, but he refused. Normally, Tanita would have argued with him about that and told him he had to listen to his doctors. But this time, she just asked him if he was sure about his decision. He was.

It was a short conversation. Travis would always end their phone calls by saying, "I love you," then telling Tanita when he would call her the next day. This time, he just said, "I love you. Goodbye." She almost called him back to find out when he would be calling again but decided against it—he needed rest.

Around 9 a.m. the next morning, Travis got out of bed to use the bathroom. His mother helped him. On his way back to bed, he had a dizzy spell and had to be helped under the covers. He closed his eyes, took a deep breath, and his heart stopped.

He was gone.

III

Strange how the mind works. The memories of April 28, 1992, are becoming increasingly clear to Tanita as time passes. For a long time, that day was a blur. Travis had cancer and was violently ill toward the end of his life, but his sudden death was a surprise to those close to him.

"It was so unexpected," said Tanita, sitting in her dorm room, filled with pictures and mementos. "He never complained, for the most part, about anything."

About the same time Travis died, Tanita was doing Spanish homework in the library and felt sick to her stomach. She gathered her books and walked back to her room. Once there, she turned on her favorite soap opera and tried to relax. The phone rang. "I was thinking, 'This is Travis,'" she recalled, "because he usually called me in between classes." She picked up the phone, but no one was on the other end. A minute later, there was a knock on the door. It was her father.

"He came in and—my dad is the kind of person who's not real sentimental—and said, 'Travis died,'" she recalled.

"That can't be true!" she screamed. "Why are you lying? That can't be true because we're getting married! That can't be true!"

Her world was spinning out of control. She called her mother, who was crying. "I don't remember what I was saying," Tanita said. "I was just yelling at the top of my lungs." She collected all her photo albums, clutched the stuffed Mickey Mouse Travis gave her and sobbed: "Take me to him! I want to see him!" They rushed down to the car where her grandparents were waiting. They drove to the Lambs's home, where Travis was lying on the living room couch.

The walk from the car to the house felt like miles. She entered the house, saw Travis, and dropped to her knees. "I sat there and I thought to myself: 'This is really happening. It's real. It's not a dream,'" she said. Travis had a smile on his face. One of his eyes was part open. Tanita reached up and closed it.

More than 1,500 mourners packed St. Edward's Church in Seattle's Rainier Valley for Travis Spring's funeral, and the procession of cars stretched all the way across the floating bridge. Several people spoke and delivered readings, including Mario Bailey, who said, "I'm going to dedicate my life and my career to

Travis because he means so much to me." The Husky coaching staff dedicated a perpetual trophy in Travis's memory, presenting the annual award to the most inspirational freshman.

Two songs were played over and over as long lines of mourners filed past the casket: Eric Clapton's "Tears in Heaven" and "It's So Hard to Say Goodbye to Yesterday" by Boyz II Men.

Tanita read from her diary, Mario Bailey and Demetrius Devers spoke. So did Joe Slye, Travis's football coach at Franklin, and Jim Brown, Travis's grandfather. Reverend Chuck McAllister read aloud a few lines Terry Spring wrote in memory of his son:

Travis, like a meteor blazing across the sky, you were brilliant.
But you were gone from us all too soon.

6

Present Not Past

Stitched in white on the shiny black national championship jackets given to each Washington player, indeed woven into the Huskies' mental tapestry, were the letters PNP.

Present Not Past.

Time to focus on the future of Husky football. A future without Steve Emtman. Without Mario Bailey. Without Keith Gilbertson. Still, a future in the footlights. College football writers in New York paid a little more attention to Washington football, so did scribes in Chicago, Dallas, and Miami. Time had come, many felt, for the Huskies to prove that 1991 was no fluke, no Andy Warholian 15 minutes of fame.

In Seattle, the Dawgs were the toast of the town. For the first time in the Don James era, the school sold every season-ticket package, and a lottery was held to distribute the remaining tickets. If you wanted to see a Husky game, you had better be prepared to pay top dollar to the scalpers on Montlake Boulevard—some of whom charged five times face value for a big game—or sit in the bottom five rows of the horseshoe, a vantage point that offers something less than a bird's-eye view.

Present Not Past might inspire a football player, but it's blasphemy for a recruiting coordinator. A national title is one heck of a trump card for luring top high school talent. The McDonald's Trophy is the equivalent of an atom bomb in the recruiting wars. But that bomb has a delayed fuse. Conventional wisdom said the recruiting dividends from the 1991 season would pay off in a year. Many high school standouts already had made their college choice before the 1992 Rose Bowl. But there were plenty of high school juniors watching Washington reach the summit, and the mailboxes at the homes of those kids were stuffed daily with recruiting letters.

That delayed response helps explain why Washington's recruiting class announced February 5, 1992, was the school's smallest ever. Just 14 recruits signed national letters of intent to play football at Washington, making the Huskies' class easily the smallest in the Pac-10. Because Washington had loaded up on players in recent years and because of reductions in allowable scholarships, the Dawgs had only 16 scholarships to give. Usually, teams are able to sign 20 or more players.

In February, the Pac-10 recommended to the NCAA that the UW be docked a scholarship because of a self-reported infraction that took place a year earlier when Patrick Kesi, an offensive line prospect who eventually signed with the Huskies, was on his recruiting trip from Honolulu. Kesi and his host, Shannon Cyrus, met up with former Husky players Ricky Andrews and Willy Galoia, both from Hawaii, and spent part of the evening together. NCAA rules bar any contact between recruits and alumni or boosters. The Pac-10 recommended the NCAA penalize the Huskies one scholarship.

James, who called the Pac-10 recommendation "rotten," said before the Rose Bowl: "I don't care what they do—public reprimand, private reprimand, whatever. It doesn't matter to me because they're wrong. This was not a case of somebody breaking a rule to get an advantage."

One Pac-10 official confided, "I think the committee saw a pattern it didn't like. It has happened before at Washington, and (the Pac-10) felt it was time to stop it by slapping their hand."

To make matters worse, changes to the NCAA recruiting rules were made, and the new stipulations hurt the Huskies. For the first time, coaches were not allowed to supervise the letter-of-intent signings. Instead, the player and his guardian(s) were required to sign the contract on their own and mail it to the institution of their choice. The rule wasn't popular with many coaches, including James, because a player might change his mind on the way to the post office.

Eric Holcomb did just that. The receiver prospect from Westlake Village, California, made an oral commitment to Washington, then made a last-second decision to attend UCLA. The same thing happened with receiver Armon Williams, who made a promise to Washington, then signed with Arizona.

Washington was on the receiving end of one of those last-second decisions, too, when wideout David Janoski, bound for Oregon State, made an eleventh-hour choice to spend his college years in Seattle.

So for the first time, coaches had to rely mainly on word of mouth about the new recruits instead of making firsthand evaluations. "I guess it would be a little like dating," James said. "We've all probably dated girls that after two or three dates, we couldn't take it anymore. It only makes sense. If you could see the individual more often, you could learn more about them."

James might not have spent much time with his 1992 freshman class, but he had reason to believe it was talent rich. Eleven members of the class were on the Western 100 team, ranked by the *Morning News Tribune* .

Among the stars of the class was Cedric White, a 6-foot-3, 275-pounder from Los Angeles, one of the country's most highly touted defensive linemen. It likely was only coincidence, but on the day that Emtman announced his intentions to leave, White made an oral commitment to attend Washington.

Jason Shelley was the offensive gem of the class. An outstanding baseball player who spent some time in the Atlanta Braves system, Shelley had electrifying talent as a wide receiver. Back home in Vallejo, California folks called Shelley "Money," hence the gold dollar-sign necklace he wore. He signed his last name $helley. *SuperPrep* Magazine regarded him as the nation's No. 2 prospect at his position.

The Dawgs also landed Theron Hill, a running back in high school who converted to H-back in college. He and Shelley would come to call each other the "Wonder Twins" and touch fists in the huddle to activate their "powers," emulating a cartoon they watched growing up.

Ted Stark became the fifth consecutive Western 100 quarterback the Huskies signed, and Tobiase Brookins provided the UW with a darting running back with a background in sprinting. Hernan Santiago, an outstanding linebacker and fullback in Lamont, California, would play offense in college.

James received oral commitments from three talented offensive linemen, yet only two, Lynn Johnson and Brad Brozaitis, were able to sign. The most highly regarded of the three, Joe Wells, had to attend a junior college because he failed to pass enough core classes at Arroyo Grande (California) High. The loss of Wells was painful: the 6-foot-4, 290-pound tackle was one of two Washington recruits who received perfect 10s in the *Long Beach (California) Press Telegram's* Best of the West poll.

The other recipient of the perfect score was Lincoln High defensive back Lawyer Malloy, the best player to come out of a Tacoma city school in a decade. A ferocious hitter, Malloy was one of two true freshmen the Huskies were seriously considering using in the fall. Shelley was the other. Plans to use Malloy were shelved after he sustained a broken bone in his foot during fall two-a-days.

Joining White on the defensive line were David Richie and Bob Sapp. Ink Aleaga and Curtis Bogan were signed to play linebacker.

II

Even without this bumper crop of fuzzy-faced freshmen, this was a new-look football team, one with diminished firepower on both sides of the ball.

"We have a long way to go," James said after one spring scrimmage. "I would assume most other teams are in the same situation we are. But we aren't even close to where we were this time last year."

For one thing, the quarterback job was up for grabs. Sure, Billy Joe Hobert was 12-0 as a starter and piloted the team to a national title, but giving Mark Brunell a chance was the only fair thing. After all, Hobert remembered how discouraging it was when Brunell had a lock on the position. There was a time Hobert considered transferring, maybe playing baseball or taking up competitive golf. He even went so far as to make some phone calls to schools. "They told me to wait until spring," he recalled. "I'm sure glad they did."

The classroom never appeared to be a problem for Hobert until he dropped out of school briefly during spring 1992, a time when his marriage was failing and his spending spree was in full swing. Ironically, at that time, a panel of Phoenix-area and national sports writers and broadcasters selected him as one of 11

Samaritan All-America college football scholar-athletes. The honorees were chosen for their "high standards of excellence in academics, citizenship, and athletics."

The football game that truly defined Hobert was the second start of his college career, when the Huskies played at Nebraska. He led the team back from a 12-point third-quarter deficit. Quite a feat for a 20-year-old kid barking signals over a roaring sea of red in Lincoln.

With less than a minute remaining in the third quarter and Nebraska leading, 21-9, the Washington offense faced a fourth-and-8 situation at the Cornhusker 30. No field-goal attempt, the Dawgs were shooting for the first down. The Huskies called a timeout, and Hobert came over to the sidelines.

The play was delivered, and as the ultra-confident sopho-more was heading back to the huddle, James reminded him, "Billy, we *need* a first down."

"NO SHIT!"

That's the chutzpah of a corporate raider, maybe a Los Angeles Raider, but not a typical sophomore drama major. Hobert showed bite to his bark, too, finding Orlando McKay for a gain of 15 yards and a first down. It was the stuff of legends. Washington went on to win, 36-21.

Hobert had a way of fearlessly speaking his mind, which made his coaches blanch and reporters smile. When he had to wear a neck roll to protect a pinched nerve, he complained: "It's a little confining. Sort of like wearing a condom."

After the California game, one of the Dawgs' two close contests in the 1991 season, he said the Huskies "should just dog the Rose Bowl" and play top-ranked Miami for the national championship. "I wouldn't even care if we went on probation." The comment didn't sit too well with his coaches, and from that point on Hobert was a little less free and easy when talking to the press. Any suggestion of giving the Granddaddy of Them All the brush-off, after all, is blasphemous in most college football circles.

Golf was a consuming passion for Hobert. He worked at the nearby Tyee Valley Golf Course during high school—a job that later would be a flashpoint of controversy because of how it was arranged—and even tried out for the UW golf team in 1992. He shot two poor rounds in tryouts and failed to make the cut.

Although coaches didn't always approve of what came out of Hobert's mouth, they really seemed to appreciate him. "I'll tell you," James said after the Rose Bowl. "When you talk about Billy Joe Hobert, you can't say enough. We're here today because of what he started against Stanford and Nebraska. We've never had a quarterback—and we've had a bunch of them in the NFL—start like he did in critical games on the road."

When spring ball came around, Hobert seemed a little sullen, certainly more reserved than he was amid the national-title season. Word circulated among Husky beat writers that he and his wife, Heather, were having some marital strife. It was a personal matter, and reporters kept clear of the subject when talking to him. More topical was the possibility of his skipping his senior year and possibly declaring himself eligible for the NFL draft after the 1992 season. He said that was a longshot at best.

"If it happens, it happens," he said. "But I'm not rated high enough nationally to be thinking about it. I saw someplace where I would be rated No. 8 among college quarterbacks by the time I'm a senior. I'm probably 12 now. . . If I'm not in the top two, there's no reason (to leave early). The only reason would be money."

Ah, money. It was later discovered that Hobert said these things while embroiled in a $17,000-per-month spending spree. Reporters had no indication of his fat wallet at the time. His life was coming apart at the seams, and his marriage was crumbling, too. "When we first got married," he said, "I thought this was going to be easy, because we got along real well and talked real easily. But I found out if you don't keep at it, you lose things quickly. My wife and I always used to talk, but during football I'd get my 'attitude,' a little adrenalized, and I didn't talk much. . . . Even after football season, I quit talking. I never let her know anything was wrong. One day I said, 'Screw it!' and took off. . . I did a lot of things I regretted. I got to a point in my life where I couldn't get any lower. . . . My conscience caught up with me. I was pretty close to saying bye-bye to everybody."

At the insistence of his wife, he reluctantly met with Dick Gohee, a Christian counselor. "I thought she wanted somebody to tell me what a sinner I was," he told Blaine Newnham. "But then I told her I'd give the guy 15 minutes and then I was leaving.

For 14 minutes, I just tolerated him, then the 15th minute I began to hear what he was saying. . . . Three hours later we were still talking when I accepted Jesus Christ. I can't tell you what it was like. I was sweating, crying. I got so emotional I went to the bathroom and vomited. But I left the house feeling the pressure of my life and all those lies were gone."

III

Brunell was far more reserved with, and somewhat more wary of, the media. His comments seldom strayed from the party line. Unfailingly courteous, he would compliment his offensive line, insist there was no quarterback controversy, and extol the virtues of taking one game at a time. Hardly illuminating stuff, but it never pissed off the coaches. Brunell dealt with the media, particularly writers, in a workmanlike way. He was friendly and made himself accessible, yet he wasn't chatty and didn't lobby for ink or airtime. He seldom flashed his more mischievous side to reporters. He rarely spoke about how, after his freshman season, he relished showing up a co-worker on a construction site who didn't believe he played for the Huskies, or how he once pulled a world-class April Fool's Day prank on lineman Todd Bridge by heisting the keys to Bridge's car and parking it a mile away from the lineman's apartment. Brunell didn't confess to that hoax until Bridge frantically picked up the phone and dialed 911.

"The difference between Mark and Billy is that Billy lets his personality out in the press," Joe Kralik said. "All the coaches tell us how to do interviews and (Brunell) does it like Interview 101. He doesn't say anything, doesn't let his emotions get into it. Just gives straight answers. He doesn't let his personality get out, so everyone thinks he's got this dry personality, a real square guy. That isn't true."

Brunell's was truly a heroic story. His right knee was shredded in spring 1991. A torn anterior cruciate ligament meant the best part of his game, his ability to scramble and improvise on the run, was gone. It was an injury that might have ended the career of a thousand other players, but Brunell was fiercely determined to come back. When he did—several months ahead of schedule— the crowd of 71,638 watching the Huskies devour Kansas State shook Husky Stadium to its foundation. He took over for Hobert on the final play of the third quarter. The significance of the moment and the accompanying response from the Washington fans could leave goose bumps on a dead man.

Brunell grew up in tiny Santa Maria, California, just north of Santa Barbara. The son of a high school baseball coach, he was a star athlete at St. Joseph's High, shining in football, basketball, and baseball. Although he was drafted by the Atlanta Braves after high school, he decided to pursue a college football career. Plenty of schools wanted him. He was one of a triumvirate of red-hot quarterback prospects to graduate from Southern California high schools in 1987. The other two were Todd Marinovich, who played at USC before leaving early for the NFL, and Brett Johnson, who played at UCLA and Michigan State. Marinovich and Johnson, both of whom hailed from heavily populated Orange County, received most of the media coverage, yet Brunell, a left-hander, was considered by many coaches to be the best player of the three. Judging by his accomplishments at Washington, Brunell proved his supporters right.

Often during his college career, Brunell was compared to San Francisco quarterback Steve Young, a fellow southpaw. Both threw a nice ball and were elusive as running backs when chased out of the pocket. When he first returned from his knee injury, Brunell was noticeably slower. Rigorous rehabilitation strengthened the joint, however, and Brunell looked closer and closer to his former self as the 1991 season rolled on. By spring 1992, he was back at full speed. Questions about the status of the knee kept coming, particularly from out-of-town media, and Brunell grew weary of answering them. He was playing well, he reasoned, why dig up the past?

"I was talking to my dad last night," said Brunell, two weeks before the 1993 Rose Bowl. "He said some guy from L.A. called and wanted to know about the knee. It was two years ago! Sure, I wear that brace still. But it's old to me. I'm ready to go on. I don't want to be considered the guy that had the knee injury and came back. I just want to be the regular old guy, like it never happened. Also, my knee feels like it's as good as new. If someone calls and wants to do a story on that, it just bugs me. I'm so sick of it.

"I could understand if I ran a 5.1 (-second) 40 or something like that. If it changed my game entirely, I could understand that."

So much about the media took time to understand. A devout Christian, Brunell would often sprinkle his comments with references to his faith or God. None of that stuff would wind up in newspapers or TV sound bites. He and teammates with similar beliefs would tie religion into their answers and reporters would nod almost dutifully as if to say, "Yeah, yeah, but what about that third-down keeper?" He got used to it. "It's not like (reporters) ignore it," he said. "It's just that nobody's really going to ask you about it. You don't get a lot of opportunities to talk about it, but it's not something that never gets mentioned."

Because of his reserved nature, Brunell was considered by some to be the antithesis of Hobert. That wasn't the case. In fact, they shared similar outlooks. Both were married. Brunell had a daughter, and Hobert had one on the way. They suited up two locker stalls apart and counted each other as friends.

"I respect the guy," Brunell said after Hobert was ruled ineligible. "I think he's a great guy, and he's fun to be with. We've never had a confrontation. Never. Nothing. I think a lot of people think that we're in two separate locker rooms. Like I've got my guys and he's got his. It's not like that at all."

That's not to say there wasn't any competitive friction between the quarterbacks. Each heard the footsteps of the other. "When we're on the field," Brunell said, "I'm looking to see what he's doing and he's looking to see what I'm doing. If we're in a scrimmage, and he took a drive down for a touchdown, and it was my turn next, I'd do anything to do the same thing.

"Even if we're just throwing a ball. If I throw a nice ball and he's up next, you can bet he'll do whatever he can to throw just as nice a ball. We got along real well, and we knew it was helping us."

Another thing that helped these quarterbacks was a stable of sure-handed receivers. Precisely what was missing from the new-look Huskies in spring 1992. Gone were Bailey, Orlando McKay, and Curtis Gaspard, a trio that accounted for 127 receptions and 1,865 yards. The Dawgs were left with a group that caught seven passes and scored once.

Third-string quarterback Eric Bjornson saw an opening. Husky coaches told the 6-foot-5 sophomore that switching to receiver might mean a crack at meaningful playing time. Otherwise, barring injuries to Hobert and Brunell, Bjornson would be an afterthought in the offense. "I started talking to my dad about it," Bjornson said. "I said, 'Shoot, no one has really proven himself at receiver. If I could be in the top three or four guys, I would be content to play receiver for a year.'"

Make no mistake, he wasn't giving up on his dreams of piloting the Husky offense. Playing receiver began as a temporary fix, but he planned to run a comeback route to quarterback. Bjornson, who held on point-after kicks, had good speed and hands so soft he could reach one up and snare a bullet pass from point-blank range. His pass routes weren't perfect but were surprisingly crisp, considering his lack of experience. The last time he ran patterns was in seventh grade, playing in a mud-ball game with his pals.

"He's going to play a lot at receiver," receivers coach Bill Wentworth predicted. "I'd like to see him stay there, purely from a selfish point of view. I think he's going to be a pretty darn good receiver, but we definitely want him to be happy."

Everyone on the team referred to Bjornson (pronounced BeYORNson) as Bornson, following the lead of Don James, who never mastered the Nordic nuances of the name.

The Huskies' most experienced returning receiver was Kralik, a close friend and teammate of Hobert's at Puyallup (Washington) High. Frequently, stories were written about the Hobert-Kralik battery, dubbed the Puyallup Connection. "Everybody is always asking me about that," Kralik complained. "I really get sick of talking about it."

Kralik looked closer to a rock musician than a football hero. He wore his dishwater blond hair long, and his curly locks spilled out the back of his helmet. He had meaty, blacksmith arms and was crafty enough to find holes in a defense. Quick with quips, he and Hobert shared a kind of honky-tonk candor that made them popular with reporters. He didn't seem to mind telling funny stories on himself.

One of his more ribald tales was particularly entertaining. It happened in Anaheim, California, while the team was preparing to play Florida in the 1989 Freedom Bowl. Kralik made the trip as a redshirt freshman. While running a reverse during practice one afternoon, he was crushed by linebacker Martin Harrison, who now plays for the San Francisco 49ers. "He drilled me," recalled Kralik, knocked unconscious by the hit. "Just *drilled* me. I watched the film the next night. I wanted to see what happened because I had no recollection."

Out cold for 30 seconds, Kralik lay face down. Finally, with the help of assistant trainer Doug Calland, he rolled over and regained consciousness.

"Do you know where you are?" Calland asked.

"Fuck, no."

"Does Anaheim, California, ring a bell?"

"No," Kralik mumbled. "Am I still a freshman?"

Dazed, he wandered over to Hobert and told him, "I want to go home." Hobert assured him they were heading right back to the hotel. "No," Kralik clarified, still unsure of where he was. "I want to go home to Puyallup."

Kralik made it to the locker room and began to undress. Linebacker James Clifford, sitting at the next stall, ribbed him. "You remember that 20 bucks you owe me?" Clifford asked, trying to keep a straight face. "You borrowed it from me last night. Where's my 20 bucks?"

The fog just beginning to clear, Kralik made it to the team dinner that night. He ate and went back to the Marriott hotel room he was sharing with Hobert. "I went to bed, and I never sleep naked, but I did that night," Kralik said. "I was so tired, and they had me so drugged up because of my concussion."

His next memory?

Bing.

The doors opened at the lobby level, exposing the elevator's cargo, a naked, suddenly lucid redshirt freshman. Some startled teammates, no doubt highly amused, chided him from the lobby, "HEY, JOE! WHAT'S GOING ON?" Kralik had no explanation. He was just as surprised as the hotel guests he shocked. "Everyone was in hysterics," he recalled. "You don't see something like that every day."

Panicked, Kralik madly punched at the elevator buttons. Anything to close the door, get back up to the eighth floor, make it to the room, get under the covers, and forget this nightmare-come-true ever happened. It was a long ride up. "What if that thing had stopped on the fourth floor and a coach wanted to get on with his wife or something like that?" Kralik asked, wincing at the thought. "I was just stark naked, dude."

At last, the doors opened on Floor Eight, and Kralik shot out. No one was walking the halls. He ran a naked bootleg back to his room and pounded on the door. Hobert answered. "JOE!" he screamed, "WHAT THE HELL ARE YOU DOING?"

"Don't talk to me," Kralik pleaded, trying to purge the memory. "Don't talk to me."

In the morning, Kralik woke up, turned to Hobert and said, "Billy, I had a dream I was outside naked last night."

"Joe, I had that same dream."

7

The Defense Never Rests

Dave Hoffmann hunkered down in his stance and tilted up on the balls of his toes, coiling himself like a steel spring ready to jackhammer some flesh. *Hit the sucker so hard he forgets his name.* His fingers slowly sliced through the air, fanning as if to feel the flow of the play. His body reacted to the snap with hair-trigger sensitivity. In a flash, he was in the backfield, helmet tracked on the quarterback like a guided missile. Then that noise, that horrifyingly delicious sound of plastic meeting plastic at full speed. *tthhWAPP.* A bug on a windshield.

Welcome to the Dawghouse, brother.

Hoffmann was, at the same time, in love with and mystified by the violence of it all. Behind that diamond-hard forehead was a mind that could look at the craziness of the game with perspective. As an inside linebacker, he did things on the field that would put him behind bars off it.

There were really two Dave Hoffmanns, something that gave him an intriguing ambivalence. A side of him was kind and unaffected, a reflection of his modest upbringing as the son of a pastor in Dallas. Some players luxuriate in the attention given them, cutting loose with flamboyant and clearly premeditated quotes that will ensure them ink in the next day's sports pages. That wasn't Hoffmann. He never seemed to get too caught up in his popularity as a Husky. He had a certain modesty to him, an old-school way. With a neck like a steel girder and a flat-top haircut that was even as a putting green, he looked like a throwback from an era when players finished a game by folding up their helmets and stuffing them in their back pockets. He had a square jaw and brutish good looks. The most distinguishing feature of his face was his broad forehead and heavy brow. As much as any could, his head looked like a weapon. As if he could tilt it forward and effortlessly knock out a row of someone's teeth with a casual bare-headed thrust. Teammates teased him about the two bony lobes above his eyes, calling him Cro-Magnon. He didn't mind. "The Lord just blessed me with a hard head," he said, smiling at the irony of the comment.

The other side of his personality surfaced when he stepped on the field. This Dave Hoffmann was frightening. The Hitman. Two hundred twenty-five pounds of angry energy looking to separate someone from his sensibilities. This beast wasn't frothing and catatonic but embraced the calculating viciousness of a serial killer. As Hoffmann put it: "I try to get myself to that fine line. There's such a fine line between having your head on top of your shoulders and being clearheaded, and being jacked up beyond belief and really being ready to play. Ready to be violent. It's a violent game.

"If you get too much on one side or the other, it can hurt you. But if you can find that fine line . . . have those aggressive feelings going through you, that's when you play the best football."

The thing Hoffmann loved about the game was the window it created that allowed him to escape the real world and enter a fantasy land of blood, brutality and high-speed collisions. He could be himself on the field, plow his head into a receiver's chest and leave him in a crumpled heap. His best hits cracked like a deer-hunting rifle. The crowd would react with a low moan that sounded like a throaty foghorn. "In society, there are special norms and things you're supposed to live by," he said. "Certain things that are right and not right. Certain ways to be polite and things like that. Kind of like rules out there. On the football field, that's all thrown out the window. . . . There are things you can do out there that obviously you couldn't do in society. You'd get in trouble for them and people would look at you as wacko. But I think that's why a lot of guys play this game, because you can do that and really go out there and be yourself and have a good time."

Hoffmann talked about learning to strike a blow as if the desire to do so was an inevitable hormonal process. A boy's voice cracks, he starts noticing girls, he's overcome with the uncontrollable urge to knock the shit out of the kid next to him. . . .

"It's all a matter of how hard you think you can strike somebody and how much you enjoy it," he explained. "Some people enjoy it more than others. I think before you even start playing football you have those feelings."

Hoffmann became a linebacker even before his father let him set foot on the field. Until he was in eighth grade, he was forbidden to play on a team. The sport was too dangerous, his parents reasoned. His mother, a nurse, knew too much about the frailty of young bones to let her little boy run wild. A time came when she didn't have much choice but to let him play. Little David had been watching pro football, watching it in a different way than his friends. They liked the way the ball spun off Roger Staubach's fingers. Hoffmann liked the way Randy White swallowed up running backs in his giant arms. "It started to get to me," he recalled. "It was contagious. It was hard to sit still on the couch. That's when I really started to beg my dad to let me play."

Hoffmann quickly grew into a fine linebacker. His family moved to San Jose, California, and he starred at Pioneer High under Coach Dan Lloyd, a former Husky linebacker who went on to play for the New York Giants and USFL's Washington Federals. Even in high school, Hoffmann's pops were thunderclaps. Lloyd truly believed that his star pupil, as a senior at Pioneer, hit just as hard as his teammates in the USFL. Just as he walked the fine line separating mania and lucidity, Hoffmann struck a balance between aggressiveness and underhanded tactics. He avoided taking cheap shots, didn't target knees, and tried to stop hitting at the sound of the whistle. That's not to say he didn't rake a few faces with his hands when he was fighting for a fumble in a pile, or talk a little smack when he dusted a running back. Those things were only natural. He couldn't completely turn off his emotional spigot. He had his limits. He abided by the instructions of defensive coordinator Jim Lambright to "Be the nastiest legal player you can be." Or, as Hoffmann put it, "Even though you're out there to be barbaric, you have to have a certain amount of class."

Hoffmann might have been the son of a pastor, but that didn't mean he passed on trash talking. Instead, he jabbered constantly, gnawing at an opponent's concentration with insult after insult.

By all accounts, he didn't use vulgar language and, after stamping a mind-altering hit on someone, Hoffmann would extend his hand, hoist the victim to his feet, and say, "God bless you, brother." Moments later, the insults would start back up. This duality, almost a comical struggle between the yin and yang of his spirit, only furthered his reputation as a psychopath on the field. Noted a teammate, "He's the meanest nice guy I've ever met."

Frequently, when Hoffmann slipped deep into his trance, his blurtings were unintelligible and sounded something like "*YAK, BROTHER! YAK!*" They spilled out of his mouth like rumbling belches. When he hit someone, anybody within a long bomb of the impact zone knew about it. Like any defensive player worth his weight in sod, Hoffmann aimed to limit an offense to three plays. Heaven forbid one of his teammates made a mistake that kept the Husky defense on the field a little longer than necessary. Hoffmann, regarded by his peers as the patriarch of the unit, didn't take kindly to mental errors. He didn't say much in the huddle after a teammate's gaffe, but he would show his disappointment with bulging eyes and exaggerated huffing, more Lamaze instructor than linebacker. The penalty was meted out not after another bad play but a good one. "If you made a good play after you screwed up, he'd come up and say, 'GOOD PLAY!' and knock the hell out of you," defensive tackle D'Marco Farr said. "Take a look at the film on the big-play reel. Watch the guys that get sacks run away from him after they get one. If you celebrate, watch out for Hoffmann, because he'll knock you senseless."

Stanford's Ed McCaffrey, an All-America receiver, found himself on the ugly end of a crash with Hoffmann during a game in 1990. The lanky junior was running a crossing route late in the game when his chin became a mite too intimate with a gold helmet. *tthhWAPP.* Suffice to say that hit, which would convince any clear-thinking human to avoid playing this game at all costs, deserves its own wing in the Husky film archives. When he finally came to, after lying in a heap for at least a minute, McCaffrey left the field with a teammate under each arm.

Hoffmann could make just about anyone see double, except when they were attempting to spell his name. Programs listed him as Hofmann, Hoffman and Hofman, seldom getting the correct spelling of two f's and two n's. Before the Husky sports information department began reminding reporters of the unusual spelling in the press notes each week, the mistake was made constantly. If a Husky game was televised, you could bet the network would screw up Hoffmann. The blunder was made across the shoulders of his first Washington jersey, issued before the spring game. He protested the gaffe by refusing to wear the jersey unless the name was covered with athletic tape.

It didn't take long for Hoffmann to make a name for himself with the Huskies. After his redshirt season in 1988, he rapidly ascended the depth chart at linebacker and replaced Chico Fraley as a starter in 1989 after Fraley went down with broken ribs in the fifth game. He went on to lead the Huskies in tackles for three consecutive years, won the Pac-10's Defensive Player of the Year award as a senior, and was one of three finalists for the Butkus Award, presented to the nation's best linebacker. He anchored Washington's linebacking corps, considered among the best in the nation, and was named to several All-America teams.

Hoffmann, whose younger brother, Steve, played on the Husky defensive line, wasn't the only heavy hitter on this defense. At his right shoulder was James Clifford, a barrel-chested senior with a fire hydrant for a neck. He had a knack for sniffing out a ball carrier. He wasn't the fastest player at his position, in part because of his reconstructed knee, but he made big plays. That he was even on the field was an accomplishment. A debilitating injury nearly snuffed his football career. He tore knee ligaments during fall practice before the 1990 season, underwent surgery, and didn't return to the lineup for a year. It was a devastating interruption for a guy who led the Pac-10 in tackles as a sophomore with 164, a number that ranked him ninth among all-time UW single-season leaders. That year, he made an astounding 27 tackles against USC. Teammates called him "The Anvil" and wondered privately if he had a sliver of mercy in his soul. "He's Charles Manson in shoulder pads," said one, asking anonymity. "He might just hit his mother if he had the chance." Coaches credited Clifford with being at the forefront of the Huskies' defensive metamorphosis from a bulky and lumbering lineup to an attacking scheme that favored smaller, quicker players. "Cliff created the attack attitude," Lambright said. "He was the catalyst while guys like Steve Emtman and Dave Hoffmann were just a couple of players."

Clifford and Hoffmann were close friends and would sit in the locker room after practice ended and their teammates were long gone. Clifford would share his fears, the ones about his never being the same player, never relocating his burst. Hoffmann would listen, then give the same advice each time: "Stay focused." But that wasn't easy, especially when Clifford's knee just wouldn't move the way it used to. Plus there was the mental aspect, the thought that one false move, one hard cut would snap those ligaments like so much cold taffy.

Doubts lingered for Clifford, even when he returned to the field in 1991 and played in all 12 games as a reserve, making 36 tackles and recovering two fumbles. Watching films of himself was frustrating, and others on campus wrote him off. "Nobody would ever say it to my face," he said. "Friends of mine would be at parties, or watching the games somewhere, and people would say: 'Clifford will never be good again. They're just giving him courtesy time.'"

After the national championship year, Clifford needed a change of scenery and decided to try his hand at baseball, a sport he hadn't played since his senior year at Seattle's Ingraham High, where he was an all-state selection and a 1988 draft pick of the Seattle Mariners. James told him that if he expected to step into a starting inside linebacker job in the fall, he couldn't turn his back on football in the spring. Clifford understood and did double-duty, practicing with both the Washington football and baseball teams in the spring. He flourished on the diamond, batting .304 with 10 home runs—the second-highest homer total in Husky history—and leading Washington to its first NCAA appearance since 1959. Again, the Mariners fell for his uncommon bat speed and drafted him. This time he signed, inking a deal to play with the Class-A Bellingham (Wash.) Mariners during the summer. His stick wasn't so torrid there. He learned that, unlike playing college ball, he couldn't get by on athletic ability alone as a pro. He finished the season with a modest .138 batting average, collecting nine hits in 65 at-bats.

The diversion let Clifford unwind and begin fall football practice with renewed enthusiasm for the game. Hillary Butler appeared to have a lock on a starting job when fall two-a-days began, but not for long. "Everyone was saying Clifford looked kind of shaky and wouldn't be back," Butler said. "They were saying, 'Hill, Hill, you might be the man.' When I saw Clifford, it didn't seem like he was ready... But sometime between the first practice and first scrimmage, he got it back. I don't know how, but he got it back. He dug deep for it."

The most intimidating member of Washington's defense was weakside linebacker Jaime Fields, whose light blue, wolflike eyes played off his coffee skin. He was listed in the press guide at 6 feet, but his compact 230-pound frame made him appear an inch or two shorter. The thick knot of muscles in his upper back almost reached his earlobes, giving him the look of a snarling pit bull.

His punishing blows were legendary, and *The Sporting News* and *Lindy's* magazines called him the hardest hitter in the country. Jesse Johnson could attest to that. The Michigan tailback caught a little swing pass in the 1992 Rose Bowl and was flattened by Fields. The shot reverberated through the stadium like a shotgun report rolling through a ravine. Farr and linebacker Chico Fraley were nearby when contact was made, but only Fraley saw the blast.

"What was that?" Farr asked, startled.

"That was Jaime."

"What'd he hit him with? A baseball bat?"

Fields headed for the sidelines, where he was met by Emtman. The two Compton Quaked and bear-hugged. The philosophy of hitting embraced by Jaime (pronounced HY-me) was simple, brutal. "When I was in high school," he said, "my coach used to say if you hit him hard enough in the head, his brain will forget he has the ball or his brain will forget he has legs." He could scare people with his maniacal stares. And his quiet way made him seem that much more pathological.

Interestingly, one of Fields's greatest ambitions was to meet Mel Kiper Jr., the ESPN personality and NFL draft analyst who was anything but tight-lipped. "I want his job," Fields told the *Post-Intelligencer*. Wanted it bad enough, in fact, that he sent Kiper an autographed picture. It seems Fields and friends grew up listening to Kiper on the radio, and they took a liking to the guy. Liked the way he judged talent. Little wonder—Kiper thought Fields would be a first-round pick if he were 6-foot-1, but since he was a tad short for a first-round linebacker, the analyst predicted he'd be drafted in the fourth or fifth round.

Starting at the other outside linebacker spot was Andy Mason, who turned down a $65,000 signing bonus from the Toronto

Blue Jays to play for the Huskies. He was drafted out of Mark Morris High in Longview, Washington, in 1989 as a power-hitting speedster. His chiseled, 6-foot-2 frame packed 240 pounds of punch. His build was ideal for the game: yard-wide shoulders, muscles clustered high on his calves like softballs, and the waistline of a New York runway model. Teammates called him "A-Bomb."

Mason had his sites set on more than a pro football career; a business management major, he suggested after the 1993 Rose Bowl that he might not even play his senior season, opting to devote more time to his studies. "I didn't want to come to the end of my football career and then, all of a sudden, get thrown out into the real world," he said.

Football, to Mason, was anything but the real world. One reporter noted A-Bomb's Robocop field attire—which included shiny black socks and bandana, hand and elbow pads—gave him the look of a "futuristic gladiator." Regarding his changing role in the defense, Mason said, "I've been David the whole time. Now, I'm Goliath." He had an undeniable panache to him and would don his double-breasted purple suit and jewelry for special occasions. When he smiled, it was the confident smile of a casino owner and would dominate his broad face. Few could match the aplomb of A-bomb. In his right ear were two gold earrings and in his left ear, one. A football-shaped pendant encrusted with 13 diamonds, matching his jersey number, hung around his neck. He was a walking Fort Knox for any mugger crazy enough to tangle with a brute who clubbed quarterbacks into submission every Saturday. His grandmother worked for the phone company and gave him a cellular phone, which he used frequently in conspicuous places. When the Huskies went to Disneyland a few days before playing Iowa in the Rose Bowl, A-bomb was spotted waiting in a food line, wearing his purple suit and gold sunglasses, gabbing on his cellular phone. Vintage Mason.

More than anyone on the Husky defense, Mason could give the opponent an earache with constant trash talking. He was, in essence, a stand-up comedian whose audience was usually prone, sometimes writhing in pain. His banter was more calculated than mere mindless babbling. "You don't want to give your opponent too much to come after you with," he explained. "But at the same time, you want to try to disrupt his flow and his thinking to where it works to your advantage." Mason was the General Schwarzkopf of cerebral strategy. Consider the punishment, both physical and mental, he doled out to Kansas State quarterback Paul Watson in 1991. The Wildcat offense moved as if knee deep in quicksand, netting minus-17 yards on the ground. Mason was no help.

"You're probably pretty scared right about now, huh?" Mason shouted to Watson as he dropped into a ferocious stance, arching his back like an alley cat.

Watson's worried eyes told the story.

"I've been pickin' on you all day," Mason ranted. "I tell you what, we're winning, I'm gonna ease up on this play. I'll go half speed."

Watson's face was that of a death-row inmate answering a last-minute call from the governor. At last, reprieve from the purple landslide. He nodded to Mason as if to say, "OK, sounds good to me." At the snap of the ball, Mason exploded into the backfield and flattened him.

"Stupid motherfucker," he crowed, shaking his head as he sauntered back to the defensive huddle.

II

The area richest with athleticism was the defensive backfield. *The Sporting News* and *Lindy's* called Washington's the best secondary in the nation. Tommie Smith was an all-state running back during his high school days in Lancaster, California, but switched to defense when he came to Seattle. Probably the best athlete on the team, Smith was quiet as a monk off the field and positively percolated with trash talk in games. "He *never* stops talking," said Mason, and, considering the source, that meant something.

Walter Bailey would man one corner and Josh Moore the other. Shane Pahukoa would play free safety, and his story was one of the team's most compelling. He, Hoffmann, Kennedy, and Brunell shared duties as co-captains and all were enormously popular both with fans and teammates.

No one on the team endured the type of tribulations Pahukoa went through as a child. The scars of his trauma will last his entire life. In 1979, while playing in the backyard of a relative's home in Vancouver, Washington, Pahukoa suffered third-degree burns on his head, neck, left hand, and body when a cousin poured gasoline onto a campfire, causing flames to leap onto Pahukoa's face. His older brother, Jeff, rolled him and pushed his head under a water faucet to extinguish the flames. That saved Shane's life. Doctors at the Portland, Oregon, hospital in which Shane stayed for two months still thought he wouldn't survive. Pahukoa's head swelled to three times its normal size after the accident. He underwent several skin grafts and had to wear a protective mask off and on for three years.

Athletics became Shane's escape. He and Jeff, two years his senior, spent most of their youth in Marysville, Washington, playing sports. Jeff played on the offensive line for the Huskies and now, the Los Angeles Rams. Shane was a two-sport star at Marysville-Pilchuck High, earning all-state recognition as a running back and averaging 11.4 points a game for the basketball team. His leaping ability was astounding, and he won a slam-dunk contest during a summer basketball camp. He turned down football scholarship offers from Brigham Young and several Northwest schools before accepting an offer from the Huskies.

Things didn't always go smoothly for Pahukoa when he came to Seattle. For his first two seasons, he was beneath Tommie Smith on the free-safety depth chart and only secured the starting job after Smith moved to strong safety. Playing on the second team didn't suit Pahukoa. "Neither of us was red-shirted," he recalled. "I felt like they were kind of wasting me. I thought I'd always be a backup.

"I went out there and gave it 75 percent. I wasn't ready to play. My grades went down. My parents will tell you. I wasn't too much (fun) to be around."

Smith had grade troubles at the end of the 1990 season, and Pahukoa stepped into the starting lineup. He never relinquished the spot, earning second-team All-Pac-10 honors during the national championship season and cementing his role as a defensive leader. His showing in the 1992 Rose Bowl, in which he dislocated his shoulder on the game's first play but refused to come out, only garnered more respect from his teammates. "We call him 'The Assassin,'" D'Marco Farr said. "He's so quiet, and you never know when he's going to come up and take your head off."

Said James of Pahukoa, "The one thing that's probably as impressive about him as anything else is, our players look up to him just from a standpoint of his toughness."

8

Law And Disorder

Kevin Conard and Vince Fudzie arrived at Washington in 1983 as two promising recruits from California. Each saw his Husky career end abruptly less than three years later after an altercation with Santa Ana (California) police.

Subjects of frequent reprimand, Conard and Fudzie were kicked off the team by Don James after an incident before the 1985 Freedom Bowl. James recommended that the school strip the two of their scholarships. Conard and Fudzie (pronounced Foo-gee) sued James and the university on grounds that they were denied due process and had their scholarships revoked unfairly. A Court of Appeals ruled that the scholarships were a protected property interest of the players, but the Washington State Supreme Court reversed that decision August 6, 1992, saying the players did not have a protected property interest in the renewal of their scholarships, which were granted for one academic year in 1983. The players hope to take the case to the U.S. Supreme Court.

The decision to revoke the scholarships was based on the Freedom Bowl incidents as well as earlier accusations of theft, intimidation, and extortion leveled against Conard and Fudzie, who were never charged in the incidents.

In that Freedom Bowl episode, the two were arrested in the early morning after exchanging words with police at the Red Onion, a Santa Ana restaurant and nightclub, and were in jail when practice started later that morning.

"I just felt whether (Fudzie) was right or wrong, he could have easily avoided the problem," James wrote in an October 1986 letter to the university director of financial aid. "Simply leave the disco. I did listen to his story as well as the arresting officer's story. But at that time I just felt he had made too many mistakes to be given another chance."

As part of a class-action discrimination suit, Conard and Fudzie won an out-of-court settlement from the Red Onion as well as the establishment's promise to address an unofficial policy of discouraging minorities from patronizing their discos.

The players also sued the Santa Ana police officers involved for assault and battery and false imprisonment in a case that is pending.

Despite having his scholarship revoked, Fudzie went on to earn his accounting degree at the school, and was the only black player from California to graduate in the 1983 recruiting class. After college, he joined the accounting firm of Deloitte and Touche in San Francisco and now works as a sports agent and business consultant.

Conard, who could not be reached for comment, transferred to San Diego State, where he played in 1987 and earned a degree in business. He works in Los Angeles as a credit-repair specialist, Fudzie said.

There is no denying Conard and Fudzie got into their fair share of conflict with authorities while at Washington.

In November 1983, Conard was arrested for using a stolen student food credit card. Fudzie also admitted to using the card, but argued the offense was justifiable. He said a Catch-22 forced him into using the card: He was told by coaches to keep meat on his frame, yet his stipend was too small for him to buy a sufficient amount of food. The two were accused of making $100 of purchases with the card, which, Fudzie said, they found.

"You've got to look at the other side," he argued. "The university, Don James, lied to me. He lied to my parents. He lied to everybody else's parents. He said, 'You eat all you can eat.' That was a blatant lie. Now, when we got there, what really happened was during the *season* you could eat all you could. After the season, you're on your own. You got approximately $36 to $40 a week to eat on.

"Have you ever tried to eat on the university campus three times a day for $6 a day? That's $2 a meal. And we're football players. On one hand, Don was telling me personally, 'Vince, you need to get bigger. Gain some weight.' Now, how the hell am I gonna gain weight if I'm not eating? How am I gonna eat (on that budget)? Basically, we're not the only ones that have ever done that. . . . There have been numerous guys on the team that have done the same thing.

"We didn't go buy stupid things; we went and bought stuff like protein shakes and bananas and honey, all things that would help you gain weight."

In 1984, university police informed James that Fudzie had broken windows in a residence hall. Actually, just one window had been broken. Police said Fudzie had been drinking and apparently was angry at a female resident when he punched through the thick, wire-reinforced glass. He sustained a gash slightly longer than an inch on his right forearm and was taken to the hospital for stitches. Fudzie disagreed with the version in the police report. He said he didn't punch the window—he stumbled back into it while roughhousing with friends.

"It was an accident that happened when we were playing around on the weekend," he said. "That was it. I paid for the window. I went to a little dormitory review of my peers and they found me innocent."

According to campus police, two students complained of harassment and intimidation by Fudzie and Conard. In one case, the two were reported to have entered a student's room and made threats of bodily harm. "Oh, hell, no," Fudzie said when asked if he was a dorm bully. "That's the thing that the black man always has to face in America. We've always been perceived by others—because we don't smile as much as maybe another race of people, or we don't talk as much, or we don't have a big happy face all the time—that we're intimidating. I mean, if you're 6-2, 230 pounds and you don't have a smile on your face, then some people are going to just naturally feel that you're intimidating."

Fudzie recalled that his position coach, Skip Hall, once told him and his fellow black linebackers that they didn't smile enough off the field. "He was *serious*," said Fudzie, his voice sounding as if the suggestion still galled him a decade later. "I was like, 'Man, you're not paying me to be a clown and run around with a big happy face on.'"

Hall, former head coach at Boise State who is now an assistant at Missouri, was in charge of player housing while at Washington. "Whenever there was a problem with any of our players, they would call me," said Hall, who did not recall the suggestion to smile more often but explained, "Maybe I was trying to get our players more involved with the students. Those guys (Conard and Fudzie) were definitely a lot of problems in a lot of different areas, and housing was just one of them."

James met with the players frequently and, true to his organized nature, kept records of every formal conversation with them. "I met with Fudzie and Conard and discussed these incidents with them," the coach said in an affidavit, "counseled them regarding their behavior and warned them of the possible sanction of being removed from the team with a loss of their scholarships and having their scholarships discontinued if such behavior continued."

According to documents   filed in King County Superior Court, Conard and Fudzie allegedly attempted to extort money from a female student, Charm Bushnell, after taking pictures of her in bed with another football player, Kevin Gogan. In a report taken to university police, Bushnell wrote Conard and Fudzie were hiding in Gogan's room while she and the player were in bed. She said Fudzie and Conard were seeking revenge after she failed to repay them $30 for their house plants, which died under her care. Gogan, a friend of Conard and Fudzie, had surreptitiously invited the two to hide in the room and watch, she said.

"Kevin Gogan and I were lying down talking," she wrote in the report. "All of a sudden, he said, 'Did you hear that?' I looked over towards where I heard the noise. I then observed Kevin Conard exit the closet area, laughing. Within a few seconds, he said, 'See? I told you we were going to get you. I told you that was going to happen if you messed with us.' Other comments were, 'Oh, is it my turn now?' Gogan was just laughing."

The woman said Fudzie left the room briefly and returned with a pocket camera. She said she tried to pull the covers over her head as Fudzie began to take pictures, but, she said, Conard attempted to pull the covers down. "I was scared," she said, adding, "Then (Gogan) said, 'Oh, just uncover your face for one picture because I want a picture of you and I to put on my lamp.'"

Fudzie said the woman invited the situation by making derogatory racial remarks about him and Conard before they hid in the room. "She came in the room and they immediately went at it," he recalled. "We started messing with Gogan. We started tickling his feet and so forth. We were just clowning around, because everybody had already slept with her before, so to see her in that way was no biggie.

"Gogan started to laugh and she all of a sudden realized what was going on. We turned the light on, and all three of us started talking about it."

In Fudzie's opinion, Bushnell wasn't frightened and seemed to enjoy having her picture taken. "She and Gogan were posing," he recalled. "Nothing nude. Nothing explicit. They both were under the covers. They had smiles on their faces. He was smiling. She was smiling. These were the pictures the police got. And the police destroyed them, because they knew, with these pictures, they had no case."

"I was continually saying no to any of (the three players') requests," she wrote. "I was scared and didn't know what was going to happen next. After the film had been used, both Vince and Kevin (Conard) were indicating deals that could be made so the photos would not be shown to anyone, or sent to my father. Vince was indicating his plants and pots were worth so much money, suggesting that if I payed (sic) the price I could have the photos and negatives. Conard said he was going to be having the pictures too, so you will have to pay me also. I don't recall whether it was Vince or Conard who said, 'Oh, we should keep at least one photo or the negatives, so that if she gets out of line we can put up a photo next to the elevator.'

"(Gogan) continued to just ly (sic) in bed. He did say, 'Oh, you guys should just leave, I'm already in trouble now. She's going to yell at me when you leave.'"

Bushnell wrote that she withdrew $30 from her bank account the next day and delivered it to Fudzie. Later that day, she met with Conard at a campus deli and purchased food for him. "Upon obtaining numerous deli items, and at the checkstand, I indicated to the checker don't ring up more than $20 worth," she wrote in her complaint. "Conard indicated to me that I really wasn't in the position to bargin (sic). The bill came to $23."

Fudzie denied ever trying to extort money from the woman. "We had more money than this girl," he said. "I've got a pretty wealthy father. Kevin's family is not poor or anything. I never had a financial problem."

The three were arrested by campus police and, after about an hour, Gogan, who is white, was released. "We figured we were about to leave, too," Fudzie said. "We left all right—we left when they took us to King County Jail." The two spent the weekend behind bars, but no further action was taken.

Archie Greenlee, who represented Fudzie and Conard when they were faced with the extortion charges, said his clients were fortunate they didn't get in more trouble. "I think they got out of those things because of, well, my skill in handling it," Greenlee said, adding, "They could have been nailed. By the same token, someone else could have been nailed. Kevin Gogan could have been nailed."

Wrote James in an affidavit: "In addition to these criminal matters, I continually had difficulty with Conard and Fudzie because of their lack of respect for service personnel and their belligerent attitudes. On October 21, 1985, I met with Conard in my office about his unacceptable behavior with equipment people. He was advised that unless he made some significant improvement concerning his attitude, effort and behavior, his aid would not be recommended for renewal. I told him I thought he was a negative force in the football program.

"Five days later," James wrote, "I met with Conard again in my office, this time because he did not report an injury and told our trainers he could not and would not practice. I told him then that because of all the problems he caused, I probably would not recommend renewal of his financial aid after the year was over."

The *coup de grace* came in Southern California before the 1985 Freedom Bowl, when Fudzie and Conard failed to show up for practice. As it happened, they were arrested after an altercation with police the night before at the Red Onion restaurant in Santa Ana. They spent the night in jail. All criminal charges were later dropped.

According to the police report (see Appendix A), Fudzie and Conard were turned back from the nightclub portion of the restaurant several times because their clothes were not in accordance with the dress code. Soon after they borrowed shirts and finally gained entrance, they were asked to leave by the management but, according to the police, refused to do so. The police report states that both players were being loud and belligerent, and at one point Conard said, "Fuck this place, fuck these honkies, let's get out of here." Police said the two finally left, and Conard's car was followed out of the parking lot by the original officers and several backup units.

The first two officers on the scene said the two players challenged them to fights on "six or seven" occasions and, when they pulled over the players, Conard got out and threw a punch. He then ran, police said, weaving a dangerous path through traffic and hopping into the car of an uninvolved motorist. Conard was ultimately pulled out of the car, subdued by several officers, and sustained a severe laceration above his left eye that required immediate medical attention.

The players spent the night in jail. Upon hearing of the arrests the next morning, James informed the two they were kicked off the team, would have to find their way back to Seattle, and would not have their scholarships renewed for the following season.

The players' version of the story is vastly different from that of the police. Fudzie pointed out several inconsistencies in the police report, including that the police never mention brandishing their handguns, even though the situation, as described by police, might have warranted that. Fudzie said the police did, in fact, have their guns drawn.

Fudzie also took umbrage to some of the street jargon attributed to him and Conard. "Honky mother fucker?" he asked. "*Honky*? I haven't used that word since the '70s. Conard didn't say that, either. He wasn't living in the '70s, either. We laughed about that. They were trying to stereotype our language—trying to say this is the way we talk—and they couldn't even get that straight." Fudzie said he and Conard received $50,000 each as part of the settlement.

Greenlee, who did not represent Fudzie and Conard in the case against the Red Onion, said the players were right in fighting what appeared to be racial discrimination but wrong in that they disobeyed James and got in a confrontational situation. "In James's case," he said, "working with what he had to work with, he was no doubt justified in doing what he did.

"Where James is pissed off with those guys down there was he *told* them not to do that. Here they went down there and got in trouble anyway. That's what James was rightfully pissed off for."

Greenlee, whose son, Tom, was an All-America defensive end at Washington in 1966, said James is anything but racist. Something that convinced Greenlee of this was the coach's treatment of "Harold" Warren Moon, a quarterback who is black and piloted the Husky offense in the mid-1970s. "That's what sold me on (James) from the very beginning when he came here," said Greenlee, who is black. "I remember people would boo (Moon) and say, 'Take him out.' At that time, there was a white quarterback (Chris Rowland) and people wanted to pull Moon out and put him in. . . . (James) didn't let the public dictate to him what to do. I remember talking to him about it once. He said, 'Well, Warren Moon is our best quarterback.' There was no question in his mind that he was playing the best man. That's the kind of guy that we want."

Going with Moon in 1975, James' first season at the school, was a gutsy move. Rowland had been the starter the year before, and James named Moon to the top job just days before the opener at Arizona State. Even though he fumbled his first snap as a starter, setting up an ASU touchdown, Moon blossomed into a Hall of Fame player for the Huskies and, after a stint in the Canadian Football League, into an All-Pro with the Houston Oilers.

After the Supreme Court decided in Washington's favor in the case of Conard and Fudzie, James said, "I feel real good about it and the university feels real good about it." When asked whether he felt the players' legal maneuvering had been a waste of everyone's time, he said, "Obviously it took a lot of lawyers' man hours and somebody must have lost some money on it. . . . I haven't lost much sleep over that issue for several years."

But that wasn't the last time James would hear from Kevin Conard and Vince Fudzie in 1992.

Not by a long shot.

9

Cheeseburgers in Paradise

Something became readily apparent to Bruce Snyder during 1992 fall football practice in Tempe. Not only did coaching at Arizona State involve juggling X's and O's, figuring how to match up a lumbering linebacker on one of his jet-quick receivers, and spending his $385,500 annual income; coaching the Sun Devils also required a little background in criminology.

From the end of 1991 until August 1992, 10 Arizona State football and basketball players were arrested for allegedly committing various crimes, including fraud, theft, and assault. "For me," ASU athletic director Charles Harris said, "this is personally offensive. There is no place for this kind of behavior. I don't care where it is. I don't care what you believe in, where you come from, or what your justification is. There is no place for it."

Summer in the sweltering SunBelt can be downright unbearable. This scrutiny was as hot as a magnifying glass focused on an ant hill. The school was being pressured by all sides, taking criticism from the media, NCAA, community members, even its own students and faculty.

Not only was the Sun Devil program unraveling like a lanced golf ball, the football team had a doozy of an opener, playing host to the defending co-national champions, the Washington Huskies. "I don't know how your week's been," moaned Snyder, addressing a handful of reporters a day before the opener. "Stephen King wrote mine."

No, King's books are more believable.

One of Snyder's most imposing problems was finding a competent quarterback, one who could keep some semblance of composure against a Washington defense that had a reputation for swallowing young signal-callers like so many chewable vitamins. Bret Powers faced the Dawgs in a 44-16 debacle the year before and looked like he might get the start again. Redshirt freshman Garrick McGee passed him on the depth chart in the fall, however, and a disgruntled Powers quit the team and enrolled at Ohio State.

McGee didn't last long as pilot of the No. 1 offense. He was faster than Powers, yet green at the helm. Predicted Snyder: "He'll get a baptism by fire, as they say, because Washington has a great, great defense."

What Snyder didn't know is McGee would *need* a great defense . . . and a sympathetic jury. A few days before the Washington game, the strong-armed freshman was accused of three counts of felony burglary, dating to the 1991 theft of T-shirts, blue jeans, and a compact-disc player. Linebacker Tim Smith also was charged with the crime and suspended from the team. "You can live a lifetime," Harris said, "and not have what happened to this program in a week."

The Arizona media didn't shadow box with the program. No punches were pulled. The night before the game, a local TV anchor said, "The fingerprinting and mug-shot pictures of ASU players are over—it's time to play football!" The station staged a tele-poll that night, giving viewers two numbers to call: one to blame the players, the other to blame the administration. The results were split down the middle.

Conceded Snyder of the chaos: "I'm stunned. I feel blindsided."

There was more misery to come. With Powers and McGee scratched from the depth chart and third-stringer Grady Benton already in trouble with the law for using a fraudulent credit card, Snyder rested the quarterbacking responsibilities on the broad shoulders of Troy Rauer (pronounced, appropriately, RAW-er), a redshirt freshman who switched from linebacker to quarterback during spring ball. Rauer had a rifle for an arm, but the site on that gun was frequently out of kilter. True, he could zip a bullet pass between the jersey numbers, but between *whose* jersey numbers wasn't always clear. "He has the strongest arm on the team," Snyder said. "I'm just not always sure where the ball is going to go."

Rauer, 19, was a last resort for the Sun Devils. Dig any deeper on the roster and things got ugly quick. Backing him up was Brad Belanger, a 5-foot-8, 150-pound walk-on from Anaheim, California. Behind him? Backup flanker Derrick Hart. Hardly the type of bench that puts a coach's mind at ease. "Troy Rauer will be the guy," Snyder stressed. "And if Troy gets hurt, we'll play Troy, anyway."

At least the defensive formations Rauer would be seeing against Washington would look somewhat familiar. Cal, during the Snyder years, emulated the Huskies' defensive schemes, and Snyder brought along that philosophy when he headed south. But for Rauer, looking down the throat of the beast that was the Dawg defense had to be like staring into a meat grinder. A meat grinder on a mission, mind you.

Pac-10 coaches chose Washington as the odds-on favorite to win a third consecutive trip to Pasadena. That would assure the Huskies of a chance to rewrite the history books: No school had ever won three straight Rose Bowls. A few had come close. USC won in 1979 and 1980, but placed a quite-mortal third in the Pac-10 in 1981, a year when the Trojans were banned from post-season play because of academic irregularities. A decade earlier, Stanford won back-to-back Rose Bowls (1971-72), but a third try at a league title proved futile, and the school finished 2-5 in the league. Of course it didn't help that the Indians, as they were called at the time, lost three factors crucial to their success: quarterback Don Bunce, Coach John Ralston, and the "Thunder Chickens" defense.

The 1992 Huskies, despite all their NFL defections, were in prime position to win a third Rose Bowl and, many felt, make a run at another national championship. The schedule certainly weighed in Washington's favor. Seven of the Huskies' 11 regular-season games would be played in Seattle. Wisconsin would come to Husky Stadium, so would Nebraska, USC, Cal, Pacific, Stanford, and Oregon State. Peppered between those games were trips to Arizona State, Oregon, Arizona, and Washington State. Still, playing the bulk of their games on the banks of Lake Washington hasn't always guaranteed success for the Dawgs. The last time Don James's team wore home uniforms seven times in a season was 1987, when the Huskies finished 7-4-1. Seven home games in 1976 translated into a 5-6 record and no bowl game.

Expectations for Washington were far higher now. The Huskies were ranked second to Miami in the preseason AP poll, with the Hurricanes receiving 43 first-place votes and 1,528 points and Washington collecting 15 first-place votes and 1,491 points. Both teams had a crack at a second consecutive undefeated season. The last Division I-A school to do so was Toledo, which had three straight from 1969 to 1971, going 11-0, 12-0, and 12-0. Before the Rockets' streak was snapped, it reached 35 games. Penn State went 11-0 in 1968 and '69, tearing off a 24-game streak in all.

But for now, the Washington Huskies had their sights set on a more attainable goal: a win at ASU.

In keeping with the team motto, Present Not Past, linebacker Dave Hoffmann decided to leave his national championship ring—the one sporting a No. 1 the size of Greater Cleveland—in Seattle rather than taking it to Tempe. "I don't go around telling other guys not to wear them or something like that," Hoffmann explained. "It's just that I want to concentrate on the here and now. And that ring doesn't have anything to do with this season."

Staying focused on the future was paramount to Walter Bailey, too, but the thought of past Arizona State games kept creeping into his mind. Who could blame him? A year earlier, Bailey intercepted the Sun Devils' first pass, and recovered a fumble on an ASU kickoff, before leaving the game with a sprained ankle. In 1990, the last time the Huskies played at Sun Devil Stadium, he picked off a pair of passes and introduced himself to a television audience in Seattle that knew him only as a seldom-used reserve. Fans would come to know him as a team cheerleader who would frequently flail his arms to beckon noise from the home crowd. Opponents would quickly discover they were dealing with a gambler, a risk-taker eager for an interception. "When the ball's thrown toward Walter," Don James once observed, "it's usually seven points in either direction."

An entertaining character and a spectacular athlete, Bailey was fluent in Bo-speak, the tendency to use the third person when referring to oneself. His mother made him a T-shirt with a block "W" on the pocket. The purple letter, trimmed with gold, looked like the one on standard Washington shirts, but upon closer inspection, written in tiny cursive after the W was "alter." Stitched on his baseball cap, "Sweet B" for Bailey. "At times you have to be confident about your abilities," he explained. "But I try not to come off on a tangent and be vocal."

In fact, he was polite to a fault, referring to reporters he knew as Mr. or Ms. so-and-so. He drew a crowd when he spoke, and his smile dominated his face the way he blanketed receivers. A popular interview before the Arizona State game, he confided: "This is one of my favorite teams to play against. It seems for Walter that big plays seem to happen against ASU. I'm ready to play football. Expect Walter to make some big plays against ASU."

The ASU coach had seen Bailey make big plays before. A year earlier, when Snyder was coaching Cal, Bailey preserved a 24-17 Washington win in Berkeley by batting down a last-second pass by Bears quarterback Mike Pawlawski at the Washington 2-yard line. Had Bailey not made that play, Washington would not have won a national title. Period. No wonder his major was drama.

A leading candidate for the Thorpe Award, given to the nation's best defensive back, Bailey was ranked the No. 1 cornerback in the country by *The Sporting News*. "That's a lot of propaganda," he said. "That's a lot of hype. It's fun to look at, but at the same time, it's fun to look at and laugh." No one laughed at Bailey's numbers in 1991. Seven times that season he picked off passes, more interceptions than any Husky since Tony Bonwell collected seven in 1972. But Bailey's feat was no solo act. He got help from his hard-charging teammates on the line. "I tell the line, 'Just gimme four seconds, baby, and we'll get a big play,'" he said. "It works both ways. They tell us (defensive backs) to give them the coverage for four seconds, and they'll get the sack. Or they get pressure up there within four seconds and we've got a pick."

Bailey, no doubt, reminded Josh Moore of these things when the defense took the field in Tempe. Moore, making his first college start, was filling some oversized cleats, those of Dana Hall. "I've prepared Josh well," Bailey announced game week. "It's going to be a big challenge for him."

Perhaps he prepared Moore too well, or didn't prepare himself well enough. Whichever, Moore wound up with four interceptions and was an All-Pac-10 honorable mention pick; Bailey picked off just two passes, five off his junior year total, and received no postseason honors, a real disappointment in light of *The Sporting News'* prediction.

The wild arm of Rauer left the Washington secondary licking its collective chops. If he tried to throw the football through the thick, 92-degree evening air at Sun Devil Stadium, Husky hands were prepared. As it happened, Moore picked off one pass in the game, strong safety Tommie Smith another, returning his 40 yards for a touchdown, negated by a clipping call on lead blocker Walter Bailey. Another apparent touchdown came when Louis Jones, Smith's backup, picked off a pass in the flat on a dead run, darting 35 yards into the end zone. Jones anticipated the play as if he was in the ASU huddle, backpedaling, then exploding forward and snatching the pass without breaking stride. The only Sun Devil to touch him was an offensive lineman who made a futile effort to nudge him out of bounds. The touchdown was called back, however, because of a roughing-the-passer penalty. A third touchdown, scored on a run by Jay Barry, was negated by a holding call.

On five quick-strike drives, the Huskies were able to put points on the board and make them stick. Those drives took an average of 1 minute, 50 seconds. The Husky offense opened the game with a ball-moving clinic, mounting a picture-perfect touchdown drive that struck a balance between acrobatic running and crisp passing. The drive included two catches by Kralik, an alert one-handed grab of a tipped ball by Bjornson, a whirling run on an option keeper by Hobert, and an 8-yard touchdown run by Jay Barry, on which he popped off right tackle, scooted around a lead block by Darius Turner, and dived across the goal line. The rout was on.

Washington cruised to a 31-7 victory, an outcome that might have been uglier had those three Husky touchdowns counted. The win was Washington's 10th consecutive on grass, plenty of which was kicked up by the cleats of the star of the game, Napoleon Kaufman, whose long runs cut a swath through the 92-degree desert air. Untouchable as a high-plains cactus, he ripped through the heart of the Sun Devil defense with runs of 63 and 70 yards. He moved as if he were floating, his feet barely doffing the grass. In all, he collected 159 yards on six carries from scrimmage, 66 on three punt returns, and a 25-yard kickoff return. The grand total—250 all-purpose yards—helped earn him Pac-10 Offensive Player of the Week.

Considered the fastest Washington player in the Don James era, Kaufman spent most of his first season standing on the sidelines with helmet on, aching to get into games. Finding him from the press box was simple—just look for the player standing closest to the field, inched out in front of his teammates. When he was inserted into games, usually on punt returns or in garbage time, there was a palpable sense of anticipation from the home crowd. His feet, as one writer described them, hit the turf like a sewing-machine needle. He had a way of taking a handoff and waiting behind the line of scrimmage, looking for a gun-sight of a crack to open, then squirting through the alleyway between two massive linemen. The quickest guy you never saw.

Recalled defensive tackle D'Marco Farr: "When Napoleon came here, a couple of us asked him if he was any good because we didn't know. He'd just say, 'Yeah, I'm all right.' We wanted to see for ourselves, so we watched his high school highlight film. It was incredible. I think I only saw him tackled twice in the whole half-hour tape. We're talking 60-, 70-, 80-yard runs, shaking people left and right, breaking touchdowns. And he's doing it here now."

The reported 40-yard dash times of Kaufman were enough to leave seasoned track coaches slack-jawed. Washington hand-timed him crossing the finish line in a sizzling 4.22 seconds. *Sports Illustrated* balked, questioning the reported times of Kaufman, Beno Bryant (4.29) and Walter Bailey (4.31). The magazine labeled the times "just plain nonsense." Clearly agitated, James snapped: "If *Sports Illustrated* said that, they are just full of shit. And you can tell them I said that. . . . Why would we inflate anything? We've got five watches going and we take the consensus time. What advantage is it to us to inflate it? The pro scouts could care less what we time a guy. They get their own times."

The magazine called the reported times "preposterous" after officials from Seiko broke down Carl Lewis's world-record 100-meter time of 9.86 seconds in the 1991 world championship, and Leroy Burrell's 9.88—the world's second-fastest time. Burrell, leading at the 40-yard point of the race, covered the distance in

4.38. But *SI*'s test was not completely fair: First, Washington players are timed by hand, not by electronic device, allowing for some discrepancy, and second, top-notch sprinters pace themselves over 100 meters, they don't use their entire burst for a 40-yard spurt. After the season, the Huskies would purchase an electronic timer, and the marks were close to those reported.

Regardless of what Kaufman's times were, ASU players didn't have a prayer of catching him. "I just found the holes and ran, that's all," he said with a shrug.

Cutting a defense to ribbons was nothing new to Kaufman, named first-team prep All-America by *USA Today* and *Parade* magazine, the No. 2-ranked running back and No. 1 recruit from California by *SuperPrep*. During his senior year at Lompoc High, he averaged 9.8 yards a carry and scored 28 touchdowns, earning California Player of the Year. Eighty-six times he reached the end zone during his high school career, eight times fewer than state-record holder Russell White, a standout tailback at Cal.

There was something more to Napoleon Kaufman than his speed and strength that brought football fans to their feet every time he touched the ball. A certain unquenchable fire that burned within him, an invincible feeling that no one, *but no one*, on that field was as good as he was. That feeling hung in the dry desert air at ASU, where he first scored with Washington leading 7-0. Hobert held the ball on an option until the last possible second before pitching it to Kaufman, who turned upfield and darted 63 yards down the Husky sidelines for the longest run of his college career. With each stride, he pulled farther and farther away from the cornerback chasing him. Lincoln Kennedy pasted a defender to the turf on the play, applying a bone-crushing block that will grace Husky highlight films for years. After crossing the goal line and hugging a teammate, Kaufman stood in the middle of the end zone and did a little dance that he was promptly flagged for, costing the Huskies 15 yards on the ensuing kickoff. The next time Kaufman touched the ball, he took a pitch from Brunell, shot down the left sideline, and cut back to the middle of the field before being tripped up at the ASU 10 by cornerback Kevin Miniefield, who dived to make a hand tackle and just nicked Kaufman's ankle. The play covered 70 yards, and Washington scored on the next down when fullback Darius Turner charged up the middle, dragging two defenders into the end zone.

Hobert completed 22 of 35 passes for 162 yards and a touchdown. On the receiving end of that 10-yard score was Bjornson, making his debut at wideout. The catch came on a broken fourth-down play when Hobert was forced out of the pocket and threw across his body, lofting a pass toward the middle of the end zone. Bjornson seemed almost nonchalant as he stepped in front of cornerback Lenny McGill to pull down the ball. "I was more excited for him to catch that touchdown than I would have been to catch it," Kralik said. "I was just going crazy. It was a play where he was the last person in the world that was going to get the ball. I was just pumped."

Confidence in Bjornson was growing by the minute. His rangy frame made him a good-sized target. "It's been kind of remarkable when you think about it," James said. "For a guy to come in there part way through spring practice and do as well as he's doing." The best-case scenario was Bjornson would develop into a receiver like Ed McCaffrey, a lanky All-America at Stanford who went on to play for the New York Giants. Back when he was a coveted quarterback prospect at Bishop O'Dowd High in Oakland, Bjornson was courted by Stanford. The Cardinal landed three quarterbacks in 1990, however, and cooled on him when he declined to make an official recruiting visit, opting to make an unofficial visit because he lived nearby. Duke, too, was interested in Bjornson, but the school was a little too far from home. "I think I got the best of both worlds," he concluded. "A great football program and a great school."

The backbone of that football program for the past two years was its defense, particularly its ability to dismantle an opponent's ground attack. That rush defense took a big hit at ASU, yielding 279 yards on the ground, more than the Huskies had given up to any team since 1989. The shoddy run support left UW defensive coaches holding their heads and longing for Steve Emtman. The one-dimensional Sun Devils offense consisted of Mario Bates, who slashed for 82 yards on 11 carries in the first half, and finished with 214 yards on 19 attempts. His 80-yard ramble was the longest run against the Huskies in nearly two years, since UCLA's Brian Brown burst up the gut and covered 88 yards of turf in Seattle in Washington's last loss. Mario Bates is the younger brother of Michael Bates, a silver medalist in the 200 meters at the 1992 Summer Olympics who was drafted as a receiver by the Seattle Seahawks but didn't sign a contract for a year, choosing to focus on track and field for a year after college.

The Husky defense would improve against the run, but the front line needed seasoning. Farr and Mike Lustyk, the interior defensive linemen, made their first career starts against ASU. "I had no clue," Farr confessed. He and Sun Devils center Toby Mills engaged in a war of words from the beginning, insulting everything from each other's mother to his dog. At one point, while Rauer was delivering the snap count, Farr turned to Lustyk and made a guess about what the play would be. Mills lifted his head to Farr, "Good call, Cheeseburger."

When the gun sounded on the third quarter, Farr began to walk downfield and felt something cool—too cold to be sweat— run down his back. He spun around to find Mills squirting a water bottle on the back of his neck.

"What are you doing, man?"

"You looked hot."

Recalled Farr: "I didn't know what to say. I didn't know if it was a joke or not. I was kind of hot, I guess."

Washington might have won its opener for the seventh consecutive season, but you might not have known it. Players were pretty quiet in the locker room as they packed their belongings for the flight back to Seattle. "We came off the field knowing we have to get work done," linebacker Dave Hoffmann explained. "We looked at each other in the eye and said, 'Let's get better.'"

10

Getting Badgered
At Home

Barry Alvarez could have picked a better place than Seattle to open Wisconsin's 1992 football season. And, given his druthers, he would have. The third-year coach of the Badgers had no interest in bringing his team into the crucible of anguish that is Husky Stadium and didn't pretend to have any.

"I'm still looking for the guy who scheduled this game," he said to the Seattle beat writers, only half jokingly. "I'm not real crazy about going up there. I don't think it's very wise to have a game like this to open your season, particularly in our situation." Wisconsin's situation: a young team that struggled to a 6-16 record during the past two years learning a new system.

The Badgers' numbers under Alvarez were somewhat deceptive. After a 1-10 debut in 1990, he coached Wisconsin to a 5-6 record the next year, the fourth-best improvement of any team in the country. Before his arrival, the Badgers had won nine games in four years. The 1991 record was the best since 1985, and the two Big Ten wins were the most in five seasons. No greenhorn, Alvarez assisted at Iowa and Notre Dame before taking the Wisconsin job.

Subtracting Washington from the Badgers' schedule, Alvarez believed, would be a plus for the Wisconsin program. The schools signed a two-game pact in 1987, three years before Alvarez arrived. That contract was renegotiated during summer 1992 at the behest of Wisconsin, allowing the Badgers to honor the first game in Seattle and schedule instead a home game against Cincinnati in '94. Washington was reluctant to let Wisconsin out of the contract because of the difficulty of finding a suitable opponent on short notice. "We had to have some game possibilities before we would agree to not play it," Don James said.

Oh, the possibilities. As it happens, Washington filled the void with a dream opponent: Miami. The Huskies and Hurricanes will meet for the first time ever in 1994 and play again in 1998, 2001, and 2002.

But allowing Wisconsin to wrangle out of the second game of the deal wasn't an optimal situation. Athletic department officials at Washington privately said the Badgers were an ideal nonconference opponent. Wisconsin plays in the Big Ten, known for its football tradition, yet was foundering. Before the Wisconsin game, the Huskies had beaten 12 consecutive Big Ten opponents since 1981, including three in Rose Bowls. The margin of victory in 10 of those 12 games was more than a touchdown.

That type of number crunching stung Fred Akers, who coached against Washington each of his four seasons at Purdue. "It wasn't much fun," conceded Akers, now living on a ranch in Austin, Texas. Like Wisconsin, the Boilermakers were amid a rebuilding period. Washington took advantage of that, winning the four games by an average score of 27-10. "We'd lose two or three starters each year," Akers said. "That was bad for morale. That was tough on us. Really was." Tougher was that Purdue could not get out of the series despite its coach's desire to do so. When told of the reworking of Wisconsin's contract, Akers said, "I wish I had an athletic director that had done that."

Hardly buoyed by that type of endorsement, Alvarez did what he had to do to prepare his players for Seattle. "We're not in a position where I think we can go out and compete with a Washington," he said Monday before the game. "But they're on the schedule, and we'll have to try to make the best of it. I'll try to use it as an experience our kids can learn from."

Washington players were learning as well. The team escaped Tempe a winner, but its play was rough hewn. "It was really ragged, which is to be expected from a first game," James confessed. "But not *that* ragged." Pollsters didn't seem to notice; the No. 2 Huskies edged closer to top-ranked Miami, which posted a 24-7 win over Iowa, and both teams pulled away from

No. 3 Notre Dame, which couldn't seem to satisfy the voters, despite thrashing Northwestern, 42-7. The Huskies were favored by 33 points over Wisconsin.

It was announced during the Wisconsin week that Jeff Bockert, a highly touted defensive end recruit when he was signed two years earlier, had transferred to Portland State.

A broken layer of slate-gray clouds hung over Husky Stadium on Saturday, September 12. It was somewhat cool, about 65 degrees. A good day to see a football game, especially in a stadium called by some, including *Sports Illustrated*, the most majestic in the land.

Sitting in the Husky press box, high over the field, is an experience few soon forget. "Breathtaking" is the most accurate way to describe the view from the box, which is suspended like a row of teeth along the roof of the stadium's south side. To reach the teeth, you take an elevator to the top floor, walk about 50 feet down an enclosed ramp, and make a right turn when you reach the rim of the world. From that vantage, you feel like a ghost, hovering high over the turf, watching plays form, crumble, form again. Sports Information Director Jim Daves likes to bring visiting reporters to the east end of the box, pointing out the spectacular view of Lake Washington and Mount Rainier. One reporter jokingly asked him if the flight path of airplanes would obstruct his view of the field.

Weak knees get weaker when the crowd cheers. Then, the box rumbles and sways enough to remind your stomach it's five stories away from its final meal. Eruptions come frequently. A recovered fumble. An interception. A touchdown.

A time-tested ritual begins the event. "Helloooo, Daaaawg fannnnss," Lou Gellermann's rich baritone voice booms over the public-address speakers. An air-raid siren spirals up to an ear-piercing crescendo and freezes there as the Huskies bound out of the locker room tunnel. The crowd roars. The band blares. The stadium shakes from its foundation to its rafters.

A crowd of 72,800, the largest for a home opener since the stadium dedication game against Stanford in 1987, filled the seats to see the Wisconsin game. More people bought tickets to this relatively insignificant game than to any home game during the national championship year. Folks were ready to see the Huskies kick off their campaign for a second title. The place boiled with anticipation.

For all the protestations of Alvarez, the scrappy Badgers put up a fight before losing, 27-10. The performance proved good enough to satisfy the cluster of about 1,000 Wisconsin fans sitting in the closed end zone. A chant began among the Badger faithful: "We covered the spread! We covered the spread!" While fairly sullen Husky supporters filed out of the stadium, the Badger band took the field and put on its "fifth-quarter" extravaganza. The boisterous crowd that remained merrily sang along as the band, led by the sousaphone section, belted out "Roll Out the Barrel" and the Budweiser theme. A beer distributor in Madison paid the band $5,000 each time it played the Bud tune, so that ditty echoed through the stadium more than a few times.

Things weren't so jovial in the Washington interview room. The Huskies were 2-0 but had yet to hit their stride, or as James put it, "We're not batting on all cylinders right now." The running game, something that decimated Arizona State, sputtered. The Dawgs gained 174 yards on the ground, but 60 of those came on a lumbering touchdown gallop by Billy Joe Hobert, on which he juked the Badger secondary with crafty hip swivels, not blinding speed. Toward the end of the run, he felt as if he was breathing swamp water. "After I got to the sideline," he said, "I asked myself, 'Why did I do that?' Everybody made fun of me after the game in the locker room. They told me it was a nasty run."

Maybe so, but none of his teammates covered as much ground that day. Kaufman was the second-leading rusher with 43 yards on seven carries. Beno Bryant, bothered by a pulled hamstring, did not play. Lacking was the churning, ram-it-down-their-throat running between the tackles, something that bleeds pressure off the passing game.

The Dawgs whipped the crowd into a frenzy early, scoring on a 34-second drive on their first possession. A slashing punt return by Napoleon Kaufman put the team in scoring position at the Badger 14, and after a 4-yard loss on first down, Hobert found Kralik in the back of the end zone with an 18-yard touchdown pass.

Wisconsin answered on its next possession, moving 65 yards in four plays and capping the drive with a 17-yard pass from Jay Macias to Tim Ware. "I made a pre-read," Macias said. "He said he should be coming open and there he was." Macias left Husky

Stadium uncowed and unconvinced that the team he had just faced was deserving of being called defending co-national champs. "I expected them to be a lot better," he said. "I was surprised how our receivers were able to beat them. Their secondary seemed a lot slower than they did on film."

Hobert was intercepted on the next series but tore off his long touchdown run on the following one. Even his coaches gave him some good-natured guff about the ramble. "We put him in the hospital two days to get oxygen," James joked the next week. "He seems to be responding."

If statistics decided football games, this one would have been a blowout. Washington led in rushing yards (174-90), passing yards (281-128), first downs (26-9), plays run (93-54), and time of possession (36:43-23:17). But the Dawgs were unable to translate those numbers into big points. Their 27 points were the fewest against a nonconference opponent in two years. Hardly an encouraging statistic with Nebraska coming to town. "If we play like this next week," Hobert groaned, "we won't be talking to the press after the game. We've got to improve."

The best way to classify Walter Bailey's day? "Forgettable" would be kind. Wisconsin receiver Lee DeRamus came to Seattle to catch Bailey's eye. As it happens, he caught his eye, his ire, and a few footballs along the way. "I just wanted to come out here and get some respect," the Badger sophomore said. "With me being a wide receiver and he being one of the best cornerbacks in the country . . . " DeRamus accounted for 70 of the Badgers' 128 receiving yards, and as for his defensive counterpart, well, no one confused Walter Bailey with Walter Mitty.

Already burned on an 18-yard touchdown pass, Bailey had a sure interception wrestled away by DeRamus, was flagged for a personal foul, gave up a 44-yard reception, and lost a huge chunk of yardage on a punt return most would deem ill-advised. Sure, he sprinkled in some good defensive plays, but Walter simply wasn't Walter. "Well," James said, "I'll tell you, he's supposed to be our best corner. He's got to play better than that. Our expectations of his play are a lot better than that."

As usual, Bailey was upbeat after the game, blaming the mistakes on a lack of patience, an inclination to gamble for the big defensive play. "I was making mistakes on plays that weren't there instead of playing it safe," he said. "At times I thought the big play would happen and it didn't come." That, of course, depended on whom you talked to. DeRamus pointed to plenty of big plays.

One series was particularly memorable. Facing a third-and-17 midway through the third quarter, the Badgers were pinned on their own 19. Jay Macias floated a pass in the direction of DeRamus, covered by Bailey. Both players caught the ball, but DeRamus pulled it away before being body-slammed. "That ball was mine," Bailey lamented. "I just let it go. . . . It slipped. I tried to grip it real hard." A scuffle erupted. Bailey, who later accused DeRamus of throwing a punch, was flagged for a personal foul. "Swinging at somebody isn't right," Bailey said. "I wouldn't swing at somebody."

When referees stepped between the two, DeRamus told Bailey, "Yo, I'm coming." He wasn't kidding. On the next play, he caught a 44-yard pass on an out-and-up route. Any ill will was left on the field as Bailey and DeRamus embraced before heading up the tunnel. No hard feelings. DeRamus felt as if he knew Bailey. After all, he had seen enough Washington films during the summer to leave Roger Ebert shifting in his seat. "I almost watched their whole season last year," he confessed. "As soon as the Arizona State game was over, I was back in the film room."

Bailey might have wanted to cover his eyes when the Wisconsin video rolled. On Husky punt returns, he replaced Kaufman—ejected for throwing a punch—and didn't have much luck. He declined to return one punt that, but for a Washington bounce into the end zone, would have been downed at the 5. On another, he tried to one-hop the ball at the 30 but missed, chased it back to the 9, and was tackled at the 5. Defending the decision, he said, "It was a heads-up play, but I didn't know where I was."

Kaufman made two errors, both of which pointed to a disturbing trend: He fumbled, and his emotions got the best of him. The fumble came on a 36-yard punt return and didn't hurt the Huskies because the ball was recovered by teammate Richard Thomas and advanced 8 yards to the Badger 14. The ejection proved more costly. Kaufman had to leave the game mid-third period after taking a swing at Wisconsin linebacker Gary Casper, who, Kaufman said, grabbed his jersey. The outburst infuriated James. "I don't think there's any question Kaufman swung back," James said. "The guy held his jersey and Kaufman swung at him. I said: 'That's real smart. That's exactly the thing to do. Swing at a guy holding your jersey and get thrown out.' . . . He's got to mature. We don't want to take a lot of excitement and exuberance away from him." The real problem, James said, was not Kaufman's age but a lack of self-control. "You look at NFL games and they're swinging at each other all game long," he said. "So you can't say it's youth. It's got to change. . . . These aren't the streets."

Far less peeved, Casper explained, "He got flustered. He probably hurt his hand more than anything."

Kaufman was sullen after the game, only making a brief stop in the interview room to give a perfunctory explanation of the ejection. Usually, he would stay longer and spend some time answering questions. Now, he just wanted to shower and leave. "I just reacted wrong," he said with a shrug. "I was very surprised I got kicked out, but what can you do?"

Washington remained No. 2 behind Miami in the AP poll, but the win over Wisconsin wasn't altogether pleasing. "If we don't improve 99 percent by next week," Hobert said, "it's going to be a cakewalk for Nebraska."

11

Saturday Night Lights

Two games into the college football season, Washington had gathered all the momentum of a glacial shift. The Huskies were 2-0, but neither win could be classified as a pounding. Both the offense and defense showed flashes of precision, but at times, each unit wobbled like a punch-drunk pug. Enough to keep the lights burning at all hours in the Tubby Graves building, where the coaches had their offices. One surety loomed: Nebraska, the 12th-ranked team in the nation, was coming to Seattle, along with ESPN, a television audience of millions, and a host of national sports writers. Why Nebraska? Why television? Why now? Such are the spoils of national acclaim.

Showtime, ready or not.

Things could have been better for the banged-up Huskies. There were two conspicuous holes in the offense; hurt were tailback Beno Bryant and guard Pete Kaligas. Still bothered by a hamstring pull, Bryant was questionable for the Nebraska game, and when he did play, he gained just 19 yards on nine carries. Kaligas, one of the team's strongest players, injured his knee in the fourth quarter of the Wisconsin game and would be out for at least a month. Strange, a guy can bench-press a quarter ton, but if he takes a hit in that soft tangle of tendons below the kneecap, it's all over. Bad knees plagued Kaligas throughout his college career.

Losing both players hurt. Each played a critical role when the Huskies battled the Cornhuskers a year earlier. In that game,

Bryant gained 139 yards rushing, and Kaligas graded out higher than any Washington lineman.

Also hobbled was tailback Jay Barry, slowed by a broken bone in his foot. He spent much of his time with a cowboy boot on one foot and a walking cast that he could remove for games on the other. Against the Cornhuskers in 1991, he rushed for 110 yards, including a game-clinching touchdown burst that covered 81 yards. But this foot injury really affected his running style. He used to be able to zip through a hole, zig right, zag left, cut as if attached to the rails of some wild carnival ride. After the injury, planting with one foot meant a jolt of pain. Finding a hole wasn't a problem, but hitting it hard and making extra yards after contact was. As James put it, "He's getting basically what's blocked for him."

The offensive line, patchwork because of injuries, yielded four sacks for minus-21 yards in the first two games, not horrible unless you consider the line gave up just six sacks for the 1991 season.

So this might not have been the best time for the Huskies to face such a formidable foe as Nebraska, yet Washington had a precedent for a seamless shift from low to high gear. The 1990 season began with lackluster wins over San Jose State and Purdue, who the Huskies slipped past by meager margins of 20-17 and 20-14, before a blockbuster victory over USC in the third game. The Trojans were pummeled, 31-0, in a game that not only indicated Washington was the front-runner in the Rose Bowl race but a national championship contender.

If that pounding was a springboard for Washington, it was a slingshot for USC coach Larry Smith, fired two years later. Many point to the debacle in Seattle as the beginning of the end for him. "I remember it was the biggest humiliation any of us can remember for a long time," Smith said. "We were so bad, we couldn't run a pattern. We went in at halftime and got ourselves together and played a respectable second half. The second quarter was a nightmare."

The Dawg defense enveloped quarterback Todd Marinovich like the smog-soaked L.A. skyline, pasting him to the floor of Husky Stadium. After the game, he slumped against his locker and answered questions through swollen lips. One could only imagine the dazed look in those eyes, hidden by dark, wraparound sunglasses. "I didn't see anything," he said, uttering words that have become part of Husky lore. "No names, no numbers. All I saw was purple." The UW defense begged for a moniker, and got one after that performance: Purple Haze. The nickname was particularly appropriate because Jimi Hendrix hailed from Seattle.

The 1992 Huskies had a role model in the 1990 team. Sure, the wins over ASU and Wisconsin were something less than awe inspiring, but beating Nebraska by any margin would leave smiles on the faces of Husky fans. However, Don James noted, those fans would have to do their part. He implored them to make more noise than ever before. "As a coach, you'd all love to play defense in a Texas A & M-type atmosphere," he said. "Where the opposing team can't hear the snap count . . . We've been asking the fans to come to play."

Pushing the anticipation for this game even higher was that it would be played at night, the first such contest in the history of Husky Stadium. Kickoff was set for 6:35 p.m. The latest start in previous years was 5 p.m. for the 1985 season opener against Oklahoma State. From the perspective of national attention, there were pros and cons to playing Nebraska under the lights; it ensured a national television audience, yet, because of early deadlines and the time difference on the West Coast, the game was less enticing to East Coast sports writers. Deadlines for morning papers usually fall around 11 p.m. to midnight, so if a Husky game begins at 9:30 p.m. E.S.T., a paper in, say, Boston will be hard-pressed to get the final score in its first edition. The Huskies also are at a geographic disadvantage as far as the national media is concerned because Seattle is so remote. Plane tickets to the Emerald City are expensive, so editors often are reluctant to send writers to Seattle to cover games, opting to use wire stories instead.

Night game or not, the Washington-Nebraska showdown was just too enticing for a cluster of national college football writers to miss. Sally Jenkins of *Sports Illustrated* came; so did Ivan Maisel of the *Dallas Morning News*, and Rick Warner, from AP's New York bureau, and *USA Today's* Mike Lopresti. In all, six AP voters—one-tenth of the total number—were in attendance.

A strong showing against the Cornhuskers would help guarantee that the Huskies' 1991 season wouldn't be dismissed as some sort of cosmic wrinkle, a fortunate fluke that allowed the school a share of the national title. Even though Washington seemed to have started the 1991 season on more of a roll, the numbers from the first two games of the 1992 season were similar: the 1991 team opened with 26- and 15-point victories over Stanford and Nebraska and was ranked fourth; the 1992 team began with 24- and 17-point wins and was ranked second.

The Cornhuskers, as usual, were reliant on a powerhouse ground game that had a knack for manufacturing long drives and keeping opposing defenses on the field. Bookend backs Calvin Jones and Derek Brown fueled the attack and rotated on every other series. These "we" backs in an I-back system were the toast of Lincoln.

Scheduled to start against Washington was Brown, a shifty slasher who ran for 1,313 yards in 1991. He attended Servite High in Orange County, California, a Jesuit school with a reputation for turning out a steady stream of Division I football players. Brown and Russell White, 1989 high school graduates, were two of the nation's most heavily recruited players. White attended Crespi High, about an hour up Interstate 5 from Servite.

The dueling rushing statistics of Brown and White were recorded in the Southland newspapers each Saturday, but the two faced each other only once, in a Southern Section playoff game. White, the nephew of Heisman Trophy winner Charles White, said of Brown, "We'll show him who's the originator and who's the impostor." By game's end, it was tough to tell. The two went juke for juke, and Brown's team won, 42-21. Brown was named Back of the Year at the Los Angeles Times prep football banquet, and a disgusted White, who won the mantle as a sophomore, got up from his table and stormed out when the presentation was being made.

Jones, Brown's counterpart in the Cornhusker offense, was a polite, soft-spoken Nebraska native. A powerful inside runner, he could lower his shoulders and bore a hole through a cinder-block defensive front. Raised in Omaha, he grew up rooting for Mike Rozier, Irving Fryar, and Turner Gill. Before his time came Johnny Rodgers, Jeff Kinney, and Rich Glover.

Creating Peterbilt-sized holes for Jones and Brown was an offensive line that 20-year coach Tom Osborne called his best ever. Three 300-pounders. A tight end who tipped the scales at

260. Good ol' farm boys looking to dent the turf in Raintown. The lighter Husky defensive line would either be forged like white-hot steel or snap like an ear of corn.

This game had the trappings of a watershed for both teams. Nebraska's proud heritage included an NCAA-record 30 consecutive winning seasons and 23 consecutive bowl berths. But in the past few years, the Cornhuskers have been notorious for folding against elite foes, losing seven of their past nine games against Top 10 teams. Beating Washington in Seattle could help shake that bugaboo. Things just had to get better. Losing sucked, and folks in Lincoln were sick and tired of watching their team choke in almost every big game. The defeats were downright ugly, just like the phone calls that Charlie McBride got after his defense—with faces as red as their Nebraska jerseys—gave up 618 yards of total offense to the Huskies in 1991. Boy, the calls were harsh. It got so bad, he had to take his home phone off the hook.

The Huskies could use the national attention to sway AP pollsters and, quite possibly, win some votes from those who had sided with Miami. The 1991 game in Lincoln was a turning point for the UW program. "The last 20 minutes against Nebraska was probably the greatest 20 minutes of football we've ever played here," James recalled. "At least since I've been here. We overcame so much to win that game."

Some of those obstacles popped up even before toe met leather. For one thing, the Huskies had no opportunity to practice under the lights. The team arrived at Memorial Stadium on Friday night and, moments later, the field was cast in darkness. The coaches found members of the stadium maintenance crew, who spent 45 minutes fiddling with switches to no avail. Irked, the Husky players and coaches packed up and left. As the buses were pulling out of the parking lot, the lights came on. Still, the team left. James joked about returning the favor when the Cornhuskers came to Seattle. "No lights Friday night," he quipped. "We're taking the guy in charge of the lights out to dinner Friday night."

No one could argue, however, that the Huskies didn't get the red-carpet treatment from Nebraska fans. Although Huskers backers pulled for their team throughout, they politely applauded the victorious Washington players as they left the field.

Football is serious business in Lincoln, but so, apparently, is gamesmanship.

Predicted *Seattle Times* columnist Blaine Newnham, "Good or bad, the people from Nebraska sitting in Husky Stadium tonight will be a little more polite and wear a little more polyester than their opposites from Washington."

The fabric in the Seattle sky on the evening of Sept. 19, 1992, was a patchwork of cumulus clouds. Not foreboding weather, but a reminder that summer nights were on the wane. Just like the lights warming up overhead, energy fairly crackled around Husky Stadium.

People like Pat Shaw, a mason from nearby Puyallup, listened to Don James's impassioned plea for fan support. Shaw knew the importance of this game and heard the request for a decibel count that would ring the ears of any self-respecting jackhammer operator. His response? Purely Pavlovian. He shaved his head and grease-painted a Husky helmet on his shiny noggin. "My girlfriend hates me," confided Shaw, a longtime fan. "But everyone here wants me to party with them. I've had free cocktails and cookies. It's great."

Shaw wasn't the only crazy one. Consider Yvonne Stahmer of Omaha, who flew to Seattle with her husband and eight friends. None had tickets to the game, which had been sold out for some time. Hey, she reasoned, there are plenty of large-screen TVs in Seattle. "It's gutsy all right," she said, all the while holding up two fingers to summon scalpers. "My mother thinks she dropped me on my head." Flying 1,500 miles without tickets isn't odd, she said. She was less than convincing. "I've had season tickets since 1965 and only missed one home game," she said. "That was for a funeral. I told my kids that when I die, 'You'd better not bury me on a Saturday. I don't want any of my friends missing a game for my funeral.' "

Paul Darlington wasn't about to die for his Dawgs, but he would make most any other sacrifice to see them. He planned to go to every 1992 Husky game, home and away, and had already been to four Rose Bowls and an Orange Bowl. "We went to Nebraska last year and they treated us royally," said Darlington, who owns 10 season tickets. "I can't remember a game as big as this one, outside of a bowl game." His purple 10-gallon cowboy hat adorned with about 30 buttons and pins proclaiming his love for the Huskies and vague disdain for anyone they play made Darlington easy to find in a crowd.

The buying and selling of tickets was done surreptitiously. The place was crawling with Seattle police officers. "It's pretty much the same today, except the prices are higher," said officer Gilbert Espinosa, estimating some folks were spending $85-$175 per ticket. He had caught four scalpers, issuing each a $250 fine. Proving the sale was tough. If the tickets were sold at face value, the transaction was aboveboard.

Cornhuskers alumni Ron and Shelly Wright, who flew in from Lake Tahoe, California, bought upper-level seats for $45 apiece. They tried to get tickets for weeks, even asking a friend who knew Nebraska athletic director Bob Devaney. No luck. Finally, they knuckled under to scalpers. Along the walk from their distant parking spot, the Wrights saw a comforting sight: Washington and Nebraska fans tailgating together. Huskies and 'Huskers? Aw, shucks. "I went to a lot of games in college when it wasn't that way," Shelly said. "I've had beer bottles thrown at me. This is the way it's supposed to be."

The anticipation fans were feeling paled in comparison to the nervous energy generated in the locker rooms. Two of the more anxious players were Husky defensive linemen D'Marco Farr and Mike Lustyk. The tandem faced the unenviable task of going toe to toe with the massive Cornhuskers line, which included guard Will Shields, winner of the 1992 Outland Trophy and called by Osborne "the best lineman I've ever coached." Farr and Lustyk, whose lockers were side by side, went through a ritual before each game. Each would help the other dress, snapping up his shoulder pads, pulling his jersey on, and lining his cheekbones with eye-black.

The two had a pact: Farr could never wear a T-shirt under his pads, even on the coldest of days, and Lustyk could never wear gloves. The superstition began two years earlier when the Huskies hosted UCLA and lost. That chilly afternoon was the first and last time Farr wore a T-shirt. "It was kind of cold," he recalled. "And I knew I wasn't going to play, so I wore it." Never again. The Dawgs had not lost since, building the nation's second-longest current winning streak at 15 games.

Farr and Lustyk walked slowly down the slanted tunnel leading to the field. Neither spoke. "We needed to conserve our energy," Farr explained. Coming out of the tunnel's mouth, they were greeted by the din of 73,333 people, the largest crowd ever to see a nonconference game at Husky Stadium and the sixth-largest crowd in school history. The roar was deafening. Under the odd glow of the lights, shadows of the players were long and thin. Colors changed in the hard glow. The pants of Husky players a rich gold, their jerseys almost black. The field, a sparkling green dance floor on a sunny day, now took on a cool emerald hue like felt on a pool table. The crowd, sheets of dark purple.

"GO!" cheered one side of the stadium.

"HUS-KIES!" answered the other side, sounding like a diabolical blast from a coal furnace.

"GO!"

"HUS-KIES!"

From the floor of the stadium, it was a surreal scene. Farr's stomach gurgled and bubbled like the innards of a Lava Lamp. Sweating already, he looked at Lustyk and nodded. Lustyk nodded back. No words were exchanged, and none needed be. More than a nicety, the nods were acknowledgments from two friends heading into a ring of fire, the same knowing glance that climbing partners might share before repelling with frayed ropes down a 20-story granite face.

"GO!"

"HUS-KIES!"

Nebraska struck the first blow of this game, stopping the Huskies on a fourth-and-1 situation in the opening period, yet the Dawgs answered with a flurry and ultimately delivered a 29-14 drubbing. Big plays on offense and a defense that had made startling strides since Wisconsin was in town won this game. The Husky defense applied a firm choke hold on a Nebraska offense that was averaging 558.5 yards a game, limiting the Cornhuskers to 309. Said James of the defensive effort, "They've got pride." More than that, they now had a performance under their belts that, according to linebacker James Clifford, "would shut some people up."

As for Farr and Lustyk? "We laid the '91 defensive team to rest tonight," Farr said. "We've always known we were good. We proved that tonight. . . . Maybe now people will stop hammering us. We've been hearing it for two weeks now that we can't do it, that we can't play like last year's D-linemen. Well, nobody can play like Steve Emtman, but we did a pretty good imitation, didn't we?"

Not bad, and the numbers reflected that. Nine times, the Cornhuskers were tackled for losses. Clifford and Farr recovered fumbles, Walter Bailey picked off a wobbly pass, and Lustyk and Dave Hoffmann deflected balls. "Our defense talked all week about needing to make some big plays today and get some points on the board," Clifford said. "We got it done tonight."

The most significant defensive lapse by Washington came in the second quarter, when Jones found a jet stream and cruised 73 yards for a touchdown, the longest run of his career.

Most of the game, the Husky defense was as rigid as an iron bar. The third time Nebraska touched the ball, late in the first quarter, the defense put on a show of force that brought the crowd to its feet. Corporate America could learn something from the precision of this attack. John Werdel, standing at the Husky 40, boomed a punt that dropped inside the Nebraska 10 and was downed by Washington's Leif Johnson at the 3. The noise made it impossible for quarterback Mike Grant to check off plays at the line, even though the Cornhusker offense was working closest to the open end of the stadium. An offensive lineman lurched forward on first down, drawing an illegal-procedure flag that moved Nebraska back to the 2. A delay-of-game penalty followed, moving the offense deeper into the hole and stirring the stadium into a boiling frenzy.

The Cornhuskers finally got the snap off, and fullback Lance Lewis tried to blast up the middle. He was knocked back for no gain, looking like a child experimenting with a fork and a wall socket. On the next play, free safety Tommie Smith nailed Mike Grant with a blindside sack in the end zone for a safety. Unblocked, Smith shot out from the right side of the defense and applied a brutal hit, the kind that sounds like a car accident or a sledge hammer crushing a can of paint.

Grant didn't seem the same after that. Gone was the confident swagger. His eyes, particularly after that rude awakening, took on a bulging, doelike quality. His worried expression whimpered, *Man, get me the hell out of here.* But there was no leaving this crucible of pain, the place Husky players referred to as the "Dawghouse." A chant thundered through the tunnel after every victory as the players shuffled up the ramp to the locker room, their cleats clicking like tap shoes on the cement.

"WHOSE HOUSE? DAWGS' HOUSE! WHOSE HOUSE? DAWGS' HOUSE!"

On this night, at least, the Dawgs' House still felt like home to Beno Bryant. Making one of his last appearances of the season, he pushed the Washington advantage to 9-0 in the second quarter with a touchdown dive over the left side of the line from a yard out. He took the handoff from Mark Brunell, who played just two series, completing each of his three pass attempts. Hobert, temporarily sidelined in the second quarter with a pinched nerve in his neck, threw for 155 yards and a touchdown on 10-of-19 passing.

Eric Bjornson, the backup quarterback-turned-receiver, shed his secret-weapon status. He caught three balls for a game-high 72 yards, making one reception that covered 31 yards and another for 25. He had a deceptive way about him that made him an unlikely football hero. Long legs made his running style look loping. He had a casual way of talking and hair long enough in back that he could pull a strand around his cheek and touch it to his mouth. Before the game, James approached the angular flanker and asked, "It's BeYORNson, right?" No more Bornson. Not on this night.

"I knew right then," Bjornson recalled, "that it was going to be a great night."

Forgetting this night would be tough for Walter Bailey, too. He set up a Washington scoring drive with less than two minutes left in the first half, picking off a pass intended for split end Trumane Bell and stepping out of bounds at the Cornhusker 47. Hobert found Matt Jones for an 8-yard completion, and after a Nebraska penalty, hit Joe Kralik with a 29-yard touchdown strike. The first option on the play was receiver Jason Shelley, but Hobert gambled on hitting Kralik over the top. Jackpot.

Extending from toes to fingertips, Kralik leaped out of the end zone to make the grab. Or *almost* make it. A touchdown was signaled, yet judging by the video replay in the press box, the ball appeared to bounce and Kralik appeared to be out of bounds when it touched his hands. Ken Wilhite, defending on the play, saw it from point-blank range. "As far as I'm concerned, it was clear the ball was not in," he said. "The ball was on the ground, and if it wasn't, he was out of bounds." The back judge shot his hands up almost instantaneously to signal a touchdown. Wilhite, stunned, complained bitterly for several seconds.

James said he couldn't see the play from his vantage point. And after the game, when Kralik was asked if he thought the catch was good, he gave no definite answer. "I'm pretty sure my knee was down (in bounds)," he said. "I don't know when the ball came out. I have to see the TV replay."

Of course, the directional TV microphones didn't pick up the exchange between Kralik and Bjornson when the close friends passed on the field. Kralik, bounding toward the sidelines, met up with Bjornson, coming on to hold for the extra-point attempt.

"What happened, dude?" said Bjornson, who, like James, couldn't see the play.

"I don't know," Kralik blurted, "but I didn't catch that motherfucker!"

Upon further review, the Pac-10 agreed. Verle Sorgen, supervisor of the league officials, said after watching the game videotape that he would not have allowed Kralik's touchdown catch. "I talked to the back judge (Dave Cutaia) and what he saw—and he was closer than we were—was that there was firm possession of the ball," he said. "I don't agree." On Monday morning, Sorgen got two telephone calls from irate Cornhuskers fans, who demanded to know how the Pac-10 could explain this miscarriage of justice.

Another call that went Washington's direction incensed Nebraska fans, too. The play in question—a fumble recovery by UW linebacker James Clifford on the first series of the second quarter. Grant, sacked for a 6-yard loss by Andy Mason, coughed up the ball at the Cornhusker 39. Clifford pounced on the fumble, although the play appeared to be over. Mason, in fact, was too preoccupied with arching back like a drum major and shooting off his invisible six-guns to notice the pigskin on the turf. "I had no clue the ball was on the ground," Mason confided. "All of a sudden I see Clifford pick it up and take off running. I wasn't thinking, 'Uh oh!' I was thinking, 'Man, that was my shot!' I could have taken off running, then the whistle blew and I thought, 'Boy, I've got to pay a little closer attention.'" Officials ruled the play a turnover, and Washington scored on a short drive.

Tacoma Morning News Tribune columnist John McGrath, noting that Kralik's touchdown catch wasn't a catch and Grant's fumble wasn't a fumble, wrote, "To say the Huskies enjoyed the consequence of every doubtful call Saturday night would be like saying that spectators get more fired up for nationally televised football games than they do for public utility-rate hearings."

After watching video from the game, Don James conceded, "Most of the questionable calls, the tough calls, went in our favor," and of Kralik's touchdown he added, "Normally, when the ball comes out that quick, you don't get the call."

Questionable calls or not, the Huskies won convincingly. The Husky special-teams units were razor sharp. Werdel averaged 45.1 yards on eight punts, and Travis Hanson made good on what James called "big, big threes," splitting the uprights with field goals of 42 and 32 yards.

The Huskies mashed Nebraska into cornmeal and did it on television sets from coast to coast. Mission accomplished. Now, there were skeptics to be silenced. Dan Raley, the *Seattle Post-Intelligencer* beat writer, predicted on a Seattle radio station earlier in the week that the Cornhuskers would win. If they didn't, Raley promised to run a mile for every point by which the Huskies won. The 29-14 final, therefore, meant 15 miles for Raley, no easy task for this former Western Washington University football player with next-to-no cartilage left in his knees. He would do his penance by running laps around nearby Greenlake.

Before heading up the tunnel after the clock expired, Hobert ran up to Raley, standing behind the west end zone.

"What size?" Hobert asked.

"Huh?"

"What size running shoes do you wear? I'm going to get you a pair."

"Hey," Raley quipped, patting his abdomen, "I need to work off this gut anyway."

The two chuckled. Hobert cultivated a special rapport with scribes. He knew what to say to get their pens moving.

Meanwhile, Cornhusker John Parrella and massive Husky Lincoln Kennedy walked off the field shoulder to shoulder. They talked and laughed as if they were reunited high school team-mates. They weren't, but they did get to know each other pretty well bashing heads that night. Kennedy peeled the purple "W" off his helmet and handed it to his new friend. That sticker would be taken back to Nebraska and adhered to Parrella's locker. A

Lincoln memorial, if you will. "When you play big games like this, you take souvenirs," explained Parrella, a senior defensive tackle. "I'll just put it on my locker and remember this as a loss—so it never happens again. They are a great team, obviously."

It is customary, immediately after games, for the Huskies to pile into the interview room, midway up the tunnel connecting the football field with Hec Edmundson Pavilion. The players get a few words from their coaches before heading up the tunnel to the locker room, off-limits to the media. James then answers questions from the media for about 10 minutes. Next, 10 to 15 players requested by the media are brought into the room for interviews.

The postgame press conference would usually begin the same way: James would take his place behind the podium on a stage and say, "Fire away." Dick Rockne, longtime beat writer from the *Seattle Times*, would ask the first question. A ritual seldom violated.

James beamed after this victory, a great win in front of a home crowd, and really, the whole country. Most of his teams make their greatest strides between the first and second games. This one grew between the second and third. Up next for Washington, a much-needed bye week, then a home game against USC. James could take a deep breath and enjoy this win. Coaches, after all, live for these moments.

James remembered the remarks made by Bob Devaney about Miami being far stronger than Washington. He gave the former Cornhusker coach a parting poke. "We're giving a game ball to Bob for the comments he made after the Orange Bowl last year," James said. "He basically said we're not in the same class as Miami. We've had that in our locker room ever since."

Six months later, when first informed of the dedication, Devaney erupted. "Don James is full of shit," he fumed. "You can tell him I said that, too. He's just got a big mouth. All I said was Miami is a better football team. If that's bad, if a person doesn't have the right to his opinion, that's a sad situation. That didn't mean Washington was bad."

12

Northern Underexposure

The TV exposure from the Nebraska game paid off. The Huskies had captured the attention of a national audience and climbed to No. 1 in the AP poll for the first time since 1984. They did so by edging Miami, which did a face plant at home against Arizona and barely escaped with an 8-7 win. Wrote Ed Sherman of the *Chicago Tribune,* "On this subject, however, there is no debate: Washington is the greatest team never seen east of the Mississippi."

But were the dividends from the attention what the Huskies needed? Was it good to be No. 1 at this point in the season? Being king of the hill is the ultimate goal of any college football team, but playing the national polls game can be a little like taking in a roller coaster at an amusement park—the ride doesn't last forever, and when it's over, there's a long line waiting to get on. The trick is to be at the front of that line when the ride ends on New Year's Day. But being the top-ranked team in football the first week of October is a weighty burden that can keep the light burning in a coach's office around the clock. As James put it: "We'll take it, but right now it doesn't mean much. It doesn't change anything."

Except the blood pressure of the players and coaching staff.

The Huskies had been No. 1 during the midseason before but were never able to cling to that tenuous position, always backsliding before the final polls were released. In 1982, the team went 6-0 and held the top ranking until a 10-3 win over Texas Tech was deemed far too feeble for the national front-runners, and Pittsburgh moved into the top spot. The following week, Washington lost to Stanford and plummeted in the polls.

More ominous, especially with USC coming to town, was Washington's short stay at the summit in 1984, when the Huskies won three games at No. 1 before being toppled by the Trojans, 16-7, in the next-to-last game of the regular season. History definitely wasn't on the Huskies' side. In the previous 19 seasons, 32 teams had been designated No. 1 in September by AP . . . and each of those 32 teams stumbled by the time the national champion was crowned. There were no gala celebrations planned when Washington moved into the top spot this time, no ticker-tape parades. Eight games remained on the schedule, and that No. 1 label hung like a target around the team's collective neck. As if there wasn't reason enough to put everything on the line to beat the snot out of the Huskies, here was one more.

Dennis Erickson sounded almost relieved when the mantle was lifted from his team. Miami could hover at No. 2, poised like a viper waiting to strike, and make its move for the title New Year's Day. Arizona made the Hurricanes look quite human, however, and would have won had Steve McLaughlin's 51-yard field-goal attempt not sailed wide by two feet on the final play of the game. The Wildcats didn't make it out of South Florida without a left-handed compliment from the frustrated Miami coach, whose team pushed its winning streak to 21 games. "If we play this way against Florida State," he said, "we won't get a first down."

It wasn't uncommon for teams to drop out of first place after lackluster wins. In the 55 years of the AP poll, a team had lost its No. 1 ranking 73 times without losing on the field. That statistic raised interesting questions about the dilemma facing coaches. They are scolded by their peers for running up the score against weaker opponents, yet punished by pollsters for not pounding those teams into the dirt. Folks who backed the Huskies didn't spend a lot of time musing over that thorny little paradox. Not until Washington dropped from the top spot later in the season would the fairness of the poll system be called into question. Now, the Huskies were No. 1 and, as far as their fans were concerned, all was right in the world of college football.

ABC decided to televise the USC game to most of the nation, announcing the choice after the Nebraska game. It was an enticing matchup. The game had become an accurate indicator of which school would represent the Pac-10 in the Rose Bowl. The winner of the past six USC-Washington games has advanced to the Rose Bowl. In the teams' 32 meetings since 1960, the Trojan-Husky winner has gone on to Pasadena 23 times (15 trips by USC, eight by Washington).

But to some Huskies, this game meant more than a Rose Bowl litmus test. Even for those who didn't set foot on the field, each game had special meaning. Each was a reminder of that simple certainty they once took for granted but now rejoiced: They were alive.

II

The metal rods that ran the length of Michael Steward's right arm and leg would be surgically removed after the 1992 football season. The nasty scars remained, as did the horrifying memories of an early morning a year earlier.

Steward, a reserve cornerback for the Huskies, will never know exactly why Rene Guzman-Velloso was driving the wrong way in the southbound fast lane of Interstate 5 near Medford, Oregon, on September 19, 1991. Police said Guzman-Velloso was intoxicated when he slammed almost head-on into a van carrying Steward, six UW teammates, and another Washington student. The police also concluded that Guzman-Velloso was trying to kill himself.

If so, he succeeded. He died at the scene.

"I feel a lot of anger toward him," Steward confessed, fingering the shiny brown scar on his arm. "From the time they told me it was a drunken driver, I couldn't believe it. I was saying to myself, 'If he wasn't dead, I wish I could kill him.' "

The accident might have killed one-third of the Huskies' prized 1991 recruiting class. Riding in the rented van were Steward, free safety Richard Washington, split end Leon Neal, split end Joel Rosborough, defensive end Doug Barnes, offensive tackle Eric Battle, cornerback Reggie Reser. All were from Los Angeles. Also in the van was Adrian Jamison, a friend of Neal's. Despite some severe injuries, each member of what the local media dubbed "The Medford Seven" returned to the team. All were reserves and spent most of the USC game on the sidelines, although Reser did start later in the season in place of Walter Bailey against Oregon State.

The memory of the accident remained hauntingly fresh a year later. The players—none of whom was on the Washington traveling squad as a true freshman—were taking advantage of a four-day break from football. School was not in session, and their teammates were in Nebraska, preparing for the game with the Cornhuskers. A whirlwind trip to Los Angeles sounded good to these homesick freshmen. If they drove all night, spelling one another behind the wheel, they might get to spend two whole days with their families and friends. So they rented the van and headed south.

The trip ended abruptly at 2:30 a.m. in tiny Talent, Oregon, when Guzman-Velloso veered out of the northbound fast lane, crossed the grass median, and plowed into the players' van. "There was a semi in front of us," recalled Rosborough, who was driving. "We just heard that semi honking. By the time we saw (Guzman-Velloso), it was too late. I tried to swerve into the grass, but it was too late."

A blinding flash of headlights. Then tumbling. So much tumbling. Like the world had snapped off its axis. "It seemed like we rolled forever," Battle remembered. "And when we stopped rolling, we slid. There was dirt and glass in our faces, our mouths."

When the crushed van finally settled on its side, all the passengers except Steward and Washington were able to climb out. Battle, wide as a door at 260 pounds, grabbed a seat belt and began to hoist himself out a broken window. In the confusion, he heard Steward.

"I could hear Mike say, 'Don't leave me!' That's when I turned back and saw the van was on fire," Battle said. "I told Mike to grab my pants in the back." Steward grabbed his shirt instead. It ripped like wet paper.

"I was trying to pull him out," Battle recalled, his voice reduced to a somber whisper, "and I could hear him screaming. We didn't know he had all those broken bones."

A state trooper extinguished the small fire. Steward, who broke the thighbone in his right leg and every bone in his right arm, was finally freed by the Jaws of Life, a hydraulic prying device. Recalled Steward, "When the ambulance driver picked me up, he said, 'Oh, my God!' When he said that, I knew it would be bad for me." Steward spent 2 1/2 months in a wheelchair. By spring practice, he could run but was the only player involved in the accident who didn't participate in contact drills.

Shortly after Washington was pulled from the van, he underwent emergency surgery. The crash left him with a broken pelvis, a cracked hip, a cracked jaw and internal bleeding. "It was the worst thing that ever happened to me," Washington said. Recuperation was painful. Doctors told him he might never walk again without a limp. Playing football again was a longshot. He spent the entire winter at home, where he and his family celebrated his graduations from wheelchair to walker, crutches to cane. "I *wanted* to get better," he said. "Maybe I was sick of everybody babying me. I wanted to play football again. I made a promise to myself that I would."

Husky coaches thought Washington had a spectacular spring. Leveled guys with his molar-rattling pops. Always around the ball. Made big plays. Washington wasn't so pleased. He felt good but complained he wasn't as strong as he once was. "As far as hitting," he said, "I can't come with it like I used to. But it's getting there. I'm gradually getting it back."

It began to come back to his teammates, too, as they tried to claw their way up a talent-rich depth chart. Still, the flashbacks lingered.

While he was regaining his strength to come back to school, Washington would watch a lot of TV. Once, he, his father, and his sister were watching "Rescue 911" at home. On the screen was a Volkswagen Rabbit, pulverized in a horrendous accident. Fire that followed the crash reduced the car to a warped, bubbling lump of metal and rubber.

"Dad," Washington asked, "do you smell that? I can."

III

Something about kicking the crap out of USC delighted the Huskies.

For the players, it reaffirmed the power shift in the Pac-10. For the fans, it was the physical embodiment of the popular Northwest tenet of California-bashing, a pursuit primarily directed at Los Angelenos who had sold their high-priced homes in the

Golden State and moved north to greener (and cheaper) pastures. Those Californians needed no prodding from the Washington Department of Licensing to change the tags on their cars. Newcomers sporting California plates got ample advice about where they should relocate next from Northwest motorists, many of whom were, of course, transplanted Californians.

But USC had changed. Once proud, the tradition of Trojan football was dimming as the floodlight of scrutiny intensified. The school that once hoarded Heisman Trophies and could dominate foes forewarned of their simple but elegant game plan of "Student Body Right" and "Student Body Left" was in turmoil. With their NFL defections, felony convictions, and the tumult surrounding Todd Marinovich, the Trojans were up to their ears in negative publicity. Said Allen Wallace, publisher of *SuperPrep* recruiting magazine and a 1974 USC alumnus, "Most people attribute SC's problems to the coaches, not the talent. Larry Smith is about as popular as (former L.A. police chief) Daryl Gates."

Two weeks before coming to Seattle, the Trojans snapped a seven-game winless streak by knocking off No. 13 Oklahoma, 20-10, on the road. It was an impressive win in which USC scored all its points in the fourth quarter and squashed the Sooners with a vice-grip defense. The Trojans, who had the same bye week as Washington, climbed to 22 in the AP poll.

The Trojan roster was speckled with world-class speed, certainly faster players than any the Huskies had faced. Some publications ranked the Trojan receiving corps as the best in the country. Split end Johnnie Morton was dangerous; so was flanker Travis Hannah. But the most exciting USC player was flanker Curtis Conway, an explosive punt returner and track man who could cover 100 meters in a scorching 10.28 seconds. He caught nine balls at Oklahoma and silenced the crowd in Norman with a 51-yard touchdown streak.

Conway and Beno Bryant were close friends, grew up near each other in South-Central L.A. and played on the same Pop Warner team. They still spent a lot of summer nights bowling together and constantly gave each other guff about their selection of schools.

Beno had a lot of friends on this USC team, a factor that might have caused him to ignore the screeching pain in his hamstring and declare himself ready to play. How could he sit out against the Trojans? Just stand there on the sidelines while the USC band blared that nauseating "Conquest" over and over and over? Take shit from his buddies all summer for wussing out on the big game? No, he was going to play.

It didn't make much difference. Bryant gained 38 yards on 10 carries and proved to be another feeble link in the Husky offense, which sputtered and coughed to 271 total yards, the second-lowest output of the season. It was a disappointing performance for an offense that, after the Nebraska game, seemed to have found its rhythm. "We've got to get this football team ready to play," James said, clearly frustrated.

This day belonged to the defense. Pahukoa stepped in front of a pass by USC quarterback Rob Johnson on the first play from scrimmage, returning it 31 yards to the 1. The crowd, already buzzing at fever pitch, erupted. He appeared to have scored—causing James to summon the kicking unit—but his dive landed inches short of the end zone. It was an ignominious beginning to a short day for Johnson, the rifle-armed younger brother of former UCLA and Michigan State quarterback Brett Johnson. A play later, Hobert connected with Matt Jones for a 1-yard touchdown pass, a somewhat unusual wrinkle in the Husky playbook. Jones, who didn't have a defender within 10 yards of him, caught the ball and celebrated by facing the fans at the closed end of the stadium, flinging his head back and shooting his arms up like a soap-box preacher delivering the Gospel.

The Trojans got the ball back and began to move it. A gain of 6 yards on a pitch to Estrus Crayton. A pass from Johnson to Conway covering 17. Crayton off tackle for 14, then 4. Johnson to Conway for 9 and . . . *boom* . . .. Tommie Smith punched the ball out of his hand. Hoffmann jumped on the fumble in the blink of a black eye. Washington took over and eight plays later, Hobert floated an 18-yard pass over the top to Kralik, who, pulling two defenders in his wake, tilted his head back and made a blind Willie Mays-style catch for a touchdown. With 5 minutes 20 seconds expired, the Husky offense had touched the ball nine times and put 14 points on the board.

GO! HUS-KIES! GO! HUS-KIES! GO! HUS-KIES! GO! HUS-KIES!

Problem was, only those at Husky Stadium saw the scoring flurry. Television coverage of the game didn't begin until two minutes remained in the first quarter. Ironically, coverage was delayed because of the length of the early game between No. 2 Miami and No. 3 Florida State, two teams Husky fans counted among the favorites of the East Coast Mafia. The switchboard at the local ABC affiliate was flooded with more than 200 angry calls. When James was told of the situation, he joked, "Maybe the nation will think we had two long marches."

But there would be no long scoring marches in this game. The Husky offense would account for just three more points in the final 58 minutes. Even those three points, which came in the third quarter on a 40-yard field goal by Travis Hanson, were generated by the defense. Mason sacked Reggie Perry on third down, forcing a fumble that was recovered by Fields. The Huskies posted a 17-10 victory but were less than overjoyed with the offensive production. As James put it, "It was Washington stopping Washington a lot."

The Trojan offense accounted for 332 yards, all but 89 of which were gained by air. A big chunk of that offense came on a defensive gaffe late in the second quarter. Perry sidestepped a charging Clifford and floated a high pass toward the middle of the field, where Pahukoa waited for his second interception like a center fielder positioning himself to catch a pop fly. He mistimed his jump and leaped at the 10, tipping the ball into the hands of Conway, who cradled it 5 yards into the end zone. It was USC's longest scoring play in two years and the Trojans' first touchdown against Washington in three games.

Perry replaced Johnson at quarterback after the starter was apparently knocked out on a first-down play in the second quarter when he was sandwiched by Fountaine, Clifford, and Fields. The Trojans were in a spread formation on the play, so there were too few blockers to clog the rushing lanes. Johnson was pummeled, but whether he was knocked unconscious was questionable. Some Huskies on the field said that when he was lying on the ground, after the body slam that sent him to the sidelines, they heard him say in frustration, "Oh, I don't need this!"

"He's not hurt," one Husky on the field announced, "he's just pissed off."

Another war was being waged between Fields and fullback Wes Bender, who made the mistake of drilling the hardest-hitting Husky after a third-quarter play was whistled dead. He was flagged for a personal foul, but Fields, who felt Bender levied a cheap shot on him earlier in the game, was still fuming. "I was hoping they were going to call a toss sweep my way," Fields said. "I was going to try and get him." Perhaps the best revenge had already come. Fields wrestled a fumble from Bender earlier in the third period, setting up Hanson's field goal.

In the interview room, Clifford wore the smile of a satisfied man as he spoke to a small group of reporters. "Frenzy," he said, as if listening to the sound of the word. "It would be nice if people said our defense ran to the ball in a frenzy. I think it would be a compliment. I'd like it to be called that." He and his teammates were certainly impressive, sacking a trio of USC quarterbacks six times for minus-57 yards. The Trojans were tackled for losses 12 times and turned the ball over five times.

Battered body or simply a bruised ego, there was no question Johnson took a throttling from a ferocious defense. "I'n a little droggy right now," he mumbled before getting on the bus, his words slurred through his torn and swollen lips. "I got a concuthion. I cut my lit 'retty 'ad with ny teeth. . . . I got hit 'y two or three guys, I don't know. I 'lacked out for a second."

Perry, usually more effective with his legs than his arm, entered for Johnson, then was replaced in the fourth quarter by Kyle Wachholtz, a 6-foot-5 redshirt freshman, when the Trojans had little time to operate and needed a pocket passer. With his team trailing by a touchdown, 17-10, Wachholtz entered and took the first live snap of his college career. He dropped back and hit Conway for a gain of 25 yards. A few plays later, he completed another pass to Conway. Soon, the Trojan offense was within 28 yards of the end zone and a touchdown and two-point conversion from toppling the nation's No. 1 team.

But Walter Bailey wouldn't let that happen. On first down, Wachholtz fired a pass into double coverage, seeking Travis Hannah. Bailey had been burned by Hannah for a 52-yard reception earlier in the game, but he wasn't going to be fooled again. "He was definitely not going to catch that ball," Bailey said later. "I knew I could make that play. When I saw that ball, I said he was *definitely* not going to catch it." Not now. Not over Sweet B. Instincts took over and Bailey stepped in front of the pass, snatching it out of the sky. Washington's 18th consecutive victory, along with the heart of every Husky football fan, was in his hands. All the unfulfilled expectations, the pointed questions from reporters, the costly coverage gambles washed away. Bailey was the hero at last. Just like old times. And he did it "Sweet B" style, too, calmly singing a tune in the huddle before he made the play.

The glee almost ended in a flash. Bailey made a blunder that might have given the Trojans two points and the ball back had an official spotted it. Instead of downing the ball in the end zone, he picked it off, celebrated with it for a moment, and tossed it to a referee. It appeared to be a safety. "I blacked out," Bailey confessed later with refreshing candor. "That was a safety, but I don't care. I was so happy to get us off the field."

The Washington offense, it seemed, had blackout spells for most of the game. The Huskies gained just 92 yards on the ground, 179 by air, and were penalized six times for 52 yards. It was the Huskies' worst rushing performance in 33 games, just eclipsing a 68-yard debacle against Cal in 1989. Also, it was the first time in 16 games an opponent had outgained the Huskies in total yards, with USC leading, 332-271. "We'd get in a rhythm, then we'd get out of it real quick," said Kralik, one of the few offensive standouts. He caught four balls for 42 yards and a touchdown and had a third-down catch that covered 32 yards negated by a holding penalty. The fruits of victory belonged to the defense. "The defense has got to feel great," Kralik said. "Offense? I don't know what to say."

Across the room, Lincoln Kennedy spouted off about the officiating. He found himself, he said, looking over his shoulder after every play, sure that the flag-happy refs had nailed him again. By his count, he was responsible for four holding calls. His normally jovial face, described by one teammate as that of an overstuffed Gary Coleman, was terse and frowning. "The refs really played a crucial role with me because they took me out of my game," he complained. "I have never been that frustrated on a football field. . . . On a frustration level of 1 to 10, I was a 13. I'd walk up to one of the referees and ask them what was going on and they'd turn and walk away." One flag in the fourth quarter was particularly deflating. The Huskies were trying to increase their 17-10 advantage and looked as though they might do so, picking up a first down at the USC 30. Then, a 7-yard run by

Kaufman was negated by a personal foul on Kennedy, whose hands slipped up the jersey and under the facemask of the player he was blocking. The call was unfair, Kennedy said. "I don't know what I'm doing wrong out there," he groaned. "I've been doing the same thing since I was a redshirt freshman. And now they're telling me I'm holding. Something's going on."

The Pac-10 didn't take kindly to the remarks. Calls are a subjective thing, and refs should have the final say. "Mr. Kennedy's remarks about the officiating were inappropriate and unfortunate," Pac-10 commissioner Tom Hansen said. "We will not permit such criticism of officials to be made to the media." James watched the films, admonished Kennedy, and said one call was deserved, another wasn't, and a third—which Kennedy claimed was his—was actually called on Matt Jones. The coach agreed with the Pac-10's stance. "Lincoln shouldn't complain to any of you people in the press," he said. "I haven't got that right, and he hasn't, either. . . . The thing that Lincoln has to remember is that when you're offensive Pac-10 Player of the Year, you've got a reputation. And anybody as big as him is going to stand out. So what happens when defensive guys get crushed? They're not going to say, 'That guy's really good and he blocked the hell out of me.' They're going to go to the umpire and say, 'That guy's holding me.' Lincoln has just got to realize that and play and not worry about it."

James was criticized by some in the media for censoring his players. A university should be, after all, a bastion for free speech. Students should be encouraged to question authority. Wrote *Seattle Times* columnist Steve Kelley: "Apparently, the Pac-10 believes a 6-foot-7, 325-pound tackle is to be seen and not heard. If he disagrees with an official, he must suffer in silence. If he believes he is wrongfully accused, he has no due process. And that is wrong. Very wrong. This is a free-speech issue, not a discipline problem."

13

I'm Not Running Things Anymore

Billy Joe Hobert chose his words carefully, or at least softened his typical sledgehammer approach to sensitive topics. He didn't like sharing the quarterback job with Mark Brunell. Nothing against Brunell, Hobert just didn't like dividing time, getting pulled for a series or two in the second quarter and knowing that coaches would evaluate the hotter hand at halftime.

Could he be replaced? The thought was upsetting and Hobert wanted to talk about it. He sat eating lunch with a handful of beat writers in the Tyee Center, which overlooks the football field, and spoke between bites of an overstuffed roast beef sandwich. "Last year," he said, "I had the team. It was my offense. Now we're splitting it up. It's not my (winning) streak. It's not really my offense. I'm not running things anymore." The notion pained him. He wanted to be back in control. Especially this week. Especially against Cal. Especially against Keith Gilbertson.

The Huskies had dominated Cal ever since the guys who would play in this game planned their Saturdays around cartoons. Washington had won the past 11 games against the Golden Bears, the Dawgs' longest winning streak against any Pac-10 opponent. During that streak, Cal went through four head coaches and was outscored by an average of 37-18 against the Huskies.

Hobert and Gilbertson had a special relationship that developed during the national championship season when the upstart sophomore was making the offensive coordinator's complex instructions come to life. The two shared more of a friendship than a typical coach-player bond. Both were straight shooters, and both had a rough edge. Wild hairs in a carefully groomed coif. Then, one day, Gilbertson was gone. He accepted the head coaching job at Cal and left without saying goodbye. Packed up his office in the middle of night to avoid any emotional farewells. Hobert didn't hear about it until he was approached on the golf course a few days later. "Someone came up to me and said, 'What do you think about Gilby taking the Cal job?'" Hobert recalled. "I said, 'He's not going to California.' I couldn't believe it." Hobert later penned his old pal a note, writing, "To win is something to die for. . . ."

Now, winning wasn't Hobert's only concern. He wanted to win on his terms, to win with the ball in his hands. "It's hard to prepare when you play for a while and come out, then go in later and read a different defense than the first time you were out there," he said. "Anybody who's seen me play knows I'm a streaky passer. I haven't had a chance to get in a streak yet. There's no continuity.

"I feel kind of lost. It's frustrating. I haven't had a chance to get on a roll. I'm not even in the same class I was in last year." More than that, Hobert said, gears were grinding all over the offense. "I personally don't feel like we're defending the No. 1 ranking," he said. "I think we're just trying to save our own butts. There were a lot of times out there when USC could have easily won that game. Luckily, the defense was good enough to take advantage of every mistake they made. But the offense wasn't. And if the offense continues to play like this, we're not going to be No. 1 at the end of the year."

It was a significant outcry in an atmosphere where talk of a quarterback controversy was treated like a three-alarm fire bell. Whenever reporters asked about any friction between the signal callers, James answered by saying any other coach would relish the dilemma of finding time for two Rose Bowl MVPs. Hobert had never lost as a starter, a stretch of 16 games. Brunell had lost just twice in 12 starts. Both boasted strong numbers, with Hobert completing 57 percent of his pass attempts (61 of 107) and Brunell completing 61 percent (23 of 38). Brunell's passing skills had sharpened since his knee injury, and Hobert had shown that he could break off a big run as he did in his 60-yard rumble down a seam in the Wisconsin secondary. "They're both great players," Gilbertson told a group of writers from his office in Berkeley. "They both deserve to play. They're both great for the Husky offense.... I'm probably scaring the hell out of the defensive staff here."

Gibertson didn't need to study miles of films for this game. He had a vivid Husky highlight loop in his mind, along with three years' worth of playbooks he committed to memory during his stint with the UW program. He knew this offense as well as anyone. Washington players complained that USC seemed to have an inside line on the Husky audible system and were able to make defensive adjustments with uncanny accuracy. Gilbertson's team would be worse. "If we do what we did against USC against Gilby," Hobert predicted, "he'll take advantage of it and eat us alive."

When Gilbertson was coaching in Seattle, there was constant speculation that he was the heir apparent to James. That, Gilbertson said, put a strain on his relationship with the rest of the coaching staff, bothered him, and bothered his wife. "There are some people who think they are in line to be the next head coach at Washington," Gilbertson said. "Any time you mention somebody else, it's derisive. I didn't want (James) thinking I was there to get his job. How could anybody enjoy that relationship? That's Don's program. He's the head coach, and he's the guy that created the environment for me to do that."

There were differences of opinion on how much of the Washington offense was developed by Gilbertson. Production had definitely fallen. The Huskies were averaging 26 points and 380 yards of offense per game, compared to 41.9 and 471 a year earlier. According to Jeff Woodruff, Gilbertson's replacement at offensive coordinator, his predecessor was responsible for about 20 percent of the Husky offensive playbook. The rest, Woodruff said, belonged to James as far back as he was coaching at Kent State. And when Woodruff took over the offense six months earlier, the team changed its snap counts, checkoffs, and entire audible system. Whether that would be a code too difficult to decipher, Hobert wasn't so sure. "It's a little bit scary because he does know our offense," he said of Gilbertson. "He invented it."

More than merely knowing the X's and O's, Gilbertson knew the tendencies of his former players. He once gave Hobert an earful over the headset for looking for Kralik, his favorite target in high school, too frequently on pass plays. "I don't care if you guys were in Boy Scouts together!" he screamed. "Start looking for some other receivers!"

Even though he was in Berkeley, Gilbertson kept close tabs on how his former team was faring. Cal had a bye the week Nebraska came to Seattle, and Gilbertson watched his old team from his living room, hooting and hollering with every big play by Washington. Husky football was still in his blood. "Some of my closest friends are on the Washington staff," he explained. "I've known Jim Lambright for about 75 years." A native of Snohomish, Gilbertson had family in the area. He joked with reporters about the availability of game tickets and that he might have to stand out on Montlake Boulevard holding up two fingers. Washington players appreciated Gilbertson's folksy sense of humor and got along with him well. There were two new coaches in the Bay area: Bill Walsh, who Gilbertson referred to as "that big shadow down the peninsula," was beginning his second stint at Stanford. Husky players were confident their former offensive coordinator had every bit the savvy of the guy with all the Super Bowl rings. "All this hype has been made about this other coach in the Bay area," Ed Cunningham said, speaking about Walsh. "People better watch out for Cal. Let Gilby get recruiting and I think Cal will be the talk of the Bay area."

Things had changed at Cal since the change at the top. Players were more relaxed and generally felt closer to him than they did to former coach Bruce Snyder, more aloof and militant. The Bay area media, too, took a liking to the new coach, even ribbing him about his portly build. As *San Francisco Chronicle* reporter Jake Curtis put it, "Gilbertson has a coach's mind, a player's outlook, and a spectator's body." On this point Gilbertson was dead serious: Cal players needed to cut down on the smack-talking and cocky swaggers when they came to Seattle this time. Before their game at Washington in 1990, they arrived wearing tiny rose stickers on their lapels and got into a war of words with the Huskies in the locker room tunnel during halftime. The Golden Bears, spanked 46-7, stashed those stickers deep in their gym bags after the game. A valuable lesson was learned. "This year we're going to be a lot more humble about ourselves," defensive end Scott Roseman vowed. "We've gone in there before with too much attitude, I believe." Said receiver Sean Dawkins, "We're going to be as focused as possible and keep our mouths shut."

Part of that attitude was because of feisty quarterback Mike Pawlawski, longer on grit than natural ability. Like Hobert, he was All-Pac-10 with a quote. But Pawlawski used up his eligibility in 1991 and the torch was passed to sophomore Dave Barr, a better passer with a blander demeanor that adhered more closely to Snyder's party line.

This Cal team, ranked 24th in the AP poll, was disciplined and featured a well-balanced offensive attack. The Bears were 3-1 with wins over San Jose State, Kansas, and Oregon State. A 41-14 loss at Purdue in the season's second game seemed an anomaly as distant as it was disappointing. A win over Washington would be a sizable step toward Pasadena for Cal, which had not played in the Rose Bowl since the 1958 season. And an offensive guru like Gilbertson could deliver the knockout punch to the Huskies, who had won four games but in each showed a vulnerability to big plays. The Dawg defense had allowed Arizona State and Nebraska touchdown runs of 80 and 73 yards, receptions of 53 and 52 yards by USC, and a 44-yard pass play by Wisconsin. The Washington offense had been inconsistent, at best, explaining why the loudest cheers were reserved for a defense that had 11 takeaways resulting in 37 points.

In 1991, Cal was unable to shut down Barry and Bryant, who gained 143 and 99 yards on the ground. But both players would watch this game in street clothes because of injuries. Kaufman, who started the season as the best third-string player in the country, was promoted to starter status. Gilbertson was left to describe to his ranks what Kaufman might look like. On film, Kaufman sometimes looked spectacular and sometimes looked more like a spectacle. He had a tendency to fumble, and some of his decisions against USC were suspect. He had a tendency to try to reverse his field when he got in trouble, something that compounded his problems at times. James was patient about his progress. "You don't want to take away a guy's creativity," the coach explained. "It's like an artist trying to paint a picture. He usually gets in the hole pretty well." There was no question Kaufman brought the fans to their feet. Whether he gained or lost yardage, his darting moves were exciting. The Husky band picked up on Napoleon-mania and played a few bars of "La Marseilles" every time he broke away for a long gain.

Kaufman had something to prove in this game. He wanted to show he could face a bona fide Heisman Trophy candidate and go step for step. And then some.

II

Russell White had seen a real live Heisman Trophy before. How many times had he wrapped his hand around the little bronze man's waist and lugged the prize off that special shelf in his Uncle Charles's home? Too many to count. He studied the contours of it. Posed for pictures with it. Rubbed it as if it was some kind of magic lamp. Dreamed.

This year, if everything clicked for Russell, he would no longer have to pretend the statue belonged to him. In his sweetest dream, folks cleared a space in the Cal trophy case for the Heisman. *His* Heisman. That would do it. That would silence those critics who blasted away at Cal three years earlier for making White, who failed to pass the Scholastic Aptitude Test on three tries, the school's first Proposition 48 player. It would quiet those who complained he didn't have the heart to persevere. That he was only in it for himself.

One month into the 1992 football season and two tailbacks had emerged as the leading candidates for the Heisman: White and San Diego State sophomore Marshall Faulk. The better numbers belonged to Faulk, who was averaging 209 rushing yards a game, but White's totals were better than respectable at 523 yards and five touchdowns in 92 carries. Besides, White had a promotional tool Faulk would never have—the Washington Huskies. A spectacular afternoon in Seattle in a game televised to 37 percent of the country could be just the campaigning White would need to make him the man to beat. A bad game, and he could hang up those cleats. "I feel I haven't had too many big games," he told writers in Seattle. "But I guess it's all what you do on national TV, or regional TV. . . . I feel I have to do well (against Washington) or I'll be out of the race."

The Cal athletic department sent Heisman voters glossy post cards showing Russell posing in uniform, clutching a football spray-painted gold, a million-dollar smile on his face, and his foot resting on a Cal helmet. Next to him were the words "White Gold." No one could ever accuse him of being insecure. Even in high school, he spoke about his athletic prowess freely and wore a brown letter jacket embroidered with the words, "With the ball, I can do it all." When he arrived at Cal and couldn't play because of his Proposition 48 status, he entertained himself by schooling some weekend warriors in a flag football game. It was a ridiculous mismatch that quickly bored him.

"What's your name?" one exhausted defender wheezed.

"Lamar," White answered, giving his middle name, later explaining, "I just wanted to see if I still had the moves and touch to do it."

Anyone in Berkeley who didn't recognize White a year later was living in a bubble or an unshakable psychedelic haze. With help from tutors, he became a decent student, and his ascent to academic mediocrity was a cause celebre for Proposition 48 proponents. For one reason or another, White was constantly in the spotlight. The power of the press wasn't lost on him, and he knew the nuances of the media game.

In his second college game, he returned a kickoff against Miami 99 yards for a touchdown, providing a few seconds of highlight video in an otherwise dismal 52-24 Hurricane rout. The outcome didn't seem so lopsided if you listened to White, who told reporters, "Take away the scoreboard and we beat them up and down the field."

Now, two years later, braggadocio wouldn't work. Cal needed to beat Washington and, for White to stay in the Heisman race, merely scoring touchdowns on the Huskies wouldn't be enough. His two previous performances against Washington were markedly different. When he first faced the Huskies in Seattle two years earlier, he gained 121 yards on 19 carries, one of only three ball carriers to break the century mark against a Washington defense that yielded an average of 66.8 yards rushing, best in the nation. Despite White's performance, Cal lost, 46-7. When the Huskies came to Berkeley in 1991, White carried the ball 15 times but managed to grind out only 55 yards. This time, he needed more than yardage; he needed to sway Heisman voters with footage worthy of a highlight film. "When I'm on TV," he said, "I have to do something that maybe somebody hasn't seen, like a one-armed catch, or maybe I have to jump over somebody to get in (the end zone) or throw a pass or something like that to catch somebody's attention." He didn't sound like a braggart saying these things but more like an executive mulling over an advertising strategy.

Little did he know his designs on the Heisman would die in Seattle with Washington's 35-16 victory. The Huskies stuffed him time after time, holding him to 18 carries for 82 yards, most of which came on a 32-yard draw in the third quarter. He complained of a groin injury after the game, saying: "As I started playing, it started nagging more and more. As a renegade, I kept on going."

White helplessly watched from the sidelines as Kaufman wrestled away the mantle of the league's best back. He carried the ball 30 times for 208 yards and two touchdowns. He left his cleat marks on the Washington record books. It was the first time a Husky had broken the 200-yard mark since Greg Lewis gained 205 against Cal in 1990 and just the third time the feat had been accomplished by a Husky in the modern era. Never had Kaufman notched 30 carries before, not even as an All-America in Lompoc. By his own reckoning, the dazzling performance silenced skeptics who called the team's smallest ball carrier too fragile and too much of a fumbler. "I've been getting a lot of criticism about my durability," he snapped after the game. "I'm getting tired of everybody saying that. I'm getting sick of it." A cluster of reporters gathered around him after the game. They all needed a Kaufman quote or two for their game stories. He answered a few questions into a television camera, but when the klieg light snapped off, Kaufman stood and walked away. Interview over. Joked one of the reporters standing by with a blank notepad, "Hey, I thought *we* were supposed to end these things."

Said James of the scatback: "There's no question the little guy did a good job. He's got such a quick start. He gives you a spark. If he gets a little step on you, he can run away from you."

That's precisely what Kaufman did to Cal cornerback Ike Booth in the second quarter, when he burst off tackle and made a head fake that left Booth pirouetting the wrong direction and allowed Kaufman a free lane to the end zone for a 36-yard score. Booth tried to capture the brevity of it all with a snap of his fingers, explaining, "He was there and then, just like that, he wasn't there."

No one pulled off a disappearing act so conspicuous as Hobert's. The passing touch that normally allowed him to zip balls into double coverage and hit receivers in full stride vanished. Betrayed by his fingertips, he not only missed on tough passes but easy ones. The opening series were ungainly portents for him. On Washington's first possession, Hobert failed to connect with Bjornson, then Kaufman, and was sacked on third down. The next series, he missed Shelley and Kralik before another third-down sack and a fumble gave Cal the ball at its 42. He completed his first pass on the opening series of the second quarter, when he found Kralik for a 13-yard gain that set up Kaufman's long touchdown run. Brunell entered midway through the period and was noticeably sharper than Hobert, although both were harassed by Cal pass rushers. The teams headed for the locker rooms at halftime deadlocked at 7-7.

The second half began for Hobert the same dismal way the first ended. Four of his five passes in the opening series fell incomplete. The ball fluttered out of his hand in a way that seemed to crystallize his fragile confidence. Once the fair prince of this stadium, he was reduced to a rube. After missing Mark Bruener on third down with a high pass over the middle, Hobert threw a tantrum by jumping up and slamming his feet down as if trying to punch holes in the turf. The crowd of 73,504 didn't mask its discontent, booing him lustily. Had everyone forgotten that he had not lost in 16 games as a starter? That just 10 months earlier, he heroically led the Huskies to their first national championship in any sport? That he was only 21 years old? It was becoming abundantly clear that, to play quarterback for the Huskies, you needed a golden arm and elephant skin for a hide. The boos angered some Washington players, who felt the fans had gotten too comfortable with easy wins, spoiled by abundant success. "I think it's real bogus," Jamal Fountaine said. "Mark Brunell gave us a Rose Bowl. Billy gave us a Rose Bowl. Our fans are spoiled. You have to throw for 400 yards to satisfy them. Be a little patient with us. We're winning."

Hobert's abysmal numbers told why for the first time since he earned the starting job he refused to be interviewed after the game. Twelve passes attempted, three completed for 36 yards. Brunell's numbers weren't much better—four of 11 for 83—but he was more effective in moving the offense and was at the helm during a 21-point surge that took up little more than five minutes in the third period. "I felt really good about this game," he said. "We moved the ball really well in the second half."

On third-and-10 in the third quarter, Brunell found Kralik for a 36-yard gain to the Cal 16. Kralik had to sacrifice his body to make the spectacular over-the-shoulder catch, extending his frame parallel to the ground before belly-flopping to the turf. "He just laid out," James gushed later. "That was a great catch, a classic catch." Two plays later, Kaufman broke a 13-yard run, and Matt Jones bashed into the end zone from the 3, giving Washington a 14-7 advantage with 6 minutes, 32 seconds to play in the quarter.

The play that followed broke the back of the Bears, and it wasn't made by the Washington offense or defense but by the special-teams unit. Cal's Lindsey Chapman waited under the towering kickoff like a center fielder, muffed the catch in the end zone and was screened away from the ball by a block from Louis Jones. Husky Russell Hairston pounced on the ball for a touchdown. Chapman was despondent after the game, accepting a hefty chunk of blame for the loss. "I saw it all the way in," he said of the ball. "I just dropped it. I tried to pick it up, but at the same time I was seeing (the Huskies) running towards me. I don't know what happened. It just took a weird bounce. . . . I feel bad about it."

Cal trimmed the advantage to 21-10 with a 35-yard field goal by Doug Brien, but Washington answered by going 74 yards in four plays in a drive punctuated by Kaufman's 14-yard touchdown run. He crossed the goal line, casually dropped the ball and, before being mobbed by teammates, fired off his imaginary pistols into the crowd. Judging by their reaction, Washington fans loved the display. The referees weren't so kind in their review, tossing a yellow flag onto his stage. Fifteen yards for excessive celebration. That was Napoleon's second such offense of the season, and James gave him a tongue-lashing when he reached the sideline. Later, after looking at video of the game, James backed off. "We can't find anything on his celebration in the end zone," James said two days later. "We did see one of their players dance in the end zone and it wasn't called . . . Napoleon shot the six guns off, but he shot them in the stands, not at any of their players. That's not illegal. It's OK to kill the fans, but don't kill the players." Any kind of celebratory dancing really rankled James. Be proud if you score a touchdown, he told his player, then get your butt off the field. He even had a private meeting with the player who choreographed the Compton Quake and un-plugged it. "The main thing is you don't want to tell your players they can't be emotional," James explained. "They have a right to be emotional. I think the (Pac-10) wants to control it, but not so often that you can't show any emotion at all."

Holding off a ranked team wasn't enough to keep the Huskies atop both polls, and although they held the No. 1 spot in the AP poll, they dropped to No. 2 to Miami in the coaches' poll. The Hurricanes had to overcome a cushy Washington lead and did so by beating Penn State by three, a week after knocking off Florida State by three. Shifts at the top at this point in the season were of little consequence to the teams involved. "There will always be a comparison until one of us loses," Miami's Dennis Erickson said. "The players can't worry about this . . . There's nothing we can do but play well and win games. The rest is in the hands of others."

A drop in the polls was not the only change the Huskies would have to adjust to. There was a far more significant shift in the works for the coming game at Oregon.

It certainly couldn't be called a quarterback keeper.

14

Nothing Civil
About This War

Even though seven games remained in the season, Washington again was consumed with the battle for No. 1. Only this time, the issue wasn't which team was atop the polls but which Husky quarterback, Billy Joe Hobert or Mark Brunell, should run the No. 1 offense.

The announcement was made by Don James at the Monday-morning press conference after the Cal game: Hobert would be replaced by Brunell for the game at Oregon. The disclosure didn't come as a shock to anyone. Hobert had been unable to locate his passing touch, and Brunell consistently had engineered scoring drives. Neither was red-hot against Cal, and their combined completion totals (seven) tied the Huskies' worst passing performance in the past 52 games, and the worst passing-yardage total in 29 games (119 yards). Hobert's tirade on the field showed that he had not only lost control of the offense, as he complained the week before the Cal game, but his emotions as well. Immediately after the game, James was characteristically tight-lipped about his plans to pick a starter. "I'm going to play who I'm going to play," he said tersely. "I'm going to substitute who I'm going to substitute. I don't care what anyone thinks. I don't want to touch that right now."

James gave word of the change Monday morning, refusing to open the floor to questions on the issue. "Brunell will start and Hobert will come in in the second quarter," he said. "I'm not going to spend a whole lot of time talking about it." He knew these situations could be explosive, and he didn't want some type of schism forming in his squad. Things were going well, even though the Huskies couldn't seem to put together a complete offensive effort. They had shown they could move the ball well on the ground and in the air, but not both in the same game. Hobert took the demotion, at least outwardly, in stride. "Obviously I'm upset," he said. "But I'm not upset with the coaches and their decision. I'm upset with the way I've been playing. Quite honestly, I don't think I deserved to start this week." There was a twinge of disbelief in Hobert's voice, as if he was on the verge of snapping out of this nightmare. How could he have known he would never start another game in his college career? "I think it's good because since I've been here, I've never had to face adversity athletically," he continued. "In the long run, I think it's going to help me out. Quite honestly, I've never failed or been demoted in anything athletically. I've never had a problem. I've always been successful. Everybody needs this as a maturation thing."

The Husky coaches based their decision to shuffle the quarterbacks on four plays made by Brunell against Cal. The first two came in the second quarter: a 47-yard pass play to Jason Shelley nullified by a holding penalty, and a 14-yard completion to Shelley on a third-down rollout. The last two came in the third quarter: the 36-yard completion to Kralik and a scramble that netted 37 yards and showed that, while he might not have had all the lateral quickness he had before knee surgery, he had the forward burst. He could still leave defenders tackling air in his jet stream.

The benching of Billy Joe was reminiscent of the quarterback situation in 1984, when the Huskies were 8-0 and ranked No. 1 by AP, and Hugh Millen was replaced by Paul Sicuro. The Hobert-Brunell case was different, however, in that there was no rotation in 1984, and Millen did not take another live snap until he came off the bench in the Orange Bowl four games later.

The Oregon game, to be played in Eugene, would be Brunell's first start since the 1991 Rose Bowl, in which he was named the game's MVP. Eighteen months had passed since he suffered the knee injury in spring ball. "I'm excited to get a chance to start again," he said. "But I don't think there's any quarterback controversy here. I think it's just a case where we have good depth at a position. We have two guys who can play; now we have to keep winning games."

Oregon was determined to end that. There has always been an intense interstate rivalry between the Huskies and Ducks, one some call as heated as USC-UCLA or Stanford-Cal. Washington had won the past three matchups with the Ducks, each of which was played in Seattle, but lost the last two times it played at Oregon (1987 and '88). The game was a sellout each year, and Interstate 5 between Seattle and Eugene was clogged by a steady caravan of motor homes and cars packed with fans.

Oregon had not hosted the nation's top-ranked team since 1972, when USC came to Eugene. On that rainy afternoon, the Trojans and Ducks were deadlocked at 0-0 for the better part of three quarters before Anthony Davis split the Oregon defense at the seams, ripping off touchdown runs of 48 and 55 yards. The Duck offense, unable to budge, turned the ball over five times and was largely to blame for the 18-0 defeat.

Like the USC team that came two decades before, the Huskies had a burner of a tailback, Kaufman, and a propensity for forcing turnovers, prying three per game from opponents. The Washington defense was beginning to harden like cement and in five games had yet to allow a point in the fourth quarter. The 1991 Huskies posted a shutout in eight of 12 fourth quarters and began the season with a seven-game streak of blanking foes in the final period. The first team to break that string was Oregon, which set up a late score with a blocked punt.

This streak of shutouts was not inconsequential, particularly to Husky coaches, who, in their desire to avoid losing a game in the fourth quarter, constructed some stiff penalties even if the team is outscored in the period. Washington players usually run a mile on Mondays, five 106-yard dashes on Tuesdays, and 10 10-yard sprints on Wednesdays. If they lose in the fourth quarter, those conditioning drills are doubled. "We talk about winning in the fourth quarter, because it means you're in shape," Jim Lambright said. "There's a certain amount of toughness involved."

The Duck offense featured two able tailbacks, Ricky Whittle and Sean Burwell, and a young quarterback, Danny O'Neil, who was coming off a 32-10 loss to USC in which he was sacked 13 times. Brooks said at least half of those sacks were a result of O'Neil running out of the pocket and trying to scramble away from pass rushers. He had some success doing that against

Arizona State, but USC players were faster. Washington players were faster still.

To confuse and find gaps in the Oregon offensive line, the Husky defensive front would make frequent line calls and constantly be shifting and stunting. The Dawgs employed the strategy every game. "We move so much," one defensive lineman quipped, "that I don't even know what we're doing half the time."

Kaufman would start in the Husky backfield, with Barry and Bryant out of action with injuries. Things were looking grimmer for Beno, who didn't make the trip to Eugene and could barely practice with the searing pain in his hamstring. "This is the worst thing that's ever happened to me," he complained. "This is my senior year." Brooks, considered a defensive whiz, had a plan for stopping Napoleon, but it involved putting 15 guys on the field. The Ducks ranked 21st nationally against the run, allowing an average of 62.5 rushing yards in their past four games. But Kaufman was quicker than any back they had faced.

It was no coincidence that the Ducks' defensive resurgence came around the time senior free safety Eric Castle returned from his bout with mononucleosis. Oregon yielded 903 yards in the season's first two games, losing to Hawaii and Stanford. Then Castle returned, and the Ducks won three of their next four games, allowing a combined 1,058 yards. Castle, an All-Pac-10 pick, was the senior statesman in a backfield that included two sophomores, strong safety Chad Cota and cornerback Herman O'Berry, and redshirt freshman cornerback Alex Molden.

Oregon was 3-3 and was a 17-point underdog but had a legitimate chance to post an upset. Autzen Stadium could be a pretty unfriendly place to play. Even though Eugene had a reputation as a tie-dyed haven for peaceniks, Oregon football fans were as boisterous and frothing as any others. When he was being recruited as a running back out of Portland, Husky fullback Matt Jones traveled to Eugene to watch the Oregon-Washington game. His older brother, Mark, was a UW linebacker at the time, and his mother, decked out in purple, watched the game in a different section of the stadium. After the game, Matt found his mother sitting on a curb in tears. Her purse had been stolen. Ducks fans swore at her and showered her with popcorn. Matt promptly committed to Washington and vowed to avenge his mother. The Ducks would get his wrath.

Only one Husky, James Clifford, had been around long enough to have played at Autzen. Only he and Brunell, a redshirt freshman the last time the Dawgs played at Oregon, knew the unbridled mania of it all. Husky Stadium seats about 25,000 more people but is more wide open and airy. Autzen is cozier, louder. Ticket demand for this game was unprecedented. To accommodate an estimated record crowd, the school installed 2,800 bleacher seats around the stadium rim, even though the average Oregon crowd was down 10,000 from a year earlier. This game was even bigger than the "Civil War," Oregon's bitter natural rivalry with Oregon State, a showdown that had grown somewhat stale because of the futility of the OSU Beavers.

Eugene, normally a quaint college town, was a zoo for the Washington game. The movie "Animal House" was filmed here, and the shenanigans of some fans rivaled those of John Belushi. "I got hit with a few things coming on the field—they were dog bones, like dog chow," Clifford recalled of the 1988 game, which Washington lost, 17-14, in front of a state-record crowd of 45,978. "Then in the parking lot, I remember three or four big trucks with stuffed Husky dogs tied to their bumpers dragging them through the parking lot. . . . We couldn't believe they were that crazy."

A raucous crowd wasn't the only thing that made playing at Oregon tough. The Omniturf field, which consists of artificial grass stretched over a thick layer of sand, also can be a problem. Most players hate the surface. Every tackle or bounce of the ball kicks up a puff of sand. Grit in mouthpieces, noses, eyes. The spongy surface is slick like wet moss, too, and every so often a player loses his footing for reasons not apparent from the stands. Several schools, including Washington State and Missouri, also have that surface on their fields.

Lincoln Kennedy heard all this and came to one conclusion: "I don't want to go down there. If I had my choice, I'd play the Oregon schools up here and WSU over here. Why? Because they don't like us . . . I'm going to keep my helmet on."

II

"HEEEYYY!" one shirtless fan crowed. *"YOU GUYS AREN'T DAWGS, YOU'RE DOG SHIT!"*

Something skittered across the end zone as the Huskies were stretching and going through drills. Was it a rock? A crushed beer cup? No, a dog biscuit, a less-than-subtle reminder of what this cluster of bleacher bums thought of Husky mystique. Lineman Frank Garcia picked up the projectile and examined it, his face equal parts fascination and disgust. So this is what Clifford was talking about. This was a red-carpet reception, Autzen-style.

What most people would see as a dog biscuit, Jim Lambright saw as an opportunity for inspiration. He grabbed it from Garcia and called the linebackers into a tight huddle. "See this?" he asked, twisting his face into a scowl as he produced the evidence. "*This* is what these people think of you! This is how much they *respect* you!"

Almost by instinct, Dave Hoffmann snatched the biscuit and stuffed it in his mouth. Turning to the section from which it was launched, he slowly chewed, swallowed, and smiled. His teeth were speckled with the stomach-churning remnants. The rabid fans in the section fell momentarily silent, perhaps sickened, or maybe enlightened with the knowledge that there was a guy on the field crazier than they were, a guy who was prepared to do anything to win this football game. "It didn't taste that bad, dude," Hoffmann confided a few months after the episode. "I mean, I wouldn't go out and buy them to munch on, but . . ."

To his teammates, Hoffmann's display was merely more evidence that linebackers tended to be a few cards shy of a full deck. As Jamal Fountaine put it, "If you were butting heads for two hours every day, you'd be eating dog biscuits, too."

Hobert showed up at the game with a new haircut, a rough-shorn flattop that didn't quite represent the height of tonsorial artistry. It looked rather as if it was cut by a blindfolded monkey with a pack of matches. He laughed about it later. "I got sick of combing it, so I cut it off," he explained. "Everybody else's hair is shorter than mine." His life had taken a pretty sharp turn the past week. He wanted a new look. He had plenty of time to show off his new coif, too, because he had no need for his helmet for much of the game. This was Brunell's show now.

Predictably, the game started with iron-bar defense. Washington tried to move the ball first. Turner for no gain. Brunell for Kaufman, incomplete (Oregon offside penalty). Brunell rolled right, tackled for no gain. Over the middle for Bjornson, incomplete. Punt.

Up yours, Huskies.

Oregon took over at its 38 and jumped offside on first down. Draw to Burwell, no gain (Washington offside penalty). O'Neil to Ferry over the middle, gain of 6. Pitch to Burwell for a yard. Burwell off right tackle on third-and-3 met by Clifford. Dropped for no gain.

Up yours, Ducks.

Washington took over after an Oregon punt and was unable to budge. Three downs and out. The Ducks didn't have the luxury of punting on their next possession. Josh Moore picked off O'Neil's third-down pass, giving Washington the ball at the Husky 47. The Huskies could do nothing, and midway through the first quarter, Brunell was 0-for-5 in passing. So much for great beginnings.

Finally, with three minutes remaining in the opening period, things started to click for the Huskies. Brunell had found his mark, drilling receivers with pinpoint touch, and the offensive line started pushing open holes for ball carriers. Three times, the Dawgs converted on third-down situations. Yardage did not come in big chunks, but bits and pieces—precisely the type of drive that sends defensive coordinators into hair-pulling fits. The 13-play march ended when Brunell faked a handoff to Matt Jones, kept the ball, and knifed into the end zone from 14 yards out. A perfectly timed play by a seasoned quarterback.

Heated exchanges between Huskies and Ducks took place on the field as well as in the stands. Jamal Fountaine felt he was held on several occasions by Oregon tackle David Collinsworth. During a timeout, the Husky defensive lineman motioned to a referee and whispered, "Hey, that guy is holding me on *every* play. Can't you do something about that?" It was not the kind of thing Fountaine wanted to announce out loud. He'd look like a tattletale.

The ref nodded and, to the horror of Fountaine, walked directly to the Duck huddle and scolded the culprit: "No. 75, No. 47 says you're holding him. Cut that out."

Fountaine cringed. The Oregon line was suddenly transformed into an underfed maternity ward. "*WWWAAAA! WWWAAA!*" they teased, doing their best impersonation of crying babies. A few falsetto voices perked up: "He's *holding* me! He's *holding* me!"

Mason, meanwhile, jabbered back at the Ducks. He had the comedy routine going and he wasn't about to lose this war of words. These guys were amateurs. "My mouth was running the whoooole time," he recalled with a smile. "I had their whole bench mad. They wanted to fight us."

His ramblings made him sound like a deranged auctioneer and even had the Oregon players fighting among themselves.

"He's killing you!" one Oregon lineman said to another.

"Shuddup!"

"Yeah," Mason chirped in, "I'm *killing* you. Listen to your man!"

"Shuddup!"

As promised, Hobert entered for two series in the second quarter and seemed to have regained some of the touch so conspicuously absent a week earlier. On his second series, he moved the ball 44 yards, connecting on passes with Kaufman and Bjornson for first downs. But his drive ended at the Duck 21, when Kaufman was tackled for no gain on a fourth-down blast.

The Huskies' next scoring drive was directed by Brunell and set up by a blocked punt, which gave Washington the ball at the Duck 25. Louis Jones burst through the Oregon line to apply the block, the first of the season for Washington. A sophomore from Los Angeles, Jones was gaining a reputation as a gonzo game-breaker on special teams. He was the one who hit Cal kick returner Lindsey Chapman in the end zone a week earlier, causing a fumble recovered for a Husky touchdown. Special teams players, regarded as kamikaze pilots in pads, had their own rules. "We make it a competition amongst ourselves," Jones explained. "On kickoff it's like, 'I'll see you down there. Party in the end zone. Who's going to get the big hit?' On punt returns it's like, 'Who's going to hold their man up the longest? Who's going to get the blocked punt?'"

Jones, one of the strongest members of the secondary, was built like a steel beam and looked like a swashbuckler after the game in billowing silk shirt and shiny black bandana. He walked out of the visitors' locker room all but unnoticed by autograph hounds. A teammate grabbed him by the shoulders, turned him toward a group of reporters, and announced: "This is the guy you want to talk to! This is my boy!" Jones looked like a kid, a little embarrassed at the introduction but just interested enough in the attention to hesitate before boarding the bus. A reporter called him over. Jones smiled, and had reason to; he played a key role in this win.

The blocked punt, it seems, was not blind luck. The man assigned to blocking Jones wasn't doing a very good job of it. "The first time I went out there," Jones said, "I noticed the guy in front of me was opening up a hole away from me. We told the coaches what was happening. They called a 10-man rush and the guy did it again. I fit through there just fine. The up-back didn't pick me up and the kicker kicked the ball from about 8 yards. I was right there to block it."

Two plays later, after a loss of six on a pitch to Kaufman, Brunell scrambled left and lofted a pass to Jason Shelley for a 31-yard touchdown. The catch was worthy of a highlight film. Shelley, a true freshman, beat cornerback Devon Hosey to the left corner of the end zone, jumped to snag the ball and, as if he had magnets in the toes of his shoes, dragged both feet before falling out of bounds.

By that point, the crowd of 47,612—the largest to gather for a sporting event in state history—was downright meek, rendered a nonfactor by a string of disappointing setbacks. Before the half, many would file out of the stadium in disgust. The coup de grace for some of them was the final play of the half, a 38-yard field goal by Travis Hanson set up by a pass from Brunell to Kralik that covered 21 yards with 11 seconds to play. Washington headed for the locker room riding a 17-0 lead.

Oregon mounted a drive midway through the third quarter which, had it been fruitful, would have put the Ducks within striking range of victory. Keeping the drive alive was a roughing-the-passer call on third-and-13 that moved the ball to the Husky 38. Completions of 12 and 15 yards gave Oregon a first-and-goal at the 10. Two plays later, Moore quashed any hopes of a comeback by picking off a pass in the end zone, his second interception of the game. O'Neil had thrown 67 consecutive passes without an interception before Washington came to town.

Mobbed by reporters after the game, Moore answered questions with a soft voice and a broad smile. "This was my best game as a Husky," he said. "I was just trying to make something happen both times." He glanced at a microphone, then up at a TV camera. "Oh, this is for TV?" he asked, momentarily preoccupied with some hectic primping as he checked his reflection in the lens. "I thought this was radio. I didn't do my hair for TV."

The second pick allowed the Huskies to preserve their shut-out, and they pushed their advantage to 24-0 with a minute to play in the third quarter when Kaufman charged over the right side for a 2-yard score. The touchdown drive covered 80 yards in six plays and was highlighted by Kaufman's 18-yard draw and a Brunell-to-Kralik bomb that covered 50 yards.

Hanson booted the extra point for Washington, but his biggest contribution was made with his hands. He latched onto Burwell on a third-quarter kick return, making what was probably a touchdown-saving tackle. Burwell, hoping to pare the Huskies' 24-0 lead, returned the kickoff 43 yards before being dragged down by Hanson at the Duck 46. "I was thinking, 'Man, he's dragging me a long way,'" said Hanson, who was pulled at least 5 yards. It wasn't exactly a textbook tackle. "I started at his hips," he explained, "and after that didn't work, I went down to his ankles." The point being, he made the tackle. "That's why we practice it," James said. "Kickers have to practice tackling. (The Ducks) were the top kickoff return team in our league, and they've been good at that for years. We did a pretty good job on it. But one play, they popped it. They've got a pretty good wedge."

Folks in the stands didn't seem too impressed with the Ducks' overall effort. Frustration was evident among the Oregon faithful, many of whom had improved their seating. The once-packed bleachers were now peppered with spectators. At one point in the fourth quarter, the Duck defense was backed up deep in its own territory. "*C'MON, CASTLE!*" screamed one fan seated close to the field, his tone suggesting he was more irritated than supportive. The Oregon free safety heard the comment and glared at the loudmouth as if to say, "Why don't you get out here, buddy?"

Then, at last, something to cheer about. Oregon kicker Tommy Thompson drilled the longest field goal in Autzen Stadium history, a 56-yarder in the fourth quarter. The Herculean boot also ended Washington's fourth-quarter shutout streak. Thompson said the kick didn't feel good when it left his foot, and he didn't even want to look up, fearing he'd see it flutter down about 15 yards shy of the goal post. "I started walking off the field and I heard the crowd," he said. "I knew I had it then."

That score further fueled Hobert's disappointment. His numbers were forgettable—three of eight for 26 yards—and he failed to direct a scoring drive in the fourth quarter, although the

Huskies did allow the final 20 seconds on the clock to run out when they had a fourth down on the Duck 1. "The way I looked at it, we lost, 3-0," Hobert said after the 24-3 victory, shaking his head in disgust. Things would only get worse for him.

James would never quite forget this game, but he'd never quite remember it, either. One play in the first quarter, a sweep by Kaufman, got the coach's attention in a big way. It was a reminder of how fast things happen on the field, how powerful these players can be. James was standing on the sidelines when Kaufman came his way, Oregon linebacker David Massey on his heels. Husky lineman Frank Garcia delivered a legal hit to Massey, bumping him toward James.

Despite his efforts to sidestep the charging bodies, James couldn't get out of the path quick enough and was smacked off his feet. A replay of the collision was gruesome. Massey's helmet bashed into the right side of James's face. The 59-year-old coach was catapulted backward to the bench. James climbed to his feet, then sagged as his knees buckled, and was helped to the bench by the Husky medical staff. They huddled around the dazed coach, who sustained cuts on his forehead and wrist from the hit, which also broke his Rolex.

The wallop also scrambled his brain a bit. After about a few moments on the bench, James returned to the sidelines to continue coaching the game. He noticed something scary. "I was coherent talking to the coaches in the press box," he recalled. "But when I said I couldn't evaluate the quarterbacks, I was serious. I knew we had some long passes, but I really didn't know who was in there throwing the ball." Moreover, he didn't know who hit him. When he spoke to the media outside the visitors' locker room after the game, he had crimson welts that looked like strawberries on his cheek and forehead, a glassy-eyed look, and seemed disoriented. What happened? "It was a sweep by Beno," he said. Beno, a reporter pointed out, didn't play in the game and was, in fact, in Seattle nursing his hamstring. "By Beno," James repeated. "He was sweeping the end and I got hit by the pursuit." Reminded again that Beno wasn't in town, James said, "Oh, it was Napoleon Kaufman."

As it happened, the collision broke James's right cheekbone and he had to undergo corrective surgery nine days later. He maintained his dry sense of humor throughout the ordeal. "I'm going to be in red for a couple of days," he joked at the Monday-morning press conference, referring to the red jerseys given to injured players. "I tell you what, that tower doesn't get hit too much.

"It was a cheap shot," he joked. "I can't eat salads. A lot of yogurt this week."

Joked his wife, Carol, about her reaction in the stands to the blindside hit: "I was thinking, you can replace a husband at midseason easier than a linebacker."

15

Of Whitewashings
And Wake-up Calls

Like James, the Huskies had undergone an accidental face-lift. Their winning streak had reached 20 games at Oregon, and they were in the thick of things for a second consecutive national championship, but they were embroiled in a game of roster roulette. Injuries were rampant. Washington began the season with a passel of qualified ball carriers. Now, with Bryant, Barry, and Turner out, running back was one of the thinnest positions on the field. Lineman Pete Kaligas (knee) also was hurt, as was Bjornson (foot), Shelley (ankle), Kralik (elbow), Kennedy (viral infection), and Clifford (shoulder).

A home game against University of the Pacific offered a reprieve before the Pac-10 showdown with Stanford, a calm before the storm. Keeping the Huskies focused would be key. "Mature players don't take days off," James said. "If you don't get better today and tomorrow, then you won't be able to beat the best teams on your schedule when they come up. . . . I'm glad we don't have to get out and prepare for a big game. It seems like we've had big game, big game, big game."

Another Washington victory was a foregone conclusion; oddsmakers refused to attach a point spread to the contest for most of the week, finally settling on a margin of 47. But that's not to say the Tigers couldn't present problems with their run-and-shoot offense, the first Washington would face in 1992. Besides, as much as the Husky coaching staff and players denied it, there was the team's position in the national polls to consider. Should the Husky starters stay in an extra quarter and ensure the team beats the sizable spread, or should gamesmanship prevail and third-stringers be inserted once the outcome has been decided?

Washington had already fallen prey to the fickle vacillations of the voters. Miami moved into a first-place tie with the Huskies in the AP poll, the first such No. 1 tie in the 51-year history of the poll. When it was suggested that the UW might have held off the Hurricanes by punching the ball in against Oregon on that final drive, James said, "If I have to run up points on a friend (Rich Brooks) to get a couple of votes in the polls, I'm not going to do it."

In another season, Washington's 6-0 start would have placed it firmly in the driver's seat for a Rose Bowl berth. But this season was different. Five schools had a chance at the Pac-10 title. The Huskies were 4-0 in league play, followed by Washington State (3-0), Stanford (2-1), USC (2-1), and Arizona (2-1-1).

Provided they could keep their players healthy, the Pacific Tigers could benefit greatly from a trip to Seattle. They could use the game as a bargaining tool for recruits, gain exposure for a school of 3,600 students, and collect a relatively lucrative payoff. While a larger school might have the clout to negotiate for half the gate receipts from the game, or about $600,000, Pacific signed a pact that would guarantee it $220,000 minus $20,000 for expenses. The rest of the gate receipts belonged to Washington. It was still a big payday for the Tigers, who collected five times less ($40,000) for Big West Conference games. Pacific is the only private school in the Big West and, in 1992, tuition cost about $15,000, a prohibitive price tag that explains why the Tigers could offer just 67 football scholarships—25 fewer than Washington and 13 fewer than any other Big West team. That $200,000 would come in handy.

Although it had not posted a winning season in 14 years, Pacific boasted a rich football history. Eddie LeBaron was the quarterback at the Stockton, California, school back when the Tigers played in bowl games like the Raisin and Grape and Optimist. That was right around the end of the 14-year stint of Amos Alonzo Stagg, the third-winningest coach in college football history. Seattle Seahawks coach Tom Flores played at Pacific; so did New York Jets coach Bruce Coslet. Pros like Bob Lee, Dick Bass, Lionel Manuel, and Mike Merriweather also donned the orange and black.

The Tiger team was coached by Chuck Shelton, an amiable, folksy fellow who took over the program in January, 1992, after spending six seasons at Utah State. He had never coached against Don James and, at least when he spoke to the Seattle media, seemed a little overwhelmed with the prospect of playing the Huskies. "They're awesome," he gushed. "The most positive thing for us about this game is that we have an open date the following week to recover. . . . I know our kids will play their hearts out, and that's the way we have to approach it. I know that if you approach this game any other way, you may not get back home. You may have to visit the hospital."

He maintained his sense of humor about the matchup, and when asked if he knew who scheduled it, he said, "I think it was my in-laws."

Despite their 2-5 record, the Tigers had some weapons on offense, particularly the threesome of quarterback Troy Kopp, receiver Aaron Turner, and running back Ryan Benjamin, all touted to receive postseason awards. Kopp, a senior from Mission Viejo, California, was a preseason All-America who received Heisman votes after the school staged a quiet "Kopp Gun of Air Pacific" campaign in 1991. In the Pacific media guide, he was referred to as "unquestionably the most publicized athlete in Pacific sports history." But publicity doesn't cure a bad ankle, and that's what Kopp sustained early in the season in a game of "wally-ball," which is volleyball played in a racquetball court. Hearing about the ankle twist didn't exactly thrill Shelton, who had expected the same type of numbers Kopp posted last year when he led the NCAA in touchdown passes with 37, finished third in total offense, and fifth in passing efficiency. "I haven't said anything about wally-ball," Shelton moaned, "because I don't think I could talk about it and keep my composure at the same time."

By establishing himself as a Heisman candidate out of a small-time football program, Kopp might have surprised some people. But he was accustomed to beating the odds. He was homeless during his early teenage years and had to fight to stay enrolled in high school. When Troy was in eighth grade, his father lost his job and failed to find steady work. The Kopp family, which included three young boys, had to spend one summer camping out on a California state beach. Troy enrolled at Mission Viejo High and made the football team. Teammates put him up in their homes for short stints. Finally, the Kopps moved back to Wisconsin, where they were from. Troy stayed in Southern California. He spent most of his high school career living in his car and friends' homes, often showering at the school gym. He was a star quarterback, rewriting the school record book, and an outstanding catcher on the baseball team, who twice was drafted by the Montreal Expos organization.

In 1989, his first football season at Pacific, he made an immediate impact. He started eight games and played in all but one. He completed 57.3 percent of his passes, a Tigers record, and threw for 1,510 yards and 11 touchdowns in what was then a pro-set offense. The next year, he became the first player in NCAA history to throw for more than 3,000 yards while playing fewer than 10 games. Just a sophomore, he was voted the Tigers' offensive team captain and MVP. During his junior season, he threw for 3,767 yards and stirred Heisman murmurs.

Now, after the wally-ball fiasco, Kopp was relegated to backing up Dave Henigan, a fourth-year junior. A left-hander, Henigan enjoyed his best season in 1989 when he threw for 835 yards as a freshman, a year before being eclipsed by Kopp's shadow.

Benjamin, built like a cinder block at 5-foot-7, 185 pounds, was an explosive offensive talent, the first Pacific player to be named a first-team AP All-America. He was a second-team selection his senior year and came into the Washington game leading the nation in all-purpose yardage, averaging 222 a game. He had played in front of big crowds before, and although he was used to playing home games in front of 13,600 people, facing the crowd of more than 70,000 expected in Seattle didn't faze him.

"To me, it's a lot like playing at Tennessee," he said of the 1990 game in Knoxville, which the Vols won, 55-37. "We didn't win when we played there, but we did do some things well."

The third link in the Tigers' offensive triumvirate was Turner, a crafty wideout who led the nation as a junior in receiving yards per game (145.8) and was second in receptions per game (8.4). He caught 92 balls for 1,604 yards and 18 touchdowns in 1991. A week before coming to Washington, Turner broke the NCAA touchdown-reception record, held by Duke's Clarkston Hines, by catching his 39th in a win over New Mexico State. Turner's hands weren't sure in every game, however. He dropped several balls in 1992, including one against UNLV that might have clinched a victory. The Tigers fell, 21-17, when a second-down pass bounced off Turner's chest at the UNLV 5-yard line with less than two minutes to play. The Rebels made an interception on the next play to secure the win. That miscue wasn't enough to rattle the confidence Tigers coaches had in Turner. "He's so elusive," Shelton said. "He makes the big catch. He runs well after the catch. And he's so intelligent about our offense."

II

Washington received two wake-up calls on game day. Both late.

The first came from Bellevue's Greenwood Inn, across Lake Washington from Husky Stadium, where the Huskies were sequestered the night before the game. The second from Pacific, which was surprisingly stout, despite losing, 31-7.

Husky players were supposed to be awakened by the front desk early enough to make an 8:30 a.m. breakfast. Instead, ringing phones shook them out of the sack at 8:45. As the players trickled into the lobby, they were met by their coaches, who had been doing quite a bit of watch-checking and foot-tapping. James, meticulous about how he divvies his time, was furious. "They got the big man mad," Matt Jones recalled. "Believe me, that won't happen again. Someone will get fired first."

The second delay was far more vexing. Washington staggered through three quarters of the game before applying the knockout punch with two touchdown drives in the fourth quarter. What was supposed to be a rout turned out to be a reality check. "Give Pacific credit," James said. "A lot of people tried to pooh-pooh them. But their guys played well. They probably played better than we did." That was particularly evident in the first quarter, when the only thing louder than the grinding gears of the Husky offense was the boos pouring down from a blood-thirsty crowd. After eight minutes, Pacific had outgained Washington, 96 yards to 29, and might have held a 6-0 edge had field-goal attempts of 42 and 49 yards been on target.

Finally, with 41 seconds remaining in the quarter, Dave Hoffmann pounced on a Benjamin fumble at the UOP 12, setting up Kaufman's 8-yard touchdown run two plays later. Kaufman proved to be one of the few bright spots in the Washington offense, collecting 128 rushing yards on 20 carries and returning three punts for a total of 60 yards. Brunell, too, did damage on the ground, scoring on runs of 13 and 3 yards. The longer of Brunell's touchdown runs punctuated a 97-yard drive, the team's longest of the season, which came early in the final period.

The crowd of 70,618 was introduced to two players likely to be keys to Washington's offensive attack of the future—running back Eteka Huckaby and receiver Theron Hill, both forced into action because of the injury situation. Huckaby, a redshirt sophomore, racked up 43 yards on eight carries and scored his first college touchdown on a 2-yard run in the fourth quarter. He carried the ball just three times in the national championship season, taking handoffs on the last play of the Arizona, Toledo, and Washington State games. When he burst across the goal line against Pacific, he didn't even realize he was in the end zone until he saw the point-after unit take the field.

Hill, a true freshman, was given the option to preserve his redshirt status or step into the receiver lineup, worn wafer-thin by injuries. He decided to play and caught an 11-yard pass from Brunell on the Dawgs' final scoring drive. Because of all the new faces on offense, Washington employed a simplified, restricted version of its playbook. "There were a lot of formations we didn't run," Woodruff explained, "a lot of types of things that we think are going to be good down the road that we didn't want to show."

Hobert slipped deeper into the morass, looking brutal in two second-quarter series in which he completed two of four passes for 10 yards and tossed one ball straight into the waiting arms of Pacific cornerback Duane Thomas. Another Hobert pass was almost intercepted. "He threw a couple of bad balls, so we decided to go with someone else," James said of Hobert, who did not return after the debacle. "I don't know about his confidence. I'm sure it's a little bit hurt, but what he needs to do is go out and practice hard and try to come out of it."

Thomas left unimpressed by the entire Husky offense. When asked whether Washington should be ranked No. 1, his response was predictable. The grin grew to a smile. The smile swelled to a chuckle. The question was a no-brainer. "No," Thomas said, shaking his head. "I don't think they should. Not No. 1." He was not alone in his beliefs. None of his teammates seemed fazed by the Huskies after the uninspired win.

Tiger awe? Naw. "I don't know what's going to happen," Kopp said. "But they're not the No. 1 team. They have a great defense, but they can be moved against." Pacific proved that, gaining 315 yards. The Tigers also scored a touchdown in the fourth quarter, something no other team had done against the Huskies. That score came with 24 seconds to play when Kopp, who saw limited action, linked with Kale Wedemeyer on a fly pattern that covered 47 yards. A moral victory. "I'm sure y'all know this," Shelton said, "There might not be a better coach than Don James. They're so complete. He's been doing it for eight or 10 years, and it doesn't happen by accident. Scoring against that team meant a lot to me. It shows some heart and determination."

The consensus among Pacific players was, without the UW's attacking defense, the Dawgs were downright toothless. "Even though they were bigger than us, we played them man up," Thomas said. "If it wasn't for their defense, a lot of teams would be able to beat this team." Hardly the words of respect Husky players might have expected. Suddenly, moving up and down in the polls wasn't the primary concern. Moving up and down the field was.

Those offensive fireworks Husky fans anticipated were absent. A telling statistic: Brunell completed each of his first four pass attempts in the first quarter for a grand total of 17 yards. He entered the game averaging 7.4 yards per completion (an average of 7 yards or better is considered good), but managed an average of 4.8 in a 5-for-6 first-half outing. The Husky offense committed three turnovers on two fumbles and an interception. "We're struggling with some missed blocks, penalties and missed calls," James said.

Many felt Pacific would be a panacea for past UW ills, a chance to rest some players and fine-tune others. This, after all, was supposed to be a stomping. "Some people," Pacific's Darius Cunnigan said with a chuckle, "said we were going to lose by 60 or 80." Granted, the Tigers didn't always line up against the best players Washington had to offer. "We're a beat-up team right now," James conceded. "Most people, when they get to this time of the season, have a lot of injuries. We tried to hold a couple guys out."

Pacific's Turner, who caught eight balls for 124 yards, said he did see new faces on defense each series, "but the defensive backs that were covering me were the same the whole game."

Benjamin, who finished with 87 yards on 24 carries, admitted he was surprised the outcome wasn't more lopsided. "When you're on the bus, you're always optimistic, hoping for the best," he said. "But realistically, we knew a win wasn't going to happen. I think we shocked people a little bit."

Even though the Huskies put on something less than a top-notch performance, folks in Pasadena were anxious to host a Rose Bowl rematch. Third-ranked Michigan was aiming for the same goal. "Truthfully?" Wolverine cornerback Alfie Burch asked. "I think about Washington every day. I want revenge and a victory." Michigan free safety Corwin Brown agreed: "We're going to play championship ball and I hope they're out there. Our offense is better, and we want to be the showcase defense everyone is talking about."

Jack French, executive director of the Pasadena Tournament of Roses Association, also lobbied for a rematch. "I'm not embarrassed to say this," he said. "I want Michigan in the Rose Bowl. I want Washington in the Rose Bowl. I am rooting for them because we want the highest-ranked teams. So I keep my fingers crossed every week.

"Right now, they're looking at Alabama in the Sugar and Texas in the Cotton, with whomever is rated highest getting Miami. And that *certainly* isn't a championship game."

By season's end, that prediction would make French blanch.

16

Lambo Vs. The Silver Fox

Some called him a traitor. Some called him an idiot. Some called him just plain honest.

"Meet Dan Raley," Ivan Maisel began his college football column in the *Dallas Morning News*, "the bravest man in America . . ."

Raley, Husky beat writer for the *Post-Intelligencer*, did the unthinkable a day after watching Washington stagger and stumble to victory over Pacific: He changed his first-place vote in the AP poll from the Huskies to Miami. "I just walked away from that game thinking this is not the No. 1 team in the country," he explained. "It was a raggedy game." Three thousand miles away, the Hurricanes ran their record to 7-0 with a 43-23 whipping of Virginia Tech. Raley watched Top 25 highlights on ESPN Saturday night and the CNN coaches show Sunday morning before calling in his votes. "I put a lot of thought into those things," he said.

Maisel called Raley at home Sunday afternoon to inform him that his decision to change No. 1 teams represented the swing vote that knocked Washington out of a first-place tie. Two of the 62 AP voters switched from Washington to Miami, and a third changed his top vote to Washington. Raley never imagined the ramifications of voting his conscience. During the next few days, he was interviewed on 10 radio talk shows and turned down five more. *Sports Illustrated* ran a note on the choice, even ESPN aired a story on it. That television interview stirred the most controversy. Raley met with a reporter representing the cable sports network, Chris Fowler, in front of Husky Stadium.

"How do you want me to do this?" Raley asked, moments before the taping. "Should I be light hearted or serious?"

"It's your call," Fowler assured him.

"OK."

The klieg light popped on. Fowler turned to Raley.

"So how did you make the decision?"

"I flipped a coin," he said with a smile.

Bad choice. He should have stuck with serious. His voice mail at the newspaper recorded a handful of nasty messages the next day. Irate Husky fans wanted to know how he could be so flippant, how he could betray the team with a coin toss. This was serious business, after all. If he couldn't grasp the importance of it, they steamed, he should relinquish his voting privileges. Hand them to someone who gives a damn. An irony struck him: These people felt he was obliged to pick Washington because he covered the school, and yet these same people complained bitterly about the East Coast Mafia shunning the Huskies because of familiarity with the Hurricanes. If anything, Raley's decision to go against the grain reminded other voters they were not duty-bound to dole out courtesy votes to the teams they covered.

Quick to discount his interest in the polls, James was ambivalent about the change at the top. "I don't know that anyone deserves to be No. 1 more than us," he said. "But I don't know if we've done anything to show we're a whole lot better than anyone else. There's some pretty good teams out there. I know Texas A & M had a little bit of a struggle, but Alabama's really good. There's a lot more games to be played."

The volume of angry calls coming into the *P-I* newsroom prompted Raley to buy an answering machine to screen calls and get his home number unlisted.

His phone might have stopped ringing, but Raley hadn't heard the last of the lambasting.

II

For all his talents as a football coach, Bill Walsh was a pretty weak sandbagger.

During a Monday press conference October 26, five days before the Huskies squared off against Stanford, the Silver Fox tried his best to blur the Huskies' focus with a little old-fashioned ego stroking. The Cardinal was ranked 15th in the nation, but you might not know it to hear the Walsh talk. "I honestly think the Huskies can look at us, then look quickly past us, because they could just roll right on through this thing like they did last year," said the coach who returned to Stanford after winning three Super Bowls with the San Francisco 49ers.

Walsh coached at Stanford in 1977 and '78 before taking an NFL job, and was rehired by the school in spring 1992. He replaced Dennis Green, who became head coach of the Minnesota Vikings. Insiders say Walsh turned down more lucrative offers from NFL teams to sign a five-year pact with Stanford, which paid him $500,000-$700,000 a year. Before Walsh showed interest in the position, the top candidate was Willie Shaw, defensive coordinator under Green. Stanford snapped up the Silver Fox so quickly that the day before Walsh was hired, Shaw was told that *he* had a lock on the job.

Like the stucco buildings on the tree-lined Palo Alto campus, Walsh had a reputation for a simple elegance. Understated but classy. He urged his players to call him Bill, and his office door was always open. Stanford players described him as the loosest coach they had ever known. Cardinal practices, as was the case with the Walsh-coached 49ers, are sans pads except for one day a week. After his hiring, donations to Stanford football went up 7 percent and season tickets increased from 21,300 to 24,408, yet home attendance sank from 52,258 to 47,374.

Stanford, a game behind Washington and tied for second in the conference with WSU, was in the Rose Bowl race. But to hear Walsh, the Cardinal would be satisfied to squeeze into an alternative bowl. Pasadena? *Pishaw.* "Looking at it realistically," he said, "if we could win two of our last four games, we would be really excited." Walsh had coached this team to big victories. Earlier in the season, the Cardinal overcame a 16-0 deficit in South Bend, Ind., scoring 33 unanswered points to post a 33-16 victory over Notre Dame. That proved to be one of the most shocking games of the season. He wept after the win.

The Cardinal defense was top-ranked in the league, rated third nationally, and was one of the main reasons Stanford was 6-2 and ranked 15th. Opponents had gained a paltry average of 123.1 rushing yards and 76.2 by air. Washington coaches and players were well aware of Walsh's magic touch, particularly when it came to designing an offense. They knew of his ability to inspire, his knack for finding soft spots in a defense, and his ability to leave coordinators kicking stones and talking to themselves. He was, in short, a mastermind.

The Cardinal ran what Walsh liked to refer to as the most complex offensive package in the country, that's college or pro football. If his players could handle a Stanford biology class, he reasoned, they could decipher the hieroglyphics in their playbooks. He might have been correct. Comprehension and execution, however, are two different things. Stanford had an offensive line some felt was overrated and receivers with, at best, decent speed. So despite featuring one of the league's best passers, Steve Stenstrom, and best all-purpose backs, Glyn Milburn, the Cardinal offense was ranked seventh in the Pac-10, tallying 332 yards and 23 points a game. "We just can't get untracked," Walsh said. "We haven't scored like we hoped and haven't sustained the attack like we hoped . . . We're going to have to play letter-perfect football and be opportunistic in playing the Huskies."

Those complaints didn't ease the mind of Jim Lambright, the Huskies' defensive coordinator, who confided: "The fact that Bill Walsh and his offensive genius will be devising a game plan against what we've done defensively worries me to death. Bill has been so successful being able to outscheme people at all levels. It makes it for me a special challenge."

Bruised ego notwithstanding, the Huskies had recuperated since their previous game. Nine Washington starters missed all or a large part of the Pacific contest, but almost all would return to face Stanford.

Lambright took over head coaching duties Monday while James underwent surgery at Swedish Hospital to repair his broken cheekbone. The shift of power was appropriate because defense would be the theme this week. The Husky defense embodied the bend-don't-break philosophy—it had allowed 310 yards a game, more yards than six other Pac-10 teams, but yielded just 9.6 points a game, making it the second-best scoring defense in the country. Washington also boasted the best turnover ratio in the nation and had scored 58 points after 10 of the 20 turnovers it had generated. Meanwhile, the Husky offense had committed a mere eight turnovers, resulting in zero points for the opposition.

The architect of Washington's attacking scheme, Lambright was largely considered a defensive guru and the heir apparent to James. He had been an assistant at the UW for 24 years and was the lone holdover from the Jim Owens era. If anyone personified Husky football, it was Lambright, first as a player, then a coach. His players called him "Lambo," as in Rambo, and he had a clenched-jaw smile and Popeye forearms. His build was sturdy, just as it was in the mid-1960s when he played on the Husky defensive line.

Lambright couldn't confine his ideas to Washington football. Teams up and down the West Coast copied the scheme he helped develop. His attacking system, designed as an answer to the trendy spread offense, was adopted by school after school. The scheme was based on the principle that applying increased pressure to the quarterback would force him to make split-second, often errant decisions. As many as nine Washington players would position themselves on the line to get in his face.

For the Stanford game, Steve Hoffmann would start on the defensive line in place of Mike Lustyk, out with a sprained ankle. It marked the second time in James's 18 years at Washington that brothers have been starters on the same team and the first time that those brothers were on the same side of the ball. Shane and Jeff Pahukoa started two years earlier, but Shane was a safety and Jeff an offensive lineman.

This game was scheduled for Halloween, as was the Stanford-Washington showdown 11 years earlier, an event that shaped history not because of what happened on the field but off it. On October 31, 1981, Husky Stadium became the birthplace of The Wave. Robb Weller, a former Washington yell leader-turned-television personality, was on the sidelines for the homecoming contest, leading the student section in some cheers. He coaxed the students to create a ripple effect by raising and lowering their arms in succession. The wave first moved up and down the section, then from one side to the other. Soon, season-ticket holders joined in and the wave carried around the stadium. A fad was born.

Rich Myhre, a sportswriter from the *Everett Herald*, witnessed the phenomenon from field level. "I can still remember many of the Husky players on the sidelines being totally distracted from the game," he said, "laughing and pointing in disbelief." Washington won that game, 42-31.

This showdown was considered a major hurdle between the Huskies and their third trip to Pasadena. And it was a hurdle many thought Washington would not conquer. The offense was too sporadic, the defense too prone to big plays. "George G. Grid," a fictitious columnist at the *Bellevue Journal American*, predicted the Dawgs would be mauled. The column runs on fall Fridays and includes light hearted predictions for high school, college, and pro football. The Huskies didn't get the joke. They had their customary team meeting at their Bellevue hotel Friday night, and Brunell brought the Grid prediction. He read it to his teammates, then tore the paper in half. "He just ripped us," Brunell recalled. "The team was pissed. We were pissed off that a Bellevue paper—sure, you can write whatever you want—but if you're a local guy, you don't just rip the damn program. That was one of the reasons we were so fired up for the game . . . It fires me up when I read something that goes against what we're trying to work toward. I was just fed up."

The weather on game day was dreary, the sky a gun-metal gray. It was the type of weather the nationwide television audience and large contingent of out-of-town writers might have expected from Seattle. In all, seven AP voters sat in the press box, including representatives from ESPN, the *Washington Post, Boston Globe, Sports Illustrated, Dallas Morning News, New York Times, New York Daily News, Chicago Tribune, Associated Press,* and *Los Angeles Times.*

As far as Washington was concerned, that travel money was well spent. The Huskies reached the pinnacle of their season that afternoon, momentarily finding that apex where all good things converge and shortcomings wash away. They walloped Stanford, 41-7, and left the Cardinal with a pretty good idea of where the mantle of the country's best team should lie. "Washington is definitely the best team I've seen," Stanford strong safety John Lynch said. "I'm just a little confused about what happened out there today. Anytime you take a beating like we did, it's not fun."

No one took a harder beating than quarterback Steve Stenstrom, protected by his offensive line the way a gauze strip holds back a locomotive. Pummeled by hit after hit, Stenstrom finally reached his limit in the second quarter when Jamal Fountaine leveled him. Stenstrom was helped to his feet and left the game with a sprained wrist and a throbbing head. "I hit him in the middle of his chest," Fountaine recalled. "And he made a little noise and fell to the ground. He had his eyes closed." The thrashing was so severe that D'Marco Farr felt his killer instinct give way to pity.

"Man, that's sad," Farr said in the defensive huddle. "They gotta take that guy out of there."

"Screw that!" Clifford snapped. "I like the guy."

Little wonder. Stenstrom had been kind to the linebackers, absorbing shoulders like a crash dummy and tossing a ball over the middle that Clifford snagged and returned for a 42-yard touchdown. That interception was caused in part by Dave Hoffmann, who knifed through the middle into the Stanford backfield and swooped in on Stenstrom like a purple vulture. Clifford, meanwhile, stepped in front of Milburn to make the play. "I figured there was somebody right behind me when I caught the ball, so I thought I might get tackled," Clifford said. "There must have been some great blocking out there because I saw the end zone and, I think, I made one cut, ran as fast as I could, and made it."

While standing on the sideline, Clifford had a premonition that he would intercept a pass. It was more a nightmare than a dream. "I thought, 'Man, I'm gonna grab it and their guy's going to come up running behind me and punch the ball out, and they're going to recover it.' I honestly was thinking that before I went out." Then, the first part of his prediction came true. He made sure the fumble wouldn't come to fruition. "The whole time down, I was trying to squeeze the ball as hard as I could."

Fountaine played the game of his life, collecting eight tackles, three for losses, and recovering a fumble. Although the rangy defensive tackle was raised in the San Francisco Bay area, he was unfazed by Walsh's reputation as a mastermind. "He could have been Pop Warner," he said. "He could have been Einstein. But he was on the sideline. He didn't catch a pass, he didn't make a play for their defense. People have got to realize we've got a good coach, too."

The Stanford offense wasn't exactly a well-oiled machine. The Cardinal accounted for 42 yards on the ground and 210 by air, turned the ball over three times and converted on just five of 17 third-down situations. "I can't really say anything positive about this day," Walsh said. "Just that we can eat our box lunches, board our plane, and soon we'll be home safe and sound."

Assuming Washington didn't already eat Stanford's lunch. The Husky defense bullied its way to the quarterback down after down, collecting seven sacks and breaking up three passes. "Today was par for the course for our offensive line," Walsh said. "They had problems everywhere. They need to move more quickly."

Milburn, a darting slasher once considered a serious contender for the Heisman, was held to 39 yards on 10 carries, a total that becomes even less impressive by subtracting a 15-yard run. He netted 18 yards on three punt returns and 52 on two kickoffs.

His counterpart in purple, Napoleon Kaufman, was far more effective. He ran for 87 yards on 11 carries against the nation's No. 3 defense, popping runs of 29 and 11 yards to set up Washington's second touchdown. His was the strategic approach of a boxer. "You come at them and at them," he said, "waiting for them to break down inside. Then you throw a little option at them outside." Toss in the hard running of Jones and Turner, the dangerous feet of Brunell, and the pass-catching ability of Kralik and newcomer Jason Shelley, who caught five balls for 117 yards against the Cardinal, and the Huskies were tough to stop. "It was a dominant performance by our offense against a strong, strong defensive football team," James said. "We haven't been lighting it up offensively, but a lot of good things happened to us today."

One of those good things was the reemergence of Hobert, who became the eighth player in UW history to pass for more than 3,000 yards when he hit Shelley for a 15-yard gain in the second quarter. Hobert's shining moment came in the fourth quarter when he turned an option keeper into a 50-yard touchdown lumber, taking advantage of big blocks by P. A. Emerson and Shelley. "Am I gonna be a tailback next week?" Hobert asked with a smile. "I don't think so. If I lost about 30 pounds and had 4.4 speed, maybe I would. But I'll take it. It was a long run, and I needed oxygen after it, but it was worth it."

The Huskies were back, and now their attack was three-pronged: defense, special teams, and at last, offense. Hobert's run was a pleasant bonus. "No one around here has given up on

Bill Hobert," James assured. ". . . Billy's a team player. He works hard and he's helping Mark.

"Hey, we need Billy on this team. No one is writing him off at all."

III

Raley made his way down to the field with a group of reporters. They took the elevator from the press box to ground level, then walked down a long aisle between two sections of season-ticket holders to the floor of the stadium. As Raley walked down the cement steps, he was spotted by a woman who evidently recognized him from the ESPN interview. "There's Dan Raley!" she screeched, pointing an accusing finger. Another woman stood and did the same. Raley lowered his head and quickened his pace. More people stood. Some began to boo. Some chanted his name. "It just shocked me," Raley said. "It was mob mentality." The rain was coming down hard now. The outcome of the game had been decided, and now many of the fans sitting in the southwest corner of the stadium turned their attention to Raley. Some yelled his name while holding up a finger in a gesture that doesn't necessarily mean "We're No. 1."

The reaction of Washington players was more civilized but still confrontational. As he was standing in the tunnel waiting for the team to walk off the field, Raley was approached by a player shrouded by a purple raincoat. The player flashed open his cape—it was Kaufman—and said, "Who are you gonna vote for now?" More Huskies asked the same question. Lincoln Kennedy inked the letters "STP" on his wrist tape. The initials stood for "Something to Prove" but could just have easily stood for "Stomp the Press." He was indignant after the game and interested in letting Raley know just how much he and his teammates appreciated the No. 2 vote. A crowd gathered around the huge tackle as he spouted off. "For the hometown beat writer to do something like that, then turn around and brag about it and talk about it is ridiculous," he said. "I know that gave some of our players inspiration today. It was really a motivating factor . . . I know I won't be doing any more interviews with the guy.

"I hope this win was impressive enough to change some of the voters' minds about us. If we can get (the No. 1) vote back from Dan Raley, that would help."

The win did convince Raley to switch back. Other voters, too, were duly impressed. Miami, which built a 32-point lead against West Virginia before giving up two late touchdowns and winning, 35-23, was bumped out of the top spot in the polls by the Huskies. Washington took a 33 1/2 to 27 1/2 advantage in first-place votes. "I told the team Thursday (the national media) would be here," James said. "I thought that was impressive. I said: 'If you want to make an impact, here's your chance. You can only go out and play, you can't vote.'"

But not every voter who spent Saturday in Seattle gave Washington the nod. "I still voted for Miami, but I was real impressed by the way Washington played," the *Boston Globe's* Mark Blaudschum said. "I can't see voting against them until they lose. But if Washington and Miami were both 12-0 at the end of the year, I'd have a difficult time splitting my vote."

Colorful tailback Beno Bryant entertained teammates and coaches with his playful crooning, but his mood darkened after injuries soured his senior season.

Lui Kit Wong

Lui Kit Wong

Michigan's Burnie Legette tried to elude defensive tackle D'Marco Farr, who said filling Steve Emtman's shoes felt like parking a Hyundai in a Cadillac's spot.

Lui Kit Wong

Stoic Coach Don James shed his steely game face and wept when the Huskies won a share of the 1992 national championship.

Lui Kit Wong

Dave Hoffmann, the son of a Texas minister, did things on the field that would have put him behind bars off of it. Teammates simultaneously loved and feared him.

Receiver Mario Bailey, who matched Michigan's Desmond Howard stat for stat in 1992, was first snubbed by Heisman Trophy voters, then by NFL scouts.

Lui Kit Wong

Futuristic gladiator Andy Mason, whose mouth moved nearly as fast as his cleats, was a master of cerebral strategy.

Lui Kit Wong

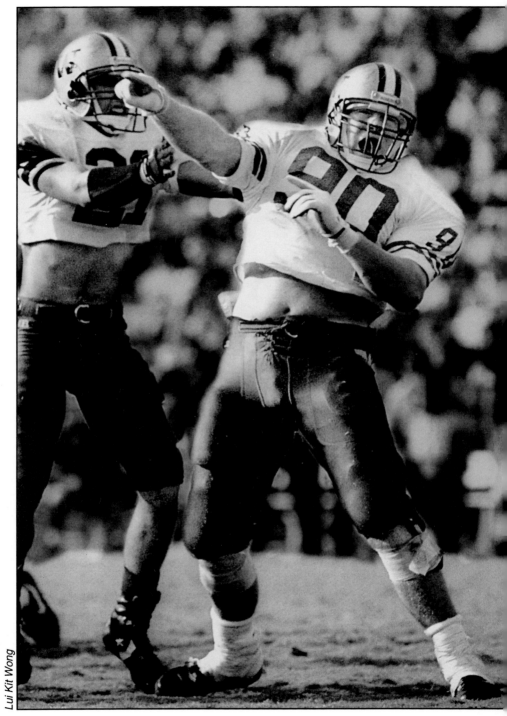

Lui Kit Wong

Emtman, No. 90, was so intent on winning he would punish teammates with a bell-ringing fist to the head when they would run drills at half-speed.

Center Ed Cunningham snapped the ball to Billy Joe Hobert throughout the national champion- ship season but later called him "an idiot" for his indiscretions.

Lui Kit Wong

Lui Kit Wong

When opposing quarterbacks threw in the direction of gambling cornerback Walter Bailey, coaches joked that it meant six points in either direction. Few Huskies on the national championship team will forget Bailey's shenanigans on the White House trip.

Bruce Terami

Redshirt freshman receiver Travis Spring, 19, died April 28, 1992 after a short bout with cancer. Husky Coach Don James called Spring's passing "one of the hardest things I've had to deal with as a football coach."

Lui Kit Wong

All-American lineman Lincoln Kennedy, a crowd favorite, flattened opponents with pancake blocks, and left coaches cringing and referees rankling when he stood up against what he viewed as on-field injustice.

Some thought quarterback Mark Brunell was the devoutly religious antithesis of his wild counterpart Hobert. Teammates knew differently.

Lui Kit Wong

Tailback Napoleon Kaufman, the fastest Husky ever, burned most who tried to catch him, but took heat from coaches for his "Compton Quakes" and spectacular end-zone jigs.

Outlaw quarterback Hobert, once a brash press darling, left Seattle questioning the scruples of a media that once adored him.

17

Behind The Scenes
Of Billygate

Steely clouds of controversy rolled in over Husky Stadium on Thursday, November 5. Bannered across the top of the *Seattle Times* that afternoon was the headline, "Huskies' Hobert got $50,000 loan." In the front-page story, Billy Joe Hobert admitted to spending the money during a three-month period in the spring in which he purchased cars, guns, stereos, golf clubs, and spent "hundreds of dollars" bankrolling wild weekends with friends. It was a stunning revelation.

Hobert's was the largest improper loan to a player ever discovered in NCAA history.

The story was not one whipped up in a few days but a month-long project piece so secret that even editors at the newspaper were not told of the subject matter, simply instructed to leave a hole for the story atop the front page. Only a handful of staff members at the newspaper knew what was coming.

At 5:30 a.m. Thursday, as the finishing touches were being applied to the piece, a desk editor approached Eric Nalder, who co-wrote the copyrighted story with Tom Farrey, and asked, "OK, Nalder, what the hell are you doing now?"

Nalder didn't answer, but a few hours later, just about every sports fan in the Seattle area would know. Paper boxes sold out in a flash. Word of the story spread quickly. The loan was one of the top stories on ESPN's broadcast that evening. The allegations were the hot topic that afternoon on KJR, a local sports radio station, and talk of them eclipsed the usual fare of Seahawks and SuperSonics chatter. The implications of the story were staggering: Would Hobert be suspended? How would the team be affected? Was probation a possibility?

More sinister notions also were discussed. Could Billy Joe have bet on Husky games? When he overthrew a wide-open receiver or gunned a ball directly into the hands of a defender, was he, heaven forbid, making a calculated error to shave points? Some believed the real conspiracy was carried out by the media. What kind of vendetta, some wondered, did the *Times* have against Washington? All was grist for the talk-show mill.

Although the newspaper really began to pour resources into this story after an informant called in October, the sports department received a strange telephone call in May. It came from someone who claimed to know Hobert but wished to remain anonymous. The person urged the reporter who answered to check the divorce papers filed by Billy Joe and Heather Hobert. Those documents would show, the caller said, that Heather wanted half the proceeds Billy Joe had received from signing with a professional agent, an act that would automatically make him ineligible to compete in an NCAA event.

The following day, the reporter checked those divorce papers, filed in Pierce County. Written in the space designated for division of assets were the words "still to come." The reporter struck up a deal with a clerk to give him a call as soon as the completed papers arrived. But before the documents were finished, the couple got back together, so the papers were never filed. It was never proven that Billy Joe had any illegal dealings with an agent, and the anonymous caller likely got the story wrong. Still, it put reporters at the newspaper on alert.

Another call came from a different informant in October. That call not only would change the life of Hobert but those of his teammates, coaches, and family. It would shake Washington football to its foundation, trigger an avalanche of allegations, and cast the hard light of reality on a football program long considered an unsullied bastion of fair play.

Like most informants or whistle-blowers, the tipster didn't have the entire story. The information was cryptic and incomplete—Hobert had taken out a $50,000 loan with 100-percent payback at 10 percent interest, and he planned to turn professional. The tipster didn't know exactly where the money was coming from but heard Hobert talking on the telephone with a golfing buddy named Rudy, who might be a longshoreman.

Hardly the stuff a newspaper can take to press, but the sliver of information did more than pique the interest of the reporter who answered the call. If true, the story was a blockbuster. NCAA rules prohibit athletes from receiving benefits not available to other students. The rule states, "a student-athlete may not receive preferential treatment, benefits or services (e.g. loans on a deferred payback basis) for his or her athletics reputation or skill or payback potential as a future professional athlete."

Farrey and Nalder were assigned to the story. Nalder was the more experienced, yet Farrey had proven he could handle tough subjects and, at 28, had won several national writing awards and established himself as one of the paper's best reporters. He came to Seattle after stints at the *St. Petersburg (Florida) Times, Miami Herald,* and *Los Angeles Times.* An enterprise and investigative reporter in sports, Farrey specialized in personality profiles, and he had done in-depth enterprise stories on athletes such as beleaguered NBA star Dale Ellis and Mike Utley, the former Detroit Lions lineman paralyzed after an on-field collision. Farrey pitched a Hobert profile to his editors in September. "I thought he wasn't the typical Washington player," he said. "He was not provincial at all. He thought big. He dreamed about being No. 1 in the country, not going to the Rose Bowl . . . I thought he was a helluva competitor, a talker. There just seemed to be something there." So Farrey was in the process of collecting random notes, quotes, and anecdotes about Hobert even before the tipster called.

Nalder, 47, was a University of Washington graduate who came to the *Seattle Times* in 1983 from the *Post-Intelligencer,* where he worked for eight years. As the *Times'* chief investigative reporter, he had a history of breaking earthshaking stories, including a series on oil tankers that won a Pulitzer Prize. Among his other stories were an investigation of alleged sexual assaults by U.S. Sen. Brock Adams; a series about bureaucratic bungling in a cancer drug program; an exposé of expense-account fraud by a member of the governor's cabinet; a probe of unsafe rocket-making plants after the *Challenger* accident; and stories that led to the closure of unsafe and unsecured nuclear weapons plants.

Although pleasant and polite, Nalder could be confrontational and had a knack for finding obscure records and prying information from otherwise airtight sources. "Anytime I deal with anyone," he said, "I want to first establish a rapport with them so I don't come on like a pit bull. However, at some point, I have to be persistent. I have to show people their options—one is, either you tell me the truth or I'm going to find it out elsewhere and you're not going to look so good. People realize that and usually choose Door No. 1."

A certain old-school editor suggested that a serious journalist should develop a hard-hitting reputation so a call to a subject gets one response: "Oh, shit! What have I done now?" Nalder had that reputation. His calls could accelerate the heart rates in courthouses, nuclear power plants, senatorial offices, and, in this case, university athletic departments. "I'm not so interested in being scary to people I call," he said. "Although I'm told that I am sometimes."

The key to breaking the Hobert story was maintaining confidentiality. There were several risks to an information leak, the most obvious being writers from a competing paper would be tipped off, and a leak could alert those people who might want to bury the truth. This story was multilayered, and getting to the heart of it would be akin to peeling an onion. The morsels of information given by the tipster were a handful of pieces in a huge jigsaw puzzle. "I've never, in my journalism career, come across a tipster who knows the whole story or has the whole story accurately," Nalder said. "Never happens. But there's usually a door opened. This was no different."

The first question to be answered: Who was Rudy? Nalder had a hunch that, because of the size of the loan, Rudy was probably retired. Not many longshoremen can afford to spend their afternoons on a golf course and grant a college kid a $50,000, no-collateral loan. Nalder called the longshoremen's union and asked if anyone there was familiar with a Rudy. Someone was and gave him the name of Rudy Martinez, a retired longshoreman. Nalder went to work, checking court records, driver's license records, anything that might shed light on who this guy was. The investigation lasted several days.

"It was," Nalder lamented, "a complete dry hole."

Nothing in the records check indicated this was the correct Rudy. Because it *wasn't*. From a face-to-face meeting with the informant, which came about a week after the initial call, Nalder learned that the Rudy in question frequented a Seattle restaurant. So Nalder went there and asked a waitress if she knew a Rudy. "Oh, sure," she said, "I know a Rudy Finne."

Everything clicked. "My first thought was, 'Damn, I had the wrong guy,' " Nalder said. Now, he had the right one. He went through the entire records process again, confident he was on the right track.

Finne, 43, was a one-time restaurateur and commercial fisherman, who in the late 1970s invested in a Tacoma restaurant that was supposed to have a cardroom. Because a gambling license was never obtained, the deal never happened. He told the newspaper he made bets on college football games before, but, "I'm no more a gambler that any Saturday-morning quarterback. I'm a fisherman-longshoreman."

In fact, Nalder discovered, Finne was a casual or part-time longshoreman. "I learned quite a bit about Rudy," he said. "There was a fishing company that went bankrupt that he was involved in. The bankruptcy records pointed in the direction of a lot of people that knew him. Indeed, people that were willing to talk to me."

Hobert and Finne (pronounced Finney) met during Hobert's sophomore year at Puyallup High. The two fostered a friendship and saw each other frequently at Tyee Valley, where Hobert worked as a greenskeeper during high school. They wagered up to $100 on golf matches, but, Hobert told the *Times*, Finne never bet on football games. "If he did it, I'd kill him," Hobert said. "Him and I are really good friends, and that's not something you go into and ask a friend to do. Everything that Rudy and I have done has been pretty much on the straight and narrow, other than gambling on golf. I don't delve into any kind of gambling other than my personal golf game."

Initially, Farrey and Nalder believed the source of the loan was Finne's father, but in speaking to sources, they learned that Finne's father was ill and probably not the lender. The reporters moved on. One person from the failed fishing business told Nalder that Finne had borrowed money on occasion from his father-in-law. Bingo. "The light went off in my head," Nalder said later. "There was the likely source of the loan."

There was more skin on this onion. The reporters neither knew the maiden name of Finne's wife nor where her father lived. It wasn't as if they could call Rudy Finne and ask him—the entire investigation was as hush-hush as possible. The operative was to gather as much information as they could without tipping off any of the key players in the deal. The reporters checked King and Pierce County marriage records, but there was no documentation for the Finnes. They then went to the state health department and got what they needed: a matrimonial license for Rudy and Jo Finne, who were married by Jo's father, Charles Rice, a nuclear engineer and lay preacher from Idaho Falls, Idaho.

As it happened, Rice was more than an everyday rocket scientist. He managed the nation's nuclear program and was president of a firm that operated a major federal nuclear research facility in Idaho Falls. After that, he worked as a consultant and assessed the safety of various commercial nuclear reactors. He was not, however, a Washington booster or alumnus. He had investments on the side and what Farrey called "a good cash flow."

A rocket scientist? If you could look beyond the serious ramifications of the simple-minded deal, you didn't have to be a rocket scientist to recognize the whole situation as downright comical. Columnist John McGrath would later write that the fiasco not only marked the downfall of Hobert but "the displacement of the rocket scientist as the last, most elite stop on the food chain. Thanks to Rice, rocket scientists now share kinship with Jethro Clampett and Gomer Pyle and anybody else who might require a cue card to get out of the rain."

Confident that they had the source of the loan, Farrey and Nalder began to build a money trail to determine where Hobert spent the cash. In a second interview, the tipster said Hobert had purchased guns during the spring. Farrey called the state Department of Licensing and learned that Hobert had purchased a pistol and rifle in late April. Farrey went to the store listed on the license, and the clerk, who recalled Hobert, pointed out the guns he bought. As it happens, he purchased a 7mm Colt 2000 semiautomatic pistol, a nasty, easily concealable weapon that cost him $477, and an M77 Ruger hunting rifle, described by one gun-store employee as the perfect rifle for hunting "little varmints like rabbits and prairie dogs."

Hobert would later admit to bringing the Colt 2000 to bars and keeping it in the glove compartment of his car for protection.

It seems university police knew of at least two Huskies with concealed-weapons permits, and Don James said he confronted the issue in spring 1992 after a handgun was found in the locker room.

Players said they needed the weapons to ward off would-be attackers, jealous of their success, at local bars and nightclubs.

"A lot of people on the team have guns," Tommie Smith said. "They just don't have them on campus. They let their (off-campus) friends keep them when they don't need them."

State Department of Licensing records showed that one player in 1992 and two in 1991 bought at least eight handguns during an 18-month span.

"You don't so much *need* a gun, but you want one," Smith said. "There have been a lot of shootings at (some nightclubs), and you need them not so much to shoot somebody, but to protect yourself . . . People are jealous of what we have and what they don't have."

The *Times* reporters were told by the informant that Hobert bought a car, and they checked the Department of Licensing for its registration. They learned that, indeed, he had paid cash for a 1991 Chevrolet Camaro in April. The tipster said Hobert spent $2,500 to reimburse his girlfriend at the time. In all, the reporters could account for about $15,000 of the money spent before approaching Hobert.

"We really couldn't go much farther," Farrey said. "We couldn't go into the paper with that. We still didn't have this loan confirmed. You kind of knew in your gut after talking to all these people that, yeah, it probably did happen . . . We really needed to get it confirmed by Hobert." The reporters were ready to make their next move: present Hobert with the information they accumulated and hope that he would come clean. Farrey said he and Nalder planned two interview sessions with the quarterback, the first with Farrey alone and the second, to be held the next night, with both reporters. The first night, Farrey said, he would get background information on him for a profile piece—stuff about growing up in Orting, Wash., his life as a Husky, general information to flesh out what type of person he was. The second night would be devoted to the loan.

This is how Farrey recalled the subject of the loan was introduced:

On the first night, Hobert mentioned that he had gotten into deep debt. "This was a subject he seemed pretty comfortable with," Farrey recalled, "more comfortable than I assumed he would be talking about it." Hobert continued, even making mention of a loan that he received, but was referring to a car loan, not the one for $50,000.

"Listen, Billy," Farrey said, stopping the interview, "We know you received not a car loan, but a *personal* loan from Charles Rice in Idaho. It was arranged through your friend Rudy Finne. We know that."

Hobert was shocked. "How did you know that?" he blurted. "Who told you that?"

Actually, Farrey knew far less about the loan than he let on. He and Nalder were almost sure a loan had been taken out, but they could not confirm the amount or any other details of the loan. Hobert, however, assumed Farrey knew everything and began to talk. "He just opened up," Farrey recalled. "He felt like he was busted."

Hobert never provided the exact dollar amount of the loan but was incredulous when Farrey asked if it was for $50,000. "Where did you get this information?" he asked again, his tone indicating the figure was on target. The two talked about the loan for about an hour. Hobert was embarrassed about borrowing the money and kept saying: "I'm stupid. I'm just stupid." He told Farrey about his problems in the spring before he found religion. Life was hell. He had marital strife and said he went on an eight-day drinking binge and entertained thoughts of suicide. Things got so heavy, he dropped out of school in the spring and had to make up the credits with summer-school courses.

Most of the particulars of how Hobert spent his money came out in the interview, and more was disclosed in a Pac-10 deposition. He borrowed $25,000 on April 19, 1992, but spent it so quickly that he requested, and received, a $15,000 check from Rice less than a month later. He bought the '91 Camaro for $11,000 and used $3,000 to replace the engine in his wife's Chevy Blazer and "$5,000 to $6,000" on a stereo for the Blazer, $2,900 to pay off his Hyundai. He spent $1,200 for car insurance, $1,000 on the guns, and $2,500 to reimburse his former girlfriend, Carisa Barrett Jacobsen. On July 19, he received his third and final check from Rice, made out for $10,000. He traded in the Camaro for a

1992 model in which he installed a $4,000 stereo system and spent much of the remaining money on golf equipment and entertaining friends.

Almost as soon as he purchased the '91 Camaro, a '92 model caught his eye. He inquired about a trade-in but was told he had put too many miles on his '91 during the three days that he owned it. The dealer later offered him $7,500 as a trade-in on the $12,300 '92 model. Hobert took the deal. "The '92 was a 25th-Anniversary edition," he explained in the deposition, "and had a commemorative marker. I thought it might be an investment. Otherwise, the cars look exactly the same. Both cars are white. I got the 1992 for prestige." Six months after Hobert purchased the 1992 model, the car was stolen and found vandalized and desecrated along a dirt road.

Hobert didn't seem to be too worried about conspicuous consumption. Having a fat wallet was a dream for a guy who grew up in a working-class family that never had too much money on hand. "I just pulled it out and paid cash wherever I went," he said. "People must have thought I was the richest guy in town until I stopped showing up at places (where) I had spent the money."

Hobert later confessed, "I told Chuck (Rice) I was going to use the money to pay bills and get back together with my wife. But I spent it because I didn't want to give her the chance to spend it . . . I was going through a real selfish, macho time, when I thought I was about to became a bachelor . . . I didn't know it at the time, but I was in some sort of deep depression. I really don't know why. I just didn't feel happy about anything I was doing. I didn't want any part of school or football or marriage."

Late in the 2 1/2-hour interview, Farrey said, he told Hobert what the coming story would discuss. "In a couple of days," he explained, "we'll write a news story about this. It's going to say that you took out a $50,000 loan that may violate NCAA rules. There's going to be a lot of attention. A lot of reporters calling. You may have to deal with it in a mass situation. Just get your facts straight, keep your composure. It will blow over. You made an error. You admit you made an error. Life will go on."

Understandably, Hobert was nervous. He later said he thought the focus of the story was going to be his conversion to Christianity. "Can't you just leave out the part about the loan?" he asked hopefully.

"Billy," Farrey explained, "my paper has invested the resources of two full-time reporters for a month. There's no way I can go back, knowing what I know about the loan, and say, 'Let's just not write about the loan.' They won't accept that."

"Yeah, I guess not."

According to Farrey, the interview was cordial, never heated, and he and Hobert shook hands when it ended. Farrey felt an adrenaline surge as he walked away from the interview. In one hand was a recorder documenting a story any sports section would put on its front page. He knew his other hand had shook that of Billy Joe Hobert, a likable kid who made a stupid mistake when money was wafted under his nose.

Hobert had a vastly different impression of the interview. He felt that he was set up by the reporters, lured into talking about the loan. "These guys have no integrity whatsoever," he said. "They came to me and were asking me a bunch of questions about my personal life . . . (they) told me they were going to do a profile on me about my personal life and how my Christian life has changed and saved my life.

"(Farrey) was asking me about my father, how I was raised, all that ... Then he says, 'Now, being a Christian, how do you accept the responsibilities of such a large loan?' I should have just ended the interview, but I didn't. When people ask questions, I usually answer 'em.

"He knew most of everything that happened before he asked me the questions. He knew about loans, cars, they had done a lot of work . . . But he kept saying, 'Billy Joe, when I write this I'll make it real sympathetic to what was going on in your life.'

"I knew I was stupid. I had no idea they knew this stuff and were just coming after me . . . I didn't know Farrey was such a sleazy weasel. I don't know what their motives were—Let's just trash Billy Joe."

Around 4 p.m. the day after the interview, Farrey called Faculty Athletic Representative Dick Dunn and told him of the story to be released in the next day's paper. Dunn thanked him for the information and called Athletic Director Barbara Hedges. About two hours later, Farrey and Nalder knocked on Hedges's office door. She invited them in, asking, "So what's this all about?" They told her as much as they knew. "I don't think Hedges knew a thing (about the loan in advance)," Farrey said. "She was completely dumbfounded."

Meanwhile, Hobert called his father, Terry, and told him what to expect. "He told me, 'Hey, Dad, there's going to be something that's hitting the fan,'" Terry Hobert told *Tacoma Morning News Tribune* reporter Don Borst. "We've all done something stupid like that . . . refinancing our house at the wrong time . . . we all make mistakes.

"He's an idealist," the elder Hobert said of his son. "He doesn't like to see the negative side of things and people. He has too much faith in people. He doesn't understand why he has to take it in the chops."

The story ran the next day and Hobert dodged the media waiting for him at the stadium that afternoon by leaving practice early. "I've got to go to my wife's Lamaze class," he explained as he lowered his head and jogged past a cluster of reporters. Hobert and the rest of the team learned before practice that the university was suspending him for the Arizona game. "It was an administrative decision," James said. "Obviously I'm disappointed, but life goes on."

Hedges defended her decision to opt for suspension, saying it would give the administration time to sort through the facts. "Right now, we've heard (Hobert's) interpretation of what he thought he could or could not do . . . We're investigating it."

One of the pressing questions that had to be answered was, when did the coaches find out about the loan? If Husky coaches were aware that Hobert took out an improper loan and did not report it to Dunn or Hedges, they were guilty of concealing information. The ramifications of such a blunder were staggering and, if that mistake was made, some type of probation was highly probable. A day after breaking the initial story, the *Seattle Times* ran a follow-up piece headlined, "Coaches Knew UW's Hobert Was Looking for Money." The story reported Jeff Woodruff and Myles Corrigan, the offensive coordinator and tight-ends coach, knew Hobert was seeking a personal loan the previous April. The quarterback had asked how to structure the loan to comply with the rules. Woodruff and Corrigan said they gave Hobert some general advice, although they did not ask the amount and terms of the loan or name of the lender. Corrigan said he heard none of the specifics of the loan and first learned of them when the story broke.

When the quarterback asked about taking out a loan in the spring, Woodruff told him to run the request through "the proper channels" and suggested he talk to Dick Baird, the recruiting director for Husky athletics and a member of the department's rules-compliance committee. Woodruff, too, talked with Baird. "I didn't take it as an interpretation, more as a clarification," Baird said of Woodruff's inquiry about the legality of a loan. "Jeff was unclear on rules regarding student loans. Jeff and Billy Joe were there, and I think Myles Corrigan for a while. It was very casual. Jeff asked, 'Can a student-athlete take out a loan?' I told him, 'Sure,' there were Guaranteed Student Loans, bank loans, et cetera, and these are the rules. And I reviewed the rules on personal loans—that they could be from family.

"I think Billy Joe originally indicated someone in his family might want to lend him money. I told him if it's a friend, it has to be established, not someone he met since he came here. It couldn't be because of athletic ability. The red flag that went up was about agents because it was right after the NFL draft. He understood it can't even be close to being an agent.

"He asked good questions. He said he didn't want to do anything wrong, but he never said he had a loan set up."

Woodruff said he was in frequent contact with Hobert during the spring and knew of his financial problems. He said Hobert told him the lender was a "family friend" not associated with the school. When the quarterback returned to school in August, he was driving his '92 Camaro. "I saw the car and asked about it," Woodruff told the *Seattle Times*. "He said he got (the loan) through a personal friend." Woodruff believed the loan was not a violation because the lender was not associated with the school and said he did not report the information to Hedges or James, his father-in-law. "A flag would have gone up with me if the person (who made the loan) was connected to the UW," Woodruff said.

In a Pac-10 deposition taken three days after the loan story was released, Woodruff clarified his comments about the car. "I never saw his car," he said. "I never asked him about it or heard him say anything. The only thing about a car I remember was that his was broken down, and I thought that was the purpose of the loan . . . The only thing he said was that he got a new stereo and he was proud of the stereo 'in my car.' That's very common—all the kids have stereos in the dorms, cars, on their shoulders."

Woodruff said nothing he saw led him to believe Hobert had come into a lot of money. ("He dressed the same. Like a gym rat.") When the quarterback dropped out of school in the spring, he also dropped out of touch with his coaches. "I tried (to reach him) constantly," Woodruff said. "I'd call his wife at work and talk to her for four or five minutes at a time. His home number changed all the time. I reached him at at least one other girl's home. I even asked her how he was doing—'I haven't seen him for a week,'—to try and get information on his mental state, what was going on in his life.

"Heather was upset, thought he needed help. Carisa said: 'Everything's great. We're in love.' I asked her to get word to him that I needed to talk to him. He didn't work out here during the summer. I was worried about his weight." Woodruff said he next heard about the loan when Hobert made passing reference to it during fall camp. "He mentioned, 'Yeah, I got a loan. Heather and I are back together,' " he said. "I spent more time on his personal life than just this. I knew they separated, got back together, who he was seeing. Most of our conversations were on that."

Woodruff said he spent "an awful lot" of time counseling Hobert during his three-year playing career, and because of the quarterback's transgressions, "I get ripped (from James) constantly. It's a daily ritual." Woodruff might have been a bit more attentive to talk of the loan during fall practice if he was aware of its amount. "If (Hobert) would have told me," he said, "I would have grabbed him around the neck and wrestled him to the ground. I don't think he's mature enough to handle anything like that."

Apparently, Charles Rice believed otherwise. Even though the Idaho scientist had no ties to the school, the loan was a violation of NCAA rules, which state that an athlete cannot receive a benefit not ordinarily available to students who are not athletes. This was clearly the case with Hobert. Had he not been a football player with the potential to make a great deal of money as a professional, he would not have received a loan that size. Although Rice said he never had a conversation with Hobert regarding his pro potential, it was obviously a consideration. "If I had seen the potential for him to become a professional musician, super scientist, or lots of other things that would have led me to believe he could pay it back, then I would have been willing to do it," he said, adding, "If he were not on a track to pay it back after he finished school, I would have been reluctant to loan him money."

Bob Oliver, director of legislative services for the NCAA, said athletic department employees, including coaches, are required to alert the athletic director or faculty representative whenever potential violations exist. "If they know something's going on," he said, "they need to get involved whatever university experts are available. The coach needs to deal with it immediately and involve the proper people."

Another director of legislative services explained schools could be penalized if staff members knew about potential violations, or *should* have known. Hedges defended the staff, saying, "I don't think anything has slipped through the cracks ... (except) possibly the interpretation of the rules by Billy."

The ramifications of an NCAA rules violation stretched far beyond the mere suspension of Hobert. The specter of game forfeitures hung over the Huskies like a mallet. There was a possibility Washington would have to forfeit each 1992 game in which Hobert played. He played in all eight. NCAA regulations stipulate that if an athlete violates a rule of amateurism or receives an extra benefit, the individual becomes ineligible at the time of the violation. Pac-10 rules state that when an ineligible competes in a contest, other than on a losing team, the outcome of the contest is subject to review by the conference. Forfeiture is one of the penalties, and the UW couldn't exactly be considered the leading candidate for a Rose Bowl berth with an 0-8 record.

A tense week passed between the time the Hobert loan story broke and the three-person Pac-10 review committee recommended the games not be forfeited. The committee, which worked out of Los Angeles, determined the violations rested completely on Hobert's shoulders. "We would be unwilling to punish an institution for something we believed to be unknown and unknowable," said Douglas Hobbs, committee spokesman and UCLA faculty representative. "That's just not the American way."

The threat of forfeiting games was real however, it would have been somewhat uncharacteristic for the NCAA to mete out such an extreme penalty. There were other cases on the books concerning ineligible players competing in which the penalties were less severe. A Colorado wide receiver, whose name was never released, dropped a class in the fall of 1992 and fell below the 12-hour term minimum. Effectively ineligible, he played in a victory over Missouri before the error was discovered, yet the Big Eight Conference did not punish Colorado. In another case, the Big Eight ruled in favor of Nebraska after it was discovered that fullback Omar Soto, slated to start in the 1992 Orange Bowl, had played in a 1986 junior college game, violating the NCAA's five-years-to-play-four rule. Like the Buffaloes, Nebraska was not punished with forfeits.

The recommendation by the Pac-10 committee was just that, a recommendation, and the first step in a three-step process to reach a final verdict. The following Sunday, the 30-member Pac-10 Council would meet in San Francisco, where the situation would be voted on again. A resolution would then be sent to the league's chief executive officers, who would make the ultimate determination by conference call.

The Pac-10 council, composed of the top three athletic administrators from each school, voted unanimously to allow Washington's eight victories to stand, and two days later, got rubber-stamp approval from the league officers. During that period, the Huskies had lost to Arizona and defeated Oregon State, a victory which ensured a third straight Rose Bowl appearance.

In short, the Huskies were bound for Pasadena with plenty of baggage in tow.

II

"If you fuck with me, you'll pay for it."

That's what Billy Joe Hobert remembers being told by Carisa Barrett Jacobsen, his girlfriend during spring 1992. They were harsh words but ones he believed. "Fucking with her" apparently meant leaving her to make amends with his wife. That's how Hobert understood it, at least. So when he learned that the newspaper knew of the loan, Carisa was on his short list of suspected informants. "She hates my guts," he confided. Her father, John Barrett, was another person Hobert thought might have tipped off the press. A friend of Hobert's at the Tyee Valley Golf Course overheard Barrett telling other golfers, "I'm going to get that SOB."

Regardless of who provided information to the media, Hobert clearly violated NCAA rules by taking out the loan. Husky players receive specific information each year regarding the do's and do nots of financial transactions. "This was not a gray-area violation," former Husky Ed Cunningham said. "Billy knew exactly what he was doing."

During the summer of 1992, each Washington booster received a letter from the school's athletic department that outlined some NCAA regulations. The letter included a copy of a newspaper story about Notre Dame linebacker Demetrius DuBose, suspended for two games after accepting a $600 loan from a Seattle couple he knew while growing up. They were Fighting Irish backers. The clippings were one of the many ways the UW tried to discourage improper activities.

"When freshmen come," James explained, "we do 10 segments covering a combination of topics like housing, NCAA rules, and philosophical rules on drugs, alcohol, fights, dorm living, phone fraud, campus theft, rape. We have a nightly, 30-minute talk during fall camp on a variety of subjects with major emphasis on agent issues. We cover the NCAA rules, but we also talk about the evils of agents. We bring in speakers from the FBI, campus, city and state police. We're getting before them as much information as possible regarding life skills and NCAA rules. We have testing for the coaches all spring long. That's got us spending more time on the rules. We know the answers, or where to get the answers."

Like all NCAA athletes, Washington football players are required to sign a statement each year that includes a promise to report any loans or income outside of normal sources (i.e., summer jobs, car loans). Players are not required to list personal loans provided they have a regular repayment schedule. Hobert's loan from Charles Rice did not have a repayment schedule per se. Player loans also are deemed improper by the NCAA if they are based on potential earnings as a professional athlete.

The notion of the loan was born sometime after the 1992 Rose Bowl. Hobert spoke at length with Finne about his financial problems while the two were golfing. "I wasn't golfing well," Hobert said, "and he asked what was bothering me. I told him I had trouble at home and explained the situation . . . A couple of days later, he said something like, 'What if I could help with something like a loan?' " Finne suggested that his father-in-law, Chuck Rice, had loaned money before and might be willing to help Hobert.

Recalled Finne: "(Hobert) owed more and more money per month than he was bringing in . . . It was common knowledge. He wasn't silent about the fact that he was financially strapped."

Rice had loaned money fairly regularly. "It's a well-known fact in the family," Finne said. "He's done it a lot of times. Billy Joe would have been the 15th person, I think. Some of the loans were for more money than Billy Joe's." Rice agreed that he had made several loans, but fewer than Finne claimed and for less money than Hobert's. "The maximum is probably in the vicinity of $5,000," he said.

Hobert first met Rice at Lofurno's restaurant in Seattle, where the two ate with Rudy and Jo Finne. The loan was not arranged over dinner. "It was kind of a get-to-know-you kind of meeting," Hobert explained. Rice was bookish, not a big football fan, in Hobert's words, "sort of a Col. Sanders-type guy." The two met again before finally setting up a $25,000 agreement at the airport before Rice was to fly back to Idaho.

"The principle thing I was interested in," Rice said, "was, is this a youngster that deserves help, as opposed to someone who was simply looking for money? . . . (I concluded) that he was a nice young fellow who had gotten in over his head in debt and that he deserved a chance to get out of it." And Rice was wealthy enough to provide that help. Hobert signed a demand note, repayable with 10 percent interest, and Rice handed him a $25,000 check as they parted.

Using a friend's computer, Finne drew up the deal. Rice was busy with an executorship and asked his son-in-law to handle the Hobert arrangements. "I asked Billy Joe if it was legal," Finne said. "He checked it out, I don't know with who. It was very standard. I talked to my attorney. I went with Billy Joe to the bank. We were blatantly and absolutely out in front with this. I didn't want to get the UW in trouble."

In mid-May, Hobert contacted Rice and asked for an additional $15,000. Finne was on a fishing trip at the time. Rice and Hobert edited the original pact, increasing the terms to $40,000. "Chuck called me and told me to make another note for $40,000," Finne recalled. "I asked him why he did that. I was mad, thought maybe Billy Joe was taking advantage of us."

That wasn't the end of the requests. In early July, Hobert penned Rice a handwritten note, clearly scribbled in haste:

Chuck,

I would like to upgrade the contract to an even $50,000 within the next couple of months. The money has to be the best thing that has happened to Heather and I. Chuck, I can honestly say that you have saved our marriage and gotten us, for the most part, out of debt. I owe you more than you can imagine and I hope I can do more than repay you with money.

Thanks a Million,
Your Grateful Friend,
Billy Joe Hobert

Rice began to get the picture. Hobert was an irresponsible college kid who had blown 40 grand. Yet there was one compelling reason to increase the agreement to $50,000: Heather Hobert was pregnant and Billy Joe indicated he needed the money for prenatal expenses. He also needed to reimburse his father for another loan. "I was not very happy with Billy Joe at that point in time," Rice said, "and could not understand how he could have gone through the amount of money he had and still have financial problems he professed to have." Rice tried to reach Finne to investigate the situation further, but the son-in-law was on a fishing trip. Rice wrote a scolding letter to Hobert and before he could mail it, Finne called back. Rice sent the letter to Finne, instead, asking him to discuss it with Hobert. The letter read:

Dear Billy Joe,

I have loaned you $40,000 without collateral to date at an interest rate of 10%. You are asking for ($10,000) more "to pay back your father and put $3,000 in the bank"! All of this in a span of time of less than 3 months.

Let me give you some economic facts of life. Nobody sits on cash (except some dumb misers that don't understand that money earns money when it's invested). So, I have some of my money invested in Government bonds that earn 8% and are increasing in value. Some other funds are invested in tax exempt bonds that net me nearly 11% and are also increasing in value. I had to either borrow against or sell some of those solid investments to lend you money. As you are possibly aware, the stock market, in which the bulk of the remainder of my funds is invested, is down by 10% since mid-January. I chose to borrow against my stocks and bonds to avoid taking a loss on the stocks or eliminate the potential gain and interest accruing on the bonds. At the interest rate on your note, I will, at best, break even if it gets repaid (you are the only collateral).

The $52,000 you are asking for in total <u>to date</u> is more than 5% of a million dollars and exceeds the maximum total amount I have either given or lent to any of my own 8 kids by nearly a factor of four, and some of my children have offered me a home for life when I get old and feeble and need it or want it. <u>For a non-business proposition, which this certainly is, I don't think it's fair to those 8 kids!</u>

What are you offering me? An unspecified increase in interest on an unsecured loan! On the basis of one evening's acquaintance and Rudy's friendship with you! Based on what appears to be your voracious appetite for money, <u>$17,500 per month,</u> it appears I have befriended a bottomless pit.

I am glad my loan is the "best thing that has ever happened to Heather and you" and that it "saved your marriage", but it didn't get you "out of debt for the most part", unless you don't consider a $50,000 loan from me to be debt. It certainly hasn't been the best thing that ever happened to me. Rudy was very upset with me when I agreed to increase the 25 to 40 and now I can't even get him to return my calls—so this whole business appears to be alienating one of my favorite people.

Over my better judgment, and especially since Rudy wanted to talk to you before I increased the loan, I am enclosing a check for the $10,000 to pay off <u>your</u> father. I sure wish you had any regard for me and my problems and future needs.

When you sign, get notarized, and return the enclosed note, I would appreciate your enclosing copies of the debts you have paid off since April 19th along with a statement of your present financial status, and your monthly income and expenses. A prudent lender would have gotten this information before the first loan.

Regards,
Chuck

Finne used his friend's computer to consolidate the final two loans and draw up a $25,000 contract. This agreement was different from the others in that it made specific mention of Hobert's pro potential, a blatant NCAA violation, and mandated he repay Rice as much as $110,000. Hobert signed the pact, Finne and notary witnessed the signing, and it was sent to Rice, who later voided the note when news of the improper loan became public. Hobert said he knew the pro-potential rules but did not read the four-paragraph pact when he signed it and had it notarized. "Billy Joe was in a super rush for the money on July 24," said Finne, adding he, too, was in a hurry and accidentally punched out "the wrong note." The agreement read:

> For value received, the undersigned promises to pay upon demand to Charles M. Rice the sum of twenty-five thousand dollars. This promissory note shall bear one and a half percent interest of any future monies received on a pro football contract.
> These are the provisions of said contract:
> A. Mr. Hobert agrees to pay Mr. Rice one hundred and ten thousand dollars maximum at one and one half percent of any future monies received on a pro football contract.
> B. Mr. Hobert has a buy out provision if he pays the note in full, two months after any such signed football contract. The buy out provision is sixty-five thousand dollars.
> C. Mr. Hobert agrees to start payments upon any monies received as a pro football player, a failure to comply with this payment plan if it results in any legal action or any added expenses will be paid by Mr. Hobert.

Rice received the agreement July 24 and phoned Finne two days later to tell him, "I have a note for $25,000 that mentions future earnings with Billy Joe's signature and it's been notarized. Something's wrong." Rice voided the contract by drawing a line through it but kept a copy in his files. Finne claimed that he had several versions of a contract on the computer and mistakenly printed the wrong one. Hobert explained he was in such a rush to get the money, he signed the pact without reading it. Finne, who said he and Rice are not too familiar with NCAA regulations, said printing the wrong contract was merely an unfortunate accident. "I love the guy," he said, referring to Hobert. "I'm not going to do anything to hurt him. Chuck Rice didn't want anything like that . . . I totally believe him when he says he didn't read it."

Were it up to Hobert, of course, none of the details of these transactions would have been released to the university. Soon after the initial story ran, he collected all the paperwork documenting his dealings with Rice and burned it. "When I realized what it was," he said, "I was so mad, I burned it. Since I had discussed it with Mrs. Hedges, I didn't think (the Pac-10) would want to see it." Rice, however, had copies of all correspondence with Hobert in his files and faxed everything to Barbara Hedges the day after the story broke. There was no evidence to suggest Rice was anything more than a casual sports fan, and one who was unfamiliar with the particulars of NCAA regulations regarding player loans. To him, lending money to Hobert was logical; after all, the kid would earn gobs of cash as a pro football player. "If I had seen the potential for him to become a professional musician, super scientist, or lots of other things that would have led me to believe he could pay it back, then I would have been willing to do it," he said. "If he were not on track to pay it back after he finished school, I would have been reluctant to loan him money."

A month after its initial story about the improper loan, the *Seattle Times* released another copyrighted story regarding Hobert. This piece said UW boosters might have violated NCAA rules by providing Hobert with a job in high school and improper financial benefits after he joined the Huskies. The focal point of the story involved Hobert's employment as a greenskeeper at the Tyee Valley Golf Course during his senior year at Puyallup High, when he was the state's top football prospect. NCAA rules say university athletic boosters and alumni "shall not be involved, directly or indirectly, in making arrangements for or giving" financial aid or other benefits to a prospect. Also, the rules specifically state an athlete cannot be offered a job before completing high school.

Hobert said he got the job because of arrangements made by Ron Crowe, the mayor of Puyallup at the time and a former Washington basketball player. Crowe recalled that Herb Mead, a prominent Husky booster, called and said, "We've got to get (Hobert) a job at the golf course." Crowe said Mead and Roy Moore, a booster who operates the golf course, worked out a job offer for Hobert. Crowe said he made no job arrangement, has never met Moore, and is not a Husky booster. Mead and Moore denied arranging the job offer.

According to the *Seattle Times* story, Hobert was paid $7 an hour, about $2 more than other first-time employees of the course. He said he received free meals at the course restaurant, a violation if the extra benefits were not ordinarily available to other students. "It's a meal here, a meal there," Hobert said. "Maybe a little bit of borrowed money."

Former managers and workers at the course said Washington football players who worked there were given special treatment, inasmuch as they weren't chastised for slow or sloppy work.

"We called them the milkmen, the milkers," said Jason Daley, a former groundskeeper. "Everybody milks their job a little bit, but these guys would take it to a whole 'nother level."

All the inquiries, the accusations, the general turmoil surrounding the improper loan had Hobert thinking about another level, too: the NFL. He could have petitioned for reinstatement to university officials, who would not have considered the petition until after the Rose Bowl, then the NCAA. "Everybody has a chance," Barbara Hedges said of a favorable verdict for Hobert. "Billy has a deadline of January 6. It was impossible for all of the review to have taken place . . . I want the best for Billy Joe. I want whatever Billy Joe thinks is best for him." At this time, that was professional football. Hobert spent some time during early December working out with former Seattle Seahawks quarterback Jim Zorn and had a private baseball workout with scout Gary Pellant of the Chicago White Sox. Hobert preferred a pro football career. "Financially, football is a lot better start for me and my family," he said.

On December 8, Hobert decided to forgo his option to petition for reinstatement and make himself eligible for the 1993 NFL draft.

Said Hobert: "I've decided to make my peace and go on."

18

Desert Swarm

The University of Arizona falls within the Tucson city limits, but a more appropriate locale for the football team might be Phoenix. After a 4-7 season in 1991, their worst since 1972, the Wildcats rose from the ashes in one season. Riding a four-game winning streak, they were a legitimate contender for a bowl berth. The No. 1 Huskies were coming to town, and Arizona had a chance to show that its 5-2-1 record and the stranglehold it put on Miami's offense in an 8-7 loss was no fluke. The turnaround in Tucson didn't surprise Don James. He could relate to the plight of UA Coach Dick Tomey.

"As I look back on my career," James said two days after the Stanford win, "it's the way you handle things when you're close to Chapter 11 in business or getting fired as a coach that determines what level you're ever going to get to. I don't think there's any question we're at the level we are because of our adversity. I saw it happen in '75 and '77. It shows that kids and coaches that turn teams don't give up."

Little did James know his own program was three days away from a maelstrom of adversity far more damaging than any single losing season. Yet even after Hobert's suspension, the Huskies showed no signs of disarray or despair. The Huskies trotted off the Arizona field Friday after the customary pre-game workout and seemed invigorated, even carefree. Maybe it was because Hobert had been reduced to something of an afterthought in the Washington offense. Maybe it was because of their roster full of seasoned players, or the daunting nature of facing Arizona in desert heat. Whatever, the loan quandary didn't seem to blur his teammates' focus on the task at hand.

"I thought we went into the Arizona game better prepared than we'd been in a while," Mark Brunell said. "I felt really good about it."

Redshirt freshman Damon Huard stepped into the backup quarterback role. He was hotly recruited out of Puyallup High, where Hobert played his prep ball, and probably had the best arm of the three. Huard's passes were so crisp, in fact, that Orlando McKay requested that he, and not Brunell or Hobert, throw him balls when pro scouts came calling. Previously relegated to mop-up duty, Huard would take snaps against Arizona only if Brunell were injured or if the Huskies were to put the game out of reach. "Mark's the guy who's going to have to get the job done," James said. "I think if he got tired and it turned out to be a warm game, it might limit his running, but I'd like to get him out there and get him tired. That means our offense is on the field a lot."

A Washington booster approached a reporter about two hours before kickoff and voiced an irony through a curled lip. "Billy Joe Hobert didn't want a quarterback rotation," he said. "Well, he got what he wanted. There is no quarterback rotation."

The absence of Hobert, and the potential for distraction, put that much more weight on thorough preparation. Arizona was no pushover; the No. 12 Wildcats were, quite literally, a few inches away from being undefeated and one of the nation's top teams. Their two losses and a tie were decided by last-minute field goals—a 47-yarder by Washington State's Aaron Price and narrow misses by UA kicker Steve McLaughlin against Oregon State and Miami. Coach Dick Tomey would sooner gaze at Medusa than back at those games. "I don't really engage in that," he said of hindsight. "I've always been a real pragmatic person as a coach. You accept what you've got. We had a lot of people around here saying, 'You guys could be 3-0 or whatever, 4-0.'

"But I told our players, 'No, you're 1-2-1, we have to understand that. We can't try to make ourselves feel good that we were close or that we could be this, we could be that; we are 1-2-1, and that's exactly what we are, and that's what we deserve to be because that's the way it happened . . . And I think that caused us to redouble our efforts to be better.'"

Pragmatism had no place in the Husky camp. At least not now. Not for this game. There would be no solving of Hobert's problems on this Saturday. The team needed to escape Seattle, the multimedia whirlwind, and the foreboding clouds of possible forfeitures. By bludgeoning the Wildcats on their home turf, Washington could send a message to Miami by proxy. The Hurricanes barely escaped the Arizona game with their collective ego intact. The Huskies could come out of this one smelling, ahem, like a rose.

"I'm not going to get into Washington-Miami," Tomey warned a group of Husky beat reporters when asked to choose which team was superior. "I don't care about that. I'm not going to answer questions about it before or after, win, lose, or draw."

Would a Washington win be an offer the East Coast Mafia couldn't refuse? Not likely. "The game will influence my vote a lot . . . if Arizona beats them," said voter Stephen Caldwell of the *Arkansas Democrat-Gazette*, adding it would take something just short of an act of God to change his No. 1 vote: "If Washington beats the dog out of them, maybe by 60 points." Loyalty to Miami was ironclad, even though the idle Hurricanes had a weaker schedule than Washington's, 23rd- to 11th-ranked in the nation. "If Washington wins, I'm certain I'll keep Miami No. 1," said Tony Barnhart of the *Atlanta Journal-Constitution*. "It would have to be something unusual. As a rule, I don't move a team out of first place when they don't play. Plus, I don't think Washington has as good a team as they did last year."

That certainly wasn't the case for Arizona. The Wildcats were spanked by the Huskies, 54-0 in 1991 and 54-10 in '90, but now boasted a team that was holding firm in the thick of the Rose Bowl race. That position would improve dramatically if Washington were forced to forfeit games because of Hobert's indiscretion. This was an Arizona team that won games with its jalapeno-hot defense, which led the nation against the run, allowing a paltry 54.9 yards a game. The anchor of that unit was defensive lineman Rob Waldrop, quietly compared to Steve Emtman. Waldrop squirmed at that. "I don't think there's any comparison," he said. "I don't think there will ever be another Emtman in this league. I'm not trying to be like him. I can't be like him. I'm just trying to be Rob Waldrop." That was enough. The 6-foot-2, 270-pound junior from Phoenix ranked second in the Pac-10 in tackles for losses (17) and fourth in sacks (eight).

Tomey, in command when young Emtman was told UA had its quota of defensive linemen, praised Waldrop but put the Washington All-America in a league of his own. "Up to this point," he said, "you'd have to say (Waldrop has) played as well as anyone—with the exception of a guy like Emtman, because he was in a different category." The Wildcats were in some pretty elite defensive categories, too: tied with Washington for second in the nation in scoring defense (9.3 points), fourth in total defense (246 yards), and fifth in turnover margin (1.38). Those numbers had been pared significantly during the winning streak, in victories over UCLA, Stanford, California, and New Mexico State. In those games, Arizona's 5-2 front clamped down on the opponents' running games like a bear trap, allowing rushing numbers 36, minus-33, 15, and 35 yards. The Wildcats yielded 2 yards on the ground to pass-happy Miami.

Things weren't nearly so good for the Wildcat defense the year before. During a game in Seattle, Waldrop fell to the Husky Stadium turf untouched and twisted his knee. He was lost for the season. The defense was a hopeless hodgepodge with Hicham El-Mashtoub starting at nose guard and Heath Bray at inside linebacker. Now, El-Mashtoub was the team's starting center and Bray a backup quarterback.

At the wheel of the Arizona offense was quarterback George Malauulu, a left-handed senior who had faced Washington so many times that Husky fans could almost pronounce his name. "It seems like we've been playing him since I've been here," James quipped. "I came in '75, so we're going to see when George got there." The Wildcats tended to keep the ball on the ground and rotated backs Ontiwaun Carter, Billy Johnson, and Chuck Levy, who had gained 640, 351, and 324 yards. Arizona had outrushed Miami, UCLA, Stanford, California, and New Mexico State.

Carter was a wisp of a back at 5-foot-11, 170 pounds, but could bench-press more than twice his weight. He was in Napoleon Kaufman's recruiting class and, like Kaufman, was recruited by USC and Washington. Both schools cooled on Carter when he failed to pass his entrance exams. "Washington didn't show they had enough confidence in me passing the SAT," said Carter, who passed with a 720 on his fourth attempt. "That kind of turned me off." But Carter wasn't atop the Huskies' wish list, anyway. They lobbied hardest for running backs Kaufman and Leon Neal. "Napoleon was always the No. 1 choice for us," James said in 1991. "We liked Carter. We thought he was a good player. I think he can play in this league."

That, Carter reckoned, was an understatement. He had an unflappable confidence that glared through his broad smile. In 1991, when Arizona was mauled at Husky Stadium, he had a memorable little scramble. "Once I hit the seam, I cut back," he recalled. "I was gone." Well, not exactly gone. Actually, he took a pitch on the Arizona 5, ran left, cut back to the middle, smacked into a referee and was gang-tackled 12 yards downfield. "That would have been my first college touchdown," he lamented later, shaking his head from side to side. Not everyone agreed. Washington had four secondary backs bracketing the run and Carter would have had to do some world-class juking to slip their grasp. The point was, he believed he could have.

The 1992 showdown in Tucson wouldn't be Carter's game, either: He would gain just 26 yards on 13 carries. But confidence like his was infectious. Sure, the Wildcats had been outscored by 98 points during their previous two meetings with Washington, but this was a new game. Victory was in reach. "Obviously, it's a tall order for us," Tomey said, "but it's one we're looking forward to ... We've (played the No. 1 team) before. But to me, the national thing is not significant this week. It's the conference." Tucson had flipped for this team, and a huge crowd swelled on game day for the homecoming parade, which wound through the heart of the campus. Folks held up signs—and middle fingers—proclaiming the Wildcats' dominance, general disdain for the Huskies, and, yes, the guilt of Washington's fallen quarterback. "Can I borrow $50,000?" one sign read, "Washington cheats to win" another read. The display was rowdy, but basically good-natured. Basketball was king here, yet football was making a run at the crown.

The scenery spectacular, the weather usually glorious, but Arizona Stadium offered the Huskies few good memories. No one on the team had ever won here. The last time Washington picked up a 'W' at Arizona Stadium was 1983, when the Wildcats were edged, 23-22. In 1987, the Huskies blew a 21-7 advantage and barely escaped this sweltering crucible with a 21-21 tie. The Huskies lost in the final seconds in 1989, 20-17.

Why was playing in Arizona so tough? The noise factor had something to do with it. The Huskies tried to prepare for the deafening din during practice by piping crowd noise through gigantic speakers, but nothing short of a Who concert could simulate this. "You couldn't hear yourself talking," Andy Mason recalled. "It was like you were a mute. You could feel your lips moving, but couldn't hear anything coming out." The afternoon was a balmy 76 degrees at kickoff, and the capacity crowd of 58,510 fans packed into Arizona Stadium pumped the decibel count through the ozone layer.

Arizona's defense dominated early on and pushed the crowd to its boiling point. Like a freak downpour in the high desert, the Wildcats closed in, soaking Washington in a flash. Kaufman, who had been recruited heavily by Arizona, might have wanted to burn the video of this game. When he tested the middle, he was met by a search party of red-white-and-blue jerseys. The same treatment awaited him when he broke for the boundaries. He had averaged 100 yards a game, yet gained only 50 here. Initially, it looked as if he might do more damage. Three plays into the game, he took a pitchout around left end for a 28-yard ramble. "I thought we'd go back to that," he said. They didn't. Kaufman went back, all right, back to Square One.

The only bright spot in Kaufman's day was the one a few million miles overhead that made him squint. He blamed his first of three fumbles on the sun. Early in the opening period, he dropped a punt at the UW 23. The ball glanced off Husky Reggie Reser's foot and bounced back to the 4, where Arizona recovered. "Out there in the pregame, we were trying to figure out what I was going to do to prevent from dropping the ball because of the sun," Kaufman said. "The sun and those high punts—that's basically what happened." The Wildcats fumbled the ball away three plays later, netting zero points from the golden opportunity, yet a tone had been set. After Josh Moore recovered the fumble at the 14, Washington mounted a 54-yard drive that ended when a fourth-and-6 pass by Brunell fell just out of reach of a diving Kralik. The two had kept the drive alive with a 17-yard completion.

Neither team put points on the board in the first quarter, and Washington's defense had made a stand of its own, holding the Wildcats to a net of 6 yards on 10 plays and no third-down conversions on three tries. The first score was set up by a Kaufman fumble, which came on a second-quarter run. On third-and-2, he charged up the middle and the ball popped out of his hands. Arizona recovered at the Husky 28. McLaughlin drilled a 34-yard field goal five plays later.

Like gasoline on hot asphalt, opportunities evaporated for the Huskies and ventures into the Arizona red zone—the area between the end zone and 20-yard line—left nary a trace on the scoreboard. Brunell engineered a drive in the second quarter that included a 31-yard pass to Mark Bruener and a 15-yard completion to Jason Shelley on fourth-and-2. The drive stalled at the Wildcat 8, and Travis Hanson set up for the field-goal attempt. An errant snap sent holder Eric Bjornson scrambling. He picked up the ball and his quarterbacking instincts kicked in. He zipped a tight spiral toward Bruener, but it was batted down at the last second and skittered across the end zone.

The Wildcats headed for the locker room, leading, 3-0. Their fans, many of whom were shirtless and grease-painted for the occasion, were frothing with excitement. Their team was 30 minutes away from knocking the college football world on its ear. The Dawgs finally scored in the third quarter when Jason Hanson booted a 24-yard field goal to forge a 3-3 tie. That score was little more than a bitter compromise for the Huskies, who had a first down on the UA 11 but were pushed back by a holding call. The teams each had one more series in the quarter before Arizona burned nearly eight minutes off the clock with a masterful, 17-play death march. McLaughlin capped that drive early in the fourth with a 20-yard chip shot.

Washington's next drive fizzled when a fumbled snap by Brunell gave Arizona the ball at the Husky 20. The Wildcats were unable to move far, but McLaughlin's foot was true on a 30-yard field goal, his third of the game.

With the clock winding down and Arizona leading by six, Washington had to scrap the running game and focus on an air strike. Brunell completed an 8-yard pass to Richard Thomas and one for 13 yards to Kralik before lofting a deep ball for Shelley. The freshman wideout grabbed the ball in full stride inside the Wildcat 20 and instantly was met by safety Tony Bouie. The ball, a kernel of popcorn, squirted out of Shelley's hands and into the arms of Arizona's Keshon Johnson.

The Huskies stopped Arizona on the ensuing drive, but Kaufman fumbled the booming punt on the Husky 6. Although he recovered the ball, his third fumble might have been the most costly. There would be no 94-yard drives against this Wildcat defense, a unit that only got tougher as the game progressed. Arizona put the game out of reach with 48 seconds to play when Malauulu charged in on a 1-yard keeper, capping a drive kept alive by a Billy Johnson run that covered 25 yards. Johnson led all rushers with 99 yards on 21 carries.

If the storm clouds swirling over the program were any distraction, Husky players weren't saying so. That's not to say Hobert was forgotten. "He's our friend and we're always going to support him," fullback Leif Johnson said. "It's kind of an uncomfortable situation because we don't know what's going to happen." But hanging this loss on the absence of one player, particularly one that had been struggling, was absurd. This was a defeat, plain and simple, and would have been one had Hobert made the trip. "It really didn't matter to us," Waldrop said. "Whatever they bring, we'll stop. Hobert, Brunell, or the third-string guy, it didn't matter."

The thing the Wildcats couldn't stop? Fans charging the field in glee. Twice, the game had to be stopped to clear the playing surface. Knowing zealots would take to the goalposts like ants to sugar, Arizona officials lowered the collapsible structures to the ground. Tucson rejoiced in the Wildcats' 16-3 throttling of the nation's No. 1 team. That ranking was one of the many distinctions the Huskies would lose; also history was the 22-game victory streak, which included 14 conference wins and 12 triumphs on the road. Suddenly, the dream of a second national title felt closer to a hangover. This team could not only be beaten, it could be spanked.

About the only thing the Huskies didn't lose was their inside track on a Rose Bowl berth. Oregon State and Washington State remained on the UW schedule, and with the help of a positive decision by the Pac-10, the Dawgs could assure themselves of a third consecutive trip to Pasadena by winning those games. That was of little consolation on this warm afternoon in the desert. "It hurts," Dave Hoffmann said. "It hurts more than I can describe. All of us are hurting, and it's going to hurt a long time."

Many Huskies seemed more stunned than frustrated or angry during postgame interviews. Some looked stunned, as if they had just witnessed a horrifying, sobering auto accident. A blank, did-I-just-see-what-I-think-I-saw stare. A photo moved on the AP wire showing a close-up of Brunell being gang-tackled by three Wildcats. His eyes were slits and his face was compressed. Clearly pained, he had the look of a man being swallowed whole by a python. The photo, run in sports pages coast to coast, was in stark contrast to standard shots of Brunell, which captured him darting through a hole, releasing a perfectly timed pitch, or pumping his fist in the end zone. But this game was unlike any in which Brunell had played. Although he had a career-best passing performance, completing 25 of 41 passing for 243 yards, the offense he piloted foundered on the ground. Arizona allowed just 90 rushing yards to a team that was averaging 208. "We've got our goal boards and we beat them in every category," Tomey said. "I told the guys this was not an upset. People have to start believing in us."

McLaughlin vowed to his roommate earlier in the week that Arizona would win the kicking game. It did. Miller punted eight times for an average of 47.3 yards, rocketing a 68-yard blast, and four times pinned the Huskies inside their 20. The Huskies started no drive beyond their 31-yard line. McLaughlin found his mark on an extra point and three field goals.

While Washington coaches and players were being interviewed on the field after the game, a small cluster of Arizona students leaned over the field-level railings and tried to get Don James's attention.

They chanted, "*WE DON'T PAY OUR QUARTERBACK! WE DON'T PAY OUR QUARTERBACK!*"

James ignored them. They continued. Finally, Dan Raley turned to them and said, "I wouldn't pay him, either. But I *would* pay that punter if I were you."

19

Bouncing Off
Rock Bottom

The second week of November was forgettable for the University of Washington. Dreams of another national title were all but extinguished by a cold shower of reality in Arizona, and the Huskies' New Year's Day plans were in the hands of a specially convened league committee. Washington tumbled to sixth in the AP poll, yet few seemed to notice; suddenly, monitoring polls became as meaningless as counting clouds.

More sobering news broke around midweek. Former Husky Scott Greenwood, a co-captain in the late 1970s, died of cancer three days after the Arizona game. Greenwood, 35, was a three-year starter at tight end and a member of Don James' original recruiting class.

On the same day Greenwood died, November 10, an unrelated press conference was held in the Tyee Center, which overlooks the football field. It was announced in that packed conference that Billy Joe Hobert had been declared ineligible by UW officials. His loan was reported to the Pac-10 as an NCAA rules violation. Live television coverage of the announcement preempted afternoon soap operas on some local stations. First Barbara Hedges and James spoke, then Hobert.

The three-member Pac-10 committee had yet to give its recommendation as to whether the Huskies should have to forfeit the eight games in which Hobert played. "It would be beyond my wildest dreams," Athletic Director Hedges said, "if this football program would have to forfeit games based on the actions of this individual. I think the facts will bear out." A day later, the committee decided to allow the school to keep all eight victories, pending approval from the Pac-10 council, then league presidents and chancellors. The council gave the recommendation the nod Sunday, a day after the OSU game, and the presidents and chancellors gave their OK the following Tuesday.

In his press conference, Hobert was emotional and somewhat defiant as he read a prepared statement and fielded questions at the podium. At times, his voice cracked. He said he resented implications that he knew he was violating NCAA rules by taking out the loan. "If I wanted to hide it, no one would have found out," he said. "It's a lot easier to go through other channels, like going to my parents and having it fall through their bank account, than directly depositing it in mine and having everything I bought put in my name." Later, however, when asked if he would do anything different if he had a chance to do it all over, he said, "Yeah, I'd hide it from you."

James said he had no indication that Hobert's lifestyle had changed during the spring. "I had no inclination he had spent one dime," he said. "Not one person came to me and said, 'Do you believe . . .?' I don't know how we could have done it without putting detectives on it.

"If we wanted, we could get into their lives so much we could take all of their freedoms away from them. We would have to get into cars, TVs, VCRs, the whole bit."

James spent part of the time in the press conference defending what he considered an attack on his credibility and integrity. Farrey and Nalder questioned when James first learned of the loan. Hedges and James insisted he first was told of the situation on November 4, a day before the story ran. The reporters said they had an interview on tape in which James confessed to knowing about the loans on November 2, two days before the story broke. That would imply James did not make an immediate effort to inform Hedges of a potential rules violation. "I didn't say that," James said to Farrey when questioned about the inconsistency. "You can't prove I said that. You *know* I didn't say that."

Hobert said he had a meeting with James the day before the Stanford game and—having been tipped off that a story was in the works—told him that reporters were checking on his bank account. Recalled James in the deposition: "It was something like, 'Coach, I think someone's investigating my bank account. They've called a couple of places I've been employed. Someone's inquiring about my bank account.' I told him there were privacy laws, they can't do that. He told me he just wanted to let me know." James said he didn't question Hobert further about the matter, such as asking him why reporters might be interested in his bank account or who told him this information.

After James left the press conference, Nalder asked Hedges about the date discrepancy.

"Are you questioning Don James's integrity?" she asked.

"He's questioning ours," Nalder said. "We *have* to question his. We'll get to the bottom of this if it takes a week, a month, or a year."

Standing away from the microphones and television cameras that once delighted him, Hobert stared at the ground, shook his head, and cracked a weak smile. This ranked among the darkest days of his life. He had been stripped of his NCAA eligibility. His spring transgressions had been exhumed and studied in some bizarre autopsy. All he could do was laugh. "If I wrote my book now," he mused to reporter Don Borst, "I'd call it 'Billy Dough—the $50,000 Man.' Has this thing gotten out of hand or what?"

II

To top off this week from hell, Walter Bailey and Eteka Huckaby were given one-game suspensions by James for missing classes. Those transgressions might have been a bigger deal any other week, but playing football now seemed little more than an afterthought. In describing the team, writers had started using words such as "beleaguered" and "embattled."

The good news for Washington? Oregon State was coming to town.

Not Stanford. Not Nebraska. Not USC. But Oregon State, the whipping boy of the Pac-10. "There's been a lot of frustrations on campus this week over what's gone on," Lincoln Kennedy said. "It's time to take it out on somebody."

Using the Beavers as a punching bag wasn't the only motivation; high stakes were riding on a win. A Washington victory and losses by Washington State and Arizona would send the Huskies on a third consecutive trip to Pasadena, provided the Pac-10 would give its blessing. Washington also could ensure itself of a Rose Bowl berth by winning its last two regular-season games, against Oregon State and Washington State. The Huskies might have had control of their own destiny in one sense, but in another, they were helpless. The media that once had praised them at almost every turn were now poking, prodding, and scouring for every possible impropriety. James told his players not to comment on the Hobert situation to reporters. Instead of attending a half-hour team meeting before Thursday's practice, Jim Lambright wandered alone through the stadium seats and practice field behind the east-end bleachers collecting his thoughts. "We've been treating this week just like any other week," he said later, "but I have to admit, it'll be nice when we can just talk about football around here. We're looking forward to getting back on the field and playing a game."

The memories of the Husky-Beavers game in 1985 haunted Lambright. Washington had been ranked No. 1 in the nation by several preseason publications that year, and the Huskies were 37-point favorites over the 2-4 Beavers. But Oregon State shocked the college football world that afternoon, blocking a punt late in the game and recovering the ball in the end zone for a 21-20 victory. "Don't think for a minute we don't remember that game," said Lambright, seven years removed from the agonizing defeat. "It still sends a chill up my spine every time I remember it."

The 1992 version of the OSU football team clung steadfastly to a wishbone offense that had netted the Beavers just two wins during Coach Jerry Pettibone's two seasons. "What this offense gives us is an opportunity to control the ball," Pettibone said, "take some time off the clock, to keep the other team's offense off the field, to move the ball, to score points, and to be competitive in the Pac-10 Conference."

If a lesson could be gleaned from the Huskies' lackluster win over Pacific, it was that no team could be overlooked. These were not the Dawgs of 1991. Washington could not console itself with the confidence that opponents might struggle gamely but would, ultimately, be steamrolled. The Beavers, too, had changed since absorbing a 58-6 pasting from Washington. "(OSU) is much better now," Lambright said. "Because they believe they can win, where a year ago they were just installing the offense and defense. Don't worry, this team (Washington) has noticed Oregon State is a lot better than last year. We know they tied Arizona and gave Washington State a great game. They demand your respect, and we're going to give it to them."

As it happens, the Beavers earned that respect. History will forget the particulars of Washington's 45-16 blowout. OSU players won't.

For the final 14 minutes of an otherwise lopsided game, the Beavers posted a moral victory by scoring touchdowns against the Huskies on consecutive drives. "We had our moments today," Pettibone said, "when we were able to move the ball against one of the best defenses in the country. We were able to play well on defense, and we were able to make some big plays with our kicking game." Most significantly, the Beavers were able to score as many as 16 points on Washington, something only Cal and Arizona had done.

Things worked in Washington's favor around the Pac-10: the Arizona Wildcats were dumped by USC, 14-7, and Washington State was on the ugly end of a 40-3 rout by Stanford. Those results garnered a third Rose Bowl berth for the Huskies. "This team has proven itself on the field," James said, "and I'm very proud of the job it has done. There are only a handful of teams that have been to three straight Rose Bowls, so they've joined a special group." Meanwhile, Big Ten champion and third-ranked Michigan tied Illinois, 22-22, to shore up its second consecutive Rose Bowl trip.

Again during the postgame press conference, James was asked if the Hobert situation distracted his players. The question agitated him. "You guys keep talking about distractions. I've read some things in the papers that are absolutely incredible . . . I mean, I don't beat my wife. There she is right back there," he said, motioning to Carol. "I don't kick the dog. I don't get mad at anybody. I don't quite understand some of the things I read."

Tension was thick, even after the Husky offense put on a show and, after the game, the crowd lingered to bid adieu to seniors who had played their last game at Husky Stadium. The atmosphere was subdued. Fans weren't about to charge the field and pull down the goalposts. "This week there was a lot of attention given to outside things, the ruling of the panel and stuff like that," Lincoln Kennedy said. "We knew that we needed to keep morale up and wanted to keep everybody together and try to make it back to Pasadena on January 1.

"The seniors wanted to come out today and set the tone and give the underclassmen some momentum to carry on the tradition. To give the fans what they pay their money for when they come to see the Huskies."

Those fans certainly didn't miss Hobert in this game. Brunell provided a good chunk of the Husky offense, scoring on runs of 6 and 3 yards and connecting with Eric Bjornson for an over-the-shoulder touchdown pass that covered 16 yards. "Brunell bought some time with his feet today," James said. "That's one thing a running quarterback can do for you. I thought he played well."

Damon Huard replaced Brunell in the third quarter and flashed his potential to the crowd of 70,149 by completing each of his three passes for a total of 92 yards, including a perfectly thrown touchdown bomb to freshman Theron Hill. That play covered 68 yards—28 more yards than the next-longest pass of the season.

Huard made a rookie mistake after the game. Not with the media. His answers were real, even insightful. He praised his teammates, downplayed his 3-for-3 passing performance, never veered from the party line. Then, the mistake: He sat in James's seat while talking to reporters. Washington's coach sat in the same corner of the interview room for his radio show after every home game. "Get out of here," James instructed Huard, chuckling and shooing the sophomore away. "I've got to work . . . You're a star, right? You play one game and you're a star?"

James was joking with the wide-grinned wunderkind. Sort of. Huard certainly had star potential, and it didn't take him long to go from sideline to spotlight. "These last couple of weeks, the opportunity has come," Huard said. "Here it is. You've always got to be ready. I just told myself that I may be third string, but every day I've got to be better. Because when my time comes, I've got to shine."

His shining moment arrived with 8:18 to play when he took a snap from the UW 31, rolled right, and gunned a perfect spiral to Hill, who never had to break stride to make the catch. "I beat him flat out," Hill said of the OSU player on his heels. "I don't mean to sound boastful, but I think I ran a nice crisp route and beat him ... This is the future. I'm the future, he's the future (pointing to Shelley), and he's the future (pointing to Huard)."

Although he didn't score, Kaufman gained 146 yards on 12 carries—a whopping 12.2 yards per attempt—and pushed his season rushing total to 997 yards. "We established the offensive tone on the first play today," he said. "The offensive unit played great. We moved the ball real well."

Washington was in control from the start, yet OSU's wishbone attack was effective at times. The Beavers outgained Washington on the ground, 251 yards to 245. The passing numbers were more indicative of the outcome: the Huskies threw for 294 yards, OSU for 9. Eight OSU ball carriers gained more than 10 yards, and Curtis Willis led all rushers with 47 yards on 11 carries. He scored the first OSU touchdown, charging 2 yards over the middle, where he met Shane Pahukoa and Dave Hoffmann at the goal line. They knocked him back, but after he had broken the plane for a score. "It was good contact," Willis said of the collision. "It didn't hurt, but it was a solid hit."

There were plenty of those in this game. Beavers quarterback Mark Olford could attest to that. He was replaced by Ian Shields during the first quarter after twisting an ankle. Late in the second quarter, Olford replaced Shields, who lost a contact lens. "This is the most physical game I've played in this year," Olford said, gingerly buttoning his shirt. "Most of the others I come out of without any soreness other than just getting tackled."

The sheer number of gang tackles impressed OSU running back Chad Paulson, held to 9 yards on six carries. "We would try to run inside and there would be a thousand guys there," he said. "Then we would go outside and there would be a thousand guys there." Paulson ranked the Husky defense as better than that of Arizona. "Washington is a lot faster (than Arizona)," he said. "They are well-coached and have a good scheme. They did some good things against the wishbone."

Strong safety Tommie Smith had one of his best days of the season. Two plays by him were particularly memorable. He foiled the Beavers' opening drive by penetrating the backfield and slapping down an Olford pitch. Smith one-hopped the ball at the OSU 23 and weaved his way to the end zone. The apparent touchdown was negated, however, because a deflected pitch cannot be advanced. The Huskies took possession at the 23, and Kaufman broke a 17-yard ramble two plays later that set up Brunell's 6-yard touchdown run.

Smith picked off an Olford pass in the second quarter after Pahukoa batted the ball in the air. "All of us seniors wanted to go out and have a good time today," said Smith, who led the Dawgs with 13 tackles. "We had made a couple of challenges last night—to show the underclassmen how to go out with a bang."

20

The Froze Bowl

Anthony McClanahan launched the first Apple Cup salvo.

The outspoken Washington State University linebacker offered a pointed critique of the Huskies. "They don't look as good on film as a lot of teams," he said. "They don't look good, period."

Let the mind games begin.

What might have read like a broadside slap by McClanahan was merely a kickoff to the barrel-chested banter the schools exchange before every Apple Cup game. Predictable as the swallows returning to Capistrano, the yearly spate of trash talking tends to add spice to sports pages on both sides of the Cascades. In the aftermath of an Apple Cup, there is no place so giddy, so whooping and raucous, as the winners' locker room. "There are four important stages in your life," former WSU guard Dan Lynch noted in 1984. "You're born, you play the Huskies, you get married, and you die."

So McClanahan's comments were just part of the good-natured quote war that goes on during game week. Everyone participates, even Don James, who quipped in 1983, "I've always felt being a Cougar prepares you well for life. You learn not to expect too much," and of facing former WSU coach Jim Walden, known for his colorful quotes, "I'm a 2,000-word underdog."

Former Cougar Mark Rypien, quarterback of the Washington Redskins, tried to reach WSU coach Mike Price by telephone five times during the 1992 Apple Cup week. The two finally hooked up Friday night, while Price was putting the finishing touches on the game plan. "I've only met the guy once, so that's how much this game means to him," Price said. "He said it can be one of the best memories you'll ever have. He said he'd been to two Super Bowls, but his best memory was walking around Seattle after winning the Apple Cup."

A win would be particularly sweet for Price, whose coaching style had been questioned for much of his four-year career at the school. His head was on the chopping block more than once. He had never beaten a Top 20 team, and living across the mountains from a school that shared a national title didn't make things any easier. Besides, when it came to tasting the fruits of an Apple Cup win, Price was overdue. He was 0-3 as a head coach against Washington, 0-6 as an assistant, and 0-2 as a Cougar player.

Now, his chance for greatness had arrived. Washington players, sobered by Billygate, weren't going to give the Cougars any bulletin-board ammunition. James put a gag order on his players that outlawed any form of Cougar-slamming. So even though McClanahan's jaw-flapping begged a retort, it didn't get one. "We know what's going to be said," James Clifford said, when told of the remark. "Washington State has said things like that in the past . . . I don't think there's a place for that in this game. You need the respect of your opponent. It doesn't make me feel good, but it doesn't do me any good to put anyone down."

James also banned talk of Pasadena. A ring company representative knocked on his door Monday morning and inquired about the desired design on the 1993 Rose Bowl rings.

"Get out of here!" James snapped. "All we want to think about is Washington State."

In a sense, the pressure was off the Huskies for this game. The team had moved up to No. 5 in the AP poll and, for the third consecutive year, the Rose Bowl race had been decided in Washington's favor by Apple Cup time. The most significant thing riding on this game for them was state bragging rights and bowl-season momentum. That meant a lot. "I'd love to go into every game for the rest of my life with a championship in my pocket and to be able to just think about the game," James said. "It probably takes a little bit of pressure off, but it's hard to put much more pressure on this game."

On Tuesday, the Huskies received final clearance from the Pac-10 to represent the conference in the Rose Bowl, yet the team wasn't off the hook: a formal investigation of the program would be conducted by the Pac-10 and probably would last for months. "Anything is possible, including forfeiture," said Tom Hansen, Pac-10 commissioner, adding, "It would have been a lot better if this had been reviewed in February or June. But it has to be addressed in the manner that it was because of the timing of the bowl ... There was some discomfort in how this had to be done."

Conference staffers David Price and Mike Matthews were instructed to do a white-glove inspection of Washington and turn over their findings to a four-person league compliance committee, which would offer a recommendation as to any penalties. News of the clearance allowed the Huskies a momentary sigh of relief, although it left open the possibility of a delayed punishment.

By most accounts, James ran a squeaky-clean program, but one league official, who requested anonymity, said the Huskies were getting a reputation for interpreting the NCAA rule book loosely, pushing regulations to the limit. "It's almost as if there is a King James Version of the rule book," the official said. "If he doesn't think it's a violation, it must not be a violation."

That comment filtered to Pullman, where it was promptly printed on T-shirts and buttons sold during game week. Emblazoned across the chest of some shirts was a gigantic $50,000 check made out to Billy Joe Hobert. The front of another shirt asked, "What's the difference between the Huskies and a 20-pound bucket of crap?" On the back, the answer: "The bucket."

Washington State fans were pumped for this game. Stakes riding on the Apple Cup were high for the Cougars, who might have been neck and neck with Washington for the Rose Bowl berth had they not lost to Stanford a week earlier. Had WSU defeated the Cardinal, it would be just the second time in history that the Apple Cup would decide which of the Washington schools would spend New Year's Day in Pasadena. Getting so close before falling short pained the Cougars. "You get a chance to go to the big one when everything else falls into place and everybody else does their job," Mike Price said. "... We're a little disappointed and discouraged right now. We're going to pout for a while."

During the course of the 1992 season, the Cougars were both awe inspiring and awful. An uninspired win over Montana in the opener was followed by more impressive victories over Arizona, Fresno State, Temple, Oregon State, and a 30-17 win over UCLA in which WSU looked like a juggernaut. A gut-wrenching game at USC gave the Cougars a slash in the loss column, and a victory over Arizona State was sandwiched by losses to Oregon and Stanford. WSU entered the Apple Cup a respectable 7-3 but in danger of missing out on a bowl berth.

For the second time in his career at Washington, senior Tommie Smith would have to sit out the game because he missed a class. "We've had a group of guys all season long who are not allowed to miss a class at all," James explained. "And when they miss them, as Smith apparently did, they don't play." Louis Jones was promoted to start at strong safety in place of Smith, who also sat out the 1990 Apple Cup because of academic problems. Jones would have his hands full.

The biggest gun in the WSU arsenal happened to be one of the most dangerous offensive weapons in the nation, rangy quarterback Drew Bledsoe. A 6-foot-5 junior, Bledsoe had a rocket launcher for a right arm and cut a commanding presence on the field. Even though he had the arm strength to overthrow anyone short of Saddam Hussein, he had struggled of late. During the Cougars' first seven games, he threw for an average of 276.2 yards, yet his average for the past three games dropped to 199.6. A strong performance in the Apple Cup would be critical for Bledsoe. There was a chance this could be his last college game because he was considering making himself eligible for the NFL draft a year early. Ultimately, he did.

While at Washington State, Bledsoe learned to hate the Huskies. Or *unlearned* to love them. Drew's father, Mac, was a Washington offensive tackle and team captain in the late 1960s. Drew chose a different path. "I had a special feeling about coming here," he said. "It's not like you can really choose between Washington and Washington State. Once you make the decision, it's all or nothing."

Washington officials had a strong inkling of which way Bledsoe would lean when he sat emotionless in Husky Stadium during a recruiting trip, watching the Dawgs whip WSU in the 1989 Apple Cup. An acrid disdain for the Huskies was already forming in the lanky slinger from Walla Walla, Wash., who also turned down a scholarship offer from Miami to play in Pullman.

During the week preceding the 1992 Apple Cup, ESPN made a blunder that was, in a word, *vidiotic*. The network ran a story on Bledsoe, identifying him as the star quarterback of the Huskies. The anchor went so far as to wish him well in the Rose Bowl. For Bledsoe, who watched the story with friends in his apartment, the gaffe crystallized the frustration he felt about the Cougars' lack of exposure. "It just shows how little respect we get around the nation," he said. "I just wanted to beat Washington more because of it."

Had Bledsoe attended Washington, his would have gone down as the best arm in Husky history. Bart Wright, a columnist in Tacoma, recalled a telephone conversation between him and his son, Jamie, a quarterback who attended football camp with Bledsoe when the two were high school juniors:

"Dad, you've *got* to see this guy. He's amazing."

"Why?"

"He can stand at the 20 and hit a receiver in the end zone!"

"Well, you can do that, Jamie. That's just 20 yards."

"No, I mean the *other* end zone."

II

Dave Hoffmann lifted back the curtains in his Moscow, Idaho, motel room Saturday morning and peered out. Snow had dusted the parking lot lightly but leaden skies indicated plenty more would fall. Hoffmann smiled.

Let it snow, brother, let it snow.

The wintery scene reminded him of those magical times he would curl up in front of the TV and watch his head-butting heroes thrash in the powder. Linemen, with churning legs and breath coming out in thick, white puffs, looked like locomotives. A hard hit would send a guy on a 10-yard slide. Now, it was Hoffmann's turn to play in the snow. Finally.

Dick Butkus, meet Dave Hoffmann. Soldier Field, welcome to Martin Stadium. "I was thinking," the Husky hitman recalled, "that this could be one of the funnest games of my life."

When Hoffmann thought of snow games, it conjured memories of Bears-Packers, not Huskies-Cougars. He wanted to forget the snowy Apple Cup of 1988, the last time the Cougars won the bitter showdown. He was a redshirt freshman that season and played no part in the debacle in which the Huskies built a 28-16 lead at halftime before losing, 32-31. While the teams were in the locker room at halftime, the snow really began to fall, and conditions approached blizzard proportions when the players emerged. Throwing the ball in that type of weather is next to impossible, so the teams resorted to their ground games. WSU began to dominate play, and ultimately outgained the Huskies, 450 yards to 282. Five Cougar turnovers kept Washington in the game. The Huskies led, 31-26, in the fourth quarter when WSU's Shawn Landrum exploded through the line to block a punt, setting up the go-ahead score. Recalled Eric Canton, then UW's punter: "All of a sudden, there was this guy taking it off my foot."

Back in Seattle, watching in anguish on dormitory TVs were several redshirt freshmen, including Hoffmann, Lincoln Kennedy, and Darius Turner. Their pain turned to frustration, then to vows of revenge, as the cameras panned the WSU sidelines capturing Cougars as they frolicked and taunted. James Clifford was the only Husky on the 1992 team to set foot on the field in the 1988 heartbreaker. "That was a pretty devastating plane ride home," he recalled. "It was so quiet. I remember thinking, 'This is the seniors' last game—they didn't have a chance to run off the field celebrating. That's not right.'" Cougars fans, their team headed to the Aloha Bowl, charged the turf and climbed on the goalposts that folded under their weight.

No, when Hoffmann gazed out at the snow blanketing the parking lot, he was not haunted by 1988. This was a new age of an attacking UW defense and precision offense. These Huskies were 3-0 against the Cougars, and the final scores didn't exactly have Hoffmann and his pals biting their nails: 20-9 in 1989, 55-10 in 1990, and 56-21 in 1991. In the experience of Hoffmann and his teammates, Washington State was more toothless nuisance than a legitimate contender for a league title, the little guy in a bar fight whose roundhouse swings are negated by an effortless straight-arm to the forehead.

The weather service predicted snow for Pullman, but who knew there would be this much of it for the Apple Cup? The skies above Martin Stadium were dark the day before the game, yet when the Huskies held a brief workout, it appeared as if the weather would hold for Saturday. "It was just perfect," Brunell said. "It was cold, but that's no big deal. The turf was fine. We had the right shoes, we weren't slipping. It was a whole different ball game the next day."

Brunell, Hoffmann, and the rest of the Huskies learned something when they took the field Saturday for pregame warm-ups: The romance of snow football is fleeting. The icy wind whistled through the stadium, turning snowflakes into pinpricks. Wet fingers swelled at the knuckles and red palms were raw with that stinging, rope-burned feel. Tight leg muscles first shivered, then quaked.

One fall to the rock-hard turf meant a soaked uniform. Not only was it tricky to run to a spot but nearly impossible to dig feet in deep enough to make a solid tackle. Making a tackle was akin to standing on roller skates at the bottom of a steep driveway and catching a runaway VW bug. For receivers, sharp cuts were impossible, making down-and-out patterns look closer to bananas than right angles. Joe Kralik called them Ivy League routes.

"It was a weird feeling," said Hoffmann, whose opinion of the white stuff plummeted faster than the thermometer. "It was like, 'Well, I'm going to do what I can on this, but this isn't what we expected.'" The slick surface negated any speed advantage the Huskies had. Running on the field felt like sprinting across a newly waxed ballroom floor in socks. "I can remember just trying to get up and go," Brunell recalled. "Just trying to get my burst going. I felt like (former Husky Cary) Conklin trying to run. It was horrible. A nightmare."

The bite in the air was more than mild; this was bitter cold. The angry, shrill wind was the worst. Restroom lines were especially long—anything to momentarily escape the elements. Tacoma columnist John McGrath, who grew up in Chicago and worked as a sportswriter there for several years, said the 1992 Apple Cup was colder than any Bears game he endured at Soldier Field. Small clusters of players, shrouded in long, hooded jackets, swarmed around heaters the way they would a fumbled ball. No fewer than 20 people were treated for exposure by the WSU Fire Department. One shirtless goofball, his brain freezer-burned, led the Husky fans in a cheer. He was later seen wrapped in a parka, teeth chattering like novelty choppers.

Jason Shelley, who grew up in Vallejo, California, had never seen snow before. He wasn't too excited to see it again. "As soon as you'd walk away from the heater on the sidelines, your hands would get cold again," he recalled. "My hands were so cold, they kept getting numb. I couldn't feel my fingers."

The press box offered safe harbor, warmth, and an odd sense of sanitized detachment. A football game was going on, but thick panes of glass and the buzz of heaters separated reporters from the action. The crowd could be heard, but not the familiar clap of shoulder pads colliding and rawboned pop of crashing helmets. More so than at other stadiums, watching the game from this press box was almost like seeing it on TV—something that could be done because ABC televised the matchup to half the country.

Among those watching in the press box was decathlete Dan O'Brien, who missed the 1992 Olympic Games but later set the world record in the event. O'Brien, who attended the University of Idaho and lived and trained in Moscow, Idaho, was an avid Cougar football fan. He came to every WSU home game but one in 1992.

"Do you consider yourself the world's greatest athlete?" a reporter sitting next to him asked.

"Nope," O'Brien said, smiling.

"Then who is?"

"The world's greatest athlete is Anthony McClanahan. That's my boy."

Right about then, the world's toughest job seemed to be keeping snow off the playing surface. Field crews worked furiously to try to keep the green turf visible. It was a losing battle; while a snowblower was pushed over one part of the field, the section that was just cleared needed another sweeping. Finally, the crew resorted to clearing off cross-field strips every 5 yards so the officials, teams, and fans could determine field position. The extreme elements made the players look like weekend warriors holding a pickup game in a ski-lodge parking lot. Even the fastest runners moved haltingly, cut gingerly. Slower players simply plodded.

Playing in snow was foreign to the Cougars, yet they seemed to take a more sanguine approach to the elements than the Huskies. Right before kickoff, several WSU players changed into high-top cleats called "Destroyers." The players said the shoes bit into the turf better than standard ones. During warm-ups, the home team formed a single-file line and gleefully took turns sliding face-first into a snow bank in the back of the end zone.

Steam curled off their bodies. The crowd, huddled shoulder to shoulder, roared with approval.

That enthusiasm carried over into the opening series, which WSU began at its 20-yard line. The Cougars moved the ball quickly, purposefully, picking up 15 yards on a personal-foul call and 20 on a completion from Bledsoe to C. J. Davis. Bledsoe, working with his back to the wind, stood tall in the pocket and delivered his bullets with the zip that would make cold, bare hands scream. On third-and-13 at the Washington 27, he again found Davis for a gain of 22. It was clear that something was missing from the Husky defense. Huge running lanes formed up the middle, and the pass rush was anything but menacing. "It seemed like (Bledsoe) had 99 seconds to throw," Jamal Fountaine would lament later. "I couldn't catch him. I couldn't touch him. I couldn't even catch his footsteps." Nor could the Huskies catch those of Shaumbe Wright-Fair, who capped the opening drive by slipping around the left side of the line and into the end zone for a 3-yard touchdown. The extra-point kick failed, but the 6-0 advantage stood for the first quarter.

Late in the period, the Huskies pushed WSU back to its 10, benefiting from a sack of Bledsoe and a holding call. After a short punt, Washington took over in Cougar territory and moved the ball with several runs and a 14-yard completion from Brunell to Damon Barry. Early in the second quarter, Brunell culminated the 13-play drive by sprinting left for a 1-yard touchdown. The point-after kick gave the Huskies a one-point edge, an advantage that encouraged James. "I thought a seven-point lead might be tough to overcome," he confided. "To tell you the truth, I thought our 7-6 lead might hold up."

A goal-line stand by the Dawgs cemented that notion. WSU mounted a drive midway through the second quarter that died at the Husky 2. Bledsoe was razor sharp during the march, completing passes to Davis, Brett Carolan, and Phillip Bobo, and moved the Cougars to the UW 9. Wright-Fair ran up the gut for 6 yards on first down, and Bledsoe did the same on second down for a yard. The Husky defense stiffened, stopping Derek Sparks for no gain on third-and-goal at the 2 and stuffing Boone Borden for a loss of 2 to get the ball back.

No one could ever quite explain what happened in the locker rooms at halftime, but the results will go down in WSU lore for as long as there is football on the Palouse. Torrey Hunter, a Cougar cornerback, will be able to tell his grandchildren a special version of the story. He and Bledsoe had a prophetic conversation while driving to class Thursday. It went something like this:

"Drew, what do you do if it snows?"

"I can throw in snow."

"Gonna change the game plan?"

"Nope."

The Cougars had an option at the start of the second half to take the ball or the wind at their back. They chose the wind. It reached speeds of 20 mph and was nearly impossible to move against. The snow was wet, soaking everything it touched, and the temperature had dropped further. The biting cold, and a Cougar scoring flurry, seemed to smother the Huskies' fire.

"They were too cold," McClanahan recalled of the Washington players. "They didn't feel like being out there. One guy said: 'Don't hit me. My hands are cold.' He was a lineman. I couldn't believe it. I told him, 'I'll hit you and warm 'em up.' He was just like a little baby. Put a little baby out in the cold with no clothes and it's gonna cry all day."

Said WSU tackle Konrad Pimiskern: "They really took themselves out of it. They were bitching about the snow the whole game. I mean, it's Apple Cup, man. You've got to go out there and beat the hell out of them. I think they lost their heart—I really do."

Lost it or had it excised with the surgical precision of a Drew Bledsoe bullet. And there were a season's worth of those laser-beam throws in the third quarter. The first time the Cougars touched the ball in the second half gave an indication of things to come. WSU started the drive at its 30, and Bledsoe hit Bobo for 10 years on first down. Wright-Fair tore off a 15-yard scamper, then a 1-yard dive. Next, Bledsoe faked a handoff and dropped back. He settled his feet and stood in the pocket for what seemed like hours. Finally, he casually unleashed a perfect spiral that cut a swath through the driving snow. As the ball made its downward arc, Bobo snared it from the sky and slid face-first into the snow bank at the base of the west goalposts. It was a highlight clip for the ages. Bobo popped to his feet, reached his arms out at his sides, and nodded his head in an exaggerated way. "Yeah, baby! Yeah, baby!" he screamed. "That's what I'm talking 'bout!"

To hear Bledsoe describe the play, it had a touch of serendipity. "I was actually looking for C. J. (Davis), but he was covered," he said. "I just put it up for grabs. If Phillip hadn't caught it, C. J. would have." Bledsoe hooked up with Calvin Schexnayder on a two-point conversion pass that put the Cougars up by a touchdown.

Washington could get nothing accomplished on the next series and punted the ball back to the Cougars. Again, Bledsoe went to work, completing passes of 17, 29, and 8 yards before finding Schexnayder with a 15-yard touchdown pass. The response from the Huskies was meek—three plays, 4 yards, a punt. WSU showed no mercy, scoring when Wright-Fair burst up a massive hole in the middle to score on a 51-yard gallop.

On the first play of the ensuing drive, Kaufman fumbled and the ball was recovered by WSU at the Washington 32. Bledsoe fumbled on the 1 four plays later but, just as these type of games go, Pimiskern was there to recover the ball in the end zone for another Cougar touchdown.

In the end, WSU had a 42-23 victory, Bledsoe threw for 260 yards, and Wright-Fair collected 194 on the ground, the most ever by a Cougar in this series. The Huskies were left to collect the shards of their shattered pride and listen to interminable analyses like those of Cougar tight end Butch Williams, who crowed: "We killed their will. In the third quarter, they were coming off the ball hard, but they weren't pursuing. It was like they were trying to make it look good."

McClanahan, who made the harsh critique early in the week, also got in the last word. Waiting to say a few words into a TV camera, he stood shirtless in the Cougar locker room, his heavily muscled upper body covered with goose bumps. His eye sockets were ringed with eye-black, a special makeover for this game. "This is the best day of my life," he gushed. "When I was born, that was a great day. When I die, that will be a great day. When I go to see The Man. But this is the best day of my life so far."

Maybe it was the thrill of the moment that had McClanahan shivering, maybe it was the chill of the elements. Probably both. "I kind of envisioned things this way," he said. "I thought about it when I was sleeping. I thought it might be a tie, a real close game. But I never thought it would be a blowout."

Neither did the Husky players, some of whom looked dazed, almost disoriented, as they left the field. Many shook the hands of their adversaries and watched with detached curiosity as WSU fans shimmied up the goalposts. This was Washington's worst defeat since a 47-14 loss at UCLA in 1987.

Carol James passed out roses to the Huskies before they stepped into the locker room. Fred Soldwedel, a representative of the Tournament of Roses, was greeted with polite applause as he presented the team with its official invitation to Pasadena. The timing couldn't have been worse. It was an awkward ceremony for both the Huskies and Soldwedel, who, one reporter noted, looked "like he had been force-fed the Granddaddy of All Banana Splits."

Meanwhile, the Cougars lobbied fiercely for a bowl berth. They were 8-3 and had beaten the nation's fifth-ranked team; the possibility of them staying home on New Year's Day was nothing short of criminal. James agreed. "If they don't get invited," the Washington coach said, "it just means that there are a number of teams that aren't near as good as Washington State who are in bowls. And that's a tragedy." Apparently, representatives of the Copper Bowl thought so, too. The next morning, the Cougars received a bid to play Utah in that Tucson, Arizona, game on December 29.

As for the Huskies, Pasadena seemed a million miles away.

21

Drug Bust: When Worlds Collide

The arrest of reserve defensive end Danianke Smith on felony drug charges sent shock waves rippling through the Washington football program, Seattle and beyond. The allegations had nothing to do with some Byzantine infraction of the NCAA rulebook; these marked the collision of Husky football and the Real World.

"We are shocked and dismayed about the events of today," Athletic Director Barbara Hedges said at a news conference.

Said Don James: "We've seen in our society the drugs get from the cities into the universities to the high schools to the elementary schools. It's frightening. Even more frightening is having a seller on your team."

And that's what the Huskies appeared to have. On the evening of November 23, 1992, Seattle police arrested Smith to culminate a seven-month investigation of narcotics and firearms dealing. In all, eight people in the Seattle area were arrested, including Smith, 22, and three former UW athletes. More than 50 Seattle officers participated in four raids.

According to the prosecution, a senior from Long Beach, California, Smith was charged with four counts of delivery of cocaine and one count of delivery of marijuana, with some of the transactions taking place at the Conibear Shellhouse, a.k.a. the crewhouse, a dormitory that mainly houses athletes and is due east of the athletic department building. In addition, he was charged with arranging the sale of an assault rifle to an undercover police officer, a case that was turned over to federal authorities. Also arrested were former Husky linebacker James Goodwin, former UW hurdler Bernard Ellison, and a former member of the basketball team, Doug Meekins, the second-leading scorer for the Huskies in 1991.

Charged with cocaine delivery were Smith (four counts), Meekins (four), Robert Fred Johnson (four), Alexandra Sandoval (three), Ellison (two), and Daphne Pie (one). John Reisig was charged with two counts of marijuana delivery. Pie was Smith's girlfriend, Johnson was a UW graduate student, Sandoval was described in court papers as Smith's drug supplier, and Reisig was a service station attendant who, according to court papers, lived with two Husky football players who were not home when the raid took place.

During the raid of Johnson's apartment, police seized 148 grams of cocaine with a street value of $14,800, as well as three scales and a .25-caliber handgun. They seized 220 grams of cocaine, valued at $22,000, at Meekins's apartment. "Because of the volume of cocaine involved," King County prosecutor Norm Maleng said, "these defendants cannot be described as small-time cocaine dealers."

Bail was set at $150,000 for Smith, who spent Thanksgiving behind bars. Distraught, his parents put up their house as collateral so that he could be bonded out of jail.

In a startling development three weeks before the case was to go to trial in late May 1993, all charges were dropped against Smith, Pie, Reisig, and Sandoval after a King County Superior Court judge found prosecutors violated court rules requiring them to disclose all information they had to Smith's attorneys. Ultimately, all charges against the three remaining suspects, Meekins, Johnson, and Ellison were dropped on the same grounds.

Defense attorneys sought dismissal of all charges on grounds that the state's key witness had a criminal record and had an undisclosed motive for going to police, something that started the investigation. The witness, Samuel Nemours, was a UW student who approached police and initially told them he was tired of working hard to get through school while athletes on scholarship were selling drugs, and expressed concern about drugs getting into the hands of children. Nemours had been in trouble with the law before; he was charged with property destruction after allegedly breaking windows on Capitol Hill and charged with harassing a 14-year-old girl in Kent, Washington.

Defense attorneys said they belatedly learned about a secondary motive that Nemours told police—that he would help them find whether two former Husky football players not charged in the case were involved in or knew anything about the disappearance and possible murder four or five years ago of his friend in Los Angeles, Marcus Pope. One of the players was identified in court papers as a past associate of Smith, and his apartment was searched by police when the arrests were made; police found amounts of suspected marijuana, but no arrest was made.

"The newly disclosed information interjects new facts into these cases shortly before the most crucial stage of this proceeding, the trial itself," Judge Joan E. DuBuque said in court papers. "Based on the issues involved in this case and the history of discovery in this case, it is apparent that none of the defense counsel will have a sufficient opportunity to adequately prepare a material part of their defense by the time of trial without waiving once again their rights to a speedy trial. Under circumstance of this case, they should not be forced to make a choice.

"After having waived their rights to a speedy trial in order to obtain discovery, these defendants have suffered impermissable prejudice by the way in which the State has managed the case and its discovery responsiblity, which directly impedes their ability to have a fair trial."

Contacted by telephone in Los Angeles, the two former Huskies accused by Nemours of possibly murdering "Marcus Pope" said they were stunned by the report, didn't know a Samuel Nemours, much less a Marcus Pope, and vehemently denied any connection with the crime that Nemours alleged.

Adding another bizarre twist to an already strange story: as of mid-May 1993, a check by the Los Angeles Police Department of city and county records showed that no missing-person or homicide reports had been filed on anyone named Marcus Pope.

Nemours, graduate of Highline High in Burien, Washington, said he was a poor student until Pope disappeared. After that, he said he "kicked his grades up" in order to be admitted to the UW, foster a friendship with the Husky players he believes were responsible for Pope's disappearance, and, finally, avenge his friend. Court papers say Nemours grades did, indeed, improve during high school.

In April 1992, Nemours notified Seattle narcotics detectives that a current Husky football player and three former athletes from the school were dealing drugs. The identity of Nemours, an acquaintance of Smith's, was initially kept secret out of concern for his safety. He did, however, agree to testify if the cases went to trial.

Alfred Matthews, King County senior deputy prosecutor, described the informant as a disgruntled student, tired of seeing athletes living lavish lifestyles. "He was irritated that he was working his ass off to get through school and these people who enjoyed scholarships were selling drugs," Matthews said. "He got angry." The student agreed to help undercover investigators arrange drug buys and to be wired to record drug-related conversations with the sellers.

An investigation was initiated and, by August, began to zero in on Smith, Sandoval, Pie, and Reisig. The informant and narcotics officers made a combined seven drug buys from Smith, many of which involved undercover narcotics investigator Todd Jakobsen.

Smith instructed Nemours and Jakobsen to page him by keying in their phone number followed by a secret code, 55, which was his Husky jersey number. According to court documents, Smith conducted drug sales out of the crewhouse and made transactions at a service station down the street from Husky Stadium and at restaurants around town.

Police said Smith tried to arrange the sale of an Uzi machine gun, but his supplier could not procure one and, instead, the supplier sold the informant an AK-47 assault rifle for $460. Smith could not conduct one alleged transaction because it was the night before the Huskies' game with Wisconsin.

According to court papers, Smith left the crewhouse after 11 p.m. bed check on September 21 to meet Jakobsen at a service station and make a $500 rock cocaine deal.

By the time Smith was arrested on November 18, he and Jakobsen were discussing a $19,000 cocaine deal, court documents said, and Smith sought the telephone number of a former Husky player who "made a run to California every other weekend to obtain 3 to 4 kilos of cocaine." That player was targeted in a raid on his Ballard apartment, yet he was not arrested because of a lack of evidence.

The arrest of Smith on drug charges jolted his teammates, most of whom knew him as hard working and likable. "I'm still in shock," Beno Bryant said a day after the arrest. "This is a shock to everyone, I'm sure . . . None of us knew anything about it. I just woke up this morning and heard about it."

Said Andy Mason: "When we traveled on the road, we were the tightest two guys. When we were in the weight room and training room, we were almost inseparable."

Smith, named Most Improved Defensive Lineman during the spring, was atop the depth chart at strongside linebacker before switching to defensive end toward the conclusion of fall camp. Said Mark Brunell, "There's not a guy on this team that doesn't like 'Nock."

That's not to say Smith never had his run-ins with authorities, including members of the Washington coaching staff. He was suspended three years earlier after grabbing the buttocks of a stewardess on the flight home after a 51-14 victory at Oregon State. Usually, the coaches sit in first class and seldom venture to the back of the plane. The stewardess who was allegedly grabbed immediately walked up to first class and told James of the incident. Fuming, he stormed to the back of the plane, demanded an explanation, and ultimately suspended Smith, who sat out the final two games of the 1989 season and 1990 spring practice.

Smith received one deferred sentence in fall 1992 for using another student's credit card, and another deferred sentence in 1990 after pleading guilty to illegally firing a gun in Seattle's Ravenna Park, and performing 100 hours of community service. The episode was described by Smith's lawyers this way: "A review of the incident shows that neither drugs nor gangs were involved, and there was no 'victim.' Mr. Smith and a friend engaged in a stupid, reckless, juvenile prank with a gun—firing it into the air. The gun, a 12-gauge shotgun, has been disposed of."

Smith accumulated 18 traffic and minor criminal violations in Seattle Municipal Court, including a minor theft at a UW dormitory in 1989.

On June 5, 1992, Smith was charged with unlawful possession of a weapon after a .38 caliber automatic pistol was found in his car. The gun was found when his car, a 1983 Blazer, was towed by university police for being illegally parked. All charges were dropped. According to documents prepared by Smith's attorneys, Smith had lent his Blazer to a friend on the previous evening, and that friend left his registered, legal handgun in the car. According to his lawyers, Smith was found not guilty, not because there was no proof that he was in his car at the time but because the gun did not belong to him, was not placed in the car by him, and he never knew of its presence in the car.

Another episode involving Smith and a gun happened July 26, 1992, and ultimately all charges against the player were dropped. In that case, Smith was charged with discharging a firearm. According to his lawyers, Smith was contacted by a friend around midnight (he was awakened from a dead sleep), and told that another friend was intoxicated and needed a ride home. Smith was able to talk to other people at the location and arrange for his drunk friend to get a ride to Smith's home. Lawyers say Smith then "did the responsible thing" and drove his friend home.

During the ride home, without warning, the friend leaned out the window and shot a handgun into the air. Smith was pulled over and the two were charged. At trial, according to Smith's lawyers, the evidence showed "beyond any question" that Smith never even knew that his friend was even armed and had nothing to do with the discharge of the firearm.

James did not know that Smith was being investigated by Seattle Police but was well aware of the player's previous brushes with the law. Because of Smith's track record, James asked that he reside on campus. "He'd been on probation," the coach said. "He had been suspended previously. He was moved back on campus because of the people he was palling around with."

Even after all of his problems, Smith was never kicked off the team.

"Philosophically," James said, "the easiest way to solve a problem with a player is to release him from the team. But you get into a whole bunch of rules and regulations regarding financial aid, so a lot of times that doesn't happen. When a player has a problem, we try to solve the problem—spend time with them and make them productive citizens.

"I went through the lawsuits with (Kevin) Conard and (Vince) Fudzie. I'm really concerned about that. That's the nature of society. If you release a player and you don't have them by rights ... If you're not sure, you're not positive and you can't give them more than rumors or innuendoes, if you release that player you're probably going to get a lawsuit.

"I'm really careful in everything I do with player suspensions. I cannot take them off scholarship, I can just recommend them to be taken off aid for the following year."

22

How Much Is That Dawgie In The Window?

Handsome "paychecks" distributed monthly. Free use of cars. Tickets to sporting events. An overflowing slush fund managed by cash-wielding boosters. Life was sweet if you played football for the University of Washington.

In 1955.

Long before the *Los Angeles Times* broke a story in December 1992 alleging UW boosters provided Husky players with bogus jobs and improper benefits, the Washington football program weathered sanctions. Contrary to the belief that college football once was an unsullied bastion of amateurism, scandals in the game predate the forward pass. Some schools would go to extreme, downright comical lengths to win games. Consider these cases:

• George Gipp, star running back for Notre Dame and namesake of the rallying cry "Win one for the Gipper," quit school in 1917 and moved to Wisconsin. Coach Knute Rockne chased him down and coerced him to reenroll. Three years later, Gipp transferred to Michigan and, again, Rockne pulled some strings to lure him back to South Bend, Indiana, arranging a special test through the school's admissions department. Rockne never did quite convince the Notre Dame literati that Gipp belonged on campus.

Why did Gipp seldom crack a book? He spent most of his free time making pocket change as a shark at a local pool hall, drinking, and betting on sporting events, including Fighting

Irish football games. Once, in the middle of one of Rockne's fire-and-brimstone halftime talks, Gipp walked out of the locker room to smoke a cigarette. Notre Dame was trailing Indiana by 10 points. "Speechless" was the way late sportswriter Paul Gallico described Rockne after Gipp's early exit.

"Why'd you leave?" an incensed Rockne asked Gipp.

"Aw," Gipp shrugged, "these pep talks are OK, Rock, I guess. But I've got $200 bet on this game, and if you think I'm lying down then you're crazy!" Gipp didn't, and Notre Dame won, 13-10.

In 1930, after Gipp's untimely death, Rockne wrote in *Collier's* magazine: "George Gipp was the greatest football player Notre Dame ever produced. Gipp had everything to make a man great—splendid physique, balanced temperament, a brilliant mind . . . his initiative and ingenuity never failed. Nor did his courage."

Evidently, Rockne would not subscribe to the notion proposed by sportswriter John Schulian: "Death is not a bar of soap."

•The first intercollegiate football game on record, Rutgers vs. Princeton in 1869, featured at least one player, and possibly three, who could have been ruled ineligible.

•In his book, *The Hundred-Yard Lie*, Rick Telander tells of a powerhouse Michigan team around the turn of the century that had seven players on its roster who had no affiliation whatsoever to the school.

•In 1896, Fielding "Hurry Up" Yost transferred from the University of West Virginia to Lafayette College in Easton, Pennsylvania, just before the school was to play the biggest game in its history, against the University of Pennsylvania. With the 6-foot, 195-pound "freshman" Yost playing tackle, Lafayette stunned Penn, 6-4, snapping a 34-game winning streak. Yost immediately transferred back to West Virginia, where he graduated a year later.

•In 1939, University of Chicago president Robert Maynard Hutchins abolished football at the school, which had a rich tradition that included the original Monsters of the Midway and the winner of the first Heisman Trophy, Jay Berwanger. When asked why he would scrap such a program, Hutchins said: "To be successful, one must cheat. Everyone is cheating, and I refuse to cheat."

The University of Washington did not refuse. Not in the mid-1950s, at least. In 1956, the Huskies were slapped with a stiff sanction because of payments and other benefits to players: The school was banned from bowl games for two years. Also during that time, no Washington team was allowed to participate in NCAA championship competition in any sport. The scandal unfolded after the firing of Coach John Cherberg, who was unpopular with some players and an assistant coach.

Cherberg, nicknamed "Cowboy Johnny," had a short fuse. When he left the program, he told the media that Washington players were receiving monthly paychecks from an organization called the Greater Washington Advertising Organization, headed by UW booster Roscoe "Torchy" Torrance, a spirited redhead who counted Bing Crosby and Bob Hope among his friends.

In television interviews, Cherberg said some players were receiving $200 a month, well above the $75 allowed by the Pacific Coast Conference, the Huskies' league at the time. Unidentified players were quoted in a *Sports Illustrated* article titled "Boosters Mess It Up at Washington," saying they received cars, free tickets, and lucrative monthly salaries. In the story, Cherberg said the men who were lavishing the gifts on his players turned them against him.

According to the *Sports Illustrated* story, "Torchy's fund is a big one—it had run in the past anywhere from $20,000 to $75,000—and he runs it pretty much as he pleases.

"Now and then, he sees a chance to make an extra pile for the fund, such as an exhibition pro football game last summer between the New York Giants and San Francisco 49ers. He talked the teams into coming to Seattle. He sold the directors of Greater Seattle Inc. on the idea of sponsoring the show. He persuaded the university regents to lend their 55,000-seat stadium for 15 percent of the gate. It was a whopping success. Each team made $36,856. The Associated Students of the University of Washington received $28,361 for stadium rental and management fees; Greater Seattle Inc. turned a profit of $7,201. After taxes, there was $28,000 left over, so Torchy, by previous agreement with Greater Seattle Inc. tucked it into the Greater Washington Advertising Fund, the purse he uses to pay Husky athletes."

For a long time, boosters were allowed to pay players, help them out of a jam with some cash, help fund trips home. But in the mid-1950s, the rules that governed how much players could receive were revamped. The change that came about was because of players such as Luther Carr.

Carr, a star at Tacoma's Lincoln High in the early '50s and one of nine children, had no money for college. He could, however, play a mean game of football. He received money to play at UCLA, but the cash was matched by the Washington Advertising Association to ensure Carr would wear the purple and gold. Just when Torrance thought a deal with Carr had been reached, the University of Illinois upped the ante by offering Carr $200 a month. Washington boosters finally landed the local talent by paying him $175 a month.

An investigation of the Washington program showed Husky players were receiving an average of $60 a month more than the maximum allotment of $75. On May 6, 1956, the Pacific Coast Conference banned the UW from sharing Rose Bowl receipts for two years and made the Huskies ineligible to play for conference titles during that period. UCLA received a similar punishment for attempting to "buy" Carr.

Three months earlier, Husky athletic director Harvey Cassill resigned after it was disclosed that a large sum of money was diverted from the proceeds of a pro football exhibition game to the Washington Advertising Association. Cassill, the AD for 10 years, was the driving force behind the construction of the upper deck on the south side of Husky Stadium. His popularity took a major hit when he fired Cherberg. After that, Cassill was beseiged at home by angry telephone calls, some of which came in the middle of the night. "The most obscene calls you ever heard," Cassill told Husky historian Dick Rockne for the book *100 Years of Husky Football*. Cassill continued, "Our phone was tapped . . . we had the telephone company run it down and untap it. It was vicious. John was out then, it was me they wanted. And they got me."

II

Nowhere is the power and influence of big-money boosters better illustrated than at the University of Southern California. There, wealthy supporters of the football program can actually "buy" a specific position by doling out a mound of money. The school offers an influential booster the opportunity to create an endowed scholarship for the football team and then claim the position of his or her choice. By donating a quarter-of-a-million dollars to the school, Richard Alden, the former executive vice president of the Hughes Corporation, "bought" the first-string center job. Now, every player who starts at center for the Trojans has Alden to thank for his scholarship.

The program is perfectly legal in terms of the NCAA and, in fact, is a point of pride for USC. The practice of endowing USC football scholarships began in 1983, when Don Winston, then in charge of academic fund-raising for the College of Arts and Sciences and currently a senior associate director of athletics, applied the concept of the endowed department chair to the football team. The cost of endowing a football scholarship is $250,000 but, Winston said, will probably be raised to $350,000 soon. The interest yielded from each donation takes care of scholarship costs. By 1987, each of the 22 starting positions had been endowed and the Trojans began to put backup positions on the sales block. Each year at team banquet the boosters get to meet the players they sponsor and, according to Winston, the players write their benefactors thank-you notes once or twice a season. An endowment for a reserve player costs just as much as one for a starter, so USC officials avoid using the terms first and second string and instead refer to the first unit as Cardinal and the second as Gold. That way, a wealthy booster can avoid the embarrassment of telling friends at a cocktail party, "You know the second-string punter? Well, that's basically *me* out there."

Winston recalls the case of Ray Irani, president of Occidental Petroleum, who wanted to donate money to the school and strengthen his ties to the football team:

"When he realized that he could endow an All-American linebacker position, he all of a sudden got an attachment," said Winston, in charge of all fund-raising for the athletic department. "It was a hands-on type of thing. He got a vested interest in it right away. Rather than asking him to just endow a scholarship, I said, 'Endow the outside linebacker position.' Junior Seau just happened to be playing at that time and he was only a sophomore. I said to (Irani), 'Hey, this guy will be an All-American next year.' Sure enough, we were right and (Irani) was happier than hell."

The starting tailback position, a plum of a purchase, has been endowed by the school in the name of Ricky Bell, the late Heisman Trophy winner. "We haven't quite gotten all the money for that," Winston said, "but we thought it was important to name it after him."

Often a former USC player will endow a position which he never reached during his days at the school. Richard Alden, the former executive vice president of the Hughes Corporation, is the benefactor for the starting center even though, as a player, he never cracked the starting lineup. "When he endowed he said, 'I was third team. Can I endow it?' " Winston recalled. "I said, 'Dick, you just became first string.' "

The program has been enormously successful at earning millions of dollars for the department. Schools that have taken USC's lead and started their own program include UCLA, Michigan, Nebraska, and Miami. Winston said he gets at least two calls a week from inquisitive athletic directors interested in starting position endowment scholarships. "I can't believe somebody else didn't think about this first," he joked, "because I'm not that smart."

Minor said Washington soon might put a similar program in place, considering Barbara Hedges, a former senior associate director of athletics at USC, has seen the system work. "We've talked about that many times," he said. "I think Barbara will institute that very soon. I'll be surprised if she doesn't."

The situation at USC exemplifies how close the ties are between influential boosters and a football team. It is a dangerous marriage. The motivation for some boosters is philanthropy, for many others it's prestige. Having the pull to get good seats at the game is one thing; having a position dedicated in your name is quite another. Six years ago, a booster could use his or her power and realm of influence to recruit high school prospects, but in 1987 the NCAA outlawed recruiting contact by boosters. Making sure overly enthusiastic supporters of the football program stay within the lines of NCAA policy can be a tough task for coaches and university administrators. The penalties for violators can be stiff. NCAA rules stipulate that a school can be held responsible for the actions of anyone who can be considered a representative of the school's athletic interests. If the NCAA finds such a representative acted improperly, the school could face sanctions ranging from reduced scholarships to a temporary television ban to a temporary ban on post season play.

The NCAA might have taken boosters out of the mix when it comes to luring recruits to a program, but once an athlete arrives at a school, he can have legal contact with boosters and participate in the summer-jobs program in which boosters arrange employment for athletes. This was the Washington program in question when the *Los Angeles Times* ran a package of copyrighted stories Dec. 9, 1992, citing five former Husky players who said they received money and favors from boosters during their college careers. The players said boosters provided them with bogus summer jobs that required little more than showing up to collect a paycheck. Such activities were apparent violations of the NCAA's "extra benefit" rule, which prohibits representatives from a school's athletic interests from providing student-athletes with benefits not ordinarily provided to the student body.

Also in this package, which took up more than two full pages, was a piece that elaborated on an excerpt from a deposition of Dr. Steve Bramwell, the Huskies' team physician and a former star halfback at the school. In court papers, Bramwell said football players sold prescription drugs given to them by members of the university's medical and training staff, a violation of federal law as well as NCAA rules.

Pac-10 assistant commissioner Jim Muldoon said the conference would investigate the reports. After information surfaced regarding Hobert's improper loan, the conference and the university began a joint investigation. Soon, however, the UW athletic department turned over the investigation to the Pac-10 to avoid public-disclosure laws that prevent the university, as a public institution, from keeping elements of the investigation confidential.

The headline bannered across the top of the *Los Angeles Times* sports page asked, "Washington: A Program Gone Awry?" The package of stories was co-written by Danny Robbins and Elliott Almond, members of the newspaper's sports investigative team. According to John Cherwa, associate sports editor for the newspaper, the story idea was generated after the verdict of the Rodney King beating trial came down.

"Elliott had this idea," Cherwa said. "We remembered a few years back when a couple of Washington football players were beaten up and arrested at a Red Onion in Orange County. We thought, 'Let's take a look back and see if there's anything there, if it's worth revisiting, or there are any parallels, ties, correlations, whatever.' When we did that, Elliott started interviewing some people and lo and behold we started to find out about a story we didn't know anything about."

The reporters interviewed more than two dozen players and others familiar with the Washington program and pored over court documents and state records. The story alleged that a Washington booster in Los Angeles had arranged summer jobs for Husky players paying as much as $10 an hour and requiring little or no work; while he was playing for the Huskies, star defensive lineman Dennis Brown had the use of a truck registered to a Washington booster and was arrested for driving under the influence of alcohol in the vehicle during the 1989 season; and through an arrangement with an assistant coach, a Husky player was able to secure a summer job in Seattle that included free lodging in an unoccupied home. The two prominent boosters in question were James W. Kenyon, a Los Angeles real estate developer, and Herb Mead, a Seattle businessman. Both had contact with players in the talent-fertile L.A. area, yet both denied providing players with cash.

Two of the former Husky players who spoke on the record to the newspaper were Vince Fudzie and Kevin Conard. That these two were part of the story raised suspicion, particularly because they lost their lawsuit against the school and ostensibly had an ax to grind with the football program. Also, neither was a starter, so it seemed odd that boosters would take pains to cater to their needs.

Discounting the testimony of Fudzie and Conard simply because they seemed to have an agenda is shortsighted. They might have had a vendetta against the program because of their failed lawsuit, yet that doesn't necessarily mean they weren't telling the truth. Consider witnesses in a mafia trial, many of whom are not presidents or priests but, themselves, hardened criminals. Mob bosses, one-way ticket up the river in hand, are seldom saved by the "ax-to-grind" defense.

Conard said Kenyon arranged two summer jobs for him. The first, cutting weeds on a Los Angeles hillside, required actual work. The second was at Cabot, Cabot and Forbes, and was far from taxing. He said he and other players would sleep, play cards, eat or lift weights while on the clock. "I remember a supervisor named Rick," he told the newspaper. "We never had a problem when he did catch us sleeping. He knew what we were there for, which was basically to do nothing. Occasionally, he would try to get us to do something with the workers on the other side (of the job site). But it wasn't an order. It was a request."

Fudzie said Kenyon got him a job as a security guard at a building in San Francisco. "Our job was to watch the building so it wouldn't fall down," Fudzie said. "We'd just take turns napping out there. I'd go in at 6 p.m., and I'd go to a club and hang out . . . We never saw anyone (supervising) around there."

Fudzie said when he needed money for car tires he asked Kenyon, who instructed his secretary to give the player $600 from the petty-cash supply. "I knew it was an NCAA violation," Fudzie said, "but I didn't care. It was what was expected (as a college football player)."

Former linebacker Corey Brown told the newspaper that Kenyon and Mead were well-known figures to Husky players. "Everyone (playing at Washington) had his own little booster," Brown said. "But everyone knew Kenyon and Mead were with the Los Angeles boys."

Supporters of Mead and Kenyon describe the two as good-hearted philanthropists with an unquenchable zeal for Husky football. "I'm one of the ultimate Husky junkies alive," Kenyon said in 1991. "I'll cut short a meeting, fly up for practice, then fly home the same day."

Players from California were critical to the Huskies' success and, therefore, Fudzie alleged, got special treatment from boosters. "Washington has to compete with SC and UCLA," he said. "If it weren't for the California players, Washington wouldn't be shit . . . I could go on and on and name players from the State of California that made Washington what they are: Spider Gaines, Jacque Robinson, Warren Moon, Michael Jackson, Reggie Rogers, and on and on.

"Now, SC and UCLA have always been known to do those recruiting violations. In order for Washington to compete with them, they had to do those sort of things for the California guys. To my knowledge, talking with other guys from the team, since the articles came out, I've come to the realization that maybe all of the Washington people or the people from Oregon weren't getting that kind of money.

"One particular incident I could think of was (former Husky linebacker) Tony Lewis. He played on the team when I was there. He was a starter. He was with me in California about a month ago. We talked about this, and he said, 'I didn't get any money, but I remember Fred Small and Scott Garnett and these other guys would always get money from Kenyon.' . . . (Washington) cannot make it by just pulling talent from the State of Washington. There's not enough talent there. There's not enough black guys with speed from the state for them to be a successful program."

Times editor Cherwa said the story included some off-the-record sources because "Washington football is so ingrained in that area that (the players) had a legitimate fear. They had a fear for their selves and being blackballed, being ostracized... One of the things we were very happy with about the story was the amount of people who spoke on the record. We used multiple sources to corroborate evidence that we already had, but we always pinned the evidence we had on someone that used their name."

According to some of the players interviewed, former defensive lineman Dennis Brown was a particular favorite of Mead's. Records in King County District Court show that Brown, who now plays for the San Francisco 49ers, was arrested in 1989 for being under the influence of alcohol while driving a Chevrolet pickup truck registered to Mead. The booster said he did not recall an arrangement that gave Brown use of the truck, adding he did not give the player special treatment.

A 1959 graduate of Washington, Mead majored in business administration. Mead was nicknamed "Deals" and conducted an unsuccessful campaign for student body president. His slogan: "Herb Mead, the man we need."

Mead made his fortune in commercial real estate and was one of the original 125 supporters who donated $50,000 in 1986 to build Husky Stadium's north deck and Tyee Center. Interestingly, Mead was close to booster "Torchy" Torrance, the main figure implicated in the 1956 sanctions. In his autobiography, Torrance wrote he passed his recruiting torch to Mead when the Washington Advertising Association scandal broke. At that time, Mead was a senior at the university, and he and John Torrance, Torchy's son, would show promising high school players around the city and try to sell them on the school. Those tours were entirely legal—boosters were allowed to recruit high school players until a rules change in 1987.

Sources close to the school described Mead as an overexuberant alum who worried the UW athletic department for years. A former Washington administrator, who asked anonymity, told the newspaper Mead was summoned to the offices of Don James and then-Athletic Director Mike Lude several times to deter improper activity. "Mike would talk to him privately and so would Don," the source said. "No question, they were fearful of him."

Said Mead in a written statement: "Whenever I have helped an athlete in the University of Washington program, I have always tried hard to stay within the rules and guidelines of the NCAA and the Pac-10."

Kenyon, too, donated $50,000 to enhance Husky Stadium with the north deck and Tyee Center. As president of Cabot, Cabot and Forbes, a giant real estate development company, Kenyon also had the resources to provide numerous Husky players with summer jobs in Southern California. The question was: Did those players have to work for their money? Kenyon said yes.

Another former player who spoke on the record to the *Los Angeles Times* was Vince Weathersby, one of Washington's all-time leading rushers and receivers, who in 1990 filed a personal-injury lawsuit against Dr. Bramwell and Washington trainers and coaches. In his suit, which he lost, Weathersby alleged negligence in the treatment of a shoulder separation he sustained during a September 19, 1987, game against Texas A & M. In June 1992, the defendants in Weathersby's case won a summary judgment in King County Superior Court.

In his case, Weathersby alleged that he needed to have shoulder surgery but instead was given medication to cope with the pain. He said he was given Tylenol-Codeine 3, which, he alleged, forced him to drop two classes because he could not stay awake. "It was not uncommon for me to doze off during class and team meetings," he said in an affidavit. "The coaching staff knew this was caused by pain medication, hence they would not reprimand me when I would doze off."

Bramwell said Weathersby was administered 12 codeine tablets during a four-month period. During a deposition, Bramwell and Larry J. Landry, Weathersby's lawyer, had the following exchange:

Question: How long does 12 tablets last?
Answer: For these guys?

Q: Yeah.

A: About 24 hours. That's if they don't sell it to somebody else.

Q: So that's done?

A: Has it been done?

Q: Yeah.

A: It has been done.

Q: How did you find out about that?

A: Well, there's lots of ways of finding out where drugs might go when you ask them and they say they lost it and you find out from another player that — there's lots of ways.

Only licensed physicians and pharmacists are allowed to sell prescription drugs, according to federal law.

In an interview with a local television station the day the story broke, Bramwell said he did not believe the newspaper's story was "correct, accurately reported or reflected the truth." He told the *Los Angeles Times* that team trainers and physicians had only heard rumors of players selling their prescribed medications and had no hard evidence that it was actually happening. "I wouldn't accuse any of the players of doing that other than it's been rumored to happen with athletes and we know it has happened with private patients," he said, adding, "We certainly try to control the amount going (out), so even if somebody was (selling the drugs), it would be at a very minimal level from us."

Bramwell later said he wasn't given time to clarify his answer in the deposition because the attorney moved to another line of questioning. "The attorney was pressing me," he said. "It could have been an incorrect statement on my part, but I told the *Los Angeles Times* reporter that I had no evidence of any athletes selling drugs. I knew of private patients who had sold prescription drugs, but not athletes . . . Besides, the athletes were getting Tylenol III, which has just about zero street value."

According to the newspaper story, the street value of one tablet of codeine is $2-$5.

Weathersby, who played in 1985-88, underwent shoulder surgery in 1988 after his senior season and left Washington in 1989 without a degree. He was not drafted by an NFL team and had an unsuccessful free-agent tryout with the Los Angeles Rams in July 1989.

In the report, Weathersby claimed he had been given cash payments totaling about $3,000 from both Kenyon and Mead during his five seasons at the school. Weathersby said he once received a payment from Kenyon in the Husky locker room after a game.

Five former Washington players told the newspaper they made as much as $10 an hour working at Cabot, Cabot and Forbes while they were playing at the school. The summer jobs included positions as messengers, laborers, and security guards. Kenyon told the newspaper that, because Cabot, Cabot and Forbes was building in 23 states, he traveled frequently and seldom had contact with Husky players while on the job. Kenyon added it would be brought to his attention when a player wasn't working hard and he would tell the player to "shape up or ship out."

Four dozen employers offered jobs to Husky players for summer 1992. Pay ranged from $5.50-an-hour restaurant jobs to $17-an-hour construction jobs. Earning money during the summer is vital for most players because they cannot receive financial help from anyone other than relatives, and the NCAA frowns upon students working during the school year. Whatever money a student-athlete makes during the year, in fact, is subtracted from the value of the scholarship. While in school, the players on scholarship receive $555 a month for housing, food, and other expenses. The small stipend opened the door to potential abuse. Most universities, including Washington, do not have a full-time coordinator for summer employment.

Said James: "I've told any person that ever hired one of my football players that if they didn't work, fire them... If you've got some kind of phony job, you're teaching them the wrong values."

Texas A & M caught the attention of the NCAA in 1991 after allegedly committing summer-job violations: An Aggie booster was accused of giving four players year-round salaries to be phantom maintenance workers. No one made those accusations against the Huskies and, after the Washington boosters story broke, several former and current UW players voiced their support of the program.

Former wide receiver Orlando McKay said Mark Brunell, his roommate, worked construction during the summer and "always was dusty and tired afterward." Running back Greg Lewis, who now plays for the Denver Broncos, worked as a school groundskeeper and on a construction site. "I had to be at work every day and worked every job hard," he said. "I've got the calluses and backaches to prove it." Said former receiver Mario Bailey: "I was an All-American and Greg Lewis was, too. Even if you're an All-American, you don't get any special privileges. Coach James keeps a tight noose on those things. If it happened, it never was to (James's) knowledge or to anybody else's knowledge. That's what I want people to understand; (Coaches) can't control everything."

Jeff Pahukoa, the former Husky offensive lineman who now plays for the Los Angeles Rams, told the *Post-Intelligencer* he heard rumors of special treatment from boosters yet never had firsthand knowledge of anyone getting it. "There was hearsay," he said, "talk about, you know, certain boosters in L.A. County who were helping. I don't know if they were giving cars or financial help, but I know they were giving them good (summer) jobs. L.A. people were getting better jobs than we were in Washington."

Pahukoa said "good jobs" meant "really good pay for a job that's not real demanding. You may get a $12-an-hour job for a job that someone could do for $6, or $10." Still, he said, he simply heard about these jobs through the rumor mill. "Who got the jobs? I don't know. Who was getting the money? I don't know. But that was the only hearsay I've ever heard."

Weathersby had more than hearsay evidence documenting a potential rules violation; he had an audiotape. He received a message on his telephone answering machine from Jim Heckman (then a son-in-law of Don James), a member of the Tyee Club booster organization, president of *SportsImage*, a Seattle-based company that designs and produces sports posters and calendars, and the publisher of *Sports Washington* magazine, a publication that is pro-Husky but has no affiliation with the school. In the recording, which Weathersby played for a few Seattle reporters, Heckman told the former player, "We can reverse this whole thing" if Weathersby would recant the statements he made about the summer jobs.

"Whether it's, hey, you're pissed off and you said those things because you're mad, and you didn't mean it," Heckman continued in the message, "it would absolutely make everyone in the community feel great if you could say it ... Or if it's, say, they misquoted me, or they manipulated me, or whatever it is, we need your help. You personally can absolutely (bleep) the Husky football program as it stands now. Or, with one phone call, we can reverse this whole thing.

"Corey Brown basically has already taken back his deal . . . Conard and Fudzie are a joke. We've got a rap sheet on them about 20 pages long . . . We're publishing police reports where they've been involved in all kinds of stuff . . . They're no problem. But you're a good guy and were successful with the Huskies, and you've got credibility."

NCAA rules stipulate that it is a violation for a representative of the university's athletic interests to encourage witnesses not to cooperate or to provide false or misleading information in an investigation.

Weathersby said he played the message for the media because he was tired of feeling pressured to change his story. "People have been saying stuff about me, about the mother of my daughter," the player told the *P-I*. "For a few days, the phone didn't stop ringing. Heckman left six or seven messages a day for several days, including one phone call at 1 a.m."

Heckman said he was told by several sources that Weathersby wanted to recant his story, and by trying to contact him, he was giving the former player a chance to do so.

"Don James told me that Weathersby wanted to change his story," Heckman said. "Weathersby had approached Don. Everyone on the inside of Husky athletics, Husky coaches and alumni, knew that Weathersby wanted to back out on the *Los Angeles Times'* story. His quote was, 'My quotes were twisted.' That's the way he talked."

The forum Heckman offered Weathersby was a special edition of *Sports Washington* titled "Witch Hunt." The 15-page issue was devoted to a detailed critique of the *Los Angeles Times* story, a piece aimed at undermining the credibility of Vince Fudzie and Kevin Conard, and several short testimonials from current and former Husky players in support of the program. By publishing the magazine, Heckman mixed an explosive brew—purporting to apply fair journalistic principles to the story despite his undeniable ties to the football program and the university through his relationship to James and the Tyee Club.

Heckman believes he knows the reason Weathersby provided the answering-machine tape to Art Thiel of the *P-I*: "The week he turned the tape over of me constantly calling him back was the same week that Kevin Conard came up and ended up visiting Weathersby. And then this tape mysteriously ended up going to Art Thiel . . . When Weathersby found out that (*Sports Washington* was) going to make one of his friends look bad, I think that's what spurred the call."

The tape was handed over to a media that, Heckman said, was itching to drag him through the mud. In the *Sports Washington* issue that preceded "Witch Hunt," he wrote an excoriating column that scolded local reporters for using what he viewed as underhanded tactics to obtain stories smearing Husky football. Born out of that column, Heckman believed, was a vendetta.

Thiel disagreed.

"There was absolutely no vendetta," he said. "Heckman simply walked into a situation that he should have known more about and didn't, for whatever reasons. In publishing, he has two severe conflicts of interest. One, he's a Tyee Club member, and two, he's James's son-in-law. Right there he's got a real problem with being objective about the story. Even if he wants to take a pro-Washington stance, he doesn't have any credibility."

"Witch Hunt" was published without Weathersby's blessing. In a letter from the publisher on the magazine's opening page, Heckman wrote that "someone had to stand up and put this controversy in perspective. In my opinion, no one in the media has done its job by covering both sides of the story fairly. Our goal with this issue is to present the other side of the story."

In presenting the other side of the story, *Sports Washington* never contacted the *Los Angeles Times* writers or editors to check if the conversations with former players were, say, tape recorded.

Heckman offered Weathersby $500 for an interview with *Sports Washington*. However, the *Los Angeles Times* erroneously reported that the publisher offered Weathersby $500 if he "would recant published remarks alleging improprieties in James' program." In late December, Heckman filed a $13 million libel suit against the newspaper and the *Washington Post* news service, seeking $1 million in actual damages and $1 million punitive damages for himself, and $10 million actual and $1 million in punitive for his publishing company, SportsImage. The *Los Angeles Times* ran a retraction for the error.

"The only part (of the story) that was brought into contention is whether Heckman basically offered a bribe to Weathersby to say everything that was said was wrong," Cherwa explained. "The matter that was taken to court is Heckman is saying that he did not physically say those words. Our contention is that it was clear that the implication was that he said that... We admitted that he did not physically say those words."

As of July 1993, no settlement had been reached, but according to a source who asked not to be identified, Heckman's attorneys were willing to settle simply for their fees, about $5,000. Heckman said an offer was made but had not been accepted. "We're at a standstill," Heckman said in late July, adding the $5,000 figure is inaccurate.

Allegations of potential NCAA violations involving Heckman did not abate after the Weathersby incident. Around mid-January 1993, reports surfaced that the publisher had allegedly encouraged Notre Dame linebacker Demetrius DuBose to transfer to Washington. If true, such activity also would be a violation of NCAA rules. DuBose, who attended O'Dea High in Seattle, already had completed his senior season for the Fighting Irish when the *Los Angeles Times* ran the story. According to sources who requested anonymity, DuBose informed Pac-10 investigators that he was told by Heckman at least twice that Washington would be a better place for him to play if he planned on returning to Seattle. Heckman described the two as good friends, and DuBose had spent part of summer 1990 working for Heckman.

Heckman said his comments to DuBose came long before 1992—when he became a Husky booster—and that the two had casual conversations about many things, including football, girls, and politics.

Two weeks after publishing the DuBose story, the Los Angeles Times ran another piece concerning Heckman. Signor Mobley, a Washington State player from Tacoma's Curtis High, told the newspaper that Heckman took him to dinner and tried to persuade him to sign with Washington in the winter of 1991, shortly after Mobley announced to the media he would sign with the Cougars. Mobley said he detailed his meetings with Heckman to Pac-10 investigator David Price during a January meeting in Pullman. Mobley said he chose Washington State over Washington because the Cougars recruited him as a defensive back, the position he played in high school, instead of a running back.

Mobley told the newspaper that in 1991 Heckman took him out to dinner at The Keg, a Tacoma restaurant, and paid for the meal. "He was saying that the University of Washington is a winning program," Mobley told the newspaper. "My high school team was a two-time state champion at the time, and he was saying, 'You don't want to go to a losing program. You still want to be with a winner.'

"And then he started saying, 'Business-wise, it's better to go to (Washington) because it's in the city. You have more (business) connections and all that.'"

Heckman denied making any such comments to Mobley, but did say he had dinner at The Keg with the player and breakfast before a Husky game with Mobley and his father, adding such contact with high school athletes was common practice for *Sports Washington* employees. "That's the type of thing our magazine has done for years," he said. "It's wide open. Getting to know people."

He said trying to coax Mobley to sign with Washington would be futile anyway because he knew Mobley's test scores were too low for UW admission standards. "Obviously, I didn't want to embarrass him," Heckman said. "I knew the guy's (Scholastic Aptitude Test) scores were extremely low and that Washington hadn't offered him a scholarship. All the alumni knew because they were all wondering, 'Hey, this big player Signor Mobley, is he going to be a Husky?' And the answer out there was, 'No.'"

Pac-10 investigators didn't take such a cut-and-dried view of the Mobley and DuBose cases. In fact, in the Notice of Charges released by the league office in June 1993, Heckman's relationships with DuBose and Mobley were thoroughly examined. According to the report, DuBose was asked if his conversations with Heckman regarding transferring to Washington were serious or merely good-natured bantering. DuBose said the banter was light, the two joked all the time, but "at some point it was the meat of our conversation," and described it as "friendly persuasion." The report also cites John Sandstrom and Todd Hubbell, former co-workers of Heckman, who indicated he was actively trying to recruit players for the school.

Herb Mead also was mentioned in the DuBose section of the report. According to former player Terrance Powe, Mead asked him to get involved with recruiting DuBose. "We were supposed to be calling (DuBose) at Notre Dame," Powe said, adding that

Mead gave him Seattle and South Bend, Indiana, telephone numbers for the linebacker. Powe said he didn't call DuBose but told Mead he did. Mead told investigators he had DuBose over for dinner once, but there was no talk of transferring.

Heckman separated from his wife, Jeni, the youngest child of Don and Carol James, in early 1992. The implication that problems with Washington football led to marital strife bothers Heckman. "That the marriage fell apart because of Husky controversy is an outright lie," he said. "It's a personal attack."

III

For Beno Bryant, December was bittersweet.

Good news for the injured running back was followed by bad: a report of a potential NCAA rules infraction that thrust him into the maelstrom ravaging the reputation of the program. Bryant, who played in only three games during the 1992 season and started just one, applied for and was granted an extra year of eligibility based on medical hardship. The team's leading rusher in 1991, Bryant received the extra year from the Pac-10 because of his continual problems with his hip and a partial tear of his left hamstring.

On December 18, the *Post-Intelligencer* reported a late-model Ford Mustang, apparently on long-term loan to Bryant by a childhood friend, was registered at the California address of a prominent professional sports agent. Bryant said the car was a loan from his friend and teammate at Los Angeles' Dorsey High, Chris Mims, a first-round draft pick of the San Diego Chargers. Bryant said he had no idea the address listed on the car's registration was that of Los Angeles sports agent Harold "Doc" Daniels, who represents Mims and has been accused in the past of using intermediaries to pass gifts and loans to college players in violation of NCAA rules. College athletes are forbidden by the NCAA to accept gifts, loans, or favors from professional agents or recruiters. There was no evidence that Daniels paid for or subsidized the car. Apparently, some reporters from other papers were aware that Beno was driving Mims's car, but the *P-I* was the first to make the Daniels connection.

In 1991, reports surfaced that football players from Clemson, Duke, and the University of Georgia received money from intermediaries working through Daniels. Also, a Los Angeles insurance broker was placed under federal investigation during summer 1992 for allegedly attempting to overbill football players—most of whom were clients of Daniels's and referred to the broker by the agent—on premiums for $1 million career-ending injury policies when they were actually insured for much less. Daniels himself was publicly reprimanded and fined $1,000 by the Georgia secretary of state's office for failing to register under the state's professional sports agent registration laws.

According to Bryant, he drove to Los Angeles in spring 1992 and his car broke down. Mims visited his home and lent him the car. "I said, 'I'm not going to take your car.' It was so nice and everything," Bryant said. "But I wasn't going to ask my mom for money."

Bryant's mother recalled the offer from Mims. "We were standing right there on the front porch," she said. "Beno's car didn't work, and his best friend tried to help him out by letting him use his car. Why would anyone try to make more of that than there is?

"You find two poor boys, one who has made it good and the other still trying to find his way through school, and one helps the other one. Chris was just doing something nice for Beno . . . They've been friends since they were 10 years old. Chris is a pro ball player now, he has other cars, and he let Beno use one."

Bryant said he was unaware the car was registered to Daniels, but said he did have two telephone conversations with the agent because "I was going to leave (Washington) this year." NCAA rules allow a player to speak with an agent, however, any verbal or written agreements between a player and an agent are forbidden.

Mims said Bryant did nothing that would jeopardize his college career. "He didn't have to ask my agent," Mims told Dan Raley. "He didn't have to ask no one. I had the money. I had the car. He could get anything he wanted from me. He didn't have to go nowhere else." He added Bryant wasn't secretive about the car, either. "He had the car all this time," he said. "If they wanted to find it, they could have found it a long time ago. It hasn't been like he's been hiding it, like it's been in a garage all this time and he just came out with it. He doesn't have to worry about it."

Indeed, Recruiting Coordinator Dick Baird questioned Bryant about the car before the story broke and was satisfied with the player's answers. "A month and a half ago, we tried to be more conscious of the kids' cars," he said. "I talked to Beno about it. The question came up. He told me the car was his friend's. I didn't think it was that unusual for a guy making a lot of money taking care of a buddy of his in the neighborhood."

When first asked about the loaner car, James said, "I don't know anything about that car. What do you want me to do, give you another rumor to print? I get 15 rumors a day. What do you want me to do about them? Address them to (the media)?"

The next day, James said he did, in fact, know about the car but declined to discuss it publicly, adding he preferred to have it handled by the investigators looking into the Washington program. "I know everything that's going on," he said. "I said I didn't know that agent. I do know what's going on and we're acting on things. We're not going to discuss it. We're going to go to the committee. We're dealing with everything."

Another report concerned several other Huskies who had routinely ignored court dates and traffic tickets, running up thousands of dollars in unpaid fines. Napoleon Kaufman, for instance, was issued three bench warrants during a four-month period.

Clearly agitated, Kaufman complained that he was being unfairly singled out. "Public figure?" he asked. "I'm 19 years old. I play football. I got a couple tickets and I need to get them taken care of. I'm doing that. I made a mistake. A lot of people make mistakes and they don't get their names in the newspaper. . . . These are personal problems, not the team's problems. There are individuals on this team, but they are things the individuals had to take care of. They're putting our team down for it, and it's not fair."

Said Barbara Hedges: "We are trying very hard to have a process of education, making sure they realize they are responsible for their own actions. If you have a ticket, you take care of it. It's that simple. Parking. Traffic. Whatever."

Hedges also indicated she believed local media were being petty by digging up any possible infraction, however picayune, and reporting on it.

"What is this?" she asked. "It's just sort of cherry pick on the Huskies these days, isn't it?"

23

Dial F For Fraud

Imagine never paying another telephone bill. Never haggling with roommates over who made this call and who made that one. Never worrying about daytime rates or cutting long-distance nighttime chats short.

Now, imagine plunking down $3,000 for a "magic" cellular phone that allows you to make as many calls as you like, as often as you like, and never runs up a bill. Free calls for life.

The offer is enticing, and it's one on which some members of the Washington football team couldn't pass. It was reported in early December that the Secret Service was investigating four or five UW football players who might have been involved in cellular phone fraud. The Secret Service would neither confirm nor deny that Huskies were involved in the investigation, but Barbara Hedges said, "We have an inquiry about potential cellular phone fraud. There is an investigation by the Secret Service and university police, and we have fully cooperated with both of those agencies . . . It is my understanding that the investigation is continuing." In early December, three Husky players admitted they and several of their teammates were questioned by the Secret Service regarding an investigation. They said Don James confiscated about a dozen telephones, many of which had been altered, at the beginning of the 1992 season, nearly a year after they were last used.

Some reporters were aware that an investigation was taking place but were holding off on a story until they could obtain more detailed information. Three weeks before the Rose Bowl, during a call-in segment on KJR radio, someone phoned in and asked, "When are you guys going to do something on the Huskies' cellular phone deal?" The show's host knew nothing of the investigation. Some Husky beat writers listening did. Convinced the caller would tip off the competition, the reporters wrote the story for the next day's edition.

The players said the cellular phones were sold to them in summer 1991 by a Seattle woman, a nonstudent whom they would not identify. She told the players the phones were obtained by a friend of hers in the industry and charged the players varying fees, starting at $100. Players said they used the phones for two or three months before they became inoperable, apparently shut off by the phone company.

According to the players, James urged them to meet individually with Secret Service agents. One meeting took place in a car parked in front of the Tubby Graves Building.

Darius Turner confirmed he was one of the players questioned. Turner said that, in exchange for talking, "they gave me amnesty." But Patrick Sullivan, assistant special-agent-in-charge of the Secret Service's Seattle field office, pointed out the Secret Service cannot grant immunity; only a U.S. attorney can do that.

Sullivan said newspapers reporting on a possible investigation made the Secret Service's job much more difficult. With advance notice, suspects can destroy or alter evidence and corroborate on stories and alibis. He also was shocked that the Husky players were so willing to divulge damaging information to the media.

"If the Secret Service interviewed you," Sullivan asked, "would you go and tell the media about it?"

According to the cellular phone industry, this type of fraud reaches out and touches cellular carriers in the United States and Canada for losses of $300 million-$600 million a year. Some in the industry estimate the annual losses are closer to $1 billion. The crime is becoming more and more commonplace in everyday society.

"When the phenomenon first started about three or four years ago, it was almost exclusively in the purview of drug dealers," Sullivan said. "No. 1, they're greedy people to start out with because they're crooks and they're thieves and they're lowlifes. They want to do anything to make money. They figure, 'Why not get a cellular telephone so I won't have to pay the bills?' No. 2, they are under the assumption that it would be impossible for the Drug Enforcement Administration or other law enforcement to either tap the phones with a court-authorized wire tap, or even trace the phone calls.

"Now, in the last year and a half, these phones have expanded beyond the drug dealers to other people, who are marketing these phones to otherwise legitimate people. Truck drivers, people on the road a lot. . . . They are marketing the phones under the guise that they've a satellite deal and these phones are hooked up to a special satellite. They are using the analogy that it's like stealing from a cable TV company. 'You're not *supposed* to do it, but it's OK.'"

The Secret Service has broken cellular phone fraud into three categories, all of which are prosecuted under the "Access Device Fraud" statute.

The first form of fraud is the most sophisticated, perhaps the most sinister, and involves altering the phones. Sometimes, a counterfeit computer chip is inserted into the phone, enabling the user to make calls that are, ostensibly, unbillable. The counterfeit chip duplicates the electronic serial number from a legitimate telephone and the phone's mobile identification number. Calls from these altered phones fool the telephone company's computer into thinking they are legitimate calls made by legitimate subscribers.

The second category involves those who subscribe to a service using a fictitious name or a real person's identity without that person knowing about it.

The third type of fraud is theft of the phone itself. This type of crime is less costly to the phone company because once the phone is reported stolen, the account is immediately canceled.

Although the crime might seem easy enough to solve because of the documentation involved (i.e., records of numbers called), that is not always the case. With the altered phones, the records are not always clear-cut and often end up in a "dead" file. The phone company must run a special computer program to capture those records, if they can be recovered at all. At the end of the month, when the company is reconciling its bills, it cannot produce those phantom records.

Altering the phones is a fairly sophisticated process, far more than other types of fraud such as stealing a checkbook and forging a signature. "The first domino that falls has to be someone that knows computers and knows cellular telephone circuitry," Sullivan said. "It's something I couldn't do, you couldn't do, without training." Once they hit the streets, the phones are usually sold for $2,500-$3,000 and come with an instruction sheet that describes how to change the serial number and mobile identification number simply by using the keypad.

"You can, theoretically, make 10 or 15 phone calls using one set of numbers," Sullivan said. "And once the phone company realizes those numbers aren't legitimate, it will shut them down. Then you can just reprogram the phone. It's like spinning the dice. You spin the dice and come up with a new set of numbers."

Fraudulent use of cellular phones is a felony under federal law and provides a minimum punishment of a $10,000 fine and/or 10 years' imprisonment. The maximum punishment under certain circumstances is 20 years in prison and a fine of $100,000 or twice the value of services fraudulently obtained.

24

Under The Microscope

By mid-December, the university had hired defense attorneys Mike Glazier and Rick Evrard to conduct an investigation of the Husky program independent of that being performed by the Pac-10. The two fostered the reputation of leaving no stone unturned when it came to scouring programs. Each was once an NCAA official and is now a member of the Kansas City, Missouri, law firm of Bond, Schoeneck and King. They are usually hired by university presidents, rather than athletics officials, and accept high-profile cases. They have a reputation for digging even deeper than traditional internal, conference, or NCAA probes, finding dirt on programs which are, by most accounts, squeaky clean. The team helps those schools through the self-reporting process as well as reforming compliance procedures.

The NCAA, as one reporter described it, is a little like the Catholic Church; sins can be atoned for through confession and penance. If a school admits to a rules violation, then takes steps to ensure it will not happen again, the association takes a somewhat forgiving stance. The University of Cincinnati brought in Glazier and Evrard when its football and basketball programs were under investigation by the NCAA. Ultimately, that investigation led to probation, yet the penalty would have been stiffer, according to Cincinnati president Joe Steger, had Glazier and Evrard not done their job. "If you aren't prepared to say you're wrong, you'd better not bring them in," Steger said. "They're going to tell it like it is."

Said Pac-10 associate commissioner David Price, "The Glazier-Evrard group is very experienced; they know what to look for and they can recognize immediately where the problems might be and how to approach things. The University of Washington could do a lot worse than to hire them."

Glazier and Evrard spearheaded a recent internal investigation of the Syracuse University men's basketball team, finding several infractions that were not previously reported. The Orangemen received a two-year probation in October of 1992, lost one scholarship for two years, and were not allowed to participate in the 1993 NCAA tournament. The investigative team also has done work for Oklahoma State, checking into its wrestling program, and Minnesota's basketball, football, and wrestling programs.

In October of 1992, the NCAA found the Clemson basketball program guilty of several violations, including altering players' transcripts, illegally recruiting, and lying to investigators. The Tigers received a two-year probation, including recruiting limitations and scholarship reductions. Because Clemson agreed to revamp its rules-compliance system, however, the NCAA didn't touch the school's television contracts or its eligibility for the postseason tournament.

The University of Pittsburgh brought in the Glazier-Evrard investigative team in February of 1991 after local media alleged recruiting violations and improper benefits to athletes by the Panther football program. After a lengthy in-house investigation, a report was submitted by the school to the NCAA, which, as of April 1992, had yet to rule on the matter. According to Pitt faculty athletic representative John Bolvin, the work of the team from Bond, Schoeneck and King convinced school officials to improve compliance procedures and change the position of compliance director from part time to full time.

"What the investigation has improved is the overall oversight of the compliance," Bolvin said. "It's improved the consistency among all sports in terms of records in recruiting, records on who has cars, records on where they live, all that kind of stuff. Then, those can be audited more easily and more quickly, whereas before you kept records for what you needed as a coach, as opposed to what an auditor had. It puts more system into it."

The investigation into the Washington program is being conducted by the Pac-10, not the NCAA. Although they are subject to review by the NCAA, the penalties levied by the Pac-10 are likely to be final. The way the NCAA might get involved is if a pattern of violations is determined or a major violation is evident. The definition of "major violation" by the NCAA is one that "provide(s) an extensive recruiting or competitive advantage." The minimum penalty for any major violation is a two-year probation and at least one year with the following sanctions: no bowls, no television, elimination of all expense-paid visits to the campus, and a prohibition to any off-campus visits by coaches. Any coaches who were involved in or knew about any major violations are to be fired or severely punished.

Determining culpability can be difficult in these investigations, according to Pac-10 commissioner Tom Hansen. "Certainly, a very obvious attempt to violate a rule is different from inadvertently violating a very minor rule," he said. "But in between there are so many shades. There are some rules where a claim of inadvertent violation wouldn't get you very far because the rule is so fundamental, so basic that anyone who is coaching at this level, they should certainly be aware of it, and the university should have educational programs for its staff members to make sure they were aware of the basic rules. There's no clear line on that point."

Hansen said the Pac-10 prides itself on its enforcement program and noted that it is the only conference in the country that will handle a major case from start to finish without involving the NCAA. "Most others, if they discover it's a major case, will send it to (NCAA headquarters in) Kansas City in a hurry," he said. Ultimately, in any case, everything must be reported to the NCAA; failure to do so is a violation. "Our people feel strongly that if there's a problem, they want the investigation done quickly, they want it done competently, and they feel more comfortable in people they know and who know them. We try to work very cooperatively without in any way holding back on something."

Most conferences back off from conducting an entire investigation, allowing the NCAA to take over, in order to preserve the relationship between the conference office and the member schools. "It's a tribute to (associate commissioner) David Price that that hasn't happened with us," Hansen said. "I have told him that that is something I would watch carefully. If I felt that was happening, we'd take that to the membership and discuss it with the membership. David is so good at this and has such a very fine hand and very measured approach that that has not been a problem. It's also a tribute to the approach of our presidents and chancellors, who have made it very clear that they are going to aggressively pursue any problems. They review all the cases, however major or minor, in one of their two annual meetings. That in itself is probably nationally leading in terms of the chief executive officers sitting down in a room together twice a year on athletic matters.

"Right from the top, there is a clear understanding that abuses and violations will not be tolerated, and they will be prosecuted, and the penalties can be severe because the presidents have said that they want that."

The Pac-10 last slapped one of its own members with a bowl-and-television ban in 1983, when Arizona was cited for several infractions and lost both. The situation hurts the entire conference, because any bowl revenue is divided among the league's 10 schools.

Arizona might have gotten the harshest penalty of any Pac-10 team in some time, yet it wasn't the last school in the league to be sanctioned by the NCAA. In 1988, California had some of its scholarships pulled because of "academic fraud and unethical conduct." Likewise, USC received scholarship cuts and had its recruiting limited in 1985 after giving players extra benefits and conducting improper recruiting practices.

A more serious penalty was levied against the USC program in 1982 after the Trojans were found guilty of ticket scalping, academic fraud, and other transgressions. After that, Southern Cal received a two-year bowl ban and a two-year television ban. Although the bowl sentence took effect immediately, the television sanctions were delayed twice; first to 1983 and '84 because of the Pac-10's television contract, then to '83 and '85 because of a court ruling. Regardless, the penalty handed down by the league was harsh.

25

The Rematch

If the season would have salvation, if the slates could be wiped clean for at least a night, it would come in Pasadena. There in Southern California, the Huskies could rediscover the fun of football, the frivolity of it all, a place where the whimsy of the Beef Bowl and Disneyland would briefly overshadow talk of Billygate and drug busts.

The long-stem roses distributed to the Apple Cup losers were of little consolation after a bitter defeat, yet when the players returned to Seattle, those feelings of frustration were largely eclipsed by a sense of anticipation. The Huskies were, after all, conference champions. A 9-2 record was nothing to scoff at; just three times in the modern era had Washington posted a better mark in the regular season.

"If you had told me before the season that we would finish 9-2 and play in the Rose Bowl," Don James noted, "I would have said, 'Let's nail it down' in August. We don't live and die with this idea of having to win a national championship."

The No. 9 Huskies would play seventh-ranked Michigan, which didn't lose any games but tied three, finishing with a record (8-0-3) more befitting an NHL team than the Big Ten's Rose Bowl representative. Like Washington, the Wolverines weren't exactly riding a crest of momentum into the match-up; Michigan's final two games were ties against Illinois (22-22) and bitter rival Ohio State (13-13). "I'm a little disappointed (about the way the season ended)," Michigan Coach Gary Moeller said. "But I'm very proud, not only to be in the Rose Bowl, but I'm also proud of what I bring to the Rose Bowl in our team . . . I think (the Huskies) are an excellent team, as good as anybody in the country, and I think Michigan is in that category, too."

The focus of Washington players underwent an abrupt shift after the debacles in Tucson and Pullman. No longer was a national title in reach, so the Huskies now set their sights on the history books. Their new goal: to become the first team in the history of the Rose Bowl to three-peat.

"When it's all said and done, I'm going to look down at my hand and have three Rose Bowl rings and a national championship ring," Lincoln Kennedy said. "I can definitely hold up my head and say I've had a great career here."

Of course, winning a third Rose Bowl ring was special, but it didn't have the romantic appeal of hoisting the McDonald's trophy and thrusting a raised index finger into a television camera. Somehow, it seemed unimaginable that a second win over Michigan would send the Dawgs into gleeful convulsions on the Rose Bowl floor. A few Compton Quakes, maybe, but it was hard to picture any Washington players pitching a tent under the Pasadena sky if they won this time. The gloom hanging over the program was too thick.

Husky players were suddenly in the peculiar position of defending their coach, a man who reached icon status in these parts while some of them were in diapers. The notion of questioning James' integrity would be ludicrous just two months earlier.

"I know Don James does a great job of playing by the rules and runs a really tight ship," Dave Hoffmann said. "I don't like anybody who tried to backstab the program." Echoed James Clifford: "Coach James runs a clean program. He's a great man. It really frustrates me that people are trying to put him down now."

James, in turn, defended his players in a Pasadena press conference that took place a month before the Rose Bowl game. "I still think it's a very clean program," he said. "A couple of young men made decisions that obviously weren't very good decisions, (but) we have a lot of great human beings on our team."

A dreary December in Seattle had the Huskies longing for the Southern California sunshine, reprieve from the rain, and a temporary escape from the white-hot scrutiny of local media. "It's going to be good to get away," Andy Mason confided. "I know when we get down there, there are going to be a whole new group of people questioning us. But at the same time, when all the crap is out of the way, you can go to Disneyland and Hollywood to do some other things."

Judging by Rose Bowl ticket sales and travel bookings, the allure of watching the Huskies play in Pasadena wasn't nearly as strong as it was a year before. Some travel agents reported a 50-percent drop in reservations from the previous Rose Bowl. "I think people in the community aren't excited because of the fact there have been a lot of questions about what's going on," Mason said. "How bad is it? Are there problems? Are they 'legit'? I think people are dealing with a lot of question marks."

Not all news was bad. Several Huskies received post-season awards. Hoffmann, Kennedy and Napoleon Kaufman were named to the All-Pac-10 first team. It was the second straight appearance on the team for Kennedy, winner of the Morris Trophy for the Pac-10's outstanding offensive lineman, and Hoffmann, named the league's Defensive Player of the Year. Florida State's Marvin Jones edged Hoffmann and Miami's Michael Barrow for the Butkus Award, presented to the nation's top linebacker. Kennedy was named to the first team of the AP All-America squad and was one of four finalists for the Lombardi Award, given to the nation's best lineman.

Still, this wasn't the same Husky team that rolled through opponents a year earlier. Michigan's squad looked far closer to its 1991 version. Elvis Grbac, seasoned by another year, piloted the Wolverine offense. He would enter this game armed with more than a playbook. Now, he knew pain. Humiliated in the 1992 Rose Bowl, he had something to prove. "January was a terrible month," he recalled. "To have a season like that and then perform horribly in the Rose Bowl really shook me up."

Cam Cameron, Michigan's quarterback coach, wanted to ensure Grbac never forgot the feeling of being unceremoniously dumped on his butt or being thrashed like a rag doll in front of millions. Cameron called the quarterback into his office, where an excruciating videotape was waiting. Spliced together were Grbac's gestures of frustration. A season's worth of lowlights, all rolled into one game.

"He just showed me dropping my head or pulling my chinstrap after a play," Grbac said. "He showed me losing my poise. He let that run for a while. Then he asked if that was the quarterback he had seen during the season.

"I didn't say anything. That hit home fairly hard. It was a learning experience. I'm going to keep it in my back pocket. If it happens again, I'll know how to react."

Problem was, Grbac no longer had Desmond Howard on the other end of his passes. His new target was Derrick Alexander, whose numbers fell short of Howard's but would frighten any semi-alert defensive coordinator: 47 receptions (26 percent of his team's total) and 11 of the Wolverines' 23 passing touchdowns. Teammates referred to the lanky junior as "Alexander the Great," in part because of his acrobatic catches but also because of his recovery from a knee injury that kept him sidelined for most of 1991.

Anchoring the Wolverine offensive line was Steve Everitt, considered by some to be the best center in the country and certainly a member of the All-Goofball team. He wore his blond hair spiked, his flannel shirts unbuttoned, and socks not at all. An art major, Everitt was so consumed by his craft that it was unclear what he enjoyed more—to draw or draw blood? He never seemed too concerned about losing his own bodily fluids. During his junior season, his jaw was shattered so badly that three titanium plates were required to repair it. "I remember looking into his eyes on the field," recalled Les Miles, Michigan's offensive line coach. "And there he was with his jaw busted, teeth knocked out, and blood spewing everywhere saying, 'I'll be OK.'"

Among Everitt's more legendary antics was the time he hiked up to the HOLLYWOOD sign in Los Angeles and scaled one of the letters. Michigan coaches chuckle about the time he showed up for winter conditioning in a string bikini or fell out of a tree when he fell asleep while deer hunting. His hijinx left friends doubled over with laughter, yet his toughness was what commanded respect.

Said Moeller: "I haven't been around a center any better than Steve Everitt."

And Michigan boasted four running backs who had a knack for finding any hole Everitt pushed open for them—Jesse Johnson, Ricky Powers, Tyrone Wheatley and Ed Davis, also known as Stanky Dog, Ricardo, Shank T and Spoonful. "Ed is a spoonful of everything," Wheatley explained. "Jesse plays like a stanky dog—a street dog, fighter and scrapper. I'm long and slender like a shank steak."

Said Johnson, "We call Powers 'Ricardo' because he wears these funny Spanish boots whenever we travel."

When asked if all four backs could conceivably start at separate Big Ten schools, Illinois Coach Lou Tepper said: "Conceivable? I'd say it's probable. You would have to go back to Alabama's national championship teams in 1978 and 1979 or the great Oklahoma wishbone teams to find anyone this deep in running backs. And to have Ricky Powers as your third-string tailback . . . I'd love it if we could get him on waivers."

Powers, first team All-Big Ten in 1991, was overtaken by Wheatley and Johnson on the depth chart after spraining his ankle. Wheatley, a sophomore, was nicknamed "Superman" in high school. He was the fastest of Michigan's backs and although he compared his build to that of a shank steak, at 6-foot-1, 225 pounds he looked closer to a porterhouse cut. The media voted him Big Ten Offensive Player of the Year after he rushed for 1,122 yards during the regular season, breaking the 100-yard mark six times and torching Iowa for 224 yards. He could cover 100 meters in a world-class 10.35 seconds. Washington players—those who watched him break free for a 53-yard touchdown run—knew the potential packed into those knotted muscles. Shank T wasn't his nickname on campus. There, friends called him "T Wheat" and "T Sweets," short for "Too Sweet."

Conditioned by facing the league's top quartet of ball carriers every day in practice, the Wolverine defense played the run well, allowing opponents an average of 89.5 yards a game and just 2.7 a carry. Forty-five times during the regular season Michigan defenders registered a sack, whereas the Wolverine offensive line yielded just eight. Less impressive against the pass, Michigan gave up an average of 206 yards a game by air. Late in the season, the Wolverines were saddled with injuries to the cornerback spots and allowed their last three opponents to complete 63 percent of their passes for an average of 223 yards a game. Especially damaging was the loss of Alfie Burch to a foot injury. The senior cornerback missed Michigan's final five games and would sit out the Rose Bowl, limiting the team's man-to-man coverage capabilities.

The emotional leader of the defense was Corwin Brown, a team captain and the starting free safety. His pregame ritual was peculiar. He would put on pads, pants and jersey, tape his hands, then sit on a bench in front of his locker and cry. Real honest-to-goodness tears would stream down his cheeks. "You know," he explained, "it's just a way of me expressing myself and showing a little bit of excitement. Some people just sit down and meditate. I just express myself in a little different way."

Brown was always a little different. When he was a kid in Chicago, his neighborhood friends called him "Corn" because, he said, "they couldn't pronounce Corwin for nothin'." That opened the door for a slew of new nicknames. "This guy, Lou, he was like, 'Well, you know, you're small. You look just like a little flake, anyway, so we're just going to call you 'Cornflakes.'" That moniker stuck and his Michigan teammates referred to him as 'Flakes,' although his reliability as a punishing tackler was anything but flaky. Still, he was burned in a big way by the Huskies in the 1992 Rose Bowl. "Actually, I've thought about (the loss) all summer, I can't lie," he confessed, adding the Huskies should have been held to 17 points, not 34. "I think we'll go out there, the offense will get another shot at them, and we'll do a lot better this time." Brown said that in September. Now, it was December, and his plan was unfolding nicely.

The confidence of Michigan players was booming; ticket sales were not. By mid-December—a time when, in any other year, Rose Bowl tickets would be snapped up in a heartbeat—Washington was still trying to unload 8,000 of the 41,000 tickets it was contractually bound to purchase. Those unsold tickets, at $46 apiece, represented a potential net loss of nearly $400,000. Michigan, allotted 21,000 tickets, reported about 5,000 tickets.

The ticket booth at the Rose Bowl is seldom open on January 1. And why should it be? More than 100,000 people filled the stadium for 28 consecutive Rose Bowl games. But this problem of unsold tickets threatened that streak. "We take a lot of pride in being sold out, so we want to help (Washington) in any way we can," said Jack French, executive director of the Rose Bowl. "I can remember only one time in the past few years that we've been faced with this problem—that was for the 1985 game, when we got down to a couple thousand and got rid of most of those, but not all, by selling them on the day of the game." Interest for that game, which featured USC vs. Ohio State, was down because the Trojans ended the regular season with losses to UCLA and Notre Dame.

Ultimately, Rose Bowl officials would resort to newspaper advertisements to sell tickets, a highly atypical and somewhat embarrassing situation for a bowl with such a proud, rich tradition. "We've never had a situation of this magnitude," French finally conceded.

In an irony of ironies, Washington State was on the verge of making money on its appearance in the Copper Bowl, which offers teams a paltry payoff compared to the Rose Bowl ($650,000 as compared to $6.9 million, shared among all the league teams), yet because of slow ticket sales, the Huskies stood to take a financial hit in Pasadena.

Empty stadium seats or not, the Husky coaches and players were determined not to allow outside distractions dampen their excitement for the game. This was, after all, the Granddaddy of Them All, and they had earned the right to play in the game. Apart from the allegations, rumors and innuendo, this was an exceptional football team that had provided years of excitement and satisfaction for its community. The Huskies refused to forget this. Dave Hoffmann refused to forget it. "Football is still football," he said. "And I'm not going to let a lot of outside things come in and ruin my focus...I don't care what the fans think. The two teams down on the field are going to think it's pretty incredible. You don't really know how it feels until you step on that field on January 1."

Just as everything else about the Rose Bowl had changed for the Huskies during the past year, so did Washington's accommodations. The team, which touched down in Southern California two weeks before the game, was no longer staying in Anaheim but in Pasadena. Whereas Anaheim is splattered with strip malls and fast-food restaurants, much of Pasadena is the well-manicured, antiseptic home of old money where lawns are putting greens and houses have maids' quarters. Husky practices now took place at Occidental College, a liberal arts school in less-affluent Eagle Rock, about five miles west of the Rose Bowl.

During their past two trips to the Rose Bowl, the Huskies practiced at Golden West Community College in Orange County, which offered about twice the amount of playing surface of

Occidental but less privacy. Fans, recruits and other interested spectators stood just off the two playing fields at Golden West. The crowds were smaller at Occidental and sat on the cement bleachers, more removed from the field. Quarterback-turned-Congressman Jack Kemp and former Washington assistant and current coach of the New Orleans Saints Jim Mora once were roommates at Occidental, a school with a rich tradition in NCAA Division III football and an enrollment of 1,700.

The workouts were crisp, spirited. Players seemed invigorated by the warm sunshine that bathed the grass field. After practice Eric Bjornson, who would switch back to quarterback in the spring, threw balls to Joe Kralik. The two stayed long after their teammates hit the locker room and treated the smattering of spectators to a vision of the future. It was a hopeful display. When the controversy faded, football would prevail.

While standing on the Occidental field, looking up at the beige stucco buildings and red-tile roofs of campus buildings, one Husky player who had evidently left his thinking cap back at the hotel had a memorable conversation with Dick Baird.

"How does this school have a football team?" the player asked.

"What?"

"I mean, how do they find enough dentists to make up a team?"

"Dentists?"

"This is Occi-dental, right?"

The exchange left Baird in stitches. Laughter felt good. It had been a while since anyone in the program had a real hearty laugh.

II

Mark Schwarz said he'll try to do another interview with Don James some time.

Good luck, Mark.

James let fly with an expletive-laced tirade when he felt badgered by the ESPN reporter two days before the Rose Bowl. Schwarz tried to draw James into a response about UW President William Gerberding's comments about the Husky program. Here's how the exchange aired on ESPN:

Schwarz: (Gerberding) used the word "embarrassing" to talk about some of the charges and the allegations against the

University of Washington football program. You know, for 17 years there hasn't been an embarrassing word said, and all of a sudden in the space of a few weeks, one thing after another. Are you embarrassed by what's happened?

James: I'm not sure what I am. Maybe "shocked" would be a better word.

Schwarz: Are you angry that he (Gerberding) would use the word "embarrassing?"

James: Absolutely not. Are you trying to get me to say something bad about my president? That's freaking ridiculous, Mark. Don't even lead your (censored by ESPN)ing questions that way. I'm not going to sit here and put up with that bull(bleep) now, I've already told you that. So don't go and do that bull(bleep). I have to live with my president, my boss, and you're going to sit here and try to get me making comments about that. That is (bleep)ing immature broadcasting.

According to one athletic department official, who requested anonymity, James used uncharacteristically foul language to taint the tape and render it unusable by ESPN. James, did, however, continue the interview and answered several other questions in a composed way. That part of the story was edited from the final product. After an editorial meeting regarding the trade, the network decided to air it. "There was a lot of doubt as to whether to use it," Schwarz said. "(We discussed) whether we should edit it or use the whole thing. We didn't want to be the arbiter of Don James. Given the fact that the athletic director would not talk to us, we felt we needed to use it."

During the traditional press conference at the Wrigley Mansion the next day, James' birthday, the coach was asked about the piece of videotape. "I didn't see it," he said. "It was extremely difficult with the line of questions . . . I was embarrassed that I got mad at a commentator. But I can also go on record as saying I will never, ever do another interview with that particular commentator."

When Don James says that, you can bank on it. So Schwarz, who works out of Los Angeles, might want to defer to another reporter when it comes to future interviews with the coach. Still, the reporter said he would try again. "I've always had a pretty good rapport with Washington," Schwarz said. "I was pretty surprised . . . We won't stop coming up there. I won't stop coming up there."

It was clear on game day that James had put everything behind him, blocked out the turbulent way the season ended, the media barrage, the ESPN tirade. It was time to play football and, some would argue, no football coach could focus on a task at hand as well as Don James. His knowledge of the game and yen for precision frightened opposing coaches. It is not an exaggeration to say when given three weeks to prepare for a college football game, James is the best in the business.

The theme of the 1993 Rose Bowl festivities was "Entertainment on Parade," which was highly appropriate for what took place on the field as well as off it. Although these were two solid football teams, the Rose Bowl didn't offer the intrigue of some other New Year's Day match-ups—Miami vs. Alabama in the Sugar Bowl to decide the national champion, Notre Dame vs. Texas A&M in the Cotton Bowl, and Georgia vs. Ohio State in the Citrus Bowl. By January 2, folks would be calling this classic in Pasadena one of the best bowl games in recent memory.

The game was a flurry of punches and counterpunches, and when the dust settled, Michigan players got their chance to celebrate as the Huskies—denied a three-peat—trudged back to the locker room. The Wolverines (9-0-3) completed their first undefeated season since 1974 by winning, 38-31, in front of an undersized crowd of 94,236. The attendance was the lowest for the Rose Bowl since the 1955 game, when 89,191 watched USC play Ohio State. Because of the ticket surplus, Rose Bowl officials gave away 2,500 tickets to families of American Service personnel in Somalia and another 2,500 to charity.

Whether they ordered it or not, the folks in that stadium were treated to what is destined to become a favorite in Ann Arbor—a bowl full of Wheatleys. Fifteen Tyrone Wheatley carries that is. Fifteen carries for 235 yards, just 12 short of Charles White's Rose Bowl rushing record. Wheatley added touchdown runs of 56, 88 and 24 yards to his personal highlight video. The sophomore got the starting nod after Wolverines tailback Jesse Johnson didn't make the trip to Southern California because of, according to Michigan officials, "social misconduct." Rumor had it he was suspended from the team after getting into a bar fight. The game ball was thrust into the capable hands of Wheatley.

Wheatley ran with it.

And ran, and ran.

He carved his own winding parade route through the Washington defense each time he touched the ball. As wide as two Napoleon Kaufmans and just as fast as one, Wheatley was unstoppable. Reporter Thomas Bonk of the *Los Angeles Times* noted the Michigan sophomore was simply a geometry lesson in cleats—the shortest distance between two goal lines was whichever way Wheatley decided to run.

Adding luster to Wheatley's heroics was that despite running rampant he was hobbled by pain.

"Somebody got me in the small of the back in the first quarter and I started having spasms," he said, cradling his Player of the Game trophy. "It was like somebody was tying a knot in my muscles. I'd have pain all down my left leg, then it would go numb. The numb was worse—it was like I couldn't feel my left foot hitting the ground."

From almost any vantage in the Rose Bowl, Wheatley looked unfettered by pain. He glided through the secondary, effortlessly juking people he shouldn't be able to effortlessly juke and making a seamless shift into fifth gear. "He's got speed and size," James noted. "He's probably 240 pounds in all the gear, and telling people to tackle him is pretty easy from the sidelines. Those runs were a combination of moves, speed and missed tackles."

Part of the difference between the 1992 and '93 Rose Bowl was the Huskies' attack defense didn't have those big bodies of Steve Emtman and Tyrone Rodgers clogging the middle. The Dawgs still overloaded on the line of scrimmage, but, as James Clifford said, "sometimes we got caught."

"Last year we confused and flustered them a lot," Clifford said. "This time, they had the right play calls for our defenses. They didn't get rattled. They were a lot more confident.

"Last year Grbac was scared to death every play. Today, nothing bothered him."

Whereas Wheatley moved the Michigan offense across large tracts of land, his counterpart, Napoleon Kaufman, sputtered and couldn't seem to find the seams he found during the regular season. He was held to 39 yards on 12 carries with a long of 5 yards. He fumbled twice—one of which became the game's only turnover and led to the Wolverines' tying touchdown in the third quarter. "It wasn't that they were so much faster," he said of the Michigan defenders, "they were just so disciplined. They never made a mistake. We couldn't run inside, and we couldn't run outside."

For the first time since his injury, Mark Brunell played without his knee brace, a decision he made earlier in the week. It was the right choice. He obviously felt unencumbered when he scrambled for 18 yards on third-and-6 to set up Washington's first touchdown. The play was a sign of things to come. The senior quarterback delivered the game of his life, surpassing the effort that earned him his first Rose Bowl MVP. He completed 18 of 30 passes for two touchdowns and 308 yards, the highest yardage total of his career. "Mark gave it his all," Jason Shelley said. "He ran the ball, he threw the ball. He did everything you could ask of him."

Except win. And the loss was what was on Brunell's mind as he walked off the field. "It's frustrating for us now because we wanted to win three in a row," he said. "Michigan is a good football club. We give a lot of credit to those guys. They played great the whole game. Those are the breaks. We have to learn from that and move on."

Only now, there was no place to move on to. Washington's turbulent season, mercifully, had come to a close. The players showered, packed their belongings, waded through the clot of reporters waiting just outside the locker room door and headed for the team bus. The mood of the Huskies wasn't dour; there was a certain sense of resignation in the air. For many, there was hope.

"This makes you work harder," said D'Marco Farr, surrounded by a huddle of reporters. "We've got a lot of emotion and energy. It makes you real big in a hurry."

Then, a guarantee: "We'll be back."

With that, the season of triumph and turmoil ended. It was a year when the Huskies' haunting slogan, Present Not Past, was more bane than blessing.

The past was more fun.

Afterword

The Husky legacy of Billy Joe Hobert, triumphant then turbulent, was punctuated by a bittersweet irony on NFL draft day: He was selected in a higher round than Mark Brunell. The Los Angeles Raiders made Hobert their second pick, the third quarterback selected in the draft. "I'm ecstatic," he said. "LA is a great place for me to get rid of the negative image that I've gotten. I can't wait to get started. The LA Raiders. Playing for Al Davis. It's fantastic."

Although the Raiders used a second-round pick on Hobert, the quarterback was actually selected in the third round. LA had the last pick in the second round, No. 57 overall, but allowed the five-minute time limit to expire. New England, which had the first pick of the third round, made its selection, then Minnesota made a selection. Finally, the Raiders chose.

"I was told that the reason I'll be playing for the Raiders was Al Davis," Hobert said. Davis, the flamboyant managing general partner, has been known to make unusual draft choices. Two years earlier, he selected USC's Todd Marinovich in the first round after Marinovich had been arrested on drug charges.

In June, 1993, Hobert inked a minor-league contract with the Chicago White Sox, even though he had not played on a baseball team since high school. He planned to play three weeks for Sarasota in the Gulf Coast Rookie League before reporting for Raider training camp. The White Sox, who reportedly gave Hobert a $75,000 signing bonus, were duly impressed when they flew him to a Class-A game prior to the baseball draft, and he went 1 for 3 with a double.

Many prognosticators regarded Brunell as the third-best quarterback in the draft behind WSU's Drew Bledsoe (taken by the New England Patriots as the first pick overall) and Notre Dame's Rick Mirer (Seattle Seahawks, second pick overall). But Brunell wasn't chosen until the second day of the draft when the Green Bay Packers selected him in the fifth round.

Green Bay wasn't shopping for a quarterback — particularly with Pro-Bowler Brett Favre, Don Majkowski, Ty Detmer and Ken O'Brien already on the roster — but Brunell was too talented a player to overlook. "I liked him in high school," Packer quarterback Coach Steve Mariucci said. "I liked what he did for the University of Washington. After our scouts and (Coach) Mike Holmgren watched him, they felt the same way. His athletic ability and style really fit our offense. We didn't feel we had to draft a quarterback, but if we were going to take a quarterback, he was the one ... When we got to the fifth round, and he was still available, we couldn't pass him up."

Lincoln Kennedy, as expected, was the first Husky to go in the draft, becoming the ninth pick overall as the Atlanta Falcons' first selection. That slot was six lower than he was touted to be selected during the fall, and Louisiana Tech's Willie Roaf was the first offensive lineman chosen. Nonetheless, Kennedy was unfazed. "I'm not disappointed by any means," he said. "I'm happy to go to Atlanta. It was more pride and a principle factor that I wanted to be the first person chosen as far as offensive linemen, but it happens like that. It's something you deal with."

The Kansas City Chiefs chose fullback Darius Turner in the sixth round, but indicated he could help the team right away due to the fact the team planned to make a switch from the one-back set to the 49ers' pro set and did not have another fullback on its roster. Two rounds earlier, the Chiefs had chosen UW linebacker Jaime Fields, whose car-accident-style collisions could not be ignored.

Linebacker Dave Hoffmann, whose love of violence belied his easy smile and placid soul, was chosen in the eighth round by the Chicago Bears. Predicted Ed Cunningham, a year of NFL experience under his belt: "They're going to love Dave Hoffmann in Chicago. He'll be a hero there."

Free-spirited cornerback Walter Bailey, safety Shane Pahukoa and running back Jay Barry went undrafted but later signed free-agent contracts with the New York Giants, New Orleans Saints and Los Angeles Rams. Tommie Smith and Mike Lustyk aimed to crack the Seahawks' roster.

Stanford Coach Bill Walsh, who long fostered a reputation as a soft-spoken sage of the game, blasted the Husky program in May during a speech to more than 100 Stanford alumni. He characterized UW football as an outlaw program and its players as "mercenaries."

"The football players there have almost no contact with the rest of the student body," Walsh said in his speech, which he delivered without notes. "They have an athletic department compound, and that's where they spend their time. When they use up their eligibility and are expected to return to society, they have none of the skills you are supposed to gain in college.

"The things I have read about Washington were devastating. They bring in football players without any kind of preparatory courses. They just throw them in and expect them to compete. How many kids are ready for that? It's no wonder only 33 percent of the football players at Washington graduate."

Walsh's excoriating comments sent shock waves throughout the coaching fraternity and beyond. Many felt he had violated an unspoken code by publicly undressing a fellow coach, Don James, and the program he built. James declined comment, and a day after Walsh's comments were printed in the *Sacramento Bee*, the Stanford coach apologized. "I can't hide from it or avoid it," Walsh said of the remarks, adding he made a personal apology to James via telephone. "The first thing I have to do, first and foremost, is apologize to the University of Washington ... I was dead wrong. I was out of line."

But Walsh, whose team would open the 1993 season at Washington, stopped short of recanting the remarks. "Somehow," he said, "I got into this and used the name University of Washington, maybe two or three times, maybe once. I talked about college football and basketball in general. I used the University of Washington to refer to them. What this writer did was combine the two in an indictment of the University of Washington . . . My mistake was to refer to the University of Washington. I shouldn't have."

A week later, the Pac-10 reprimanded Walsh for making the comments. "College athletics is a highly competitive enterprise," Commissioner Tom Hansen said. "Our member institutions have made it clear in conference legislation that they expect each of their representatives to conduct himself or herself with collegiality and mutual respect."

On June 21, the Pac-10 issued its Notice of Charges in late June, outlining the findings of the league's six-month investigation of the Husky program. The media was presented with the meaty, 100-plus-page document four days later, and read of charges involving Billy Joe Hobert, Husky boosters and manipulated expense reports by "student hosts."

"I'll be frank," Don James said. "I read this and was very disturbed by the first part. Then when I read the responses of the people that were named, I felt much better."

The report made no conclusions on the allegations, which if proven could result in a ban on bowl games and television appearances, and a loss of some future scholarships. Said David Berst, NCAA assistant executive director for enforcement: "If there are major penalties, it is at least a year of post-season sanctions."

Washington officials had until July 31 to respond to the allegations, whereupon a four-person Pac-10 compliance committee would make a reccommendation on actions to be taken Aug. 9-10 in San Francisco. That reccommendation would be passed along to the 30-person Pac-10 council, which would accept the reccommendation or offer another solution August 21 in San Francisco. The following day, league chancellors and presidents would vote on the matter and pass the case on for review by the NCAA.

Appendix A

This is the transcript of a report filed by the Santa Ana, California, police officers who arrested Husky players Vince Fudzie and Kevin Conard at the Red Onion restaurant December 22, 1985. All charges were dropped against Fudzie and Conard, who later sued the restaurant for discriminatory practices and received an undisclosed settlement. A civil case against the arresting officers is pending in Orange County (California) Superior Court.

On Sunday, 12/22/85, at approximately 2305 hours, myself and Officer Bertagna were at the Red Onion, 101 E. Sandpointe, in regards to a routine bar check. Upon entering the restaurant lounge area, located on the southwest portion of the establishment, both officers were contacted by a Miss Burns and a Mr. Raymer told us that two male black subjects were refused entry into the establishment approximately 45 minutes ago due to dress code violations and that the two subjects were presently in the lounge area after sneaking in by unknown means. Mr. Raymer requested Officer Bertagna's and my assistance in escorting the two subjects out of the establishment.

As I approached the two subjects, located in the lounge, Mr. Raymer was talking to the subjects and asking them if they would please leave the establishment as they did not have the proper dress code. As Mr. Raymer was talking to the subjects, I heard him several times ask the subjects in a polite manner, saying, "Sir,

I am sorry that you don't understand, but this is the policy of the establishment." As Mr. Raymer was talking, one subject, later identified as Kevin Conard, was very loud and belligerent towards Mr. Raymer and several times said, "Fuck this place, fuck these honkies, let's get out of here." However, as Conard was saying these statements, he was still seated on the barstool and not leaving. Mr. Raymer asked Officer Bertagna and I to ask the subjects to leave as they were no longer wanted in the establishment and were starting to create a scene at the lounge whereupon approximately 20 to 30 people were starting to circle around the area as they heard Conard and his friend, later identified as Vince Fudzie, becoming loud and very, very boisterous.

Officer Bertagna and I then stepped within approximately two feet of the subjects and asked them to leave the establishment per the management. Both Conard and Fudzie got up off their barstools and approached Officer Bertagna and I, and Conard, in a very threatening manner due to his size of 6-feet-4 and approximately 240 pounds, stepped up to Officer Bertagna, looking down on him, said, "Ain't no white honkie gonna be able to kick me out of this place." Officer Bertagna and I backed up for our safety and also for an avenue that both Conard and Fudzie could leave in a peaceful manner, however Conard continued to challenge both Officer Bertagna and I. Conard and Fudzie walked approximately 15 feet into the lobby area, stopped and turned again on Officer Bertagna and I and Conard again said, "You think you're bad mother fuckers. Take that badge and your gun off and you ain't shit. I'll kick your ass right here." Officer Bertagna said, "Just step outside and leave this business." Conard refused to leave and again, looking at Officer Bertagna, challenged him to fight by saying, "I'll kick your ass. You can't do anything about it because I know my rights and I'll sue you and I'll have that badge."

Suspect #2, Fudzie, also was telling me to, "Back off or I'll kick your ass." Both Fudzie and Conard then started to walk backwards towards the exit door, however continued to yell and scream at officers to "take our shit off and let's get it on." By this time, there were approximately 30 people that had started to gather around us again as the two subjects were yelling and screaming at the officers. However, Officer Bertagna and I realized that for the subjects and for officer safety, a confrontation inside the bar would not be safe. We continued to ask the two subjects to leave the establishment and after approximately a couple of minutes, the subjects got to the exit door. As we started to walk out with them, Fudzie turned suddenly, to which I pushed him out the door, along with Officer Bertagna. Both officers felt that Fudzie may have been attempting to strike the officers as he turned so suddenly.

Conard took several steps outside of the exit doors and stepped towards Officer Bertagna in a threatening manner and said, "Okay, mother fucker, now we are outside, so let's get it on." Due to the enormous size of Conard and his muscular build, Officer Bertagna and I both drew our batons out of their rings, however, kept them down towards our waist areas. As Officer Bertagna and I had our batons out, Conard said, "What are you going to do now, hit me with your baton? Come on, put your baton down and then let's get it on, you honkie mother fucker."

It was at this point that both Conard and Fudzie slowly started to walk away, however at this point, Conard had challenged both Officer Bertagna and I to fight and to "kick our ass" approximately six to seven times. Suspect #2, Fudzie, has challenged me approximately two to three times inside the bar and at the exit doors. At this point, I requested several additional officers due to the size of Conard and Fudzie as they were going to be placed under arrest for challenging to fight.

As the units started to respond, we slowly walked Conard and Fudzie in an easterly direction through the parking lot towards their car. It should be noted that alcohol was not detected on either suspect as they spoke to us inside the bar.

As Officer Bertagna and I walked the suspects into the parking lot, several patrons from the Red Onion came out of the establishment as Conard and Fudzie were still yelling very loudly at the officers and challenging us to fight. For officer safety and the safety of both Conard and Fudzie, Officer Bertagna and I decided to wait until backup units arrived to attempt to take the suspects into custody without any violence or further fighting due to the fact that they had already challenged us so many times. Several minutes later, both subjects approached a white vinyl over red or maroon Cadillac that was parked on the southeast portion of the parking lot.

As Conard started to open the driver's car door with a set of keys which did open the car, Conard turned to Officer Bertagna and I and said, "Now's your last chance, chumps. Are we going to get it on or what?" Officer Bertagna and I told Conard again to just leave the area with no further comment. Fudzie got into the front passenger's side of the vehicle and the vehicle started up and proceeded in a northbound direction through the parking lot. At the same time, several responding backup units arrived.

We told the backup officers a quick rundown of the situation and that we were going to arrest Conard and Fudzie for (challenging to fight), however we wanted to do it out of the parking lot area in a safer location.

After Officer Bertagna and I told the backup units of our intentions, Officer Davies was the first unit to respond and was instructed to make a traffic stop on the vehicle pointed out to him that had just left at the extreme northeast portion of the parking lot. The other backup units were Officer Bartholeme, Officer Pierson, Officer J. Esparza and Officer Bertagna and I. Officer Bertagna and I got into the back seat of Officer Pierson's patrol unit and Officer Davies full overhead red and blue lights were seen activated on his police car at the stop light at the northeast corner of MacArthur and Sandpointe. Officer Keith Eldridge was also present.

The suspect vehicle failed to stop for Officer Davies and, approximately ten to fifteen seconds later, the turn light turned green and suspect vehicle made a left or westbound turn onto MacArthur from the parking lot. The vehicle continued at approximately 25 MPH in a westbound direction in the outside #2 lane, still continuing to fail to yield to Officer Davies' police unit. As the vehicle slowly approached Main Street, I also heard a siren activate two or three times in short bursts. At Main Street, the westbound traffic of MacArthur had a red light, however the vehicle slowed down but would not pull over to the right.

A backup unit, Officer Eldridge, pulled in front of the suspect vehicle in a blocking manner so the vehicle could not proceed either west or make a right or leftbound turn onto Main. I approached the passenger side of the vehicle in order to take suspect Fudzie into custody and open the front passenger door of the vehicle. I told Fudzie to get out of the car as he was under arrest and Fudzie attempted to lock himself into the vehicle by grabbing onto the door and outside window panel of the vehicle. I grabbed Fudzie by the collar of his shirt in order to take him to the ground and place him under arrest, which was done. Fudzie had to be dragged out of the car at this point in order to make the arrest, however was not struck in any manner and was handcuffed with little resistance.

I then looked up and noticed Conard, who was on the driver's side of the rear portion of the car, still becoming belligerent with Officers Davies and several other officers present. Conard looked at me and said, "What the fuck is going on here? Why are you harassing us again?" I told Conard to step to the sidewalk for his own safety and officer safety due to the possibility of oncoming traffic hitting either him or officers present. I stepped to the north sidewalk area of the intersection and told Conard that he was under arrest at which point Conard took a fighting stance and very quickly jabbed out with his left fist, striking me in the face. As Conard started to swing, I reacted and stepped backwards, just catching the end of his fist as it struck my lower lip. After Conard struck me, and as I stepped back in a defensive manner, I withdrew my baton from its ring again at which point Conard took off running eastbound on foot through traffic.

While chasing suspect Conard, several cars screeched to a halt and had to pull off to the right in order to avoid hitting either myself or pursuing officers. At one point, Conard stopped a small import vehicle and opened the driver's side of the door and jumped inside. The driver of the vehicle, described only as a male Hispanic, approximately 50 years old, was not involved in the incident whatsoever and was trying to get Conard out of his car, however due to Conard's extreme size and strength, could not do so. The male subject did manage to turn his car off, however and Conard was kicking at officers trying to get him out of the car and managed to start the vehicle up momentarily and attempted to put the vehicle into drive. However, I was able to put my nightstick through the open driver's door, through the spoked steering wheel and Conard could not get the vehicle to start again.

After several attempts of getting Conard out of the car, during which time he was continually kicking and striking at officers, we were finally able to drag Conard out of the subject's car. After getting Conard out of the car, the male subject, who was visibly scared and shaken, said, "Can I go, can I go?" I told the subject to go ahead and leave the area. Due to still fighting with Conard and attempting to take him into custody, we were unable to have the time to tell the subject to stand by and wait for officers in regards to obtaining a statement or getting information about him. However, again, it should be noted that the subject was in no way involved in the incident with Conard as far as being a friend or accomplice, etc.

As Conard fell to the pavement several times while attempting to fight with and attempting to run again from the officers, again he did trip and fall down several times and had to be physically jumped on by approximately five officers present. Due to Conard's strength, the only way officers could take him into custody was by mass weight of laying down on him. Approximately one minute later, Conard was finally taken into custody, however due to his upper body strength and size, one set of handcuffs could not be used in order to handcuff him and two sets had to be used. It should be noted that Officer Bertagna was struck in the ribs by Conard, with his fist, during the scuffle and attempt to take him into custody.

Both arrestees were then transported to the Santa Ana Police Department for processing, prior to being booked at the Orange County Jail. Arrestee Conard suffered a minor contusion to the face and head area and was transported to Western Medical Center by Officer Lofton for medical treatment.

At approximately 0200 hours, I contacted a doctor at Western Medical Center and was told that Conard received two internal and several external stitches above the left eyebrow area, and was in the process of being X-rayed and if the X-rays checked okay, he would be medically released into our custody.

Due to the extremely hostile and violent nature of both subjects, no interview was conducted of them and no statements obtained as well as any Miranda warning.

Officer Bertagna conducted a records and warrant check which proved to be negative for outstanding warrants on either subject through NCIC or local. In addition, neither subject had any contact with the Santa Ana Police Department.

Appendix B

The following is a police affidavit taken from the Certification for Determination of Probable Cause against Danianke Smith, arrested November 19, 1992, on four counts of distribution of cocaine.

The Seattle Police Department Narcotics Section has been investigating, the narcotics trafficking activity of the defendants Danianke Smith, Alexandra Sandoval, John Reisig, and Daphne Pie. A confidential informant who is willing to testify in court has assisted narcotics detectives with their investigation. This confidential informant is a student at the University of Washington and associated with several people who sell illegal narcotics. Several of these people are current and former athletes. Many of these transactions were recorded on audio and video tape.

COUNT I

The informant and defendant Danianke Smith have known each other from their contacts at the University of Washington Huskies football team. Smith's jersey number is 55. During their association, Smith has told the informant that he should call him any time he wanted to buy cocaine. Smith provided the informant with his telephone number.

On August 17, 1992, the informant telephoned Smith at his residence that he shares with his girlfriend, Daphne Pie. Pie answered the phone and explained that Smith was at the crewhouse, the University of Washington athletes' dormitory and training camp. She told the informant she would ask Smith to contact the informant.

Later that day, the informant telephoned Smith at the crewhouse. The informant told Smith he wanted to purchase $500 worth of narcotics. Smith told the informant that he would have to contact his supplier to arrange the sale and said he would call the informant back. Smith asked the informant for his pager number and told the informant that when he paged him, he would also code in his jersey number, 55, in addition to his telephone number, so that the informant would know who paged him. The pager number the informant gave Smith actually belonged to Seattle Police Narcotics Detective Jakobsen.

On August 18, 1992, the informant telephoned Smith at his residence and at the crewhouse and left messages for Smith to call him.

On August 19, 1992, Smith telephoned the informant from the crewhouse and explained that he was having difficulty setting up the deal with his supplier because, when she tried to reach him, he was at practice. Smith told the informant that when he finally contacted her, he would page the informant and enter his code number, 55, along with his supplier's telephone number.

On August 20, 1992, at about 10:16 p.m., the informant finally contacted Smith at the crewhouse. Smith explained that he had just gotten off the phone with his supplier and had told her to page the informant. Smith also urged the informant to directly telephone his supplier and gave the informant her telephone number.

The informant telephoned Smith's supplier, defendant Alexandra Sandoval, a few minutes later. The informant told her that he wanted to buy $500 worth of rock cocaine. Sandoval referred to her earlier conversation with Smith about the transaction, and told the informant to telephone her the following day.

On August 21, 1992, the informant telephoned Sandoval who told him that she was waiting to hear back from Smith and still looking for someone to fill the order. Sandoval called the informant a short time later and said that she had found the narcotics, but that she would have to take the informant's money first, get the drugs, and then return with them. The informant and Sandoval discussed whether Smith should be present when the exchange was made. The informant told Sandoval that he would trust her and they arranged to meet at the Kidd Valley restaurant near Greenlake in Seattle, King County, Washington. The informant was searched for contraband with negative results, and the police gave him the money. Sandoval arrived at the agreed location driving a black Honda Civic. The informant gave her the money and she left to obtain the drugs. They met later on the overpass at Oaktree Plaza, which crosses over Aurora Avenue in Seattle. Sandoval gave the informant 12.2 grams of rock cocaine concealed in a bottle. The informant was again searched with negative results, and handed over the narcotics. The narcotics were submitted to the Washington State Patrol Crime Laboratory for analysis and were determined to contain cocaine, a controlled substance.

COUNT II

Between August 31, 1992, and September 17, 1992, the informant contacted Pie, Smith, and Sandoval in an effort to set up the purchase of $500 worth of cocaine and an Uzi machine gun.

On August 31, 1992, the informant contacted Pie and spoke to her about Smith selling him guns and dope. Pie agreed to contact Smith and relay the message.

On September 8, 1992, and on September 9, 1992, the informant telephoned Smith at his residence and spoke with Pie. They discussed the purchase of cocaine from Smith. On each date, after speaking with Pie, the informant contacted Smith at the crewhouse and discussed details for the purchase of the gun and cocaine. Smith said he was having difficulty setting up the deal.

On September 10, 1992, the informant spoke with Smith several times. Smith said he had contacted his gun supplier and that the informant could purchase an Uzi machine gun. Smith provided the informant with the gun supplier's name and phone number.

On September 11, 1992, the informant called Smith, who said he could not set up the cocaine deal that night because he had an early curfew due to a football game the next day. Later that night, however, Smith's gun supplier sold the informant an AK assault rifle for $460. The gun supplier had been unable to procure a machine gun.

After the informant purchased the rifle, he returned home and got a message that he was to call Smith at 546-XXXX. The informant recognized that this was Sandoval's telephone number. The informant called Sandoval, who told the informant that Smith had set up the deal with her, but the only way she could get the cocaine was for the informant to front her the money. The informant objected to this plan.

Between September 11, 1992, and September 16, 1992, the informant had several conversations with Smith about how the narcotics transaction would take place. Eventually it was arranged that the informant would meet Smith in a parking lot at Northeast 45th and Eighth Northeast in Seattle, and give Smith $500. At the agreed time, the informant saw Sandoval drive Smith into the parking lot. The informant gave Smith $500 and showed the defendants where the informant lived so that they could deliver the cocaine at that address later that day. No cocaine delivery was made.

On September 17, 1992, the informant contacted Sandoval, who told the informant that she had gotten the cocaine and that she was taking it over to Smith's dormitory room. The informant telephoned Smith who confirmed that this was the plan and told the informant he should go to room No. 256 at the crewhouse.

The informant was searched for contraband with negative results before he met Sandoval and Smith in the dormitory room. Smith told the informant to wait there and the two left the room. A few minutes later, they returned to the room and Sandoval handed the informant the cocaine. Smith asked the informant if he knew anyone else he could sell cocaine to. They all left the dormitory. The informant was again searched for contraband with negative results, and handed the narcotics over to police. The narcotics were submitted to the Washington State Patrol Crime Laboratory and were determined to contain cocaine, a controlled substance.

COUNT III

The informant introduced undercover Police Narcotics Detective Jakobsen to Danianke Smith and told him that Jakobsen would be interested in purchasing narcotics from him.

During the early evening hours on September 21, 1992, Detective Jakobsen had several telephone conversations with

Smith and told him he was interested in buying $500 worth of cocaine. Smith told Jakobsen that after his 11 p.m. bed check, he would leave the dormitory and meet him at a Texaco station at Montlake Boulevard East and East Roanoke in Seattle.

Jakobsen arrived at the scene with undercover Police Detective Suzuki and parked his car. While there, they saw a man driving a red Datsun station wagon park near the gas pumps. Shortly after midnight, on September 22, 1992, Danianke Smith arrived at the gas station in a Ford Escort driven by a female.

Smith then got out of his car and stood in front of Detective Jakobsen's vehicle next to some telephone booths. Jakobsen got out of the car and called Smith by his nickname. Smith acknowledged Jakobsen and explained he had to get the cocaine from his supplier, nodding towards the man standing next to the station wagon. Smith asked Jakobsen if he had the money and Jakobsen said that he did. Smith suggested that they drive down the street to do the deal. Jakobsen declined, stating that he preferred to do the deal out in the open, since he did not know him very well.

Smith walked over to his supplier, who opened up the hood of his vehicle. They conversed with one another for several minutes. The supplier and Smith entered the vehicle. A brief time later, the supplier and Smith got out of the car. The supplier went into the store. While there, Smith again tried to convince Jakobsen to do the deal down the street. Jakobsen declined because he did not know them well. Jakobsen then agreed to drive up the street one block and do the deal. Smith went into the store where his supplier was and then got into the car with his female companion. Jakobsen followed Smith up the street two blocks and then got out of their cars. As they stood on the planting strip, Smith removed a large rock of cocaine weighing about 10 grams from his pocket, handed it to Jakobsen, and asked how it was. Jakobsen said it looked like "bunk," but Smith assured him it was good and that if he was dissatisfied with it, to let him know. Jakobsen gave Smith $500 in exchange for the cocaine. Smith told Jakobsen to call him any time if he needed something else. Jakobsen replied that he would probably need a half ounce of cocaine two to three times a week, and Smith said it would be no problem.

The narcotics were submitted to the Washington State Patrol Crime Laboratory for analysis and were determined to contain cocaine, a controlled substance.

COUNT IV

On September 23, 1992, Detective Jakobsen had three telephone conversations with Smith for the purpose of arranging the purchase of $500 worth of rock cocaine. During these phone conversations, it was decided that Jakobsen would meet with Smith in his room at the University of Washington crewhouse.

Jakobsen arrived there at about 9 p.m. and Smith said he did not have the cocaine yet but that he expected his supplier to arrive soon. At about 9:25 p.m., Smith had a phone conversation with his supplier and they agreed that Smith would meet the supplier at the Red Robin restaurant at Northgate. Jakobsen agreed to give Smith the $500 so that Smith could acquire the cocaine from his supplier and told Smith he would return to the crewhouse at 10 p.m.

At about 10:05 p.m., Jakobsen saw Smith driving a Ford Escort through the parking lot. He recognized the vehicle from the transaction on September 22, 1992. Jakobsen allowed Smith some time to get to his room and met him a few minutes later. Smith said, "It's behind the compact discs," nodding his head towards the compact discs on the shelf above the desk area. Jakobsen retrieved a baggie of cocaine weighing about 12 grams. Smith told Jakobsen to call him if he needed more.

The narcotics were submitted to the Washington State Patrol Crime Laboratory for analysis and were determined to contain cocaine, a controlled substance.

COUNT V

On September 30, 1992, Seattle Police Detective Jakobsen telephoned Smith at his dormitory room and arranged to purchase $400 worth of cocaine for $250. This amount included Smith's $50 fee for setting up the deal. Smith told Jakobsen to meet him in his new dormitory room at the crewhouse.

At about 10:20 p.m., Jakobsen arrived at Smith's room. Smith was the only one there. While they waited for his supplier, Smith left the room to find out if Jakobsen could purchase some marijuana from a teammate. The teammate was not in his room and a short time later, defendant Alexandra Sandoval arrived. Smith locked the door after her and introduced her to Jakobsen. Sandoval removed the rock cocaine from her purse and said there was $460 worth of rock there. Jakobsen gave her $200 and she left under Smith's escort.

Smith returned to his room. Jakobsen handed Smith the $50 and Smith said, "Yeah, from now on we'll do that. I'll get you a good deal and you can pay me extra." These conversations were recorded.

The cocaine weighed about 3.4 grams and field tested positive for cocaine.

COUNT VI

On November 18, 1992, Detective Jakobsen was visiting Smith at the crewhouse. There he discussed buying one kilo of cocaine. Smith said he could arrange the sale of a kilo for $19,000. Detective Jakobsen heard Smith ask several people if they had a former Husky's telephone number. Smith finally obtained the former Husky's telephone number and spoke with him. Smith told Jakobsen that the former Husky made a run to California every other weekend to obtain three to four kilos of cocaine and that they would be able to do the kilo deal after he got his supply on November 22, 1992.

Smith also told Detective Jakobsen that he had people who had marijuana for sale if he wanted any. Detective Jakobsen said he wanted to buy some marijuana. Smith picked up the telephone in his room, spoke to someone, and arranged for the sale of $100 worth of marijuana. They drove to 9724 Sand Point Way Northeast in Seattle. During the ride there, Smith told Detective Jakobsen that he would have to give him some money for setting up the deal. Detective Jakobsen agreed to do so. When they arrived at that location Smith told Jakobsen to park.

Once inside the residence Smith introduced him to defendant John Reisig. Jakobsen saw Reisig retrieve the marijuana from the TV room just to the right of the front door. Another person was in a TV room where Jakobsen saw a large marijuana bong in plain view. Reisig sold Jakobsen three one-eighth ounce bags of marijuana for $100 and said any time Jakobsen needed more to get in touch with Smith. Jakobsen gave Smith $20 for setting up the deal. The narcotics tested field positive for marijuana.

COUNT VII

On November 19, 1992, Detective Jakobsen telephoned Smith and said he wanted to buy some more marijuana. Smith told Jakobsen to come over. Jakobsen arrived at Smith's room at the crewhouse at about 8:30 p.m. Smith explained that they would be meeting "them" at the Ram Sports Bar in University Village. They drove over, leaving a friend of Smith's in the car.

When they entered the bar they saw Reisig sitting at a table. They joined him and Smith asked Reisig if he still had a quarter pound of marijuana left because Jakobsen had told him he knew someone who wanted to buy that amount. Reisig said that he did not but that he was going to resupply over the weekend. Reisig added that he was only interested in selling ounces. Jakobsen said he had a friend who wanted to buy a large amount on Monday.

Jakobsen told the group that he was going outside to tell Smith's friend, who was still waiting in the car, to come into the bar and join them. Reisig said he would accompany Jakobsen and followed him outside. Reisig caught up with Jakobsen and took him over to his Suburu station wagon. Reisig pulled out three baggies of marijuana from the driver's door and gave them to Jakobsen in exchange for $125. Jakobsen asked him if he could contact him on Monday [November 23, 1992] to buy a larger amount. Reisig said yes and to give him a call. He gave Jakobsen his telephone number. The narcotics field tested positive for marijuana.

Smith and Reisig were arrested on November 23, 1992, by Seattle Police Officers.

Bail in the amount of $150,000 is requested on Smith and Sandoval. Both are facing ten years in prison if convicted. Bail in the amount of $10,000 is requested on Reisig, who faces six months in jail.

Appendix C

The following is the opinion written by Judge Joan DuBuque of King County Superior Court regarding the Danianke Smith drug case and its ultimate dismissal:

I—CASE BACKGROUND

This case involves charges filed on November 24, 1992 against the four named defendants. These charges were filed as a result of a seven month undercover investigation conducted by the Seattle Police Department using the services of a confidential informant, Mr. Samuel Nemours. The informant's identity has been known to the defense since early on after the arrests and charges were made. At a press conference called shortly after the charges were filed, the Prosecutor's office characterized its informant as a University of Washington (U of W) student who was tired of seeing athletes on scholarships selling drugs while he was working hard to get through school.

This case has been pending since November 24, 1992. The case scheduling hearing has been continued a number of times at defense counsel request, with speedy trial waivers, in order to obtain necessary discovery including wiretap recordings, transcripts, authorizations and records reflecting judicial review for purposes of trial preparation and plea negotiations.

On March 16, 1993 a trial date of April 27, 1993 was set by the Chief Criminal Judge. Shortly thereafter, the case was preassigned to this court. On April 1, 1993 a status conference was held and the court set a new trial date of May 28, 1993. The court and all counsel discussed the provision of remaining transcripts and proof of judicial review of the wiretapped conversations. The court set pretrial motions for hearing on April 13, 1993. All parties had filed a number of pretrial motions and/or advised the court of a number of pretrial motions including defense motions to dismiss for failure of the State to provide requested discovery.

On April 13, 1993 the court heard motions relating to the disclosure of University of Washington (U of W) school records on Mr. Nemours (subpoenaed by Mr. Smith's counsel) and all the defendants (subpoenaed by the State), obtaining records of all payments made to Mr. Nemours by the Seattle Police Department (subpoenaed by Mr. Smith's counsel), amending the information as to Mr. Smith, and compelling the State to provide discovery relating to Mr. Smith's predisposition in light of an asserted entrapment defense set forth in Mr. Smith's earlier filed Omnibus application.

On April 13, 1993 the court made a number of rulings relating to discovery matters, many of which are detailed below. Additionally, the court requested that the State review the Omnibus applications which had been filed by each of the defendants and provide the information sought, or indicate that it did not exist.

The court set a date of May 4, 1993 for additional hearings on pretrial matters. On April 30, 1993 the court received renewed and supplemental motions to dismiss this case filed by defense counsel on the basis of discovery violations by the State. On May 4, 1993 the court received the transcripts of the interviews with Detective Jakobsen and Mr. Nemours. On May 4 and May 5, the court conducted hearings relating solely to the dismissal of this case. It is within this context that the following findings are made:

II—FINDINGS

1.0 <u>Mr. Nemours Motive</u>. Since at least the fall of 1992, if not before, the lead Detective on this case knew of the "Marcus Pope" motive. By December, 1992 the motive was mentioned briefly to Mr. O'Toole in a joint meeting between Detective Jakobsen and Mr. Nemours.

1.1 Since December 8, 1992 defense counsel made specific requests of the State for discovery relating to Mr. Nemours' reasons for cooperating with the police. (Robinson letters of December 8, 1992, February 5, 1993, February 26, 1993.) A significant issue at the April 13, 1993 hearing related to disclosure of Mr. Nemours' University of Washington (U of W) records to explore the claimed motive publicly announced by the State in November, 1992.

1.2 On April 30, 1993, during an interview of Mr. Nemours, the defense learned for the first time of the claimed: "Marcus Pope" motive. The defense also learned for the first time that Mr. Nemours had discussed this motive with Mr. O'Toole on March 18, 1993 in a joint meeting with Detective Jakobsen. While Mr. O'Toole told Mr. Nemours he would have to disclose this to the defense, Mr. O'Toole did not disclose it to any defense counsel. During the interview he was asked about the reasons Mr. Nemours cooperated with police. He did not disclose the "Marcus Pope" motive when asked about Mr. Nemours' motive for volunteering to cooperate with the police. Detective Jakobsen, who asked about the State's representation that Mr. Nemours' motive for volunteering was because he was a good student and upset about the drug trade, said the following:

> "Um, Sam told me that, that, that that was one of his reasons. As he said the very first time we met him, that was one of his reasons. There were other reasons. I relayed those messages to Ellen O'Neill Stephens."

1.3 The claimed "Marcus Pope" motivation involves a highly unusual story including allegations that associates of Danianke Smith were responsible for the murder in Los Angeles, California of a Marcus Pope some four or five years ago. Mr. Pope was Mr. Nemours' friend. Mr. Nemours stated in his interview, that he had planned, since he was a sophomore or junior in high school, to try to get into the U of W, get close to these people who he knew would be athletes at the U of W, and find out who was responsible. To do this, he "kicked his grades up" the last two years of high school. On May 4, 1993 the court released to all counsel a copy of Mr. Nemours' high school transcript which lends credence to his improved grades.

1.4 This information, when coupled with other statements and actions of Mr. Nemours during 1992 and the police investigation raises significant and substantial questions relating to his motive, veracity and reliability. It may well be highly exculpatory in that Mr. Nemours' credibility is a key issue in this case. He is a key State's witness and provided the basis upon which many of the wiretap authorizations were obtained.

2.0 <u>Criminal History and Aukeen District Court Case</u>. Since December 3, 1992 the defense has repeatedly sought any information relating to the criminal records and convictions of Mr. Nemours. As of May 4, 1993 the State had not produced any criminal history information.

2.1 On December 3, 1992 in a meeting with prosecutors Al Matthews, Ellen O'Neill Stephens and Scott O'Toole and Mr. Smith's counsel, Mr. Smith's counsel were advised that Mr. Nemours may not have any criminal history.

2.2 Through independent investigation Mr. Smith's defense counsel later discovered, via a private investigator, that the King County Prosecutors office had filed criminal charges in Aukeen District Court on March 15, 1992 to which Mr. Nemours pled guilty on April 29, 1992. As late as March 31, 1992, the State, via a letter from Mr. O'Toole, advised the defense that it knew of no other criminal record of Mr. Nemours, aside from what the defense had discovered in Aukeen District Court. On April 30, 1993 Mr. Nemours, in his interview, disclosed the existence of a municipal court misdemeanor. On April 29, 1993 Detective Jakobsen disclosed this misdemeanor but stated he had checked it out and that Sam had only been a witness. On May 4 or 5, 1993 this court ordered that the Seattle Police Department confidential file on Mr. Nemours be produced to the court as it recalled seeing a records check on Mr. Nemours relating to his criminal history. That file was produced and contained a records check on Mr. Nemours dated April 24, 1992 which included the municipal misdemeanor case and reference to an anti-harassment no-contact order issued against Mr. Nemours involving the victims in the Aukeen District Court case. The court ordered release of this information to the defense.

2.3 The failure to provide the criminal history as to the municipal court case is not in and of itself significant. The failure to prove records and information relating to the Aukeen records is a different matter.

3.0 <u>Aukeen Records, Pre-sentence Report and State's file in State vs. Nemours</u>. The defense made repeated specific requests of the State for any information, documentary or otherwise, that related to Mr. Nemours' reasons for cooperation, credibility, any promises and/or benefits given or received by him for his cooperation.

3.1 Once the defense independently discovered the existence of the Aukeen conviction, it specifically requested production of Mr. Nemours' pre-sentence report from the State. It was not produced. On April 13, 1993 the State, via a letter from Mr. O'Toole stated the Aukeen court would not release it. On April 23, 1993 the court faxed a copy of its earlier Order requiring production of the report to the Aukeen court. On April 26, 1993 the court issued a subpoena duces tecum to the Aukeen court, along with an explanatory letter, seeking production of the pre-sentence report. On April 29, 1993 the court's bailiff was advised by the sentencing Judge, Judge Eide, that the State had a copy of the pre-sentence report at Mr. Nemours' sentencing date of March 17, 1993. On May 4, 1993 the court advised all counsel of the communication relayed by Judge Eide.

3.2 On May 4, 1993 Mr. O'Toole advised the court that the State did not have the pre-sentence report and that Judge Eide had taken possession of the State's file the previous week. On May 5, 1993 shortly before the commencement of the morning court session, the court spoke directly with Judge Eide who reiterated that the State had a copy of the pre-sentence report and that he had not taken the State's file. On May 5, 1993 this court ordered Mr. O'Toole to investigate and to provide the court with the entire State file by the afternoon or provide an explanation. At the commencement of the afternoon session, Mr. O'Toole advised the court that the State's file was being messengered to the court and that the State had misfiled it in the court file.

3.3 At 3:00 p.m. the court received the State's file and reviewed it in camera. The State's file contained two copies of the pre-sentencing report; one with Ms. O'Neill Stephen's name handwritten on it. The report is dated November 30, 1992. In that report, the probation officer recommends that Mr. Nemours receive "the maximum" sentence of two years suspended on certain conditions. That actual sentence imposed on Mr. Nemours, when he was sentenced, was a one year deferred sentence, a $150 fine, and continuation of the no-contact order with the victims.

3.4 During the course of the hearings conducted on May 4, 1993 there were conflicting recollections as to when the State and the Detective became aware of Mr. Nemours' Aukeen case and as to when the Detective made the prosecutors directly involved in this case aware of the Aukeen case. It is apparent that the State should have known of these charges since March 15, 1992 the date it filed them.

3.5 The State's file also contained information dating back to February, 1992 and continuing up until December, 1992 that are relevant to the issues of Mr. Nemours' credibility, veracity, actions, his contact with the Seattle Police Department, and potential additional reasons for his cooperation. It is of note that Mr. Nemours' original appearance for arraignment on these charges occurred on April 23, 1992, one day before he signed his cooperation agreement with the Seattle Police. He pled guilty on April 29, 1992, was scheduled to be sentenced on December 4, 1992 but that sentencing was continued as a result of a motion he filed pro se, on December 4, 1992.

3.6 The original of the pro se pleading filed by Mr. Nemours was in the State's file. According to defense counsel that pleading was not provided pursuant to the subpoena duces tecum it had earlier issued for the entire court file. The failure to file this in the court file was probably an inadvertent mistake by the State.

3.7 The pro se pleading, filed by Mr. Nemours, is dated December 4, 1992. Detective Jakobsen's name, business and pager telephone numbers are handwritten on that document. Detective Jakobsen has acknowledged that he had contact with the Aukeen prosecutor in late November or early December, 1992 to find out what was going on with Nemours' case and advised the prosecutor of Mr. Nemours' cooperation with the police but did not seek any favors on his behalf.

3.8 The pleading written by Mr. Nemours, as best can be deciphered, is a request to withdraw his guilty plea entered on April 29, 1992 and accuses the officer assigned to the case of being a "liar." It is a rambling document that reflects some unique thought processes. It is prohibitive with regard to Mr. Nemours' reasons for cooperation and reliability as an informant in light of other information that has come to light via discovery in this case.

3.9 It is apparent that the State failed to exercise due diligence to discover information contained within its own files, on its informant, that directly bears on the credibility and reliability of this witness, in spite of direct and repeated requests for this information.

4.0 <u>Motions With Regard to U of W School Records</u>. In January, 1993 the defense issued a subpoena to the U of W for Mr. Nemours' school records. On March 15, 1993 Mr. O'Toole filed a motion for protective order to prevent disclosure of these records setting it for hearing on March 22, 1993. That hearing was continued and set before this court for April 13, 1993.

4.1 On March 30, 1993 the State delivered subpoenas to the U of W seeking the academic records of all four co-defendants. This subpoena sought the identical information sought by defense counsel on Mr. Nemours. All defendants sought to quash the subpoena of their records.

4.2 In the affidavit in support of a protective order, Mr. O'Toole stated that because of Mr. Nemours' location outside the state and his lack of financial resources he could not afford to hire a counsel or formally object to the subpoena. Mr. Nemours never filed any written objection nor did he advise the U of W of any objection to the release of his school records, although he was made aware of the request by Detective Jakobsen in early March, 1993.

4.3 The defense filed a memorandum vigorously objecting to the State's acting as Mr. Nemours' representative in light of no response by Mr. Nemours himself and also advised the court that Mr. Nemours was in Seattle on March 17, 1993 as he was sentenced in Aukeen District Court on that day. This had been discovered by independent defense investigation subsequent to the filing of the State's motion for protective order.

4.4 On April 13, 1993 the court heard the matter. Mr. O'Toole argued the motion on behalf of the State. The court expressed concerns that Mr. Nemours had not appeared in any fashion to personally express any objections to the subpoena and that someone in the prosecutor's office had to have been aware of his presence in Seattle on March 17, 1993.

4.5 On April 13, 1993 the court ordered production of Mr. Nemours' school records for an in camera review. The court also quashed the subpoenas with regards to all defendants' U of W school records. Two of the defendants had never attended the school.

4.6 On April 30, 1993 via material submitted by defense counsel, the court learned, for the first time that Mr. O'Toole knew prior to the filing of his March 15, 1993 affidavit that Mr.

Nemours was coming to Seattle. In fact, Mr. O'Toole met with Mr. Nemours on March 18, 1993 in his office. Mr. Nemours was in Seattle for four or five days.

5.0 Payments, Benefits to Mr. Nemours. Since the inception of this case, defense counsel has repeatedly sought all information and documentary evidence relating to any payments made in the past or in the future to Mr. Nemours for his cooperation, his relation to any governmental agencies, and any benefits or promises given to him.

5.1 While the State disclosed the total amount of approximately $6,100 paid to Mr. Nemours to defense counsel, it stated it could not provide any vouchers or documentary proof of payment because the Seattle Police Department refused to make those records available. The defense issued a subpoena for those records with a return date before this court on April 13, 1993.

5.2 On April 13, 1993 this court ordered the police department to provide records of any and all payments, including the timing and amounts, made to Mr. Nemours since April, 1992 for an in camera review. The records produced and released to counsel reflect payments ending in January, 1993.

5.3 On April 29, 1993, in his interview, Detective Jakobsen stated that Detective Hawkes had paid the $150 fine for Mr. Nemours when he was sentenced on March 17, 1993. He characterized it as a loan which was paid back on April 28, 1993. He stated he believed it was paid out of Seattle Police Department funds but was unsure. No record or document evidencing this payment or loan was provided to the court for its in camera review. The defense was not apprised of this payment or loan until April 29, 1993.

5.4 During the course of Detective Jakobsen's interview he was asked about any payments Mr. Nemours may have received and/or may be receiving from any other governmental agencies for his cooperation as an informant in other cases. Mr. O'Toole advised the Detective not to answer.

5.5 Information about the financial benefits an informant has received, is continuing to receive, and may receive in the future is relevant and pertinent in a criminal trial in which his testimony plays a crucial part. This is information that has been specifically sought by defense counsel since the initial stages of this case (see letters referenced above).

6.0 <u>Wiretap Recordings, Authorizations, Documents Evidencing Judicial Review</u>. A significant portion of the State's case involves wiretap recordings obtained during the course of the seven-month investigation. Approximately 22 authorizations were obtained resulting in 18 recorded conversations.

6.1 The defense has sought transcripts of the tapes, the authorization approved pursuant to RCW 9.73.230, and proof of judicial review, as is required by statute.

6.2 On February 16, 1993 this court heard a contested motion for continuance of the case scheduling hearing sought by the defendants. The stated basis for the continuance primarily related to defense counsel claims that they had not yet obtained the complete authorizations and proof of judicial review or the transcripts which Mr. O'Toole promised to provide. Mr. Al Matthews appeared on behalf of the State and objected to any continuance representing that discovery was complete, that the defendants had the tapes, and that the defendants could make their own transcripts. This court granted the continuance noting, inter alia, that production of documents reflecting judicial review should not be difficult as it was required by statute.

6.3 At the April 1, 1993 status conference held by this court these issues were raised again. The court was advised that Mr. O'Toole had been working cooperatively with the defense to provide the remaining discovery related to the tapes. Defense counsel advised the court that they had sought verification that the statutorily required judicial review had occurred on all tapes by contacting the Office of the Administrator for the Court (with whom each law enforcement agency is to file a monthly report relating to authorizations granted each month) and found no record of judicial review. Mr. Smith's counsel met with Municipal Court Judge Stephen Schaefer, who allowed them to review the authorizations. However, they were unable to obtain copies. On April 22, 1993 the documents were produced pursuant to a subpoena duces tecum issued by this court and copies were subsequently provided to all counsel.

7.0 <u>Predisposition of Danianke Smith</u>. Mr. Smith's counsel, since December, 1992 has sought information from the State concerning any information it had relating to any alleged predisposition on the part of Mr. Smith. On April 13, 1993 this court heard a contested motion on this issue. In light of the assertion of an entrapment defense on Mr. Smith's behalf, the court ordered disclosure of this information.

7.1 Mr. O'Toole expressed reservations to the court, at that hearing, because the State had promised confidentiality to certain persons. This issue was again raised in the interview of Detective Jakobsen. Mr. O'Toole advised the court that the State did not intend to use any of this information. He reiterated that position during the course of the hearing on May 4, 1993.

8.0 <u>Statements of Danianke Smith</u>. Through independent investigation, Mr. Smith's attorneys discovered in March, 1993 that statements of Mr. Smith occurring in conversations with Detective Jakobsen and/or Mr. Nemours on November 22 and 23, 1993 were used by Detective Jakobsen to obtain a search warrant on Terrance Powe's house which was executed on November 23, 1992.

8.1 These statements had not been provided in any discovery given to any of the defendants by the State. Exhibits 1 and 2 admitted during the hearing on May 4, 1993 to bear on this issue. Exhibit #1 is what was provided via discovery. Exhibit #2 is the application for the search warrant which contains Mr. Smith's statements.

8.2 Ms. Ellen O'Neill Stephens was aware of these statements as she was present when Detective Jakobsen obtained the search warrant and assisted him in its preparation. Ms. O'Neill Stephens prepared the Information and Certification for Determination of Probable Cause in the charges before this court.

8.3 Mr. O'Toole was not aware of these statements until March 30, 1993 when defense counsel brought this to his attention. These statements were clearly subject to disclosure to all of the defendants.

III—Analysis and Conclusions

The dismissal of criminal charges is an extraordinary and drastic remedy. It is not lightly undertaken; however, it is this court's opinion that such an action is appropriate in this particular case given the totality of the circumstances relating to the State's mismanagement of this case.

The court concludes that the State has inexcusably failed to act with due diligence in providing discovery and information required to be produced under its obligations pursuant to CrR 4.7 and constitutionally recognized obligations to provide material that is favorable to the accused and material to his or her guilt or punishment. Brady v. Maryland 373 US 83 (1963); Davis v. Alaska 415 US 308 (1974); United States v. Bagley 473 US 667 (1985); State v. Price 94 Wn.2d. 810 (1980); State v. Sherman 59 Wn.App. 763 (1990); State v. Blackwell 120 Wn.2d. 822 (1993).

The State controlled the timing of the filing of these criminal charges. In a case such as this, where the investigation has been ongoing over a seven month period of time and which included the joint involvement of prosecuting and police authorities, the State should have prepared and managed its case sufficiently, including compliance with its discovery obligations, so that it was ready to proceed to trial within the defendants rights to a speedy trial. For the record, it is apparent that this is not the case.

The State possesses significant power and resources in its decisions to investigate, prepare for, and prosecute criminal activity. The recognition of this power underlies the burden of proof it carries and its unequal burden with regard to discovery. It is extremely disturbing that much of the information that has come to light has been through the efforts of the defense counsel, and primarily from the only defendant able to retain private counsel.

There are troubling aspects to the State's management of this case. While one prosecutor agrees to provide transcripts of taped conversations (which ultimately would be offered at trial) another later asserts that the defense should make their own transcripts. While one division of the office is stating that the informant may have no criminal history, another division is actively prosecuting the informant, has documents unfavorable to that informant in its file, and the police have information about additional criminal history in their files. Once defense counsel subpoenas the school records of the informant, the State files a motion to prevent their release, then serves a subpoena on the same institution for exactly the same records on all four defendants. At the hearing on this motion, the State fails to advise the court that it knew before it filed its affidavit that the informant would be in the state on March 17, 1993. One prosecutor is personally present when statements of one defendant are used as the basis for a search warrant in a connected case, yet this information is not provided in discovery. Prosecutors and police were aware of additional motives for the informant's cooperation but do not disclose the substance of this information until April 30, 1993 via the informant's interview.

The cumulative effect of this has significantly affected the defendant's rights to a fair trial and a trial with an adequately prepared defense counsel for the following reasons.

Any material that tends to be exculpatory as to a defendant or which reflects on bias, credibility or ulterior motives of a state witness must be disclosed as soon as the State becomes aware of it. This requires that the State act with all due diligence and also that it reviews its files to discover information within its possession, control, and knowledge. CrR 4.7 (c) (3); State v. DeWilde 12 Wn.App. 255 (1974); State v. Oughton 26 Wn.App. 74 (1990); Davis v. Alaska, supra.

Much of the material recently disclosed goes to the State's knowledge of Mr. Nemours' criminal history, his credibility and most significantly, his reasons for cooperating with the police (including motives of revenge, benefits and promises). All of this information has been within the State's control for a significant period of time and was not provided to the defense.

It was the State who chose to characterize the reasons for Mr. Nemours' cooperation with the police. Now just three weeks before trial, the defense is provided information which requires them to explore entirely new avenues of investigation on the key state witness. The credibility, reliability, veracity, and the reason(s) Mr. Nemours cooperated with the police is crucial to this case as it may well be determinative of guilt or innocence of these defendants. It is also important as Mr. Nemours provided the information to support probable cause determinations for issuance of wiretap interceptions.

Tremendous energy and resources have been invested in the discovery process in this case over the past 5-1/2 months. Unlike the situation in State v. Blackwell, supra, much of the material sought and/or undisclosed here was required to be provided pursuant to CrR 4.7, was ordered to be provided by specific court orders or, as noted above, related directly to the reliability of the key witness.

The newly disclosed information interjects new facts into these cases shortly before the most crucial stage of this proceeding, the trial itself. Based on the issues involved in this case and the history of discovery in this case, it is apparent that none of the defense counsel will have a sufficient opportunity to adequately prepare a material part of their defense by the time of trial without waiving once again their rights to a speedy trial. Under circumstance of this case, they should not be forced to make that choice.

After having waived their rights to a speedy trial in order to obtain discovery, these defendants have suffered impermissible prejudice by the way in which the State has managed the case and its discovery responsibility, which directly impedes their ability to have a fair trial.

It is the court's determination that such a showing has been made as to warrant a dismissal pursuant to CrR 8.3 (b). An appropriate order should issue.

Appendix D

The following is an excerpt from Seattle Times *reporter Tom Farrey's interview with University of Washington quarterback Billy Joe Hobert and concerns Hobert's procurement of an improper $50,000 loan from Charles Rice of Idaho:*

Farrey: You took the car loan out?

Hobert: I took the loan and my wife's savings and bought the '91 (Camaro). I had it for, I don't know, a very short period of time. And the '92 came, actually it was already sitting there, I just never test drove it. They aren't very different. Well, they're not really different body styles. They're the exact same cars except the 25th Anniversary one has a little patch inside. A 25-cent patch. So basically I could have lied, taken the 25-cent patch, put it on the '91. But no, I had to get the whole new car. Then I figured, what the heck, I'm making payments anyway so I might as well just do it. It was all a prestige thing to me. Stupid. I'm just dumb, let's put it that way.

F: How much does the '91 cost?

H: $8,000, something like that.

F: And the '92?

H: $12,400, something like that.

F: Yeah?

H: And I owe $6,600 still on the '92, at least $6,600. But payments are pretty good, though, it's a 5-year plan, about $197-a-month, but I can't afford it with a kid on the way.

F: Now, you financed the second car, but the first car, did you finance that one, or did you buy that one outright?

H: Well, with the loan and the $2,500 from my wife that I wasted — she had more than $2,500, but that's what I ended up spending on the car. She didn't even know about it. I mean, she knew about it, we were splitting up when I bought it. I brought it by to show it to her and she was like (Hobert makes a very shocked face).

F: Where did you get the loan from?

H: A private business guy. That's all personal stuff. I mean, to take out a loan, you don't have to report it to the IRS, right? Because you're paying interest, paying on the loan, I don't know. That's something I've got to find out, too, because I can't claim it on my tax forms. I didn't think you had to on a loan because it's not income anyway.

F: So anyway, you got it through a private businessman?

H: Yeah.

F: You care to tell me who that might be?

H: Well, it's a guy named Chuck Rice. Nobody knows who he is. It's a golfing buddy of mine. Actually, his son's a golfing buddy of mine that I've known since I was 12, well, ninth grade. No, it's my sophomore year is what it was, when I started golfing up at SeaTac. That's where I met this guy. We golfed for years. Then when my wife and I split up — I don't want to get into the story because as soon as somebody finds out I took a loan there's going to be a big investigation — there's nothing illegal about it. I just don't want people to find out how stupid I was financially.

F: Billy, you know those questions have been out there for a while.

H: Oh, I have no problem with the questions. But people assume alumni are involved, and this guy (Rice) has nothing to do with the UW. It's strictly a business loan on 10-percent interest, and I've got to pay it back with interest by the end of the year.

F: By the end of the year?

H: Well, at least half of it. You see, he's a friend of mine and he's been pretty, ah . . . I'm at a loss for words tonight . . . he's been very lenient because he knows that I have no money because he knows I blew all the money I had. If he wanted to, he could take my butt to the cleaners. I'm glad he's a friend. Hopefully, he'll wait until I get done with school and get a job before I can start making the full payments. But I've got to make payments for the interest from a legal standpoint. I have to say the money I borrowed wasn't the smartest thing I've done, but I ended up blowing it, and now I've got all these bills and nothing to show for it.

F: How much was the loan for?

H: That's a personal matter, but it was more than what I should have taken out, and that's as far as I'll go as far as that's concerned.

F: $50,000?

H: It wasn't that much. Where'd you hear that much?

F: Poking around.

H: No, the most I've ever borrowed from that guy—again, I'd like not to get into the situation, it's a bad deal, people are going to realize that Billy Joe Hobert's not the best businessman if things get out.

F: I know.

H: Where are you from?

F: *The Seattle Times.*

H: Oh, yeah.

Notice Of Charges

I. Background

This case was triggered by a copyrighted news report from the *Seattle Times* on November 5, 1992, that Billy Joe Hobert, Washington's starting quarterback and the 1992 Rose Bowl Most Valuable Player, had received three loans totaling $50,000 from the father-in-law of a friend. Washington authorities immediately contacted the Pacific-10 Conference office, and Associate Commissioner, David Price was brought to campus to help determine Hobert's eligibility status. Hobert was suspended from competition by the University pending the outcome of the investigation. After Hobert produced loan papers that indicated at least one of the loans was based on his potential as a professional athlete, the University declared him permanently ineligible. No attempt was made by the University to seek restoration of his eligibility through the NCAA.

A spate of media stories followed the announcement of Hobert's ineligibility, and on December 9, 1992, the *Los Angeles Times* published articles alleging that several NCAA violations had occurred in the Washington football program. The Pacific-10 Conference continued its inquiry into the case, and the University engaged the Kansas City branch of the law firm of Bond, Schoeneck and King to conduct an investigation. The University's instructions to the law firm was "to leave no stone unturned in your investigation."

II. Scope of the Investigation

During the course of the investigation, more than 225 people were interviewed. The Conference office and the Bond, Schoeneck and King investigative team headed by Michael S. Glazier, a former NCAA enforcement staff member, collaborated on most interviews and shared information openly.

III. Overview of the Allegations

The allegations in this Notice of Charges fall into seven categories:

- The Hobert loan.
- Employment of Prospective and Enrolled UW Student Athletes by Roy Moore at Tyee Valley Golf Course.
- Employment of Prospective and Enrolled UW Student-Athletes by Jim Kenyon in Los Angeles.
- Incidents Involving Herb Mead and Clint Mead.
- Incidents Involving Jim Heckman.
- Entertainment and Meals on Recruiting Visits.
- Miscellaneous Allegations.

IV. The Allegations

A. The Hobert Loan [NCAA Bylaw 12.1.2-(m)]

1. **It is alleged that UW student-athlete Billy Joe Hobert (Puyallup, WA) received three loans totaling $50,000 in the spring and summer of 1992 ($25,000 in April, $10,000 in May, and $15,000 in June), based on his potential earnings as a professional football player.**

   The Conference reviewed a report on this issue at a special meeting in November 1992, the report is attached as Exhibit No. 1.

   The only additional matter of consequence learned by the Conference was that Don James, UW Head Football Coach, kept notes of his October 28, 1992, and November 4, 1992 conversations with Hobert which confirmed his previous statements. Copies of the notes are attached in Exhibit No. 2.

B. Employment at Tyee Valley Golf Course

1. [NCAA Bylaws 13.1.2.1, 13.1.2.3-(f), 13.2.4.1]

It is alleged that Ray Moore, a representative of the University's athletics interests, arranged employment for UW prospective student-athlete Billy Joe Hobert (Puyallup, WA) at the Tyee Valley Golf Course during the summer of 1988 prior to the beginning of Hobert's senior year in high school.

NCAA rules do not permit an institution (including representatives of its athletics interests) to arrange employment for a prospective student-athlete unless the employment begins following completion of the prospect's senior year in high school. Moore was a representative of UW's athletics interests in 1988, since he was a member of the Tyee Club (the institution's athletics booster group), had employed UW student-athletes prior to that time, and had recruited on behalf of the University's football program before the NCAA's "booster ban" was implemented in 1987.

Hobert completed his *junior* year in high school in the spring of 1988 after leading his Puyallup High School football team to the state championship. He reported that he had been working at a department store in Puyallup for minimum wage in 1988 and had a conversation with Ron Crowe, a broadcaster of Hobert's high school games, about obtaining a better paying job. Hobert told Crowe he was interested in golf. Crowe later suggested that he apply at a golf course for a job. Hobert went to Tyee Valley Golf Course (located adjacent to SeaTac International Airport, about 25 miles from Puyallup) after first applying at River Bend Golf Course. He reported he filled out an application for the Tyee Valley job and was hired by Jo Ann Peterson.

Crowe recalled having a conversation with Hobert at the Puyallup department store when Hobert said he was very interested in golf. That conversation planted a seed in Crowe's mind, and at a later time (Crowe thought it was at a Seattle Supersonics basketball game), he told Herb Mead, a UW booster, that Hobert was looking for a golf job. Mead suggested that Hobert apply at Kent Municipal or Tyee Valley. Crowe said he mentioned Mead's remark to Hobert, but thought nothing more about it. Crowe said he has never met Ray Moore, the owner of Tyee Valley Golf Course, and did not call Moore on Hobert's behalf.

Mead remembered he had a brief conversation with Crowe and thinks it occurred at a Sonics game during the spring of 1988. When Crowe said that Hobert was looking for summer employment and was interested in golf, Mead mentioned that Hobert should check out the City of Kent and Tyee Valley Golf Courses. He didn't know if there was any follow-up, and said his only association with Hobert's job was to pass on a name.

Jo Ann Peterson said she did not hire Hobert and she assumed Moore did. She recalled that Moore brought Hobert to her and told her to put him on the payroll. "I never hired anyone on the grounds crew the whole time I was there," she emphasized. "I hired concessions people and restaurant workers, but I had nothing to do with hiring the grounds people." She said that if Moore did not hire Hobert, Mark Dolejsi would have. (Shannon Daley-Tillman, a Tyee Valley Golf Course employee, said Peterson told her at the time that Moore had hired Hobert.)

Roy Moore originally reported that Jo Ann Peterson had hired Hobert in July 1988. In a subsequent conversation, he stated he did not recall being personally involved with Hobert's hiring, but that Peterson's recollection may have been correct. Moore said he does not know Ron Crowe, and he had no conversations with Herb Mead about hiring Hobert. He also reported that neither Hobert or Joe Kralik was required to complete an employment application form, because the forms were not required for seasonal employees. (Copies of letter from Moore to David Price and Richard J. Dunn, UW Faculty Athletics Representative, concerning the employment are included in Exhibit No. 3.)

Mark Dolejsi was the greens superintendent at Tyee Valley Golf Course until December of 1989. He said he did not hire Hobert. "He was hired through the office and sent to me," Dolejsi said. He said other people, not just football players, also were hired by the front office and sent to him.

Dick Crowe, Ron's brother, reported that he and his brother played golf with Hobert at The Classics Golf Course following the 1992 Rose Bowl. Dick asked his brother about Hobert's job at Tyee, and Ron replied, "We helped him get the job at Tyee." Crowe asked his brother who "we" was, and his brother replied, "a guy at the U." Ron went on to state "I just referred him out there." Dick said Ron did not identify who the "guy at the U" was, but he since has learned that his brother was referring to Herb Mead. Dick said Ron has known Mead since he was a student at the University, and that Mead sometimes provides Ron with UW football tickets in good locations.

Approximately one month after Hobert was hired, <u>Joe Kralik</u>, a senior-to-be at Puyallup HS and current member of the UW football team, was hired on Hobert's recommendation. Kralik at this time was transferring from Sumner High School to Puyallup High School and had not played football the previous year because of a serious injury. Two year later, Damon Huard was hired on Kralik's recommendation.

Mead and Moore clearly are "representatives of the University's athletics interests" under NCAA rules. Ron Crowe's status, on the other hand, is open to debate. Crowe attended Washington and played on the men's basketball team for two years before transferring to Western Washington, from which he graduated. He is not a member of any UW booster club and says he has never donated to the UW beyond giving a $100 check to the Marv Harshman retirement fund when Harshman retired as Husky men's basketball coach. Crowe was the mayor of Puyallup in 1988, as well as a broadcaster for the Puyallup High School football games. Crowe indicates that when UW recruited Damon Huard, Hobert's successor at quarterback at Puyallup HS, he sometimes would kid Huard at postgame parties by saying such things as "We'd love to see you at UW," and once made a point of wearing a UW sweater to a party at the Huard's house, mentioning to Huard that he would like to see him play at the University.

2. **[NCAA Bylaws 13.2.1 and 16.12.2.1]**

    It is alleged that Roy Moore, a representative of the University's athletics interests, provided free meals, to UW student-athletes Billy Joe Hobert (Puyallup, WA), during the summers of 1989 and 1991 and Joe Kralik (Puyallup, WA), during the summers of 1989, 1990, and 1991 when they were employed at the Tyee Valley Golf Course.

Roy Moore reported that Hobert and Kralik approached him during the summer of 1989 and asked why they did not receive year-end bonuses like other grounds crew employees. Moore was concerned that providing Hobert and Kralik bonuses would be against NCAA rules, but felt that because they were not receiving a bonus and other company benefits, they could receive a "meal allowance" (i.e., free meals). (See Moore's statement in Exhibit No. 3). Moore stated that the other grounds crew employees did not receive free meals but did receive a 25% discount on their meals. Moore also reported that Damon Huard (a UW prospective student-athlete who worked in the summer of 1991) did not receive a meal allowance because he did not ask for it.

When asked about free meals at the golf course, Hobert explained that he thought he deserved a bonus because other members of the grounds crew received them. When he asked Moore about getting a bonus, Moore told Hobert he would receive a meal allowance instead. He claimed he received one free meal a day.

Joe Kralik said that he understood he and Hobert received meal allowances because they were not allowed to participate in the bonus program.

Shannon Daley-Tillman was restaurant manager at Tyee Valley from 1986 to mid-1989 and assistant general manager from mid-1989 to January 1991. She said that it was policy at Tyee that all restaurant employees and management personnel received free meals. Other than the football players, all other employees, including grounds crew members, received a 25 percent discount on meals eaten at the Tyee restaurant but did not receive bonuses. She also said that football players ate much larger meals than other employees. Hobert and Kralik once informed her they were on a high carbohydrate diet for football training and ordered very large breakfasts. She said the average price of a breakfast at Tyee was approximately four dollars while the average price of a breakfast for a football player was between $10 and $14.

Doug and Sue Schafer, who ran the pro shop, reported that some full-time workers received bonuses, but seasonal workers did not. They noted that their son did not get a bonus when he was employed on a seasonal basis, and neither did Doug

Stuns, the son of their partner in the pro shop. Among the seasonal workers, only the football players got free meals, according to the Schafers.

Mark Dolejsi, who left in December 1989, said he never received a bonus. The bonuses started about the time he left and were characterized as incentive bonuses.

Damon Huard said he ate at the Tyee restaurant when he worked at the golf course in the summer of 1990, but he does not know if the meals were free. He did not pay for the meals at the time he ate them, and does not remember if they were deducted from his paycheck. He said he just went along with what the other employees were doing. He could not remember if he signed for what he ate. (Moore reported that Huard did not receive a meal allowance.)

Mike Ewaliko, a current UW football player, worked at Tyee Valley GC in the summers of 1990, 1991, and 1992. He assured that the cost of meals were taken out of his paycheck because his check was so small at time, but he has no clue as to how the meal costs were handled.

3.   [NCAA Bylaws 12.4.1 and 13.2.1]

It is alleged that UW prospective and enrolled student-athletes Billy Joe Hobert (Puyallup, WA) and Joe Kralik (Puyallup, WA) were paid wages exceeding that paid to other employees with like experience and responsibilities at the Tyee Valley Golf Course in the summers of 1988 and 1989.

Roy Moore reported that in the summer of 1988, Hobert and Kralik were paid $8.00 an hour, which would have been the middle range of wages for seasonal grounds crew employees. He said some grounds crew members were paid $6 per hour and others were paid as much as $10 per hour. He raised Hobert's and Kralik's rate to $10 per hour during the summer of 1989. He reported that Doug Stuns and Jay Cruz were two individuals who were paid less than Hobert and Kralik when they started. Both started at Tyee approximately 5-6 months before Hobert was hired, and both agreed to be paid at the $5-6 per hour rate, Moore said.

Doug Stuns worked on the grounds crew sporadically for

several years and said he was paid $7 per hour while working on the grounds crew during 1989 and 1990. He stated that he believed he was paid in the mid to high range for grounds crew employees because he was an experienced golfer and also was knowledgeable about grooming and caring for a golf course. He said he had much experience working on the grounds crew and could operate all of the machinery involved in grooming the golf course.

Jay Cruz reported he first began working at Tyee in 1988 and his beginning rate of pay was $6 per hour. He had no prior grounds crew experience. He stated his pay was raised to $6.50 per hour after a few months. He left Tyee to do construction work in late 1988.

Doug and Sue Schafer reported that John Schafer, their son, worked on the grounds crew in the summer of 1992 for a short period. He made $6.00 per hour, according to them.

Shannon Daley-Tillman, the Tyee Valley restaurant manager at the time, said her son, Jason, had been employed at Tyee since he was 12 years old. She stated that even though Jason had more grounds-keeping experience than Hobert and was the same age as Hobert, he earned approximately $2 less per hour than Hobert. This changed in 1990 when Jason was promoted to the weekend manager position and received an approximate $1.75 per hour raise. She stated she believed that Jason was then earning approximately the same as the football players.

C. **Employment in Los Angeles**

1. **[NCAA Bylaw 12.4.1]**

   It is alleged that on numerous occasions over several years, James W. Kenyon, a representative of the University's athletics interests, provided UW student-athletes pay for work not performed while they were employed by him at Cabot, Cabot and Forbes Company in Los Angeles.

   Jim Kenyon reported that he hired numerous UW student-athletes during the summers when he was president of Cabot, Cabot and Forbes (CC&F), a commercial real estate development firm. He was removed as president of the company in April 1989 but continued to serve as a consultant through December 1989.

Kenyon stated that he met with each student-athlete who worked in his office and told him the following rules: (1) that they would be paid by the hour, (2) that is they did not work, they would not be paid, and (3) that they were to leave Kenyon's full-time staff alone and not harass or bother their co-workers. Kenyon said there was no question in his mind that the student-athletes knew they were expected to work for their pay, but he also realized that some of the student-athletes could have abused the system. He noted that the players completed their own time cards and he assumed they completed them accurately. He reported he frequently was absent from the office and would not be in a position to notice if the players were always present.

Employment records for the downtown Los Angeles office of CC&F have been sent to the main office in Boston, which has been reduced to a skeleton crew. Attempts to obtain the records were unsuccessful. (A copy of a letter from Patrick Walsh, Kenyon's attorney, more fully explaining Kenyon's position is attached as Exhibit No. 4.)

Kevin Conard played football for Washington in 1983-85 before being dismissed from the team. He said he worked for CC&F during the summers of 1983, 1984, and 1985 at project sites, but never worked downtown. He claimed the work got progressively easier each summer. By 1985, the players often would check in and immediately leave, then come back later and check out, he reported.

Vince Fudzie played football with the Huskies in 1983-85 before being dismissed from the team. Fudzie reported he worked for CC&F (Torrance site) for a brief period during the summer of 1985 and was paid for work he performed and for work he didn't perform. He said that the UW players either "basically sat around [on the job] and drank sodas, or hung out, or didn't go [to work] at all for most of the summer." He said that one of the jobs they were supposed to do was sweep up the dust made by the construction. He said the players either didn't sweep or didn't show up but they got paid on Fridays either every week or every other week. Fudzie said he made

$10 per hour for 40 hours per week for the job in Los Angeles.

Vince Weathersby played for Washington in 1985-88 and is the UW's third-leading career rusher. Unlike Conard and Fudzie, he worked in the downtown CC&F office most of the time. When he was asked about the accuracy of the *Los Angeles Times* article, Weathersby said it was true that he pretty much just showed up for work. He said he was present at work for eight hours, but there was not much to do considering there were about eight players doing the same thing. Asked about not even showing up on certain weeks except to get his paycheck, Weathersby said there were a couple of times that he worked maybe just two days during the week. "It was me taking advantage of the situation: he said. "I'd go in on Monday and Tuesday and sit around and do nothing." Weathersby would then not report to work on Wednesday or Thursday, and would go in Friday to get his paycheck.

- Liz Lundin, an accountant at the Bellevue CC&F office, reported that when Weathersby first came to work at that office, he stated that he didn't work in Los Angeles but still was paid, and he wasn't planning to work in Bellevue but still expected to get paid. Lundin said Weathersby was set straight by Bob MacMillan, the Seattle regional manager. MacMillan said he told Weathersby if he didn't work, he would not be paid. He said Weathersby had been sent to him by Herb Mead, and he called Mead, who told him that Weathersby should be required to work. MacMillan also related Weatherby's statement to Kenyon, who told MacMillan that Weathersby was entitled to anything.

[It should be noted that Conard, Fudzie, and Weathersby all have been involved unsuccessfully in lawsuits against Washington. Conard and Fudzie were dismissed from the team prior to the 1985 Freedom Bowl and their scholarships were not renewed for the 1986-87 academic year. They sued for damages alleging breach of contract by UW and intentional interference with contractual relations by Coach Don James and UW. Weathersby filed a personal injury suit against UW and Steven T. Bramwell, team physician, in 1990. The defendants won a summary judgment.]

Ron Caldwell was a top basketball recruit for UW in 1986 after leading Los Angeles Crenshaw High School to California state prep championships in 1985 and 1986. His college career was hampered by a knee injury he suffered as a freshman and although he remained with the team until the 1988-89 season, he never regained his previous skills.

Caldwell reported that he worked for the downtown Los Angeles office of CC&F in 1986 and for the first month to six weeks worked hard. He noticed, however, that the football players did not spend much time at the office and did not seem to be working hard when they were there. In late July or early August 1986, after the UW football players left for Seattle for preseason practice, Caldwell said that Kenyon called him into his office and told him to take the rest of the summer off and get into shape. From that moment, Caldwell reported, he worked very few hours and still collected a $400 paycheck each Friday.

Caldwell said that he attended summer school at West Los Angeles Community College in the summer of 1987 and Santa Monica City College in the summer of 1988 while continuing to work for CC&F and receiving $400 per week. He went to summer school five days a week and could not possibly have been working eight-hour day shifts, he said.

- Genever Caldwell, Ron's mother, said that she was opposed to the job that her son had because he "wasn't putting in the time" and "was just collecting a check." She said her son often would do no more than go downtown on Friday to pick up his money. She said he spent more time on the job when he first started. She thought that after he had worked for a while and found there was nothing to do, he just decided not to go in. She thought he still occasionally went to work but his work consisted of little more than "shooting the breeze" with other athletes who also were employed there and answering the telephone. (It should be noted that Ron Caldwell did not reside with his mother during this time, but that she says she talked with him frequently.)

- Darnell Smith, Genever Caldwell's brother, reported that Ron Caldwell resided with him during Caldwell's senior year in high school and during the summers of 1986 and 1987. While he knew little abut the CC&F job, Smith said that Caldwell did not keep normal hours and often came home during the early part of the afternoon. He confirmed that Caldwell attended summer school classes at West Los Angeles Community College in 1987.

- <u>Anthony Jenkins</u> played basketball for Washington in 1987-88-89 before transferring to UC Riverside, from which he graduated in 1992. He reported he worked for CC&F in the summers of 1987 and 1988. Jenkins said he did not know Ron Caldwell well until the end of the summer of 1987 because Caldwell was not around the CC&F office until his summer school classes ended.

<u>Dennis Brown</u> played football for Washington in 1986-87-88-89. He worked for CC&F in the downtown Los Angeles office during the summer of 1986 and during every vacation period when he returned to Los Angeles until he finished college in 1989. His duties consisted of running errands, washing cars, stocking office supplies, and performing an assortment of odd jobs. Brown went to the office daily and put in his time, but said that many of the players did not. He was living with this grandmother at the time, and she kept on him to "get to work" constantly. Brown said there were several UW players who would come in only occasionally, but that they received full pay anyway.

<u>Terrance Powe</u> played football for Washington in 1987-88-89-90. He reported that when he was being recruited in the 1986-87 academic year, he received telephone calls from UW boosters Jim Kenyon and Herb Mead (it was legal for boosters to telephone recruits at the time), who told him they had a job waiting for him in Los Angeles which would pay $10 per hour.

Powe reported that he worked for the downtown Los Angeles office of CC&F during the summers of 1987, 1988, and 1989, as well as most school vacation breaks during that time period. Powe said that he originally put in his time. When he observed that Caldwell was not working and was still collecting his paycheck, he asked Caldwell how he could receive his weekly paycheck even though he was doing very little work at the office. Caldwell told Powe it was not necessary to work, and that Kenyon had told him just to work out and stay in shape and he could still collect a weekly check.

Powe said he then went to Kenyon and told him he could not get in shape because he was working so much. Kenyon told

Powe that it was not necessary for him to come to the office, but he should work out and get in shape but he still would be paid each Friday. After that conversation, Powe said he did little or no work for the remainder of the summer but continued to receive his $400 paycheck.

Powe reported that during school vacation breaks, he would call Kenyon's secretary from Seattle to tell her that he would be coming to work during the vacation period. The secretary apparently thought he was coming to Los Angeles, he said. He would tell her that he would be coming into the office on Friday. He then went to Los Angeles, reported to work on Friday and received a check for the full week.

Powe also said his routine for post-Christmas work would be to work in Los Angeles Monday through Thursday of the first week of UW classes, then go to Seattle to attend classes on Friday, since a student had to be in school by Friday of the first week of classes in order to remain enrolled. This procedure would enable a player to receive pay from Kenyon for the first week of classes.

- Gloria Jamison, Powe's mother, reported that Powe frequently returned home from work early. He told her he was still receiving full pay. Terrance told her that other players were not going in all of the time. She thought Corey Brown was one of the others. He said that hardly any of the players went to work all the time. Football players were at her house all the time, she said. They joked about working, how much fun they were having and how much money they were making, she said. "I didn't like it, because I have to go to work every day and if I don't work, I don't get paid." She thought it sent a bad signal to the players. She also said that Powe had mentioned he was getting paid during school breaks and she recalled some occasions he did not go to work during break period.

- James Sawyer played football for the Huskies in 1987 and 1988. During the spring break of 1989, Sawyer went to Los Angeles with Powe. Sawyer stayed with Powe and said Powe did not work during the week. On Friday of that week, Powe took Sawyer to the Wilshire office of Cabot, Cabot and Forbes, where Powe received a check. Sawyer believes the check was for Powe's supposed work that week. Sawyer did not see Powe receive the check, but sat in the outer office while Powe went in and got the check. <u>1. Name</u> another UW football player, also was in the office at the time, and Sawyer assumes that he was there to pick up a check as well.

<u>Corey Brown</u> worked for the downtown CC&F office during the summers of 1987 and 1988, as well as during several vacation school breaks over those two years. While he refused to speak on the record investigators, he stated that whatever his mother would tell him would be accurate.

<u>Delores Peters</u>, Corey Brown's mother, reported she had been unhappy about her son's employment at CC&F. She explained that it appeared that her son had not been supervised, that he was at home more than he was at his job, and that there were several days when he did not even report to work. She said, however, that regardless of the amount of time her son put in, he was paid $400 per week. Peters reported that she became so disillusioned about the arrangements that she called the receptionist and talked to her about making her son's employment more of a responsible work program. The receptionist informed her that there was often not enough work for her son and the other summer employees to stay busy, and nothing changed.

Peters said she could not understand why the work program was so unsupervised, particularly for workers of such a young age. She said Corey often would go to work at 10 to 11 in the morning and would be back home by 3 in the afternoon. She said it seemed like he was at home more than he was at work during regular work hours.

Peters also reported that it was her understanding Brown and other players called the CC&F office ahead of time during school breaks to report about when they would be in Los Angeles. Peters said she understood that the young men were paid for the entire period of the time they were in Los Angeles during the breaks, whether they reported to work or not.

<u>Anthony Jenkins</u> (see above under Ron Caldwell) said he worked "pretty close" to 40 hours a week during the summers of 1987 and 1988 but that no one kept track of the hours and he figured he probably worked about seven hours a day instead of eight. He said he usually reported between 8 and 9 and left

between 4 and 5. He reported he left early a few times because there was not enough to do. When that happened, he still got paid for the full week. Sometimes he would work out with Caldwell at UCLA, or in a private club in Culver City where Caldwell held a membership, from approximately 11 a.m. to 1 p.m. before returning to work.

Doug Meekins was a "partial qualifier" who graduated from Los Angeles Crenshaw High School in 1988. He did not practice or compete during the 1988-89 basketball season at UW as required under NCAA rules, then was a member of the basketball team for the next three seasons. He worked at the CC&F downtown LA office in the summer of 1988 as well as all school vacation breaks during the 1988-89 academic year.

Meekins stated he did very little work his first week on the job, reporting for only about an hour a day. He said he probably worked only 4-5 hours that week. On Friday of that first week, he reported that Jim Kenyon pulled him aside in the lobby of the office and told him he did not need to come to work every day, but he could just come in on Fridays and collect his paycheck. He said Kenyon was just passing through the lobby and no one else was nearby. Meekins agreed "and went about my business." Meekins reported that he received $400 per week by check for the time he would "pop in about an hour at a time" during the week, then would come in on Friday and get his paycheck.

Meekins reported that Terrance Powe, Corey Brown, Ron Caldwell, Vince Weathersby and Dennis Brown all worked at CC&F when he did. Meekins did not have a set time to come to work, and said he never went to work any earlier than noon. He did not know if all the other UW student-athletes had the same arrangements he had where he could be paid and not have to report for work, but said that Powe, Corey Brown, Caldwell, and 1. Name did and basically went to work only on Fridays.

Meekins stated that the same procedures also applied when he worked at CC&F during Thanksgiving 1988, Christmas 1988 and spring break of 1989. He was paid $10 per hour but did not report to work. He would contact Kenyon's secretary when he arrived in Los Angeles, then go to the office on Friday to receive a $400 paycheck.

• Irene Meekins, Doug Meekin's mother, said she was aware that Meekins was not working a full day because there was not enough work for the players to do. She knew that Meekins was going to work, but said that on some days there was nothing to do, so the players were dismissed. She stated that Meekins may have mentioned to her that he didn't have to go to work on some days. She said that she "wished that they would hire me," given the work load.

Wilson "Beno" Bryant, a senior on the UW football team this fall, reported that he worked at CC&F downtown office in the summer of 1989 for a couple of weeks. He did not work eight hours per day, but came in about moon and left about 5:00 p.m. He said he was paid only for the hours he worked, and not paid for work he did not perform. he said he was paid in cash by Kenyon.

Mary Trout was Kenyon's secretary and responsible for supervising the players when Kenyon was not present. She reported that the players were not always working, but were available when needed. She acknowledged that a player might not show up "once in a while" if he had a doctor's appointment, etc., and would still get paid, but said the players normally were present.

Joyce Hendricks, who worked for CC&F from 1978 until April 1989, said the UW athletes performed very few duties. She said they would do some errands, mostly driving. She said the company already had two full-time messengers. "So there was not a whole lot for the athletes to do," she said. Hendricks reported that there were days the players did not come to work. She said that the players didn't work from 9 to 5, and they often left work early. "I do know that they got their money every week," she said. "When it was time to get paid, everybody showed up." That occurred on Friday. She said they got paid $10 an hour.

Felicia Davis, Hendricks' daughter, worked for CC&F during the summer of 1987 as a temporary employee, then was hired full-time upon graduation from high school in 1988. She left the company in February 1989. She was asked if the UW players kept "9 to 5" hours. Davis said they were usually at work by 11 a.m. — not 9 a.m. — and would leave around 3 p.m. She said they joked about the lack of work and the easy jobs. "They thought they had cool jobs," she said.

2. **[NCAA Bylaw 12.4.1]**

   It is alleged that during the summers of 1991 and 1992, and the spring of 1991, James W. Kenyon, a representative of the University's athletics interests, provided Wilson "Beno" Bryant (Los Angeles, CA), a UW student-athlete, with pay for work not performed while Bryant was employed by Kenyon at the Jim Kenyon Company offices in Los Angeles.

   Wilson "Beno" Bryant reported that he worked at the Kenyon Company in Century City during the summers of 1991 and 1992, as well as during the spring break of 1991 and made approximately $400 per week. He said his hours were from 11:00 a.m. to whenever he finished his work, the latest being 4:30-5:00 p.m. He did not work on Fridays but went to the office to collect his wages, which were paid in cash by Kenyon. He said that Damon Mack and Darius Turner also worked for the Kenyon Company in 1991. If he did not have additional work to do during the day, he was allowed to leave early.

   Jim Kenyon stated that Bryant did work for his company during the summers of 1991 and 1992, but that he (Kenyon) was traveling extensively during those summers and was not in a position to supervise Bryant. He believed Bryant had been required to complete timesheets and he presumed Bryant had worked full 40-hour weeks. He said Bryant did work for him during the spring of 1991.

3. **[NCAA Bylaw 16.12.2.2.2]**

   It is alleged that on numerous occasions over several years, Jim Kenyon, a representative of the University's athletics interests, and other office personnel at the Cabot, Cabot and Forbes offices in Los Angeles permitted UW student-athletes who were employed at the office to make long-distance personal telephone calls at no charge to the young men.

   Terrance Powe and Ron Caldwell both reported that UW student-athletes were placed in a room with a telephone when they worked at the CC&F downtown Los Angeles office. They said the players made long-distance personal telephone calls on a regular basis. (A photograph supplied by Powe of players sitting in a conference-style room with a telephone is listed as 5-1 in Exhibit No. 5.)

Dennis Brown, who worked for CC&F in the summer of 1986 and during numerous vacation periods during the academic year, reported that the players made long-distance personal telephone calls to Seattle. He remembered that Kenyon became angry on one occasion when he received an "outrageous phone bill," and told the players to cut back on the use of the phone.

Kenyon acknowledged that a telephone was accessible to the players. He acknowledged that players could have used the telephone to make personal, long-distance calls, but they were not supposed to. He said the players were told not to make personal long-distance calls. Kenyon was asked if anyone monitored the phone bill, and he said they did not. He said that in the real estate business the telephone was used considerably and was a necessary, if expensive, business expense.

D. Incidents Involving Herb Mead and/or Clint Mead

(A letter from Ronald Neubauer, the Meads' attorney, explaining the Meads' position on the following allegations is attached as Exhibit No. 6.)

1. [NCAA Bylaw 13.2.1]

It is alleged that during January and February 1989, Clint Mead, a representative of the University's athletics interests, talked with Johnnie Morton (Torrance, CA), a prospective student-athlete, and led Morton to believe that if Morton enrolled at the University, he would be provided extra benefits by Herb Mead, Clint's father.

During the time of the allegations, Morton was a highly recruited high school senior at South High School in Torrance, California, and Clint Mead was a senior student at the University of Washington.

Morton reported that prior to his official visit, he received a few recruiting telephone calls from Clint Mead. On his official visit to UW, and after dinner at a seafood restaurant one evening, he was picked up by Clint and driven to the Mead home, a high-school highlights tape of his was playing on the videotape player. Dennis Brown, a defensive lineman on the UW football team, and his girl friend were present. Morton said he talked with Brown, who told him if he came to Seattle, Herb Mead would take care of him. (Morton was shown a photograph of Herb Mead and said he had never met the man.)

Morton reported that after returning home from his official visit, Clint Mead continued to call him at an accelerated pace. (It was permissible at that time for college students to make recruiting telephone calls.) At some point during the process — Morton said it occurred during the ride to Mead's house during his official visit, but later reported he thought it occurred after he had returned home from his visit — Clint told him Clint's father would adopt Morton, and that would permit the Meads to provide benefits to Morton that they couldn't otherwise. Morton reported that Clint told him that he would be "taken care of" in the same manner that they "took care of" Dennis Brown.

Morton said that the closer it came to the initial National Letter of Intent signing date, the more intense Clint's calls became. He said shortly after he made his decision to attend USC, Clint called him and offered to fly down with a National Letter of Intent in hand if Morton would sign with Washington. Morton told him he was fairly certain he would sign with USC, and nothing came of the proposal.

Danielle Nancarrow, Morton's girl friend at the time, said Clint Mead called Morton frequently. Upon his return from his visit, Morton told her he had gone to the Mead's home. Morton told her that Clint Mead told him that Herb Mead would "adopt" Morton if he attended the University. Morton explained to her that this represented a legal way to get Morton whatever he wanted.

Dennis Brown vaguely remembered meeting Morton at the Mead home during Morton's recruiting visit. He knew nothing about Clint Mead telling Morton he would be "taken care of," but said it would not surprise him because Herb Mead promised Brown he would be "taken care of" when he was being recruited by UW. Brown said the promises were unfulfilled. For example, Mead would have Brown chop some wood and would tell Brown that he would be paid for it, but when Brown asked for payment, Mead said it was against NCAA rules.

Brown said that Herb Mead did not take care of him, although that was a common belief. Brown indicated he wouldn't have told Morton that he was being "taken care of," in part because he was disgusted with the entire recruiting scene.

Clint Mead acknowledged that he had talked by telephone with Morton on several occasions, but denied making any improper recruiting inducements to Morton. He said that he developed a rapport with Morton and that Morton called him about three days after he signed with USC to indicate he had made a mistake. Clint told Morton that changing his mind would not be in his best interest, and that he should stick with his decision to attend USC. Clint said he wrote a letter to Morton after Morton had signed with USC (a copy of the draft he provided is attached as Exhibit 7), and noted that he had written that "you have a family in Seattle." He said Morton may have misconstrued those words to mean that he was being adopted. Both Clint and Herb adamantly denied that there was ever any conversation with Morton to the effect that he would be adopted by the Meads or that he would "be taken care of."

2.   [NCAA Bylaws 13.01.5.1 and 13.1.1.1]

It is alleged that on at least one occasion during early 1989, Herb Mead, a representative of the University's athletics interests, talked by telephone with Johnnie Morton (Torrance, CA), a prospective student-athlete.

Johnnie Morton reported that on one and possibly two occasions during his recruitment by Washington in early 1989, he spoke by telephone with Herb Mead, who encouraged him to attend Washington. He said it sounded like Mead was at an airport or outdoors, because there was a lot of static on the line. He remembers that Mead asked him if he liked steaks.

Herb Mead stated that since the NCAA rule changed (effective August 1, 1987) to prevent boosters from telephoning prospects, he has made no such recruiting telephone calls. He said it might have been possible that he would have answered the telephone if a prospect had called Clint when Clint was a UW student, but he did not recall ever talking by telephone with Johnnie Morton.

3.   [NCAA Bylaw 13.2.1]

It is alleged that during January and February 1989, Clint Mead, a representative of the University's athletics interests, talked by telephone with Danielle Nancarrow (Torrance, CA) and led her to believe that if she accompanied Johnnie Morton, a prospective student-athlete, to the University of Washington, she would be provided a job, an apartment with a roommate and would be enrolled in a local junior college.

Danielle Nancarrow said she was dating Johnnie Morton when he was recruited by Washington. Clint Mead, whom she described as a son of an alumnus at Washington, called her a couple of times just before Morton signed a National Letter of Intent with USC. He told her if Morton signed with Washington, he would get her a job, find a roommate for her to live with, and get her enrolled in a Seattle junior college. He did not say anything about her apartment being free, but indicated it would be located near the University.

Tom Nancarrow, father of Danielle and a detective in the Torrance police department, said Danielle mentioned to him that she was offered a job in Seattle if Morton attended Washington. He told her he thought it was a bad idea. They didn't discuss it further.

Clint Mead acknowledged that he had talked with Danielle Nancarrow at times when he visited by telephone with Johnnie Morton, but said he never made any offers to her. He said Nancarrow wanted to accompany Morton to Seattle if Morton attended Washington, and he informed her generally of the job market and rental market, but never promised her a job or an apartment. He said he probably mentioned the presence of a local junior college, but said he does not even know where it is located.

4. [NCAA Bylaws 13.01.5.1 and 13.1.2.1]

It is alleged that in August 1989, Herb Mead, a representative of the University's athletic interests, spoke with D'Marco Farr (San Pablo, CA), a prospective student-athlete, outside the locker room following Farr's participation in the California All-Star Shrine football game in Pasadena, CA.

D'Marco Farr is a senior at UW and a member of the football

team. Farr's brother, Andre, was recruited by Washington in 1987 but enrolled at UCLA. Farr said he talked with Herb Mead every once in awhile over the phone when his brother was being recruited. He originally said he met Mead in the locker room at the California High School All-Star Shrine game in the Rose Bowl in early August prior to his freshman year at UW. Mead grabbed Farr's stomach and told him to lose weight before he came to Washington. Farr didn't know who the person was until his mother told him.

Herb Mead reported that he attended the 1989 High School All-Star Shrine Football Game in Pasadena, and found himself next to Farr as they were walking toward the locker room. He would not have known it was Farr except for his jersey number. Mead made a casual greeting and they separated.

Farr later provided a corrected version of his story through Mead. He said the meeting occurred near the vicinity of the entrance to the north locker room, and that Mead patted his stomach and said, "You should work this off before reporting to football camp." Farr asked his brother and mother who the person was, and his mother identified him as Herb Mead. Farr then went "across the way," introduced himself, and asked if Mead knew where he could work for a couple of days in Seattle before fall camp started. He did not work for Mead that summer. (A copy of Farr's statement is attached as Exhibit No. 8.)

5.   **[NCAA Bylaw 16.12.2.4]**

It is alleged that during the summer of 1991, UW student-athlete Mario Bailey (Seattle, WA) was employed by Jim Heckman, a representative of the University's athletics interests, through a special arrangement in which Bailey was paid by Herb Mead, a representative of the University's athletics interests, from Mead's personal funds.

Jim Heckman is the president of *Sports Washington* magazine. He reported that he made an agreement with 7-11 stores in Washington to display his magazine, and hired Demetrius DuBose, a freshman at Notre Dame, in the summer of 1990 to drive around to make sure that the magazine was displayed properly in the stores. Heckman had DuBose, and later Mario Bailey in 1991 and Napolean Kaufman in 1992, go to the 7-11 stores during the summer to check the magazine's display racks.

Heckman reported that the money used to pay Bailey came from a loan from Herb Mead, and he had promissory notes to prove it. Mead paid Bailey to assure himself that Bailey actually performed the work. Heckman did not have the money to hire Bailey because he was starting his NFL Exclusive magazine and his financial resources were stretched to the limit. Mead's involvement was the easiest answer.

Herb Mead explained that he had helped Heckman in his business previously by purchasing some subscriptions to his magazine and giving them to people as gifts. Heckman then told Mead he needed to hire someone to put the magazine racks in the 7-11 stores and Mead agreed to make a loan available. However, when he learned that a student-athlete (Bailey) would be hired, he wanted to be sure everything would be legitimate, so the arrangement was made that he would pay Bailey directly. He described Heckman as "hard-charging, but young." Mead said a separate promissory note was executed for each check Bailey received, and the notes were paid off before the issue became public. He stressed that the reason for his paying Bailey directly was so he could be assured that no problems occurred.

[Heckman's statement and copies of the loan papers for the Bailey hiring are attached as Exhibit No. 9.]

6. **[NCAA Bylaws 13.5.5 and 13.7.5.1]**

It is alleged that during the 1987-88 and 1988-89 academic years, Herb Mead, a representative of the University's athletics interests, provided food and drinks at his house for prospective student-athletes making official visits to the University and their student hosts.

Terrance Powe reported that he occasionally took recruits to Herb Mead's house when he served as a student host during the 1987-88 and 1988-89 academic years. He said that there would be catered food available, and the recruits could play video games and call home.

Dennis Brown reported that when he took a recruit to the Mead home, there was usually pizza available.

Corey Brown told David Price and Mike Glazier that he took various recruits to Herb Mead's house when he served as a student host in 1987-88 and 1988-89, and that food was "probably" available.

Clint Mead reported that he had a Super Bowl party in January of 1988 and had a few friends come to his house for food and drinks. He said some UW football players showed up and they might have had some recruits with them, but he does not recall who the recruits were.

A copy of a photograph provided by Powe, which shows players and recruits eating catered food at what he says is the Mead home, is attached as Photograph 5-2 in Exhibit No. 5.

[NOTE: The following allegation is made on the basis that it represents a "blatant disregard" for NCAA rules and thus qualified for an extension of the statute of limitations under NCAA Bylaw 32.2.5.2]

7.   **[NCAA Bylaw 13.2.1]**

It is alleged that Herb Mead, a representative of the University's athletics interests, provided airline transportation for prospective student-athletes Terrance Powe (Los Angeles, CA) and Corey Brown (Los Angeles, CA) to attend the 1987 UW spring football game. Further, it is alleged that Clint Mead, a representative of the University's athletics interests, arranged for prospective student-athletes Terrance Powe (Los Angeles, CA) and Corey Brown (Los Angeles, CA) to reside at the Phi Delta Theta fraternity house when the two prospects visited Washington in April of 1987. Additionally, it is alleged that Clint Mead provided local transportation to the two prospects and purchased UW souvenirs for Powe at The Tequila Club. Finally, it is alleged that Powe was entertained for dinner at Herb Mead's home during the visit.

With regard to the airline transportation:

Terrance Powe reported that after he had signed a National Letter of Intent with Washington in the spring of 1987, he was contacted by Herb Mead (at the time, it was permissible under

NCAA rules for "boosters" to make in-person and telephonic contacts with recruits). Mead invited Powe to come to Seattle for the spring football game and Powe assumed Mead would arrange for transportation. Powe reported that a round-trip airline ticket was sent to him and he used the ticket to fly to Seattle for the weekend. He does not know specifically how the ticket was delivered, but said he returned home from school one day and the ticket was there. Powe stated he always assumed that Mead sent the ticket.

- <u>Gloria Jamison</u>, Powe's mother, said she recalled that Powe received an airline ticket to Seattle in the spring of 1987 via overnight express service. She does not recall who paid for the ticket, but says that she knows that neither she nor Powe's father paid for it, and that Powe went to Seattle. She was under the impression that "Mr. Mead" had extended the invitation to come to the spring game.

<u>Corey Brown</u> originally would not go on the record, but said what his mother told investigators was true. However, on June 10, 1993, Herb Mead, Clint Mead and their attorney, Ron Neubauer, met with Brown and provided him with several affidavits to consider signing. Brown told them he would not sign the affidavits but would consider drafting and signing his own statement. Brown returned home, signed a hand-written statement later that night and gave it to Clint Mead the following morning. The statement was delivered by David Price the afternoon of June 11 by Herb Mead and Neubauer. (A copy of the statement is attached as Exhibit 10.) "I have been told that it has been claimed that Herb Mead may have provided me with airline tickets to Seattle for the spring football game in 1987," his statement read. "That was six years ago and I can't remember who paid for my plane ticket. If Herb Mead would have paid for the plane ticket, I would probably remember."

On June 13, 1993, David Price and Mike Glazier interviewed Brown by telephone. He reported that he talked with Herb Mead and Larry Slade, former UW assistant coach, about going to Seattle to see the 1987 UW spring football game "to see the type of competition I had." He did not remember any discussion with either person about how he would get to Seattle. He received an airline ticket through the mail, but did not know who sent it and did not recall who paid for the ticket. Brown said he did not pay for it.

- Corey Brown's mother, <u>Delores Peters</u>, was interviewed earlier and recalled that Corey was flown to Seattle in the spring of 1987. She said she was certain she did not purchase the ticket nor did her son, and she assumed that someone connected with the football program paid his expenses.

<u>Herb Mead</u> reported that although he knew that Powe and Corey Brown attended the 1987 spring football game, he had no part in arranging or financing their transportation to Seattle. On June 14, he voluntarily submitted to a polygraph examination and was asked a series of questions with a "yes" or "no" response. The examiner reported that "based upon the review of the polygraph charts, it is this examiner's opinion that Mr. Herb Mead was truthful in responding to the aforementioned relevant questions and was not involved in forwarding the alleged airline tickets to Mr. Powe or Mr. Brown in the spring of 1987."

With regard to the remainder of the allegation:

The source of the information is Powe, who supplied investigators with photographs of the visit. (Copies of the photographs are attached as Exhibit 5.)

<u>Powe</u> reported that during a telephone call in 1987, Herb Mead mentioned the possibility of Powe's going to the spring game. Mead said Powe could stay with Mead's son, Clint, at Clint's fraternity house. Mead also told Powe he would be picked up at the airport.

Powe said he flew to Seattle and was met at the airport by Cort Mead, Clint Mead's brother, at the baggage claim area. He had not met Cort previously, and Cort approached Powe and introduced himself. Cort drove him to the Mead's home in a black Chevrolet Blazer. Powe said that Corey Brown flew to Seattle on a separate flight that same afternoon and he understood Brown was transported to the Mead home by Clint Mead. Powe reported he and Brown had dinner with the Mead family at the house on Friday night before going to Clint's fraternity house, Phi Delta Theta, where they spent the night. On Saturday morning, Clint took Powe and Brown to Seattle Memorial

Stadium to watch the UW spring football game. The game was played at Memorial Stadium because Husky Stadium was under construction at the time. Powe said he talked with several UW coaches before and after the game. On Saturday night, Powe had pizza with Clint and partied. He said it was no secret that he and Brown were staying at the fraternity, and they jokingly told people at the fraternity that they were professional football players.

Powe reported that before taking them to the airport for their return trip on Sunday, Clint drove Brown and him to the Tequila Club, a store in the University district that sells UW clothing and merchandise. Powe reported that he got some souvenirs for his mother, girl friend and himself, and that Clint paid for the purchases. Powe said he took approximately $200 worth of souvenirs back to Los Angeles for his family and friends.

- Gloria Jamison, Powe's mother, said she recalled one occasion when Powe came home from Seattle with "T-shirts, hats, stuff like that." He brought one T-shirt especially for her, a white T-shirt with a large "W" on the front. She believed Powe told her that he had gone to a school store to get some of the merchandise and to a Banana Republic store for the remainder of the purchases. She had the impression that the merchandise was given to Powe, but said she did not get into the specifics with Powe about which individuals did things for him.

Corey Brown originally would not speak on the record to investigators. His June 10 statement addressed several of the issues (see Exhibit 10). On June 13, he was interviewed by Price and Glazier. The following is a brief summary of this testimony:

△ Souvenirs:

In his signed statement, Brown said he did not recall Clint Mead purchasing any souvenirs for him. He said he purchased souvenirs from his own money "and without contribution whatsoever from Clint Mead or anyone else associated with the University of Washington."

To Price and Glazier, Brown said that he and Powe were driven to the Tequila Club by Clint Mead. Brown purchased a UW hat and a pair of Husky boxer shorts and paid for them himself. He could not recall Clint Mead purchasing him anything at the Tequila Club. He did not know whether Clint Mead made purchases for Powe, but said Powe was present at the store and left with several purchases.

△   Telephone calls from Mead's home:

In his signed statement, Brown reported he did not recall making telephone calls to his girlfriends in California.

To Price and Glazier, Brown reported he did not remember phone calls to girl friends in California because his girlfriend did not live in California. He did not believe he called her from Mead's house. He did indicate that he may have called recruits from Mead's house, but not when Mead was present, and said that Mead had never told him to call a recruit. He said he was given a list of recruits to call by the coaches and he felt he did not have to ask Mead if he could use his phone to call a recruit. He also reported having a telephone credit card given to him by his ex-girlfriend.

△   Meal at Mead's home:

In his signed statement, Brown reported that he did not recall and did not believe "we" had a meal at Clint Mead's house:

To Price and Glazier, Brown reported that he had arrived in Seattle later than Powe, and was picked up at the airport by a girlfriend who lived in Seattle. She either drove him to the Mead home or to the fraternity house. He believed he may have eaten on the plane and said he did not recall having dinner at the Mead house. He said he could have had a snack at the Mead home. "I'm not saying I had a snack, but if I would have, it probably would have been chicken," he said.

△   Staying at the fraternity house:

Brown told Price and Glazier that he and Powe stayed in Clint Mead's room at the fraternity house Friday and Saturday nights, and were not charged for the room. He said he had some meals, which were free, and claimed that he and Powe received a free pizza because it was delivered more than 30 minutes after it was ordered.

- <u>Delores Peters</u>, Brown's mother, said Corey told her he stayed in a fraternity house when he went to Seattle during the spring of 1987, but she did not know how his expenses were paid. She assumed someone connected with the football program paid his expenses. She recalled that her son purchased a T-shirt or hat while he was in Seattle, but does not know if he made the purchase himself or if someone provided him with the money.

<u>Clint Mead</u> did not recall picking Powe or Brown up at the airport and transporting them to his home, or their being at his home that trip. He did know that Powe and Brown stayed at his fraternity house on Friday night, but said that was normal occurrence during the rush process and both were potential members. He acknowledged that he had taken them to the Tequila Club, but denied purchasing any souvenirs or other merchandise for them.

<u>Herb Mead</u> recalled seeing Powe and Brown at the 1987 spring game, but did not remember them being at his house on that occasion, although he says they could have "dropped by." He did not believe that they ate at the Mead home.

E. Incidents Involving Jim Heckman

Jim Heckman started *Sports Washington*, a magazine that covers athletics in the State of Washington, in 1987 while a student at the University of Washington. He married Jeni James, UW football coach Don James' daughter, in December 1990, and became a member of the Tyee Club in 1992.

As a young publisher with limited funds, Heckman believed that it was necessary to take a different approach to covering athletics. Therefore, he concentrated on getting close to the athletes and telling their stories. His modus operandi, he said, was to cultivate a close relationship with athletes, and in so doing he spent a great deal of time and engaged in extended conversations with them. He stressed that he did not recruit for the University of Washington or any other college. (A copy of a letter from Heckman to David Price more fully explaining his position is attached as Exhibit No. 11.)

It also should be noted that Heckman rarely wrote stories for his magazine during this time period. He said he often would interview high school players and turn his notes over to others on the staff, who would write the stories.

1.   [NCAA Bylaws 13.01.5.1, 13.1.1.3 and 13.1.2.1]

It is alleged that Jim Heckman, a representative of the University's athletics interests, contacted prospective student-athlete Demetrius DuBose (Seattle, WA) in January 1989 and encouraged him to renege on his verbal commitment to attend the University of Notre Dame and instead enroll at the University of Washington; additionally, while employing DuBose during the summer of 1990, Heckman encouraged DuBose to transfer from Notre Dame to Washington.

Demetrius DuBose reported that Heckman called after DuBose verbally committed to Notre Dame during his senior year in high school. Heckman had done an article on him earlier, DuBose said. They talked about what DuBose wanted to do for the future. DuBose said Heckman was just being a friend. He talked about what DuBose had to offer his community, since he knew DuBose was interested in politics. DuBose thought Heckman was doing a follow-up article on the earlier story on him.

The two had lunch at a restaurant somewhere in the University district. Heckman paid. DuBose said Heckman talked to him about how Heckman initially wanted to attend Washington State and how he had discussed his future with a UW booster, then changed his mind and attended UW. "In retrospect, I think he was trying to get me to change my mind," DuBose said. They also had a casual conversation about Notre Dame.

That one event was the beginning of a series of communication, DuBose said. The two became friends and talked often. But DuBose thought that Heckman later was trying to get him to change his mind about attending Notre Dame. Heckman told DuBose that UW took care of its alums. DuBose remembered that statement distinctly. Heckman told DuBose what UW could do to help someone after they had left the school. Heckman outlined many situations where UW alums were helped after finishing school and staying in the community.

DuBose enrolled at Notre Dame but maintained contact with Heckman, who continued to call him. After DuBose's freshman year at Notre Dame, he worked for Heckman during the summer of 1990 publishing programs for the Goodwill Games. DuBose told Heckman he was coming home for the summer, and Heckman offered him the job. The Photo of the Day was his particular responsibility, and he said the work was a fulfilling experience.

DuBose said when he was working for Heckman that summer, he met several UW people and it became apparent to him that they wanted him to transfer to UW. Heckman took DuBose to dinner at Herb Mead's house on one occasion. The setting was very uncomfortable to DuBose. DuBose acknowledged that he was not happy at Notre Dame, and that was apparent to Heckman and Mead. "We talked about some things that could happen if I were to stay in Seattle," DuBose said. Was it specifically suggested that DuBose transfer? "It was not clearly stated," DuBose replied, but it was contained in underlying conversations. "We did discuss it." DuBose was told something along the lines that, "If you leave, a job will be waiting for you." No specific job was mentioned, but he understood, that the job would be with Heckman or with Mead.

DuBose was asked if the conversations with Heckman were serious or if they involved good-natured bantering. DuBose said Heckman's statements were made in a good-natured, joshing way. The two were joking all the time. "We did talk about it (DuBose's transferring to UW) a lot," DuBose said. "At some point it was the meat of our conversation." He described it as a "kind of friendly persuasion" and said "the message was clear."

John Sandstrom, who worked for Costacos Publishing when it shared offices with Heckman's company, reported he had numerous conversations with Heckman. Sandstrom reported that Heckman told him that he was recruiting players for

Washington, although Sandstrom was under the impression that the UW coaches did know he was doing it. Sandstrom reported Heckman talked openly about recruiting DuBose when DuBose was working for Heckman in the summer of 1990 after DuBose went to Notre Dame. Sandstrom reported Heckman told him DuBose was considering transferring from Notre Dame to Washington and that Heckman thought he could talk DuBose into the transfer. He remembered Heckman saying that DuBose was "on the ropes" and "if I keep talking, I think I can talk him into transferring."

Todd Hubbell, who worked for Heckman from January 1989 through November 1991, reported one of his major concerns while working for the magazine was that Heckman used his position at the magazine to make contacts with Washington recruits. He emphasized that Heckman was not a writer, but was a publisher, business manager and salesman with no journalistic training. However, Heckman would contact high school athletes, then ask writers to follow up. He said Heckman rarely provided notes of his conversations with the recruits to writers. He suggested that Heckman may actually have been trying to recruit these prospects for Washington under the guise of being a journalist.

Hubbell remembered Heckman telephoning DuBose in South Bend and offering him a job, then telling others in the office that "we are going to get to him to jump to Washington." At the time, Hubbell did not pay much attention, but during the summer he noticed Heckman making strong bantering comments suggesting that DuBose should transfer. Heckman told DuBose that Washington was going to become the national champions, that he could play on defense with Steve Emtman, and that UW boosters took care of former UW players in the community. Hubbell said the comments were made in both jocular and serious ways.

Terrance Powe reported that Herb Mead tried to get him involved with recruiting DuBose. "We were supposed to be calling him at Notre Dame," Powe said. Mead told Powe to call DuBose and try to persuade him to transfer. Powe reported that Mead gave Powe the Seattle and South Bend telephone numbers for DuBose. Powe did not call DuBose but told Mead that he did.

Jim Heckman reported that he has an excellent relationship with DuBose, built over the years. He said he talked with DuBose numerous times, as he did with various high school players at that time, and established a solid friendship. When he obtained the program rights to the Goodwill Games, he hired DuBose, who was finishing his freshman year at Notre Dame, and the two worked together almost 24 hours a day for the duration of the Games. He said DuBose and he were on the same softball team, and went to Clint Mead's house after one game to raid the refrigerator. He said there was general bantering and kidding about DuBose's attending Notre Dame, but it was done in good nature. He considers it "ironic and pathetic" that anyone would question him about his outstanding relationship with DuBose.

Herb Mead recalled DuBose being at the house one evening but stressed that there was no talk about transferring. He said that there was friendly discussions comparing Washington's football program with Notre Dame's, but it was not serious talk.

DuBose contacted David Price at the Pacific-10 Conference office on Friday, June 11, 1993, the day after Price informed Heckman that an allegation would be made. DuBose, who earlier would not meet with University investigators, sent via facsimile machine a statement refuting the allegation. It is attached as Exhibit No. 12.

2.   [NCAA Bylaws 13.01.5.1, 13.1.1.3 and 13.1.2.1]

It is alleged that in January 1991, Jim Heckman, a representative of the University's athletics, contacted prospective student-athlete Lake Dawson (Federal Way, WA) and encouraged him to commit to the University of Washington instead of the University of Notre Dame.

Lake Dawson is a football player at the University of Notre Dame from the Seattle suburb of Federal Way. He reported that after his senior season in high school, he received a telephone call from Jim Heckman notifying him that he had been named prep athlete of the month by Heckman's *Sports Washington* magazine. A few days later, Heckman called again and scheduled an interview over dinner at a local restaurant. While Heckman talked positively about the University of Washington at the dinner, Dawson did not believe Heckman was trying to persuade him to attend UW.

Dawson reported that sometime later prior to National Letter of Intent signing date, Heckman called to tell him about Notre Dame's returning receivers against whom Dawson would have to compete if signed with the Irish. Heckman provided detailed information about Notre Dame's depth chart and returning players. Dawson specifically recalled that Heckman told him that Washington needed a receiver of his size and speed.

<u>Jim Sandstrom</u> reported that when Dawson was in high school, Heckman mentioned on a few occasions that he was recruiting Dawson for the University. Sandstrom remembered Dawson well, possibly because Dawson was a highly recruited player from Federal Way. He recalled that on one occasion Heckman reported he was going to take Dawson out so other recruiters could not contact him. Sandstrom did not remember how close that incident was to National Letter of Intent signing date. He assumed that Heckman was telling the truth, although he believed that Heckman tended to boast a bit.

<u>Jim Heckman</u> acknowledged talking with Dawson. However, he did not believe he became a UW representative until he married Jeni James in December 1990, or until he paid $150 a year to the Tyee Club in the summer of 1992. He became extra careful at that time. When he started his magazine, he spent considerable time talking with prep players. His questions usually were aimed at what college the player was planning to attend, and most of his dealings with the players was of an inquisitive nature. He said when he talked to Dawson, he did not think he was doing anything wrong. He was just 23 years old at the time. He said he was not involved with the athletics programs as a student and did not know Mike Lude. "My relationship with the University was nil," he said.

3. **[NCAA Bylaws 13.01.5.1, 13.1.1.3 and 13.1.2.1]**

    It is alleged that Jim Heckman, a representative of the University's athletics interests, contacted prospective student-athlete Singor Mobley (Tacoma, WA) in January 1991 and encouraged him to renege on a verbal commitment to attend Washington State University and instead enroll at the University of Washington; further, Heckman provided NFL posters to Mobley at no cost to the young man.

<u>Singor Mobley</u> reported that during the 1990 football season, he and his father, Eugene Mobley, went to Jim Heckman's office before a UW football game. Heckman called him and arranged an interview. They agreed to meet in front of Nordstrom's in the SeaTac Mall at 10:00 a.m. Singor and his father drove to the mall and met Heckman, who drove them to his office. Upon his arrival, Singor was interviewed by Mike Olson, editor of *Sports Washington*, for about 30-45 minutes. No photographs were taken. Heckman then showed the Mobleys around the building, and took them to the basement where there was a large supply of NFL posters. Heckman told Singor he could have any poster he wanted, and Singor selected about five posters. One was of Lawrence Taylor and one was of Ronnie Lott. Heckman rolled them up and put them in a box for Mobley, who took them home and hung a couple of them in his bedroom. Heckman then drove the Mobleys to a Husky football game, sat with them during the first half of the game, then drove them home after the game.

Mobley additionally reported that after he had visited Washington State, he called UW Coach Randy Hart and informed Hart he had committed to WSU. About two days later he got a call from Jim Heckman, publisher of *Sports Washington* magazine. Heckman said he wanted to take Mobley out to dinner and help him change his mind on what school he would attend. Heckman picked Mobley up at his house and drove him to a restaurant in Tacoma. Heckman then started talking about why Mobley should go to UW and "we could get it in the paper how we could tell people why I changed my mind. I was pretty shocked. I said I wasn't sure about that. I told him I did not agree with him." Heckman said Mobley should go to UW if he wanted to go to the Rose Bowl. Mobley replied that he really didn't want to attend Washington. "He kept trying to force the issue," Mobley said. "I wanted to get away from home and to get away from the city."

Mobley said when they arrived at the Mobley house after the meal, Heckman came in and sat down at the dining room table with a pen and notepad, and said he would write a story. Even then, he was telling Mobley why he should change his mind about attending WSU. "He said I came from a winning high school, and why should I go to a losing college or university. I told him I was upset. I was pretty shocked."

<u>Eugene Mobley</u>, Singor's father, confirmed that he and Singor had gone to a Husky football game with Heckman. The Mobleys went to the mall near SeaTac airport to meet Heckman outside a Nordstrom's store. Heckman drove them to his office, where Singor was interviewed for a story. Heckman took them to the basement where there were a lot of NFL posters, and permitted Singor to take some posters. Eugene said Singor selected posters of Bo Jackson, Ronnie Lott, and Lawrence Taylor. Singor hung them in his room later.

<u>Lilian Mobley</u>, Singor's mother, reported she was not home when Singor went to dinner with Heckman, but that she talked with Singor about it later. When Singor reported that Heckman would provide him with a full-page story in his magazine if he changed his mind and decided to enroll at UW, she became excited and asked if he would do it. Singor replied that he wanted to attend Washington State, not UW. She showed David Price a larger poster of Bo Jackson hanging on Singor's bedroom wall, and showed him the markings where she said a large poster of Lawrence Taylor had been hung before she took it down.

<u>Bob Lucey</u>, Tacoma Curtis High School head football coach, said he recalled the incident because "we never had a writer take a player out to dinner" and thus it stuck in his mind. He said that Mobley told him Heckman kept talking to him about his decision to attend WSU. Mobley indicated that it sounded strange because Heckman kept trying to talk him out of the decision. Lucey said Mobley made the statement shortly after the incident.

<u>Jim Sandstrom</u> said that he recalls Singor Mobley's name, but does not recall that Heckman made the same type of boasts about recruiting Mobley as he did of DuBose and Dawson. He did recall that Heckman told him Mobley could not get into the University.

<u>Jim Heckman</u> adamantly denied attempting to recruit Mobley. He said that it was well known that Mobley <u>2. Individual Privacy</u> to enroll at Washington or earn a scholarship, and that as a positive person he would never approach a person with a statement to the effect that "you have made a mistake." He reported that he and Mobley had an excellent conversation,

and that Mobley enjoyed himself so much that he asked Heckman to take him by his girlfriend's house. Heckman also notes that Mobley was prominently featured in *Sports Washington* recruiting issue later that spring as a key WSU recruit.

F.   **Use of Recruiting Funds**

1.   **[NCAA Bylaw 13.7.5.5, 13.7.5.8 and 16.12.2.1]**

It is alleged that on several occasions, student hosts provided cash or souvenirs to prospective student-athletes making official visits to the University; further, in some instances the student hosts kept part of the entertainment or meal money. Specific examples are set forth below.

a.   It is alleged that during the 1987-88 and 1988-89 academic years, UW student-athlete Dennis Brown (Long Beach, CA) provided false receipts for meals when he entertained recruits on their official visits, claiming greater expenses than he had and keeping the excess money.

Dennis Brown played football at UW in 1986-87-88-89 and currently is with the San Francisco 49ers. He reported that he served as a student host during his first two or three years at Washington and sometimes turned in bogus receipts to the coaches. He said he would purchase a pizza or fast food meal and then turn in a receipt for a much larger figure. He had a friend at the Red Robin restaurant who would let him eat free, and he would then turn in a receipt for the meal. Brown said he always kept the leftover money and never gave any of it to a recruit.

After signing a statement that contained the above comment, Brown said he did not turn in bogus receipts for meals, but just for snacks from the $20 per day entertainment money.

b.   It is alleged UW student-athlete Terrance Powe (Los Angeles, CA) regularly split entertainment/meal money with prospective student-athletes or purchased souvenirs for recruits during the 1987-88 and 1988-89 academic years when he served as a student host.

The source of this information was <u>Powe</u>, who was a member of the Husky football team for four years (1987-90). He reported that he sometimes gave money to the recruit he was hosting, or, instead of spending all of the money, he would keep some of it for himself. Consequently, many of the receipts he submitted to the coaches were false. He reported that the coaches were not concerned about where the money was spent, or how it was spent, as long as there were receipts which indicated that the money was spent legitimately. He said he had no problem splitting the money with recruits, and usually gave $20 to $40 to the recruit. He would give the recruits the options of what they could do—they could go to a nice restaurant, go partying, or simply split the money.

Powe said he often purchased souvenirs, including clothing or other merchandise containing a UW logo, for recruits, and sometimes gave money directly to the recruits to allow them to purchase the merchandise.

Powe reported he would complete blank receipts to cover the extra expenses. He had seen coaches pull out blank receipts and give them to players to be filled out, or fill out a receipt themselves.

c. **It is alleged UW student-athlete James Sawyer (San Jose, CA) split extra entertainment/meal money with prospective student-athletes when he served as a student host; specifically, Sawyer provided prospective student-athlete Keith Reynolds (Oakland, CA) with approximately $80 during Reynolds' official visit of January 13-14, 1989, and Reynolds used part of the money to purchase a sweatsuit.**

<u>Reynolds</u>, who attends Washington State, reported that when he went on his visit, he was hosted by a wide receiver from San Jose (Sawyer). On the first evening shortly after they had met at a dinner at the Space Needle restaurant, Sawyer gave Reynolds $20, saying "here's your money for the weekend." Reynolds thought nothing of it, since he had a similar experience during a visit to another (non Pac-10) institution.

Reynolds reported that on the second day of his visit,

Sawyer told him he was going to tell Coach Dave Christensen that they wanted to eat an expensive meal, and that Reynolds should agree if asked. Sawyer then went to Christensen, who reached into his inside coat pocket and pulled out an envelope with money in it. According to Reynolds, Christensen gave Sawyer at least $100 in $20 bills. Reynolds said he, Sawyer and Sawyer's roommate, a wide receiver with a shaven head who wore Number 86 (LaMar Mitchell) went to dinner at a Red Robin restaurant. After eating, the three split the excess money. Reynolds used his money to buy a white cotton sweatsuit with a cartoon caricature on the shirt and "Washington Huskies" on the leg. He wore it on the plane home, then gave it to his brother, Claude, after he decided to attend Washington State.

Claude Reynolds reported that Keith had come home with a white sweatsuit and had given it to him at a later date. He said he still has possession of the sweatsuit.

Sawyer said he did not recall Reynolds specifically, but he would buy a cheap meal and turn in a more expensive receipt, splitting the money with his recruit, when he served as a student host.

Sawyer reported that he provided money to other recruits when he served as a student host by turning in false receipts for meals and claiming a higher expense than the meals cost. He cited such an instance when he hosted 1. Name a prospective student-athlete from (1. Hometown) who later attended 1. college location .

1. Graduated from college location reported that he was hosted at UW by Aaron Pierce and Sawyer, but he did not recall receiving any cash during the visit.

d. It is alleged that UW student-athlete 1. Name (Hometown) purchased a UW souvenir T-shirt for prospective student-athlete Errol Sapp (Carson, CA) during Sapp's official visit to the University January 6-8, 1989.

Errol Sapp, who made an official visit to UW at the same time as Johnnie Morton, played football at Arizona as a freshman before becoming ineligible. He reported that 1.

<u>Name</u> had some spending money but made it clear that the money was not for Sapp personally. However, he told Sapp that they had not spent all of the money at the end of the visit and asked Sapp what he wanted to do with the rest. Sapp said that he had <u>1. Student</u> purchase him a Washington T-shirt, which he described as white with a circle on the front with a Husky dog inside the circle. He did not recall the cost of the shirt, but said <u>1. Name</u> paid in cash. He later gave the shirt to a former girlfriend who now resides in Oregon.

<u>1. Name</u> denied purchasing a T-shirt for Sapp.

e.   It is alleged <u>1. Name (Hometown)</u> provided prospective student-athlete Mondala Wilkins (San Diego, CA) with approximately $50 cash during Wilkins' official visit of January 14-16, 1990.

<u>Wilkins</u>, who attended Washington for two quarters during the 1990-91 academic year before returning home, reported that after he and <u>1. Name</u> ate at the Red Robin restaurant on the first night of his visit, <u>1. Name</u> gave him approximately $20-30 in cash. He reported that on the second night <u>1. Name</u> gave him another $20-30, and they ate two large pizzas in <u>1. Name</u> room.

The expense form for Wilkins' visit shows $81.00 for dinner (blank receipt) on the first night and $79.50 for dinner (Westin) on the second night.

<u>1. Name</u> denied the allegation.

f.   It is alleged <u>1. Name (Hometown)</u> provided prospective student-athlete Terry Vaughn (Oceanside, CA) with approximately $80 during Vaughn's official visit of January 19-21, 1990, and Vaughn used the money to purchase souvenirs.

<u>Vaughn</u> is a student-athlete at Arizona. He recalled that on Friday, his student host <u>1. Name</u> (he did not know his last name) said that the two of them would return to a shopping district near Many Towers to buy souvenirs for him. He said they never had a chance to go back to the district, so on Sunday, just before Vaughn left Seattle <u>1. Name</u> apolo-

gized for not buying souvenirs, and gave Vaughn $80-90 near the hotel to purchase souvenirs for himself. Vaughn said he kept the money instead of buying souvenirs. Vaughn said 1. Name did not say where he got the money. Vaughn reported it was the last time he saw 1. Name during the visit.

1. Name the UW student-athlete who served as Vaughn's host, could not be located.

g.   It is alleged 1. Name purchased two posters for prospective student-athlete Ontiwaun Carter (Granada Hills, CA) during Carter's official visit of January 12-14, 1990.

Carter, currently a student-athlete at Arizona, reported that on Saturday morning, 1. Name took him to a mall near the campus. Carter explained that at some earlier point during his visit, 1. Name said words to him to the effect of, "Whatever you want or need, let me know." He said while at the mall 1. Name purchased two posters for him: one featured Deion Sanders and the other Neal Anderson, two NFL players. Carter said the posters currently are hanging in his apartment. He did not recall the cost of the posters, but said that 1. Name paid for them with cash.

h.   It alleged 1. Name provided $10 cash to prospective student-athlete Fred Edwards (San Diego, CA) during Edwards' official visit of January 17-19, 1992.

Edwards, currently a student-athlete at San Diego State, reported that 1. Name gave him $10 on Saturday night at 1. Student name house. 1. Name told Edwards that he had received $10 from players when he was being recruited, and advised Edwards that whenever he went on a trip, he should be sure to get his money "because its yours." He used the money to buy something to drink that night.

Attempts to talk to 1. Name were unsuccessful.

2.   [NCAA Constitution 2.1]

It is alleged that as a result of the allegations set forth in Section F-1 of this Notice of Charges, as well as a review of the recruiting expense forms by the University's internal auditor and the Pacific-10 Conference Associate Commissioner, the University of Washington demonstrated a lack of institutional control in the accountability of expenses during official visits by football recruits during the 1987-92 time period.

While conducting in-person interviews with UW recruits who enrolled at other West Coast institutions, it became apparent to Pac-10 and University investigators that the provision of entertainment monies to UW student hosts was subject to potential abuse. A limited number of recruits reported they had received either cash or souvenirs from hosts while on official visits to UW. Three UW student hosts acknowledged abusing the system.

When the issue was brought to the attention of the University administration, a review of the football recruiting expense forms was conducted by UW internal auditors.

A significant flaw in the system was that the coaches provided cash to student hosts for meals the coaches did not attend. The student host was required to return with a meal receipt to provide to the coach, who would include the receipt on his expense form.

This system failed, however, due to the following circumstances:

- The coach often departed campus for off-campus recruiting activities at the end of the weekend and did not complete the expense form for several days.

- Many of the receipts turned in by student hosts were blank.

- In some cases, a substitute receipt had to be utilized when either the coach or student host lost a receipt.

- The system was open to manipulation by a student host, who could eat an inexpensive meal with a recruit but turn in a receipt for a more expensive meal.

The coaches told University auditors that because they often immediately left the campus on recruiting trips following a recruiting weekend, they were forced into a position of recreating expenses for a portion of the weekend upon their return home. They acknowledged that they filled in blank receipts and/or used substitute receipts to make the dollar figures balance. They recognized that some receipts were not identified with the proper meal, the proper day or occasionally even with the proper recruit. They insisted, however, that they did not personally benefit and did not believe that their players benefited.

In light of the coaches' testimony to the auditor, it is impossible to make a blanket determination that coaches, recruits or student hosts benefited from manipulation of the recruiting expense forms. At the same time, the recruiting expense forms are so defective that they are virtually worthless as a record or even a reflection of the recruiting weekend. A charge of a lack of institutional control in this area thus appears justified.

G. Miscellaneous

1. **[NCAA Bylaw 16.12.2.4]**

   It is alleged that Billy Joe Hobert (Puyallup, WA), a UW student-athlete, was provided free golf fees by Dick Crowe and Ron Crowe at Linden Country Club in December 1991 and at The Classics Golf Course in January 1992; additionally, Hobert was hosted for breakfast by the Crowes at The Classics.

   <u>Ron Crowe</u> reported that he knew Hobert liked to play golf, so at the end of the regular season and before the 1992 Rose Bowl, he invited Hobert to be his guest at the Linden Golf Club, where Ron's brother, Dick, is a member. Since Linden is a private club, Ron said either he or his brother paid for all of the expenses. While playing Linden, Ron mentioned he would like Hobert to play with him and his brother again after the Rose Bowl at The Classics Golf Course. Ron said when they played, either he or his brother picked up the greens fees (approximately $70) but he thought Hobert may have paid for the cart he shared with Ron.

   <u>Dick Crowe</u> said that his brother, Ron, arranged for a foursome at the Linden Golf Course in Puyallup and he paid the fees. They only played nine holes, but Dick believed he paid a full fare of $24. Dick said his business partner, Tom Reynolds, is a big Husky fan and he asked Ron to arrange another golf game

with Hobert at The Classics sometime after the 1992 Rose Bowl so that Reynolds could play. He does not recall who paid the fees, but assumes he would have because he asked his brother to set up the game with Hobert. If he did not pay, he believes Ron did, because he does not think Reynolds or Hobert paid.

2. [NCAA Bylaw 16.12.2.4]

    It is alleged that Billy Joe Hobert (Puyallup, WA), a student-athlete, was provided a free jacket for KXRX radio station after the 1992 Rose Bowl.

    John Maynard and Robin Erickson of KXRX reported that they knew Hobert was interested in broadcasting and contacted Cindy Holt in the UW department of athletics to arrange an interview. Hobert then agreed to three interviews over a period of time. Larry Ferro, the station's marketing director, thought it would be good for the radio station to use Hobert as a publicity gimmick. They purchased a personalized jacket for him. Cindy Holt does not recall the incident, but says she would have arranged the interviews.

3. [NCAA Bylaw 16.12.2.4]

    It is alleged that Darius Turner (Gardena, CA), a UW student-athlete, used his athletics reputation to receive free goods and services from a local gas service station while enrolled at the University.

    This allegation resulted from a story in the *Seattle Post-Intelligencer* of March 8, 1993. Darius Turner reported that he did tell the *Post-Intelligencer* that he received free tire rotations and oil changes from a local Goodyear store at Eighth Avenue and Northgate Way. He knew the manager (Jeff) and received free service on one or two occasions. Turner said Jeff might have asked him to autograph a football or poster in return.

4. [NCAA Bylaws 13.4.2-(g) and 13.75.8]

    It is alleged that fruit baskets and "Welcome to Washington" placards regularly have been provided to prospective student-athletes by Seattle area hotels when the prospects make official visits to the University.

Several recruits indicated that fruit baskets and "Welcome to Washington" placards were in their hotel rooms when they arrived on their official visits. The placards were personalized, and they took them home as a souvenir of the visit

5.   [NCAA Bylaws 15.1 and 15.2.6]

It is alleged that D'Marco Farr (San Pablo, CA), a UW student-athlete, was employed by Jim Summers, a representative of the University's athletics interests, during the first two weeks of the 1991 spring quarter at a time when Farr was not enrolled in classes; further, the employment income caused Farr to exceed the "full grant-in-aid" limits permitted under NCAA rules for the 1990-91 academic year.

D'Marco Farr reported that he had a debt he had to repay before he could enroll in the University for the spring quarter of 1991, and that he worked for Herb Mead for two weeks to earn enough money to pay off the debt. Farr stated that he worked at the Eastside Catholic High School, and the principal kept track of his hours. University records indicate that Farr received a full athletic grant-in-aid in the spring of 1991.

Herb Mead reported that he recalled Farr owed a debt of approximately $420 that he had to settle before he could enroll one spring term. He did not recall Farr working for him, and said he did not employ players to work at the Eastside Catholic High School. He recalled checking to make sure when Farr had earned sufficient wages to pay the debt, asking the employee to pay Farr, and telling Farr to take care of the debt immediately and get enrolled in school.

Jim Summers said that he hired Farr after receiving a call from Mead, but did not recall the precise timing of the employment.